Politics and Partnerships

Politics and Partnerships

*The Role of Voluntary Associations in
America's Political Past and Present*

EDITED BY ELISABETH S. CLEMENS
AND DOUG GUTHRIE

THE UNIVERSITY OF CHICAGO PRESS   CHICAGO AND LONDON

Elisabeth S. Clemens is professor and director of graduate studies in the Department of Sociology at the University of Chicago. **Doug Guthrie** is professor of sociology at New York University with a joint appointment in the Department of Management and Organization at the Stern School of Business.

The University of Chicago Press, Chicago 60637
The University of Chicago Press, Ltd., London
© 2010 by The University of Chicago
All rights reserved. Published 2010
Printed in the United States of America

16 15 14 13 12 11 10   1 2 3 4 5

ISBN-13: 978-0-226-10996-1 (cloth)
ISBN-13: 978-0-226-10997-8 (paper)
ISBN-10: 0-226-10996-8 (cloth)
ISBN-10: 0-226-10997-6 (paper)

♾ The paper used in this publication meets the minimum requirements of the American National Standard for Information Sciences—Permanence of Paper for Printed Library Materials, ANSI Z39.48-1992.

Library of Congress Cataloging-in-Publication Data

Politics and partnerships : the role of voluntary associations in America's political past and present / edited by Elisabeth S. Clemens and Doug Guthrie.
    p. cm.
    Includes bibliographical references.
    ISBN-13: 978-0-226-10996-1 (cloth : alk. paper)
    ISBN-10: 0-226-10996-8 (cloth : alk. paper)
    ISBN-13: 978-0-226-10997-8 (pbk. : alk. paper)
    ISBN-10: 0-226-10997-6 (pbk. : alk. paper)
    1. Voluntarism—Political aspects—United States.   2. Voluntarism—United States—History.   3. Civil society—United States.   4. Charities—Political aspects—United States.   5. Nonprofit organizations—United States—Political activity.   6. Religion and civil society—United States.   I. Clemens, Elisabeth Stephanie, 1958–   II. Guthrie, Doug, 1969–
    HN90.V64P66 2010
    322—dc22
                                                                2009026984

Contents

Acknowledgments

This volume began with an act of generosity that funded the Committee on Philanthropy and the Third Sector of the Social Sciences Research Council. Originally anonymous, that donor is now public as Atlantic Philanthropies. SSRC has been a wonderful home for the project, providing scholarly conversation, excellent company, and practical support from Craig Calhoun, Steve Heydemann, Amy Withers, and Holly Danzeisen. In addition to choreographing the annual meetings to select fellows and gatherings of fellows for a daylong symposium each autumn, the SSRC also made possible a final capstone conference at the Villa Sassetti of the La Pietra Estate in Florence. We would like to thank New York University's Office of Global Education for help in coordinating and hosting this event.

The chapters in this volume began as papers for that conference and were greatly enriched by presentations by other fellows and invited scholars: Sada Aksartova, Elizabeth Bloodgood, Dorothea Browder, Christopher Capozzola, Mihir Desai, Keri-Nicole Dillman, Nicole Esparza, Erzébet Farzekas, Pamela Freese, Brendan Goff, Daniel Hungerman, Michael Jo, Caroline Lee, Simon Lee, Sandra Levitsky, Thomas Medvetz, Amanda Moniz, Sandra Moog, Stephen Porter, Kenneth Prewitt, Lester Salamon, Natalia Sarkisian, John Slocum, David Strang, Tracy Steffes, Erika Summers-Effler, Ann Swidler, and Jonathan VanAntwerpen. A much longer list of fellows, committee members, and guests contributed to the ongoing conversations that carried from one gathering to the next, fueling a lively set of debates. We are particularly grateful to David Hammack and Steve Heydemann, our collaborators in organizing the capstone conference and coeditors of the companion volume, *Globalization, Philanthropy, and Civil Society: Projecting Institutional Logics Abroad* (Indiana University Press, 2009).

CHAPTER ONE

Introduction: Politics and Partnerships

Elisabeth S. Clemens and Doug Guthrie

Public debate is now full of the language of philanthropy and voluntarism. From both major American political parties, there are calls for new kinds of partnerships between government and nonprofit—as well as "faith-based"—organizations to provide services and support. In his famous "1,000 Points of Light" speech in 1989, President George H. W. Bush declared that public goods should be produced by a "readiness and ability of every individual and every institution in America to initiate action as 'a point of light'; meaningful one-to-one engagement in the lives of others is now required to overcome our most serious national problems." Arguing that charitable action and the provision of public goods should be by individuals and community-based rather than federally funded, Bush called for "a movement that is grassroots and community-based rather than devised in and imposed from Washington, a movement that does not compensate people with federal dollars for what should be an obligation of citizenship."[1] Today more than ever, individual citizens are urged to volunteer, to donate, to participate in their local communities. In times of crisis, calls for public service multiply, signaling that voluntary effort is understood as a necessary supplement to government action. And recently, in the face of international criticisms

---

1. Bush, George H.W. 1989. "White House Fact Sheet on the 1,000 Points of Light Initiative." George Bush Presidential Library.

of the relatively low level of development aid provided by the U.S. government, one prominent theme in the heated response has highlighted the scale of private donations from Americans to disaster relief, an outpouring of voluntary giving that is taken as one of the defining features of the nation's civic culture.

Yet despite the fact that volunteerism, charity, and nonprofit organizations seem to be almost everywhere in public policy debates, it has been surprisingly difficult to conceptualize their role in American governance. Among political scientists, the analysis of American politics and political history has focused on formal political institutions and electoral behavior, too often overlooking the extragovernmental organizations that are critical sites for political mobilization and public provision. Among sociologists, nonprofit organizations are most often addressed in the context of either social movements or social service. The emphasis on opposition to authority in the former and on professions in the latter has combined to obstruct a clear analysis of how nonprofits are implicated in electoral politics, policy formation, and relations of ruling. Nor have these literatures fully engaged the role of firms and markets as contributors, competitors, and substitutes for voluntary efforts. Finally, those working within the worlds of nonprofit organizations and philanthropy have been reluctant to acknowledge the more political aspects of their activities. Chastened by a history of congressional investigations and threats to their tax-exempt status, advocates and practitioners have obscured—and even avoided (Berry 2003)—forms of political activity that may be quite acceptable within the constraints of the law.

Given the heightened prominence of nonprofit organizations and philanthropic endeavors in public affairs, this fragmented and confused understanding of the role of voluntary associations in American governance has become more difficult to ignore. The ramifying system of public-private partnerships in social provision demands systematic recognition in political analysis, but that recognition cannot begin with the premise that such arrangements are entirely novel. A sustained analysis of the reasons why such arrangements have succeeded and failed—and for whom—in the past can inform contemporary efforts to understand and transform contemporary systems of governance in the United States.

Politics and Partnerships contributes to this project by combining a reconsideration of the place of voluntary associations in American political history with informed analyses of contemporary experiments in reconfiguring the role of such associations in policy formation and public provision. Once relations among government agencies, voluntary or civic associations, and even private firms are placed front and center, their history is transfigured from the development of three distinctive domains to a process of contestation over the legitimacy of organizational forms, their respective jurisdictions, and their interdependencies. This reframing focuses attention on the complex, compound, or networked character of American governance in which voluntary associations and nonprofit organizations play an important part, variously described as "mediating organizations," "heterarchic governance," or "triadic exchange" by our contributors (see chapters by Omri Elisha, Michael McQuarrie, and Nicole Marwell). The seemingly distinct and apolitical character of nonprofits that informs the "three sector" model—state, market, voluntary sector—is itself the product of a particular period of American history (see Elisabeth Clemens, chapter 4, and Alice O'Connor, chapter 5), a moment of settlement that is once again challenged by the increasingly visible interpenetration of publicly funded, philanthropically supported, and entrepreneurial projects.

Voluntary Associations in America's Political Past

Although the trinity of state, market, and nonprofit sectors does not fully capture the organizational and political history of the United States, it can nevertheless generate a set of orienting questions about the development of voluntary associations. When and why were some voluntary associations, characterized by relatively independent and distinctive streams of resources, relatively unengaged with either business or public endeavors? When was mingling of money or effort among diverse organizations condemned or praised? Posed from the perspective of firms and state agencies, when and why did such organizations encourage or depend on collaboration with organizations that were understood as voluntary, as significantly different in their defining motivations and responsibilities? When and why did voluntary associations adopt increasingly corporate forms in their structure and practice?

Such questions highlight the emergent character of distinctively "voluntary" organizations in early American history. While many projects of mutual self-help and collective altruism bubbled up through the informal networks of community and kin, such endeavors could become durable entities only through a political act: the granting of a charter. Charters granted organizations a form of legal personhood, allowing the organization itself to make contracts, to hold funds, and to own real estate (see Johann Neem, chapter 2). If organizations are to thrive, they—like Virginia Woolf's women—need rooms of their own. But such charters were not granted lightly. Political elites were extremely wary of dispersing these privileges. For collective enterprises that were not explicitly involved in trade, the granting of a charter required a credible claim that the organization would somehow contribute to the public good. And the associations themselves were not free to define that public good, as well-intentioned religious groups found when President Washington sharply dismissed their offer to raise donations to provide a ransom for Americans taken in the Barbary Coast (Allison 1995). Thus both the fact of and the rationale for a charter were deeply political and, consequently, tightly held by government elites.

In the first decades after independence, charters were not widely granted, but voluntary associations and philanthropic projects soon came to play a significant role in the economic development of the relatively new nation, providing vehicles for the accumulation of liquid capital that could be invested in fledgling industries. In New York, the Society for the Prevention of Pauperism sponsored the creation of the Savings Bank of New York to serve the city's poor and working classes; the bank grew rapidly, serving as one of the major debt holders for the Erie Canal. In Boston, the Massachusetts Hospital Life Insurance Company managed the funds and endowments for many institutions and was a source of credit for the state's textile industry, "siphoning charitable, religious, and educational endowments into regional economic development" (McCarthy 2003, 90–93). For individuals, particularly women and others excluded from many political and economic endeavors, voluntary associations provided important opportunities to cultivate management and financial skills as well as to construct careers for women supporting themselves and their families.

If the financial resources of voluntary associations supported economic development, their direct efforts were more visibly important in the field of social provision and public policy. Rather than building public institutions supported by public funds, many states in the North chose to provide public subsidies to private charitable organizations serving orphans, needy widows, the working poor, and other classes deemed

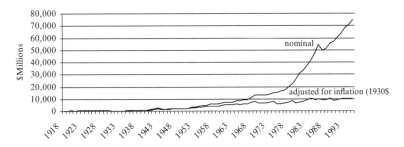

FIGURE I.I. Charitable contributions by individuals.

worthy of support (Clemens 2006; Fitzgerald 2006).[2] Voluntary associations also served as vehicles for political action and advocacy. Associations mobilized Americans across the nation—enfranchised men as well as disenfranchised women and blacks—in support of Sunday schools, temperance, abolition, women's rights, and a host of other proposed remedies to the ills of society (McCarthy 2003; Young 2002). Waves of such political activity reshaped the American party system—first through the mobilization of abolitionists, later through insurgencies sustained by labor, agrarian, and women's associations (Clemens 1997; Sanders 1999). From the late nineteenth century well past the middle of the twentieth, large voluntary associations provided critical vehicles for mobilizing public opinion and sustaining political careers (Skocpol 2003), as well as an infrastructure of insurance, medical care, and general support (Beito 2000).

But just as voluntary associations were put to ever new uses by different groups and individuals, the organizations themselves changed in character. In part, this was a simple result of increasing financial resources. Wartime appeals to voluntarism and the intensification of federal income taxation during World War I combined with the federal charitable deduction for individuals (and, as of the mid-1930s, for corporations) to encourage increased levels of charitable contribution. When adjusted to constant dollars, both individual (figures 1.1 and 1.2) and corporate contributions (figures 1.3 and 1.4) in the period after World War II represent a fundamentally different resource environment from

2. States in the South and the Midwest were less likely to develop extensive subsidy systems. See both Hall (1987) and McCarthy (2003) on this point.

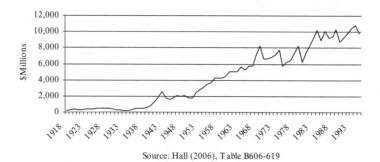

Source: Hall (2006), Table B606-619

FIGURE 1.2. Charitable contributions by individuals (adjusted 1918 dollars).

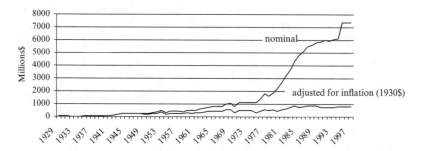

FIGURE 1.3. Growth in corporate philanthropy.

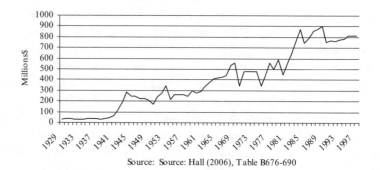

Source: Source: Hall (2006), Table B676-690

FIGURE 1.4. Growth in corporate philanthropy (adjusted 1930 dollars).

that of the 1930s and before. By the 1950s, Arthur M. Schlesinger Sr. remarked on the "fabulous dimensions" of American philanthropy (Cutlip
1965, 477), as private institutions—particularly universities, colleges, and
hospitals—built impressive endowments. Increased resources also contributed to growth in the numbers of nonprofit, voluntary, and religious

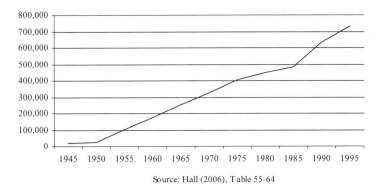

Source: Hall (2006), Table 55-64

FIGURE 1.5. Number of charitable and nonprofit organizations.

entities (figure 1.5), although these trends may also reflect the increasing likelihood that associations would acquire formal legal standing.

Charitable organizations also increasingly responded to the ideals of professionalism, often minimizing the role of volunteers and the embedding of agencies in local communities as professional managers gained greater control (e.g., Davis 1967; Oates 2003; Watson 1922). The rise of "scientific charity" in the early twentieth century transformed the relationship of volunteers to organizational governance as well as to the intended beneficiaries of their actions. A parallel change marked the more political advocacy groups that followed a shift "from membership to management" (Skocpol 2003). Charitable or nonprofit organizations (to use a term that began to gain currency after World War II) diverged ever further from the ideal of voluntary civic engagement that continues to inform many celebratory claims for the sector.

This partial decoupling of voluntary associations from popular civic participation was only one aspect of the shifting alignment of these formally private organizations with governmental institutions and activities. Major political cleavages turned on the desired relationship between private efforts and public programs, with Herbert Hoover championing his "American system" or associational state as a model of governance resting on the capacity for private action to address many social needs. Given the strength of Hoover's identification with voluntary efforts— first in wartime efforts to aid refugees and provide food relief, then as secretary of commerce collaborating with the Red Cross to respond to the devastating Mississippi River Flood of 1927, and finally as president calling for private efforts to manage the devastation of the drought in the

South and unemployment that would become the Great Depression—it has often been assumed that the Roosevelt administration's mark was made primarily in the establishment of fully public entitlements and the marginalization of private charity.

However, the expansion of governmental intervention in social provision from the New Deal forward did not constitute the creation of a sharply delimited bureaucratic state. Even during the 1930s, the full-blown backlash against public subsidies to private charities was short-lived and, by mid-decade, new streams of federal funds began to flow to private nonprofit organizations (Hammack 1999). By the postwar era, these new financial arrangements were taken up as a strategy for building a private alternative to further expansion of federal programs or, failing that, as a means for channeling government funds through private organizations. During the 1950s, new spending initiatives in health care took the form of novel collaborations between government and business—often with the aim of constructing not-for-profit hospitals (Scott et al. 2000, 189–90, 252–58). With the social programs of the Great Society and War on Poverty, collaborations between government agencies and nonprofit organizations multiplied in efforts to both avoid the politically controversial expansion of state bureaucracies and to allow for the "maximum feasible participation" of the poor as well as their advocates (Smith and Lipsky 1993). Yet for all this expansion, the increasing interdependence of government programs and nonprofit—or "charitable"—organizations did not fully penetrate the political consciousness of the time. Thus, in the 1980s, when President Reagan proposed to significantly cut government social spending on the grounds that nonprofits could take care of the needy, the modern field of nonprofit scholarship took off in an effort to document the extent to which the nonprofit sector was dependent on government support (Salamon and Abramson 1982).

The Nonprofit Sector in America's Political Present and Future

Although the current moment is not unprecedented in the interpenetration of voluntary, governmental, and market-oriented organizations, the present debate is significantly more conscious of the interrelationships among these allegedly distinct sectors of society. Policy advocacy is often entwined with claims for the distinctive virtue of one or another organizational vehicle for social provision—the efficiency of business organizations, the altruism of voluntary organizations, the values of "faith-based" programs, or the accountability and universality of fully public programs. However, the current era maintains a much clearer focus on the ways in which these sectors are forming partnerships that are transforming the distinctive nature of each of them.

Many forces have contributed to the transformation of this sector, and a number of important studies have examined the forces in some detail (e.g., Salamon 2002). Three key changes make up the complex configurations in which many nonprofits now operate. First, the transformation of the welfare state over this period has driven fundamental changes in the nonprofit sector. In the era of the receding welfare state, nonprofits have taken on new roles in the provision of public goods, and they have also become engaged in new models for generating funds. While they have lost major sources of funding in the form of grants from federal, state, and local governments, in some sectors nonprofit organizations have responded to the new models of tax credits and fee-for-services in ways that have dramatically changed the operation of nonprofit organizations. Second, new organizational forms have emerged in this period. Most important, the 1980s saw the rise and proliferation of intermediaries—organizations that play a role in brokering relationships between corporations and large foundations on the one hand and nonprofit organizations on the other. Third, funding from the philanthropic community has shifted in ways that have created new pressures and new levels of accountability for nonprofit organizations. This pressure comes from changes in the priorities of independent foundations, but it also comes from the growth in funding from the corporate sector. As funders of nonprofit activities, independent foundations, corporate foundations, and corporations themselves all place greater demands for an accounting of practical and measurable outcomes for the activities of nonprofit organizations, and these pressures have fundamentally changed the ways that nonprofit organizations operate today.

Although these changes embody the ongoing political struggles over the place of nonprofits in the organization of governance, they are also shaped by the increasing salience of firms and markets in many aspects of social life. Of course, commercial concerns have long impinged on the world of voluntary associations: mutual benefit societies sought to buf-

fer workers and farmers from the risks of illness and accident, capitalist enterprise provided the endowments that sustained philanthropy, and
employers monitored the generosity of charities to ensure that they did
not undermine the need for workers to sell their labor on the market.
But in the last two decades of the twentieth century, business increasingly influenced the nonprofit sector in two relatively new ways. First,
markets gained ascendance as *the* normative model not only for business
transactions but for virtually all aspects of economic, social, and political
life in the United States. Second, corporations increasingly sought—and
secured—control over the social agencies that would offer public goods.
In the past, the nonprofit community was to some extent immune from
these general trends. As the "third" or semiautonomous sector, it had
defined itself as a field in which private individuals or groups took independent action, spurred by motives ranging from traditional charity
to social change. Yet this relative autonomy has been increasingly challenged, as the nonprofit sector today has become subject to market logics and corporate control at the same time that it continues to be shaped
by the interplay of voluntary associations and government programs and
policies.

Greater Funding, Greater Competition

As with so many political and organizational developments, it is often easiest to begin by following the money. This is certainly the case
when it comes to understanding the impact of increasing corporate influence on the nonprofit sector and on the relationships between nonprofits and government programs. This influence is somewhat paradoxical; at the same time that business fortunes (along with changes in tax
law) fueled a great expansion of the philanthropic world (and foundations are a major funder of nonprofits), this growth in available resources
has been counterbalanced by increasing demands for business-like accountability and competition. With respect to money alone, the potential
pool for the funding of nonprofit organizations reached an all-time high
at the dawn of the twenty-first century. The economic downturns of 1987
and 2001 notwithstanding, the period in between marked the longest
period of sustained economic growth in the twentieth century for the
U.S. economy, and the accompanying rise in wealth led to a proliferation

of independent, corporate, and community foundations.[3] As the number of foundations in the United States more than doubled at the end of the twentieth century—rising from 21,877 in 1975 to 50,201 in 1999 (figure 1.6)—the overall growth in foundation giving during the same period rose from $1.9 billion in 1975 to $23.3 billion in 1999, a growth of over 1,200 percent in the period, or almost 400 percent in inflation-adjusted dollars (figure 1.7).

Yet, while more money became available for "third sector" funding—from individual and corporate contributions (see figures 1.2 and 1.4) as well as foundation grants—the nonprofit sector faced serious challenges, particularly from the parallel retreat of the federal government as a funder of social programs, many of which were implemented by nonprofit entities. In the early 1980s, changes in government policy—guided by the Reagan administration but carried out at federal, state, and local levels—led to a rapid decline in public funding (in the form of grants) for nonprofit organizations (Salamon 2002). This shift came as part of a more general trend toward the rolling back of the welfare state in order to replace that apparatus with voluntary support from charitable associations.

The conventional wisdom that emerged during this period asserted that a reduction in taxes and welfare-state burdens would lead to an increase in philanthropic and charitable giving. However, this view of the tradeoff between taxes and charitable donations, while popular, is not supported by research, at least not for the corporate sector. Indeed, a number of studies have shown that as taxation declines, so does philanthropic giving (Schwartz 1966; Burt 1983; Bakija and Slemrod 1996).[4] At the same time, competition from the private sector for the income that fee-for-service models (one of the key funding models that replaced federal and state grants) could generate left nonprofits controlling less and less of public-goods services and income. The squeeze in funding, coupled with competition from the for-profit sector and a number of scan-

---

3. The financial crisis of 2008 has interrupted this trend. Foundation and institutional endowments have declined sharply, as have corporate revenues. Thus, nonprofit organizations have seen a decline in foundation and corporate donations at the same time that the demand has increased sharply for many of the social services provided by nonprofit agencies.

4. This association is well-documented across a variety of econometric studies in this line of research. The argument most commonly advanced to explain this association is simple: with taxes, potential givers—individuals or corporations—have incentives to give because of tax write-offs; without taxes, there is no opportunity for write-offs. The result is a decline in giving.

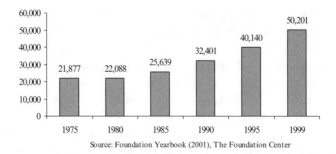

Source: Foundation Yearbook (2001), The Foundation Center

FIGURE I.6. Growth in U.S. foundation population.

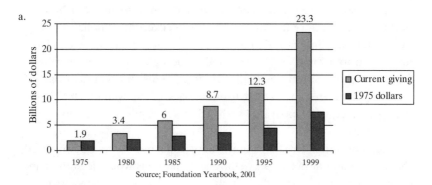

Source; Foundation Yearbook, 2001

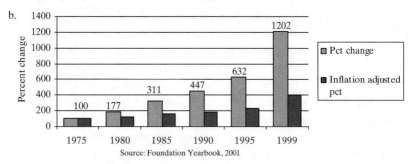

Source: Foundation Yearbook, 2001

FIGURE I.7. Growth in foundation giving. (a) Billions of dollars (b) Percentage change

dals at large-scale nonprofits, brought about a crisis of legitimacy in this sector. These challenges were met by some organizations within the non-profit sector, but only with the emergence of new organizational forms and the adoption of a new set of practices that allow nonprofit organizations to operate successfully in the changing context.

Although governmental funding of the nonprofit sector declined in the form of grants for individual organizations, their access to public resources was not shut off completely. Instead, grants for nonprofit organizations were replaced with a variety of incentive-based funding systems, such as tax credits and vouchers. These types of systems differ from a welfare-state redistribution system and grants from the federal government in a few key ways. First, in a tax credit or voucher system, funding does not pass through the government; instead it flows directly into a pool of potential resources for which organizations can compete. Second, access to these funds is often not limited to nonprofit organizations. In other words, where governmental grants were available only to nonprofit organizations, tax credit and voucher systems are often open to all types of organizations (nonprofit, for-profit, and governmental agencies). As such, competition for these resources is often much more aggressive than is the case when the eligible pool is limited to the nonprofit sector. Third, these systems often facilitate, and in some cases encourage, public-private partnerships in order to put together the most competitive coalition.

To illustrate the changing dynamic relationships among government, corporate, and nonprofit actors, we use the example of the role of the nonprofit sector in the provision of low-income housing, an issue that is explored in greater detail in chapter 9. For years before the 1980s, low-income community development was funded through a combination of Section 8 direct subsidies and Community Development Block Grants. However, in the mid-1980s, a radical transformation took place in the provision of public housing in the United States. With the declining budgets of the Department of Housing and Urban Development and, specifically, the discontinuation of the budget line for new Section 8 housing, the development of federally subsidized low-income housing in the United States had come to a virtual standstill. Direct federal subsidies were replaced by an institution called the Low-Income Housing Tax Credit (LIHTC). The LIHTC dramatically changed the orientation of local community developers—community development corporations—giving them incentives to work with private developers, banks, and corporations to stitch together deals that would eventually fully replace government set-asides.

Under this system, tax credits are allocated to states by the IRS at $1.75 per person in the state population. Corporations provide capital through a syndicator, a type of organization that arose in the 1980s as the financial institution that transforms tax credits that originate with the sponsor into capital that comes from the corporate sector. In return, corporations receive a dollar-for-dollar credit against bottom-line tax liability. This system is now a central feature of the flow of resources around low-income housing and a central feature of hidden corporate welfare. Through this system, corporate resources then flow into development deals, where they are put together with other financing sources, namely, financing from banks, foundations, intermediaries, and public money, where it is available. These deals require a sponsor, who initially applies for tax credits from the state housing finance commissions; these sponsors can be for-profit developers, nonprofit organizations, or a local housing authority. The deals require various sources of public and private funding that are then stitched together into extremely complex and, consequently, very asset-intensive deals. More important, they bring for-profit developers into the mix with nonprofit community developers: if nonprofit developers want to play ball with the new tax credit system, they must build ties with for-profit developers in order to compete with the most efficient (and asset-rich) groups that are proposing deals in search of tax credits; they must conceive of deals that allow them to draw financing from banks, funds from large corporations, and funding from major foundations. And they must give up the key community development agendas around which many of these nonprofit organizations have been built, thereby undermining the claim made by so many nonprofits to foster civic participation and generating complexity that challenges government oversight.

Our example of the partnerships emerging in low-income housing illuminates a second key institutional shift in corporate-community relations, the emergence of "intermediaries"—institutions that arose in the 1980s to serve as the interface between corporations and large-scale foundations on the one hand, and small-scale nonprofit organizations on the other. In 1979, the Ford Foundation set aside $10 million to fund a nonprofit organization, the Local Initiative Support Corporation (LISC), which would have as its central mission community development through an emphasis on low-income housing. Set up to work with local nonprofit organizations, LISC's mission was to serve as the initiator of local development projects with technical, training, project, and operating support for local nonprofits. Serving as an intermediary between nonprofits and various funders from foundations to corporations, LISC grew quickly in its scope and mission, working as an intermediary between the corporate community, banks, and the nonprofits representing local neighborhoods and communities. In 1982, a similar organization—the Enterprise Foundation—was founded by developer Jim Rouse, which also had as its core mission the economic development of local communities. These two organizations became models for a number of other organizations that have stepped into the intermediary role. The most important of these is the United Way, which has transformed its role vis-à-vis the nonprofit community in many metropolitan areas. For example, in Atlanta the United Way has virtually abandoned its "partner organization" funding model, working instead as an intermediary between the corporate community and the nonprofit community organizations in the area. In many metropolitan areas, local-level intermediaries have also emerged to serve similar functions. These organizations not only serve as the interface between the corporations and nonprofit organizations but they also serve as institutions of control. As the emerging controllers of resource distribution, the agendas of the intermediary organizations often transfer to the agendas of the nonprofit organizations in the community as well. For example, in Cleveland, the most powerful intermediary that controls corporate and large-scale foundation funding for nonprofits is Neighborhood Progress, Inc., which "supports" all the nonprofit organizations in its community (figure 1.8). However, a deeper analysis of NPI will reveal that the organization was actually founded as a program sponsored by Cleveland Tomorrow, the primary corporate body shaping government-corporate-nonprofit relations in Cleveland. Thus, the main organizational body that is setting the agenda for corporate-governmental relations is also funding the main intermediary that is controlling the distribution of resources from corporations and foundations to nonprofit organizations. The result is an arrangement that bears little resemblance to a clean division of labor among three distinct sectors; instead, corporations, government agencies, and foundations, as well as nonprofits, are linked together in a complex network that provides a public good—affordable housing—in a form that may not be recognizable as public or private or charitable.

A third critical change that has transformed the activities of nonprofit organizations in the current era has to do with accountability. Increasingly today, funding organizations—be they corporations, independent foundations, or intermediaries (which are often regranting)—are inter-

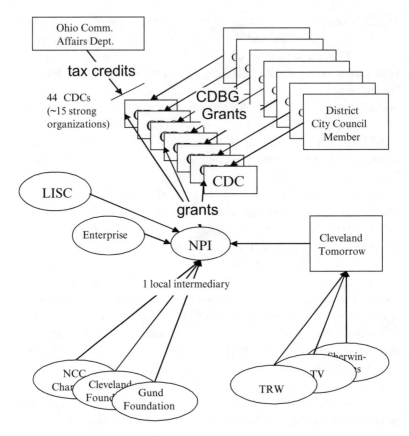

FIGURE 1.8. Corporate control through a local intermediary (NPI) in Cleveland, 2002.

ested in results. Many funders today are only interested in funding non-profit organizations that can demonstrate their efficacy in some measurable way. There are many ways this accountability phenomenon has played out. First of all, on the funding side, this phenomenon has led to a number of institutional changes in the ways that governments, foundations, and intermediaries monitor and measure success. As Salamon (2002, 17) describes it, "The key to this model is an investment approach to grant-making that calls on philanthropic institutions to invest in organizations rather than individual programs, to take a more active hand in organizational governance and operations, and to insist on measurable results." However, beyond the funding side, this new logic has transferred into the ways that nonprofits operate. Nonprofits today think primarily about the ways in which they can demonstrate the results of the programs for which they were funded. The implications are real, because nonprofit organizations have a diminishing opportunity to apply for operational funding. As Smith et al. (2002) explains, "The impact on nonprofit agencies is substantial, since they do not have the unrestricted dollars needed to support difficult-to-fund activities such as administration." Corporate models of accountability may also resonate with other cultural tropes, whether of personal responsibility or the Christian understandings of accountability that figure prominently in Omri Elisha's account of one megachurch and its commitment to urban revitalization (chapter 10).

These examples taken from housing policy capture something of the complex renegotiations of relationships among firms, foundations, government agencies, and nonprofit organizations that are central to contemporary policy debates in the United States. At times, these renegotiations may appear as straightforward capture or domination of one organizational field by another. In many policy domains, for example, corporations have been able to impose a market logic on nonprofit organizations. They have achieved this goal through direct funding (and the creation of accountability standards for receiving these funds) and through the influence (and creation) of intermediary organizations that have a direct effect on how nonprofit organizations behave. While financial crises may undercut business influence through direct contributions, models of accountability and transparency remain important carriers of business methods. Nonprofit organizations have also been shaped in the last twenty-five years by the changes in the welfare state, the emergence of new organizational forms that both fund and monitor the ways they behave, and by a new emphasis on accountability that fundamentally shapes the way they operate. The dependence of nonprofit organizations on public funds, however, changes the stakes in political advocacy and the cultivation of political sponsorship. Thus the current moment in the history of American governance represents yet another variation on the long-contested relationships among voluntary, entrepreneurial, and governmental activity.

In the changes described above, two aspects of the perspective we present here deserve underscoring. First, our perspective emphasizes the linkages between sectors as much as the distinctions among the sectors. These linkages are dynamic and constantly evolving and the ties across the sectors shape the organizations within them. For example, in

James Evans's account of the rise of nonprofit research institutes (chapter 6), we find a group of nonprofit organizations that were created as a response to the shortcomings of the market that ultimately retreat from the market in terms of the logic of how they operate. This is a fascinating account that gives us much to think about in terms of the ties between industry and the nonprofit sector, where market logics prevail, and the ways in which organizations respond to market failures. Second, it is important to note that the transformations we have described above are part of a *dynamic* system of interaction among government, corporate, and nonprofit organizations. An important part of the dynamic historical account we are presenting here focuses on the process of change that has helped to transform the organizations in these sectors and the relationships among them. Social movements have long been a driving force in the evolution of American society, and many of the processes of change we are pointing to here highlight the overlap between the social movement forces and the transformation of organizations in the three sectors. As in the case of the Community Development Corporations (CDCs) and Community Based Organizations (CBOs) described in the chapters by Michael McQuarrie (chapter 9) and Nicole Marwell (chapter 8), there are clear linkages between the social movements for community-based housing development and the organizational forms that each of these authors study. We see similar dynamics with social movements and organizational change in the example of Tepeyac (described by Alyshia Gálvez, chapter 11), from an organization under the Catholic Church to a rather unique organizational form—a grassroots transnational organization. But this story is about more than just the ties between nonprofit organizations and the social movements of which they are a part. It is also about social trends in religion that have supported the growth of "megachurches" in American society over the last fifty years, examined by Omri Elisha. In each of these chapters, we find clear examples of the importance of studying the spaces between sectors, and the ways in which the evolving linkages across sectors are shaping the organizations within the sectors in profound ways.

Overview of the Book

Our task in this book is to retrace the major lines of that history and to address the practical, analytical, and normative implications of the current moment. In this introductory essay, we have tried to establish "politics and partnerships" as a distinctive problematic for the nonprofit literature as well as for research in American political development. These questions are not simply of interest to scholars, inasmuch as they engage the very real stakes involved in the changing nonprofit sector of the past two decades, in the efforts to fundamentally reorganize relationships among government agencies, markets, and nonprofit organizations in American public policy.

The first two sections of the volume will address the deep roots of "politics and partnerships" in American history. Johann Neem (history, Western Washington University) addresses how the development of voluntary associations and corporations created tensions with the project of creating a unifying national culture in the era immediately following the American Revolution. As state leaders confronted emerging political and religious pluralism, they imposed starker boundaries between state institutions and civil society, which, somewhat ironically, created a situation in which civic organizations provided vehicles for the fuller development of American nationalism through the early nineteenth century. Yet civic and voluntary organizations remained politically problematic. Thus, what has been described as a domain of *voluntary* activity has been grounded in a pervasive legal framework, supported by the coercive powers of the state.

Rather than being a timeless feature of the American polity, the legal and organizational frameworks for the construction of private associations and charities were worked out in successive political conflicts and social experiments. Against this background of a well-developed field of associations and charities, the development of the modern American welfare state appears in a different light. Thus, the remaining chapters in this section will address the expansion of state capacity through the twentieth century in conjunction with the enrollment of private organizations—or even their creation—in the implementation of public policies. These arrangements are particularly important for understanding how Americans were constituted as objects of public or philanthropic intervention as well as citizens capable of self-government. In addressing problems such as poverty and race relations, for example, philanthropists claimed a public role for themselves. Mark Hendrickson (history, Colorado State University) argues that labor and economic experts in nongovernmental organizations were responsible for taking on the issues that the government was unwilling to tackle itself, such as the length of the workday and the claims of black workers. Foundations provided an alternative arena for policy formation, if not necessarily adoption. Although philanthropists and charities often spoke as altruistic proponents of the public good, they and their organizations were also political entities. With the onset of the drought and industrial unemployment that began the Great Depression, the role of private charity—and of the Red Cross in particular—became intensely politicized, leading to a dramatic (if temporary) drawing of a bright line between government funding and private charitable organizations. Elisabeth Clemens (sociology, University of Chicago) traces events "in the shadow of the New Deal" as the institutionalization of new public programs established a new division of labor between government and charity, a reconfiguration that, in turn, transformed charitable organizations into those nonprofit organizations that would become vital partners in the expansion of public intervention during the 1960s (Smith and Lipsky 1993).

Not all philanthropists were of one mind on this partnership between private efforts and government programs, however. The second set of chapters addresses the relation of business to the nonprofit sector. Alice O'Connor (history, University of California—Santa Barbara) reconstructs the conservative reaction to the alliance of liberal foundations and the federal government in the War on Poverty, a reaction that consolidated the rightward turn in American politics while creating new opportunities for incorporating market ideologies and practices in the domain of foundations and nonprofit organizations.

The prominence of models drawn from business extends well beyond social welfare policy. Across a wide range of policy domains, new arrangements are emerging that are not private, because they would not exist without public money; yet, they are not public, because they rely heavily on private financing and provision and complex relationships among a variety of private actors. Drawing on a large survey of corporate practices in the area of corporate philanthropy, Doug Guthrie (management and sociology, New York University) explores the giving priorities of corporations in the United States. He shows, for example, that higher tax rates at the state level increase corporate philanthropic giving; publicly traded corporations give significantly more to international causes (and less to their localities) than their private counterparts; corporations with formal offices dedicated to corporate philanthropy give significantly more than their counterparts without formal offices devoted to the task; and corporations with female CEOs direct a higher percentage of their giving to their localities than organizations run by male CEOs. James Evans (sociology, University of Chicago) explores the implications for these arrangements in a field long dominated by some of the largest and most prominent nonprofit organizations in the country: research universities. How do public and private research and development initiatives interact to transform basic research in agricultural biotechnology?

In the United States, this distinctively heterogeneous system of governance has set the terms for its own transformation and a dramatic reorganization of the delivery of public goods over the past twenty-five years. As welfare states retreat and a market logic increasingly shapes the delivery of public goods, funding from philanthropic organizations and other private sources is playing an increasingly large role in issues of social welfare. At the same time, these new relationships can potentially transform the civic organizations now charged with new public roles. Nicole Marwell (sociology, Columbia University) uses her research on New York community organizations to explore how and when these new funding relationships facilitate the "re-politicization" of social service and advocacy groups. The transformations driven by contemporary public policy and novel forms of religious organization are considerably more complex than simple phrases such as the "privatization of public goods" or "public-private partnerships" portray. In a study of the nonprofit role in public housing programs, Michael McQuarrie (sociology, University of California—Davis) examines these public-private partnerships and the increasing corporatization of the nonprofit sector in this field. Central to such new arrangements for providing goods that were previously the responsibility of welfare states are financial mechanisms that have given rise to entirely new industries. For example, in the United States it has become increasingly popular to use tax credits for corporations as a way of raising funding for the development of a variety of public goods, from low-income housing to funding for schools to the subsidization of business in low-income areas. As with faith-based spending programs, these new business models make normative claims for particular types of organizations, hybrid arrangements that can draw on the virtues of civil society, the market, and government alike. But, by privileging business models, such policy initiatives have the potential to depoliticize community advocacy organizations, long important players in local urban policy.

Over much of the twentieth century, relations between the federal government and the varied population of nonprofit organizations and foundations were repeatedly contested and reconfigured. Perhaps nowhere has this intertwining of politics and voluntarism been more controversial than in the realm of religion. Although much of the public commentary has focused on the faith-based initiatives supported by the administration of George W. Bush, both Omri Elisha (anthropology, School of American Research) and Alyshia Gálvez (anthropology, Seton Hall University) document how religious organizations serve as vehicles or arenas for engagement with social issues. Elisha traces the rewarding but fraught relationships between a relatively well-off congregation and an inner-city revitalization effort in Kentucky. Here, congregations become vehicles of social policy, and business firms are instruments of religious purpose. Finally, Gálvez documents how religious confraternities in New York City served as vehicles for the political empowerment of undocumented Mexican immigrants and, in the wake of the September 11 attacks on the World Trade Center, how they were themselves transformed into service providers and political lobbies for members and their survivors who were not citizens and, because undocumented, not easily added to the official roster of victims. As Gálvez illustrates, the interrelationship between nonprofits and state agencies does not only constitute individuals as citizens but establishes the conditions for the transformation of formal political institutions and voluntary organizations.

* * *

Since the time of de Tocqueville, scholars have been interested in the associational life that forms the fabric of American society. Nonprofit organizations have played significant roles in the emergence of many different aspects of the American welfare and workplace structure that is in place today. Yet, in recent years, the nature of the American nonprofit sector has taken on a new and different form. In the era of the receding welfare state, nonprofits have been forced to rely more heavily on funding from the private sector, and these partnerships have, in many cases, led to new organizational incentives and even new organizational forms and practices. In the chapters that follow, the contributors to *Politics and Partnerships* explore these issues and many more. We bring these chapters together to consider both the historical roles of the nonprofit sector in American society and the ways in which nonprofits have been transformed in the last quarter century.

References

Allison, Robert J. 1995. *The Crescent Obscured: The United States and the Muslim World, 1776–1815.* New York: Oxford University Press.

Bakija, Jon, and Joel Slemrod. 1996. *Taxing Ourselves: A Citizen's Guide to the Debate over Taxes.* Cambridge: MIT Press.

Beito, David T. 2000. *From Mutual Aid to the Welfare State: Fraternal Societies and Social Services, 1890–1967.* Chapel Hill: University of North Carolina Press.

Berry, Jeffrey M., with David F. Arons. 2003. *A Voice for Nonprofits.* Washington, D.C.: Brookings Institution Press.

Burt, Ronald. 1983. *Corporate Profits and Cooptation: Networks of Market Constraints and Directorate Ties in the American Economy.* New York: Academic Press.

Bush, George H.W. 1989. "White House Fact Sheet on the 1,000 Points of Light Initiative." George Bush Presidential Library, http://bushlibrary.tamu.edu/research/papers/1989.html.

Clemens, Elisabeth S. 1997. *The People's Lobby: Organizational Innovation and the Rise of Interest Group Politics in the United States, 1890–1925.* Chicago: University of Chicago Press.

———. 2006. "Lineages of the Rube Goldberg State: Building and Blurring Public Programs, 1900–1940." In *Rethinking Political Institutions: The Art of the State,* edited by Ian Shapiro, Stephen Skowronek, and Daniel Galvin. New York: New York University Press.

Cutlip, Scott M. 1965. *Fund Raising in the United States: Its Role in America's Philanthropy.* New Brunswick, N.J.: Rutgers University Press.

Davis, Allen Freeman. 1967. *Spearheads for Reform: The Social Settlements and the Progressive Movement, 1890–1914.* New York: Oxford University Press.

Fitzgerald, Maureen. 2006. *Habits of Compassion: Irish Catholic Nuns and the Origins of New York's Welfare System, 1830–1920.* Urbana: University of Illinois Press.

Hall, Peter Dobkin. 1987. "A Historical Overview of the Private Nonprofit Sector." In *The Nonprofit Sector: A Research Handbook,* edited by Walter W. Powell, 3–26. New Haven: Yale University Press.

———. 2006. "Nonprofit, Voluntary, and Religious Entities." In *Historical Statistics of the United States: Earliest Times to Present,* edited by Susan Carter, Scott Sigmund Gartner, Michael R. Haines, Alan L. Olmstead, Richard Sutch, and Gavin Wright. New York: Cambridge University Press.

Hammack, David. 1999. "Foundations in the American Polity, 1900–1950." In *Philanthropic Foundations: New Scholarship, New Possibilities,* edited by Ellen Condliffe Lagemann. Bloomington: Indiana University Press.

McCarthy, Kathleen D. 2003. *American Creed: Philanthropy and the Rise of Civil Society, 1700–1865.* Chicago: University of Chicago Press.

Oates, Mary J. 2003. "Faith and Good Works: Catholic Giving and Taking." In *Charity, Philanthropy, and Civility in American History,* edited by Lawrence J. Friedman and Mark D. McGarvie. New York: Cambridge University Press.

Salamon, Lester M. 2002. *The State of Nonprofit America.* Washington, D.C.: Brookings Institution Press.

Salamon, Lester M., and Alan J. Abramson. 1982. *The Federal Budget and the Nonprofit Sector.* Washington, D.C.: Urban Institute Press.

Sanders, Elizabeth. 1999. *Roots of Reform: Farmers, Workers, and the American State, 1877–1917.* Chicago: University of Chicago Press.

Schwartz, R. A. 1966. "Corporate Philanthropic Contributions." *Journal of Finance* 23: 479–97.

Scott, W. Richard, Martin Ruef, Peter J. Mendel, and Carol A. Caronna. 2000. *Institutional Change and Healthcare Organizations: From Professional Dominance to Managed Care.* Chicago: University of Chicago Press.

Skocpol, Theda. 2003. *Diminished Democracy: From Membership to Management in American Civic Life.* Norman: University of Oklahoma Press.

Smith, Steven Rathgeb, and Michael Lipsky. 1993. *Nonprofits for Hire: The Welfare State in the Age of Contracting.* Cambridge: Harvard University Press.

Watson, Frank Dekker. 1922. *The Charity Organization Movement in the United States: A Study in American Philanthropy.* New York: Macmillan Company.

Young, Michael. 2002. "Confessional Protest: The Religious Birth of U.S. National Social Movements." *American Sociological Review* 67: 660–88.

PART I

Of, By, and Instead of Politics

Americans have always and easily formed associations. This claim is central to the celebratory story often told about American politics and civil society. Grounded in a stylized reading of Alexis de Tocqueville's classic *Democracy in America,* this story portrays voluntary associations as an expression of conditions in the New World and a guarantee of the continued health of the new democracy. Associations, in this view, are "schools for citizenship" in which Americans overcome excessive individualism, forge social ties with others, and master Robert's Rules of Order and the other basic skills required for democratic participation.

However influential, this account overlooks the political contention required to establish the legal and institutional framework within which an associational world could come to flourish. Although citizen associations had been central to the revolutionary enterprise, leaders of the newly founded republic were less than unanimously enthusiastic about continuing to legitimate independent civic organizations. This antipathy, however, was eroded through sustained conflicts over the relation of dissenting congregations to established churches and over the granting of corporate charters to private organizations. In the process, Johann Neem argues, civic organizations came to serve as a vehicle for cultivating expansive social ties that would in turn sustain an emergent understanding of genuinely national citizenship. This political role of private associations was, however, a mixed blessing, as civic organizations first amplified dissension over abolition and then, after the Civil War, provided a setting in which ties between the antagonistic sections could be restored.

This capacity both to contain and amplify social conflict was not limited to the large, membership-based associations so characteristic of the nineteenth century. At the turn of the century, the large foundation emerged as a new species of private but civic organization. Just as large membership associations had constituted a kind of polity outside of formal politics, so too foundations were a vehicle for addressing issues that were either too controversial or too difficult to be managed through the usual challenges of administrative and electoral politics. Organizations such as the Russell Sage Foundation and the National Bureau of Economic Research devoted themselves to documenting problems of the industrializing economy and, in the process, were sometimes able to recast destabilizing political demands into technical problems of business efficiency. As Mark Hendrickson illustrates through a comparison of foundation efforts to institute the eight-hour day in the steel industry and to protect the rights of African American workers, these nonprofit research efforts were able to address issues "disregarded by the state." Questions that might have been addressed through public debate or electoral competition were, instead, transformed into the technical language of expert research.

If nonprofit organizations could serve as vehicles for politics by other means, they could also serve as nongovernmental extensions of governance. Although its scope would expand massively by the late twentieth century, the practice of channeling public funds to private charitable organizations was well established before the century began. Thus, the great episodes of twentieth-century state-building—world war, depression, and a second world war—were always already embedded in complex relationships between associational and governmental means for organizing social efforts. At the center of these struggles was the American Red Cross, a federally chartered charitable corporation grounded in small-scale volunteer chapters throughout the nation. As Elisabeth Clemens explains "In the Shadow of the New Deal," the challenges of the Depression first tarnished the reputation of voluntary efforts and then made clear the limited capacity of public agencies to match the scale of need in a national crisis. The resulting conflicts over the appropriate role of private voluntary organizations and government agencies transformed the world of private charity inherited from the nineteenth century and created the framework for a recognizable "nonprofit" sector in the postwar era.

From Tocqueville's time to our own, the place of voluntary associations in the American polity has been contested. Yet once the basic framework for associationalism was in place, these not-quite-public organizations would become a persistent part of political mobilization and the arrangements of governance. By the years after the Second World War, this ongoing debate would produce a settlement in the form of the seemingly apolitical "independent" or third sector. Yet, as will be evident in the remainder of this book, recent decades have revived the dynamic negotiations and challenges as to the place of voluntary associations in American life.

CHAPTER TWO

Civil Society and American Nationalism, 1776–1865

Johann N. Neem

It is often assumed that the American voluntary tradition emerged in opposition to, or at least independent of, the state. Since Alexis de Tocqueville's observation that "Americans of all ages, all conditions, and all minds are constantly joining together in groups," scholars and citizens have assumed that voluntary associations and private nonprofit institutions are an American substitute for state action (Tocqueville 2004 [1835, 1840], 595–99). During the Cold War in particular, scholars emphasized the multiple ways in which associations and private institutions acted as buffers against the expansion of state power (Ciepley 2001). Recent work has challenged these conclusions by exploring how the state and its institutions shaped the development of American civil society—by providing federal patronage, and by determining what kinds of associations merited corporate charters, what privileges charters would convey, and to what extent freedom of association should be protected (Schudson 1994; John 1995, 1997; Novak 2001; Skocpol 2003; Starr 2004). Correcting for past assumptions, recent scholarship tilts to the other extreme, emphasizing civil society's dependence on the state.

This chapter offers another perspective by examining the role of civil society in fostering American nationalism. Nationalism, according to Charles Taylor, is vital to modern liberal democracies. In fact, because democracies rely on voluntary consent they require from citizens "much more solidarity and much more commitment to one another in our joint political project than was demanded by the hierarchical and authoritarian societies of yesteryear." In a democracy, persuasion must be used instead of force or violence to achieve one's political goals. For a citizen to be willing to sacrifice her immediate goals, she must consider herself part of an "ongoing collective agency" (Taylor 2003). Without some emotional or affectionate bond—without nationalism—citizens will have little reason to put aside their immediate interests and desires for the good of the whole, including the rule of law: "Only those with a supermuscular Kantian conscience would be willing to knuckle under to a majority with which they felt no links" (Taylor 1995). Similarly, Craig Calhoun argues that democratic politics "requires thinking of 'the people' as active and coherent, and oneself as both a member and an agent" (Calhoun 2007, 147).

Without nationalism, nation-states would not be able to maintain social order over their territories and democratic politics would be threatened. Many scholars have therefore concluded that nationalism is a top-down affair. Since the state seems to be a primary beneficiary of nationalist sentiment, they argue, the state has been the primary agent in fomenting nationalism among its citizens (Gellner 1983; Hobsbawm and Ranger 1983). Nationalism, from this perspective, is a means of justifying existing political power structures by convincing residents of a particular territory that they are members of a shared cultural unit. Certainly, this is in part true: all states, including the United States, have actively sought to use their institutions—none more than public schools—to foster patriotism. But I suggest that American nationalism also developed from the grass roots, in civil society, as much as through state action.

Organizations in civil society were vital to the development of American nationalism.[1] Civic organizers constructed national institutions that connected people throughout the Union, giving Americans a sense of membership in the nation. If Benedict Anderson (1983) is correct that the nation is an "imagined community" that depends on the circulation of print culture to give people throughout a territory the sense of participating in a common political and culture life, it was not the American state(s) but privately organized voluntary associations that most effectively laid these foundations. The development of nationalism as an

---

1. Here I move beyond Merle Curti's (1958) classic formulation that philanthropy is both expressive of and formative of an American national character. My argument is that philanthropic efforts were themselves vital to the very possibility of an American character.

imagined community relies on the formation of local mediating institutions. For an imagined community to take hold, imagination has to
be reinforced by regular activity at the local level (Verba, Schlozman,
and Brady 1995; Skocpol and Fiorina 1999; Putnam 2000). In order for
American nationalism to develop, the state had to permit civic organizers to establish translocal associations that combined print culture with
local activity.

If modern democratic states depend on nationalism, and nationalism
is fostered at least in part within civil society, the relationship between
the state and civil society is rendered more complex. When the post-
revolutionary American state(s) sought to limit the expansion of civil society in the name of republican unity, they also inhibited the development
of nationalism. Only once the state backed off and allowed citizens to organize themselves did a truly vibrant civil society—the kind Tocqueville
witnessed—develop. Between the 1810s and 1840s, this vibrant civil society provided the organizational webs that linked citizens together into an
imagined community. Yet precisely because the nation was constituted
both by the state and by the grassroots institutional networks of civil society, it was vulnerable to persistent lines of schism generated within associations. As sectional conflict heightened during the crisis leading to
civil war, America's civic associations fragmented. The state, dependent
on the loyalties generated in a civil society that it regulated but no longer
controlled, was a victim of this fragmentation. Unable to check the sectional division of America's voluntary sector, and with it the national loyalties of its citizens, the state found itself incapable of holding the Union
together except through the exercise of large-scale military force. On the
eve of the Civil War, many Americans understood that the fragmentation of the polity had begun in civil society—that the very associations
that had forged national unity were now tearing the state apart.

Civil Society from the Top Down

Writers often assume—following Tocqueville—that the emergence of a
vibrant civil society in the United States grew out of the principles of
1776 (Tocqueville 2004 [1835, 1840], 180–84). Voluntary associations, according to this assumption, are as American as apple pie. In fact, the
postrevolutionary state governments hoped to prevent the spread of voluntary associations and nonprofit institutions. Although the Revolution

was carried out by voluntary associations—committees of correspondence, the militia, Congress—leaders worried that if the people continued to form associations they might destabilize the new regimes. The Revolution taught leaders how dangerous "self-created" associations could be. If voluntary associations had helped Americans overthrow British power, imagine the threat they might pose to the new, and fragile, state and federal governments (Neem 2008; Harris 2005). As late as 1822, as the number of voluntary associations expanded, Thomas Jefferson recalled that such associations had been necessary when "the government had combined against the rights of the people," but the 1770s "were days which no man would wish to see a second time." He feared that the proliferation of voluntary associations would lead again to revolution, this time against legitimate republican governments (Peterson 1984, 1454–55).

The Revolution's principles also worked against the development of an independent civil society. Americans believed that the purpose of government was to serve the common good. Drawing from the republican tradition, leaders argued that citizens should put the public interest ahead of their own interests (Wood 1969, 1991). They worried that if citizens formed associations, the result would be fragmentation, with each association promoting its own interests instead of the common good. But American leaders also understood that citizens must learn to think of themselves as part of the new national community. The common good would result not from an abstract commitment to universal principles, but rather through the state's effort to foster a community of affection (Bullock 1996; Burstein 2001). Leaders thus encouraged those political, economic, and social institutions that built common bonds between citizens. In order to ensure that all institutions worked to create a single community, however, they also used state power to determine which associations and institutions were legitimate.

The states hoped to use their control over civil society to foster social, political, and economic unity. State leaders considered all associations and corporations to be public bodies that must serve the common good. For example, state leaders generally supported the expansion of the Freemasons, believing that the organization encouraged fraternal ties of affection between members that would strengthen the community (Bullock 1996; Brooke 1996). In contrast, they condemned the fraternal Society of the Cincinnati out of fear that it would create a hereditary aristocracy with interests distinct from those of the people (Davies 1948;

Myers 1983; Harris 1995). New Englanders bolstered support for the public parochial church in order to promulgate shared moral values learned in common institutions. Connecticut, New Hampshire, and Massachusetts each granted the parochial church tax support until 1818, 1819, and 1833, respectively. Corporations, whether nonprofit or for-profit, were chartered to serve the public good. New England and the middle Atlantic states chartered hundreds of new corporations to provide such public goods as transportation, education, banking, and charity (Handlin and Handlin 1969; Hartz 1948; Seavoy 1982; Hall 1987, 1988; Novak 1996).

Although states encouraged institutions and associations that served the common good, they also sought to ensure that no rival associations were formed. States justified denying legal privileges or ideological legitimacy to specific associations when they threatened to fragment the community. To a surprising extent, states sought to manage civil society in order to protect the common good from pluralism, in contrast to how we often speak of associations today. In the South, for example, states chartered few corporations, out of fear that corporate proprietors would place their own interests ahead of the people's (Campbell 1973; Hall 1992, 20–32; McCarthy 2003, 78–97). Virginia and New York both repealed the Elizabethan Statute for Charitable Uses following the Revolution in order to prevent the formation of trusts beyond state (i.e., the people's) control (Wyllie 1959; Hall 1982; Katz, Sullivan, and Beach 1985; Hall 1992, 30–31). It is well known that American leaders were hostile to political parties. When the Jeffersonians formed "democratic societies" in the 1790s, Federalist leaders condemned them as factions that would divide the people into competing interests (Hofstadter 1969; Koschnik 2001, 2007; Neem 2003). New England limited the legal privileges of dissenting churches in order to protect the parochial church's ability to shape and to represent a united community. In the middle Atlantic states, religious pluralism prevented such a path. In the South, where the Anglican Church had been the established church, the Revolution undermined an institution identified with the Old Regime. In Virginia, however, disestablishment was interpreted in such a manner as to prevent any voluntary church from gaining legal privileges (McLoughlin 1971; Buckley 2000, 45–49; McGarvie 2004). Journeymen's societies—or early labor unions—were constantly condemned for promoting private interests at the public's expense (Tomlins 1993; Neem 2003).

At the federal level, President George Washington and his treasury secretary, Alexander Hamilton, hoped to use the state—and its institutions—to foster loyalty to the new government. The Constitution established what one historian has called a "roof without walls" (Murrin 1987). There was little holding Americans together as a nation either structurally or ideologically. Hamilton recognized that new political and economic institutions were needed to cement the Union together. He supported the formation of a national bank to create a national economy, and proposed establishing a "Society for the Establishment of Useful Manufactures" to encourage American industry and the development of a vibrant domestic market that would tie Americans' interests to the nation's. Hamilton's proposals were resisted by those, such as Thomas Jefferson, who believed that the federal government should not have too much power vis-à-vis the states. These debates spurred the growth of political parties and threatened Washington's and Hamilton's vision of a single united nation. Washington condemned parties and blamed them for the violence of the Whiskey Rebellion. Later, Federalists under President John Adams would pass the Sedition Act to silence Republican organizations. In his 1796 Farewell Address, Washington implored Americans to unite around the new government and centralized economic and political institutions. He hoped that citizens' "sympathy and interest" would remind them that they were "citizens . . . of a common country . . . [which] has a right to concentrate your affections" (Rhodehamel 1997, 965; Matson and Onuf 1990; Elkins and McKitrick 1993, 460–88; Minicucci 2001).

Fragmentation

The top-down model of civil society depended on a state that encouraged certain institutions and limited others. The emergence of partisan conflict in the 1790s made this project more difficult. The growth of the Republican Party meant that Federalists could no longer claim to speak for all the people. Moreover, as party competition intensified, Federalists and Republicans constructed state and national organizations to run candidates for office (Cunningham 1963; Fischer 1965; Hofstadter 1969; Elkins and McKitrick 1993; Koschnik 2007). Continuous party conflict ensured that no leaders could speak for an undivided community.

In New England, dissenting churches—such as the Baptists and Methodists—posed similar challenges to state efforts to create a single community. State leaders tried to prevent the spread of dissenting churches by denying them legal privileges. In 1810, Massachusetts's Federalist chief justice rejected the claim that the state must grant legal rights to any church as "too absurd to be admitted." Dissenters—and Republicans—responded that the state did not have a right to decide who could or could not form a legal church. These conflicts ultimately led to disestablishment and the fragmentation of the community into competing denominations (McLoughlin 1971; Neem 2008).

Partisan and religious conflict spurred legal change. So long as a single party dominated a state, it had no incentive to distinguish between the state and civil society. Associations were only chartered if they served the state's (the people's) interests, and they were usually managed by the same people who held political office. As parties competed for state control, members of both parties recognized the virtue of limiting the state's authority over associations and corporations. The most famous conflict occurred over Dartmouth College in New Hampshire. In this case, Republicans controlled the state and sought to use their power to alter Dartmouth's charter. Federalists controlled Dartmouth and refused to allow the state to take over. The case ended up in the U.S. Supreme Court where Chief Justice John Marshall ruled that charters were contracts that limited the state's authority over corporations. The case transformed civil society–state relations by extending constitutional protection to (now private) nonprofit corporations and associations (Hall 1992; Hammack 1998, 123–41; McGarvie 1999, 2004; Neem 2008, chap. 3).

Following *Dartmouth College,* new ideas and laws were needed for an increasingly independent civil society. During the second party system, Democrats worried about what Adam Smith called "the corporation spirit." They opposed public monopolies and pushed for general incorporation laws. They claimed that no group of individuals deserved special legal privileges from the state. If corporations were to be permitted, all citizens should have equal access to corporate privileges. Their ideas were given expression in the U.S. Supreme Court's 1837 *Charles River Bridge* decision. In that case, Democratic Chief Justice Roger B. Taney argued that monopolies hindered progress. Instead, the state should allow any person to form an association and rely on competition in the market to promote the common good (Kutler 1971).

Whigs, the Democrats' opponents, also developed new ideas. Unlike Democrats, they did not support competition for its own sake. Whigs supported a more active state, yet in a partisan environment Whigs also sought better control over their institutions. They followed the logic of

Dartmouth College and defended the autonomy of nonprofit institutions from the state. They argued that private institutions such as colleges served the common good best when they were not subject to the give-and-take of politics. Although their ideals differed dramatically from the Democrats, they led to a similar conclusion: corporations and associations must be granted independence from the state (Dalzell 1987, 113–63; Hall 1992, 170–87).

As leaders of both parties converged around the importance of protecting the boundary between civil society and the state, states passed new laws. Democrats supported general incorporation laws, often with Whig support, as in an amendment to New York's constitution requiring that all new corporations be formed under general laws (Campbell 1973; Seavoy 1982). Many states also granted their courts equity jurisdiction so they could enforce and oversee private trusts. Massachusetts granted its citizens broad authority to form trusts, whereas New York and Pennsylvania limited the amount of capital a trust could hold out of continued fear of private institutions. In 1844, the U.S. Supreme Court ruled that it had the authority to recognize charitable trusts, granting trusts legal existence in federal common law (Wyllie 1959; Hall 1982; Katz, Sullivan, and Beach 1985; Hall 1992, 30–31). By the 1840s, then, a new ideological and legal framework had been developed that enabled citizens to form associations, trusts, and corporations that were relatively independent of the state.

Civil Society from the Bottom Up

National identity is not just imaginary; it must be made manifest in the daily lives of citizens. Paradoxically, American national identity developed not in spite of but because of the fragmentation of the people into competing parties and denominations. As political leaders stopped trying to prevent associations, the number of associations increased dramatically. Voluntary associations provided their members with concrete settings in which national identification could be constructed and maintained. New translocal communities were established that were united by social and political bonds stronger than those the state had been able to create, and thus they more successfully fostered a sense of nationhood. These associations had myriad purposes; most were not explicitly committed to promoting nationalism. But, by establishing national institutions that included thousands of Americans across the continent, they effectively brought ordinary people, including women and African Americans, into the imagined and actual life of the nation (Appleby, 2000, 194–238; McCarthy 2003).

Political parties were one of the most important building blocks for American nationhood. It was no easy task to develop political identities around the new national government. First, politicians from different states had to learn to trust each other (Trees 2000; Freeman 2001). Second, voters had to think of themselves as participating in national affairs. The formation of parties proved vital to both phenomena by connecting both elites and voters into translocal associations with shared interests and ideologies. Although parties had initially been resisted because they fragmented the public, the realities of political conflict made their emergence unavoidable. The emergence of a functioning party system did indeed fracture the voting public ideologically, but it also made possible the formation of new institutional and ideological links between sections of the new nation. During the first party system, a new partisan press broadcast national issues to thousands of voters (Pasley 2001; Starr 2004). Party leaders also hosted banquets, parades, and organized militias that fostered a sense of partisan—and *national*—identity. Although parties provided alternative visions of what it meant to be American, they still encouraged voters to think of themselves as American (Waldstreicher 1997; Newman 1997; Ryan 1997; Robertson 2001; Koschnik 2007). The partisan press helped build national identity even as it fomented conflict. "Newspapers," David Paul Nord (1991, 395) writes, "were the organizers of faction and sedition. Yet, in their efforts to subvert the state, they helped to build the nation."

The second party system built on these foundations. In January 1827, New Yorker Martin Van Buren proposed a new party, the Democrats, that would help ease sectional tensions. Van Buren understood that even if parties offered distinct visions of what it meant to be an American, so long as they were national in scope they would weaken sectional identities and strengthen the nation (Holt 1978, 20–21; Watson 1990, 87–88). During the era of the second party system, Democrats and Whigs did indeed offer alternative notions of Americanness that produced both intense partisan conflict and deeper commitment to the nation (Welter 1975; Howe 1979; Baker 1983; Kohl 1989). The number of newspapers continued to increase. Parties developed more elaborate machinery to bring out new voters in a mass democracy. They instituted conventions to allow voters to participate directly in choosing national candidates (McKormick 1966; Silbey, Bogue, and Flanigan 1978; Skocpol 2003, 36–37). Election days became festive events where beer flowed and party leaders promised patronage to their loyal supporters (Silbey 1985; Schudson 1998; Altschuler and Blumin 2000). In parades and other events, voters linked local activity to national goals (Baker 1983; Ryan 1997). As more Americans read about and participated in partisan events, they connected their own interests and values to national politics.

Religious leaders were the second important set of organizers. Their denominational and reform associations linked thousands of men and women together across space. And, like parties, evangelicals relied on print culture and local organization to give members a sense of shared participation in a common cause. As Theda Skocpol (2003, 23–24) has written, nineteenth-century voluntary associations "brought citizens together across class lines while linking thousands of local groups to one another and to representatively governed centers of state and national activity." Disestablishment was a particularly important force for spurring organizational development. Since all states except Connecticut, New Hampshire, and Massachusetts disestablished the church immediately following the Revolution, competing religious denominations had an incentive to organize in order to win more converts. Moreover, as Americans moved west, ministers sought to ensure that they had access to churches. As a result, every American denomination developed national organizations to manage their affairs as well as missionary societies to send ministers to the underserved regions of the West. The need for ministers in the West was so urgent that Congregationalists and Presbyterians agreed in 1801 to share pulpits (Mead 1963, 103–33; Mathews 1969; Wright 1992, 77–95; McCarthy 2003, 49–77).

The spread of evangelical associations was also vital to the development of American nationalism. The Second Great Awakening produced what Donald Mathews calls an "organizing process" that forged ties between religious people in the North, South, and West (Mathews 1969; Kuykendall 1982; Lebsock 1984, 195–236; Irons 2003, 96–134; Lockley 2007). The first major national institution was the American Bible Society, established in New York City in 1816. Others soon followed, including the American Board of Commissioners for Foreign Missions, the New England (later American) Tract Society, the American Education Society, the American Temperance Society, and the American Home Missionary Society. Together, these organizations formed what one historian has called an "evangelical united front" to battle the evils of ir-religion and to urge ordinary men and women to work to better their communities (Griffin 1960; Foster 1960). National organizations encour-aged ever-increasing numbers of local associations during the 1820s and 1830s; by 1837 the American Bible Society claimed over nine hundred auxiliary associations, the American Board counted sixteen hundred in 1839, while the American Tract Society included over three thousand. In 1835, the American Temperance Society boasted five thousand local chapters and over a million members. Thanks in part to hired agents, the American Anti-Slavery Society could claim thirteen hundred chapters and 250,000 members in 1838.[2]

Evangelicals and party leaders relied on print culture to spread the word. Evangelicals were on the front lines of a print revolution that made cheap printed material available to more and more Americans. Their agents distributed or sold Bibles and cheap tracts throughout the nation (Nord 1991, 1995; Wosh 1994). Most important were annual re-ports, a new form of print literature that proved central to creating trans-local imagined communities. At first, annual reports were distributed solely to an association's trustees. They were read at board meetings to a small circle. As associations expanded, their membership rosters grew to include people scattered throughout the nation. Annual reports helped build trust between distant members and the central institution. To do so, the reports changed. Early reports were primarily about ad-ministration. By the 1820s and 1830s, however, reports took a more nar-rative form aimed at a general readership. Reports carried stories about the successes of the past year, often with vivid examples. These stories helped make local members participants in a shared cause. In addition, reports began listing local societies and their annual contributions to ex-hibit how national (and sometimes international) work depended on lo-cal efforts. Association officers consciously used reports to develop ties between themselves and their constituents. Annual reports also helped show citizens how to organize associations. Annual reports fostered na-tional identity by linking local activity to a national institution and set of causes (Neem 2008, chap. 4).[3]

2. For statistics, see Griffin 1960, 83; Strong 1910, 145; Wright 1992, 5; Abzug 1994, 90; Walters 1978, 80–81.

3. As Michael Warner (1990, xiii) argues, "It becomes possible to imagine oneself, in the act of read-ing, becoming part of an arena of the national people that cannot be realized except through such me-diating imaginings."

Both political leaders and religious reformers relied on local activity combined with print culture to develop organizations that were national in scope. They organized not to promote harmony but to compete against each other. Parties sought to win elections, and they relied on their local chapters as well as the press to convince voters to support them over their opponents. Similarly, religious leaders competed with each other for converts and, in their reform associations, hoped to create a more Christian America even when doing so brought them into conflict with political leaders and other citizens. The antebellum era was characterized by both high social capital and intense divisions. Nonetheless, competition and fragmentation provided an impetus for organization, and these organizations helped Americans from all regions participate in a national cultural life. Even elite institutions such as Harvard and Yale, despite lacking a grassroots base, contributed to the development of American national identity by opening themselves up to youth from around the country and providing a common set of experiences and values among future economic, political, and social leaders (Scott 1978; Hall 1982, 151–77).

Although the state(s) had originally hindered the development of a vibrant independent civic sector by limiting the freedom of association, in other ways it proved more conducive. In fact, some have argued that the emergence of a national public sphere of print and association was produced by the state (Skocpol, Ganz, and Munson 2000; Novak 2001; Starr 2004). A more moderate claim is that the state set the parameters for a national public sphere but did not explicitly constitute it.[4] First, the federal government built a national postal service and offered discounted rates to newspapers. The postal service aided organizers' efforts to reach a national audience and, in doing so, facilitated the formation of a national imagined community, as Richard R. John argues (John 1995; Skocpol, Ganz, and Munson 2003; Starr 2004). Second, state support for internal improvements—turnpikes, canals, and railroads—helped create a domestic economic market that linked Americans together, while also providing an infrastructure for civic organizers as they constructed translocal associations. Responding to opponents of federally funded internal improvements, Senator John C. Calhoun noted that "whatever

---

4. Novak (2001) is correct that state laws governing associations, especially as defined in acts of incorporation and judicial decisions, shaped what groups could do. Nonetheless, the state proved less effective at fostering a vibrant civil society when it sought to control and limit associational life than when it allowed citizens the freedom to form their own associations.

impedes the intercourse of the extremes with . . . the centre of the republic, weakens the Union." He urged Americans to "bind the republic
together with a perfect system of roads and canals" (Potter 1976, 7–17,
at 9; see also Larson 2001; Minicucci 2001, 264–67). Third, by protecting the independence of nonprofit corporations after *Dartmouth College,* the state ensured that citizens would feel confident giving money to
chartered institutions and associations. Fourth, whether states granted
their courts equity privileges affected the development of elite institutions (Hall 1982, 1987). The 1844 U.S. Supreme Court's decision in the
Girard Will case extended federal support for such institutions (Wyllie
1959; Campbell 1973). Finally, the very existence of a national state set
boundaries on citizens' outlooks; although some reformers participated
in international causes, most limited their sphere of action and imagination to the nation itself.

Sectional Conflict and Civil War

As sectional conflict between the North and the South intensified in the
1850s, the structural forces holding the Union together fractured. National organizations divided regionally, and, in the process, severed the
institutional networks that tied Americans together into one people. At
the same time, while Northerners emphasized the importance of a national economy, the South became convinced that its own economic
interests—dependent on exporting cotton to England—lay outside the
Union. Increasingly, Southern political economists argued in favor of
free trade and criticized Northern efforts to use tariffs to protect domestic manufactures and cultivate a domestic market. Southerners accused
Northerners of placing their own economic interests ahead of those of
the South. Northerners responded that they sought to develop an in-
terdependent national market in which the South produced cotton, the
West staple goods, and the North manufactures. The nation would then
be a self-sufficient and harmonious economic entity. Southerners coun-
tered that the North could not and did not consume enough cotton; free
trade with Britain was vital to Southern economic health (Schoen 2003,
2004; Onuf and Onuf 2006).

Just as Southerners denied the economic value of the Union, political and religious fragmentation would make it easier for Southerners
to deny the political and cultural value of the Union. Sectional conflicts

over slavery produced major schisms in the nation's three largest Protestant denominations. In the 1830s and 1840s, Presbyterians, Methodists, and Baptists all divided regionally over their churches' official position regarding the morality of slavery (Smith 1972, 74–128; Goen 1985; Snay 1993). These divisions were often framed around theological or church governance questions but they ultimately concerned whether the church should sanction slavery and slaveholders. If the formation of national denominational and reform associations had proven vital to national identity, the severing of these bonds helped make possible new sectional feelings that in time would contribute to the Civil War.

In the 1830s, Northern evangelicals had started to consider slavery un-Christian just as Southern evangelicals were articulating a proslavery Christianity in the wake of Nat Turner's 1831 rebellion (Irons 2008). These distinct ideological paths forced slavery into the national religious forums of every denomination. Presbyterians first fractured in 1837 between Old School and New School factions. The issue here was largely theological. Old School Presbyterians were critical of the New School's downplaying of original sin and conversion and the New School's emphasis on good works (through reform organizations) rather than faith alone. But the division took place on largely sectional grounds, and slavery was a factor. In 1856, the Southern presbytery of Lexington stated that its members legitimately could hold slaves. The General Assembly of the New School Presbyterians condemned the proclamation in 1857 and, in turn, twenty-one Southern and border presbyteries left to form a new synod. The Methodists fractured in 1844 over whether their governing council could discipline a minister for holding slaves. Baptists lacked central governing councils, but their missionary society divided in 1845 when Northern Baptists admitted that they would not be willing to allow slaveholders to serve as missionaries (Smith 1972; Goen 1985; Snay 1993).

Political and religious leaders understood that the division of the churches was a bad omen for the future of the Union. As one historian argues, "The contention that the denominational schisms foreshadowed political disunion rested on the assumption that religious unity provided an important moral bond that held the political union together" (Snay 1993, 140). In April 1845, Senator Henry Clay commented:

> Indeed, scarcely any public occurrence has happened for a long time that gave
> me so much real concern and pain as the menaced separation of the Church,

by a line throwing all the Free States on one side, and all the Slave States on the other.

I will not say that such a separation would necessarily produce a dissolution of the political union of these States; but the example would be fraught with imminent danger, and, in co-operation with other causes unfortunately existing, its tendency on the stability of the Confederacy would be perilous and alarming. (Goen 1985, 100–101)

Senator John C. Calhoun agreed with Clay in a speech delivered on March 4, 1850:

The cords that bind the States together are not only many, but various in character. Some are spiritual or ecclesiastical; some political; others social. . . . The strongest of those of a spiritual and ecclesiastical nature, consisted in the unity of the great religious denominations, all of which originally embraced the whole Union. All these denominations, with the exception, perhaps, of the Catholics, were organized very much upon the principle of our political institutions. . . . [their denominational and voluntary associations] contributed greatly to strengthen the bonds of Union. The ties which had held each denomination together formed a strong cord to hold the whole Union together; but, powerful as they were, they have not been able to resist the explosive effect of slavery agitation.

The first of these cords, which snapped, under its explosive force, was that of the powerful Methodist Episcopal Church . . .

The next cord that snapped was that of the Baptists. . . .

If the agitation goes on, the same force, acting with increased intensity, as has been shown, will finally snap every cord, when nothing will be left to hold the States together except force. (Goen 1985, 104–5)

It was clear to many observers that the institutional networks that made national identity possible were now fraying.

Following the church schisms, the parties themselves fragmented. During the 1850s, the second party system broke down. Regional economic divisions combined with increasingly divisive debates over slavery and westward expansion to divide the political nation in half. Moreover, following the demise of the Whig Party, the new Republican coalition made no serious effort to build a base in the South. Composed of advocates of free labor, Republicans believed that the westward expansion of slavery would use up land that should go to independent farmers. Their platform thus had little appeal to Southerners, but it drew in many anti-slavery politicians and voters (Foner 1995). The Democrats also divided between Southerners who demanded a proslavery plank in the party platform and Northerners who refused to support such a plank. In 1860, Democrats ran different candidates in the North and the South. Commenting on the fragmentation of the Democrats, a Virginia newspaper correctly observed, "The division of the Democratic party by a geographical line upon the question of slavery, is the most ominous disaster that can happen to the country. When this bond is broken what remains to hold us together? What other national organization can take the place of the Democratic party, in case it is broken and scattered? This is a serious question, not only for Democrats, but for all men" (Staunton *Valley Observer,* May 8, 1860, as quoted in Ayers, 2003, 62–63).

In the 1860 election, Abraham Lincoln was elected without a single Southern electoral vote. Southerners did not consider his election legitimate since Republicans had no ties to the South. The sectional division of national parties opened the door to secession as politicians no longer had an incentive to seek national unity. The regional fragmentation of parties proves how important their national networks were to holding the Union together, and how the demise of these institutions enabled sectional tensions to lead to a civil war (Potter 1976, 224–65, 405–7; Holt 1978; Gienapp 1996).

During the Civil War, sectional institutional networks proved vital to sustaining nationalism. Southern proslavery ministers not only defended slavery but exhorted Southerners to fight and reassured them that their god was on their side. Southern ministers argued that America's role as the Redeemer Nation now belonged to the Confederacy. Northern ministers did the same for their side (Smith 1972, 166–207; Goen 1985, 109–40; Snay 1993, 151–218; Irons 2008; Rubin 2005, 34–42). Northern political parties and evangelical voluntary associations, including the U.S. Sanitary Commission, sustained Northern support for the war and cooperated with the state to mobilize citizens and resources (Carwardine 2003, 257–96; McCarthy 2003, 192–200). Equally important in the North were both popular and elite Union clubs that connected loyalty to the nation with support for the Republican Party and the North's goals in the war (Lawson 2002). Without strong ties to their fellow citizens in the other region, neither politicians and voters nor ministers and congregants had much incentive to promote intersectional harmony. Their imagined communities were circumscribed by the institutions to which they belonged. For Northerners, moreover, they connected their sectional values with the nation's (Lawson 2002; Carwardine 2003; Onuf and Onuf 2006). Certainly, the closer one got to the boundary between the North and the South, the more interaction (economic, cultural, and religious) there was between the regions, the more hesitancy and uncertainty remained, and the more willing citizens were to seek compromise (Ayers 2003). But the only major group to continue to voice loud opposition to the Republicans' policies concerning slavery and secession were some Northern Democrats, and they were also the only political leaders in the North that remained tied to organizational networks in the South.

Conclusion

Following the Civil War, the emergence of a nationally integrated market dominated by corporate capitalism challenged the ability of local communities to manage their own affairs. The new market left many Americans feeling dislocated and seeking new ways to situate themselves in an increasingly complex society (Wiebe 1967). The state provided one context by which Americans could orient themselves, but voluntary associations again proved equally important. Political parties connected some Americans into national political units competing for power. Middle-class Americans also formed professional organizations that weakened their local ties while basing their local authority, status, and identity on their membership in national associations (Wiebe 1967). The Populist Party, the female suffrage and temperance movements, the Farmers Alliance and the Grange, and labor unions helped Americans resurrect the idea of "the people" as an imagined community in the minds of many Americans (Clemens 1997; Kazin 1995). And, finally, the decades between the Civil War and the turn of the century saw the growth of national federated fraternal associations. These associations provided members social insurance in an era before a viable government safety net, but they also provided sites for sociability. Despite their diversity and their tendency to divide people into competing communities locally, they connected Americans nationally, reinforcing a sense of the nation in the wake of civil war (Skocpol 2003; Kaufman 2003; Beito 2000; Putnam and Gamm 1999). Civil society thus once again helped forge national identity through its overlapping institutional networks, laying a foundation for the subsequent expansion of federal power as Americans adapted to a national economy increasingly carried out by large corporations.

The emergence of American national identity in civil society following the Revolution, and then civil society's role in fragmenting the Union, provides three lessons. First, people are members of those communities into which they are tied by institutions. For the United States, grassroots efforts by political and religious organizers proved as important as the state in developing these institutions. Second, to a certain degree, Revolutionary-era leaders were correct that shared institutions are vital to fostering national ties. Once parties and denominations fractured regionally, civil war was made more likely. Parties and denominations fragmented over public issues and, sometimes, over internal ones specific to their particular communities. The result was the same, however: regional divisions that weakened the bonds linking citizens together in civil society. As Craig Calhoun (1997, 103; see also Potter 1962) observes, "The discourse of nationalism can be employed equally in the service of unification or secession." This is particularly true when there are no strong countervailing structures—economic, political, and cultural institutions—to link people together (see Dahl 1967, 288–89, 311–15, 338–70, on the importance of crosscutting cleavages). Finally, pluralism encourages the growth of national identity by fostering myriad groups in which loyalties are cultivated. But the lessons are paradoxical. If the state could not impose national identity from the top down, how should it prevent its own demise if grassroots efforts cease to promote unity? Should the state limit associations when they endanger the viability of the nation? Or should our definition of nationhood be more flexible and permit new national groups, when they get a sense of themselves as such, to alter existing political structures?

References

Abzug, Robert H. 1994. *Cosmos Crumbling: American Reform and the Religious Imagination.* New York: Oxford University Press.

Altschuler, Glenn C., and Stuart M. Blumin. 2000. *Rude Republic: Americans and Their Politics in the Nineteenth Century.* Princeton: Princeton University Press.

Anderson, Benedict. 1983. *Imagined Communities: Reflections on the Origin and Spread of Nationalism.* London: Verso.

Appleby, Joyce. 2000. *Inheriting the Revolution: The First Generation of Americans*. Cambridge: Harvard University Press.

Arieli, Yehoshua. 1964. *Individualism and Nationalism in American Ideology*. Cambridge: Harvard University Press.

Ayers, Edward L. 2003. *In the Presence of Mine Enemies: War in the Heart of America, 1859–1863*. New York: W. W. Norton.

Baker, Jean H. 1983. *The Affairs of Party: The Political Culture of Northern Democrats in the Mid-Nineteenth Century*. Ithaca: Cornell University Press.

Beito, David T. 2000. *From Mutual Aid to the Welfare State: Fraternal Societies and Social Services, 1890–1967*. Chapel Hill: University of North Carolina Press.

Breen, T. H. 2004. *The Marketplace of Revolution: How Consumer Politics Shaped American Independence*. New York: Oxford University Press.

Brooke, John L. 1996. "Ancient Lodges and Self-Created Societies: Voluntary Association and the Public Sphere in the Early Republic." In *Launching the Extended Republic: The Federalist Era*, edited by Ronald Hoffman and Peter J. Albert, 273–377. Charlottesville: University of Virginia Press.

Buckley, Thomas E., S.J. 2000. "The Use and Abuse of Jefferson's Statute: Separating Church and State in Nineteenth-Century Virginia." In *Religion and the New Republic: Faith in the Founding of America*, edited by James H. Hutson, 41–63. Lanham, Md.: Rowman and Littlefield.

Bullock, Steven C. 1996. *Revolutionary Brotherhood: Freemasonry and the Transformation of the American Social Order, 1730–1840*. Chapel Hill: University of North Carolina Press.

Burstein, Andrew. 2001. "The Political Character of Sympathy." *Journal of the Early Republic* 21, no. 4 (Winter): 601–32.

Calhoun, Craig J. 1997. *Nationalism*. Minneapolis: University of Minnesota Press.

———. 2007. *Nations Matter: Culture, History, and the Cosmopolitan Dream*. London: Routledge.

Campbell, Bruce A. 1973. "Law and Experience in the Early Republic: The Evolution of the *Dartmouth College* Doctrine, 1780–1819." PhD diss., Michigan State University.

Carwardine, Richard. 2003. *Lincoln*. London: Pearson-Longman.

Ciepley, David. 2001. "Why the State Was Dropped in the First Place: A Prequel to Skocpol's 'Bringing the State Back In'." *Critical Review* 14, nos. 2–3: 157–213.

Clemens, Elisabeth S. 1997. *The People's Lobby: Organizational Innovation and the Rise of Interest Group Politics in the United States, 1880–1925*. Chicago: University of Chicago Press.

Cunningham, Noble, Jr. 1963. *The Jeffersonian Republicans in Power: Party Operations, 1801–1809*. Chapel Hill: University of North Carolina Press.

Curti, Merle. 1958. "American Philanthropy and the National Character." *American Quarterly* 10, no. 4 (Winter): 420–37.

Dahl, Robert A. 1967. *Pluralist Democracy in the United States: Conflict and Consensus*. Chicago: Rand McNally.

Dalzell, Robert F., Jr. 1987. *Enterprising Elite: The Boston Associates and the World They Made.* Cambridge: Harvard University Press.

Davies, Wallace Evan. 1948. "The Society of the Cincinnati in New England, 1783–1800." *William and Mary Quarterly* 5, no. 1 (January): 3–25.

Elkins, Stanley, and Eric McKitrick. 1993. *The Age of Federalism.* New York: Oxford University Press.

Fischer, David Hackett. 1965. *The Revolution in American Conservatism: The Federalist Party in the Era of Jeffersonian Democracy.* New York: Harper and Row.

Foner, Eric. 1995. *Free Soil, Free Labor, Free Men: The Ideology of the Republican Party before the Civil War.* New York: Oxford University Press.

Foster, Charles. 1960. *An Errand of Mercy: The Evangelical United Front, 1790–1825.* Chapel Hill: University of North Carolina Press.

Freeman, Joanne B. 2001. *Affairs of Honor: National Politics in the New Republic.* New Haven: Yale University Press.

Gellner, Ernest. 1983. *Nations and Nationalism.* Ithaca: Cornell University Press.

Gienapp, William E. 1996. "The Crisis of American Democracy: The Political System and the Coming of the Civil War." In *Why the Civil War Came,* edited by Gabor S. Boritt, 79–124. New York: Oxford University Press.

Goen, C. C. 1985. *Broken Churches, Broken Nation: Denominational Schisms and the Coming of the American Civil War.* Macon, Ga.: Mercer.

Griffin, Clifford S. 1960. *Their Brothers' Keepers: Moral Stewardship in the United States, 1800–1865.* New Brunswick, N.J.: Rutgers University Press.

Hall, Peter Dobkin. 1982. *The Organization of American Culture, 1700–1900: Private Institutions, Elites, and the Origins of American Nationality.* New York: New York University Press.

———. 1987. "A Historical Overview of the Private Nonprofit Sector." In *The Nonprofit Sector: A Research Handbook,* edited by Walter Powell, 33–65. New Haven: Yale University Press.

———. 1988. "Organizational Values and the Origins of the Corporation in Connecticut, 1760–1860." *Connecticut History* 29: 63–90.

———. 1992. *Inventing the Nonprofit Sector and Other Essays on Philanthropy, Voluntarism, and Nonprofit Organizations.* Baltimore: Johns Hopkins University Press.

Hammack, David C., ed. 1998. *Making the Nonprofit Sector in the United States: A Reader.* Bloomington: Indiana University Press.

Handlin, Oscar, and Mary F. Handlin. 1969. *Commonwealth: A Study of the Role of Government in the American Economy: Massachusetts, 1774–1861.* Revised edition. Cambridge: Harvard University Press.

Harris, Marc L. 1995. "'Cement to the Union': The Society of the Cincinnati and the Limits of Fraternal Sociability." *Proceedings of the Massachusetts Historical Society* 10: 115–40.

———. 2005. "Civil Society in Post-Revolutionary America." In *Empire and Nation: The American Revolution in the Atlantic World,* edited by Eliga H. Gould and Peter S. Onuf, 197–216. Baltimore: Johns Hopkins University Press.

Hartz, Louis. 1948. *Economic Policy and Democratic Thought: Pennsylvania, 1776–1860*. Cambridge: Harvard University Press.

Herbst, Jürgen. 1982. *From Crisis to Crisis: American College Government, 1613–1819*. Cambridge: Harvard University Press.

Hobsbawm, Eric. 1993. *Nations and Nationalism since 1780: Programme, Myth, Reality*. New York: Cambridge University Press.

Hobsbawm, Eric, and Terence Ranger. 1983. *The Invention of Tradition*. New York: Cambridge University Press.

Hofstadter, Richard. 1969. *The Idea of a Party System: The Rise of Legitimate Opposition in the United States, 1780–1840*. Berkeley: University of California Press.

Holt, Michael F. 1978. *The Political Crisis of the 1850s*. New York: Wiley.

Howe, Daniel Walker. 1979. *The Political Culture of the American Whigs*. Chicago: University of Chicago Press.

Irons, Charles F. 2008. *The Origins of Proslavery Christianity: White and Black Evangelicals in Colonial and Antebellum Virginia*. Chapel Hill: University of North Carolina Press.

John, Richard. 1995. *Spreading the News: The American Postal Service and Disorder in American History*. Cambridge: Harvard University Press.

———. 1997. "Governmental Institutions as Agents of Change: Rethinking American Political Development in the Early Republic, 1787–1835." *Studies in American Political Development* 11, no. 2 (Fall): 347–80.

Katz, Stanley, Barry Sullivan, and C. Paul Beach. 1985. "Legal Change and Legal Autonomy: Charitable Trusts in New York, 1777–1893." *Law and History Review* 3, no. 1: 51–89.

Kaufman, Jason. 2003. *For the Common Good? American Civic Life and the Golden Age of Fraternity*. New York: Oxford University Press.

Kazin, Michael. 1995. *The Populist Persuasion: An American History*. New York: Basic Books.

Kohl, Lawrence F. 1989. *The Politics of Individualism: Parties and the American Character in the Jacksonian Era*. New York: Oxford University Press.

Koschnik, Albrecht. 2001. "The Democratic Societies of Philadelphia and the Limits of the Public Sphere, circa 1793–1795." *William and Mary Quarterly*, 3rd. ser., 68, no. 3 (July): 615–36.

———. 2007. *"Let a Common Interest Bind Us Together": Associations, Partisanship, and Culture in Philadelphia, 1775–1850*. Charlottesville: University of Virginia Press.

Kutler, Stanley. 1971. *Privilege and Creative Destruction: The Charles River Bridge Case*. Philadelphia: Lippincott.

Kuykendall, John W. 1982. *Southern Enterprize: The Work of National Evangelical Societies in the Antebellum South*. Westport, Conn.: Greenwood.

Larson, John Lauritz. 2001. *Internal Improvement: National Public Works and the Promise of Popular Government in the Early United States*. Chapel Hill: University of North Carolina Press.

Lawson, Melinda. 2002. *Patriot Fires: Forging a New American Nationalism in the Civil War North*. Lawrence: University Press of Kansas.

Lebsock, Suzanne. 1984. *The Free Women of Petersburg: Status and Culture in a Southern Town, 1784–1860.* New York: W. W. Norton.

Lockley, Timothy James. 2007. *Welfare and Charity in the Antebellum South.* Gainesville: University Press of Florida.

Mathews, Donald G. 1969. "The Second Great Awakening as an Organizing Process, 1780–1830: An Hypothesis." *American Quarterly* 21, no. 1 (Spring): 23–43.

Matson, Cathy, and Peter S. Onuf. 1990. *A Union of Interests: Political and Economic Thought in Revolutionary America.* Lawrence: University Press of Kansas.

McCarthy, Kathleen D. 2003. *American Creed: Philanthropy and the Rise of Civil Society.* Chicago: University of Chicago Press.

McCormick, Richard P. 1966. *The Second American Party System: Party Formation in the Jacksonian Era.* Chapel Hill: University of North Carolina Press.

McGarvie, Mark D. 1999. "Creating Roles for Religion and Philanthropy in a Secular Nation: The *Dartmouth College* Case and the Design of Civil Society in the Early Republic." *Journal of College and University Law* 25, no. 3: 527–68.

———. 2004. *One Nation under Law: America's Early Struggles to Separate Church and State.* DeKalb: Northern Illinois University Press.

McLoughlin, William G. 1971. *New England Dissent, 1630–1833: The Baptists and the Separation of Church and State.* 2 vols. Cambridge: Harvard University Press.

Mead, Sidney. 1963. *The Lively Experiment: The Shaping of Christianity in America.* New York: Harper and Row.

Minicucci, Stephen. 2001. "The 'Cement of Interest': Interest-Based Models of Nation-Building in the Early Republic." *Social Science History* 25: 247–74.

Murrin, John M. 1987. "A Roof without Walls: The Dilemma of American National Identity." In *Beyond Confederation: Origins of the Constitution and American National Identity,* edited by Richard R. Beeman, Stephen Botein, and Edward C. Carter, 333–48. Chapel Hill: University of North Carolina Press.

Myers, Minor, Jr. 1983. *Liberty without Anarchy: A History of the Society of the Cincinnati.* Charlottesville: University of Virginia Press.

Neem, Johann N. 2003. "Freedom of Association in the Early Republic: The Republican Party, the Whiskey Rebellion, and the Philadelphia and New York Cordwainers' Cases." *Pennsylvania Magazine of History and Biography* 127, no. 3 (July): 259–90.

———. 2008. *Creating a Nation of Joiners: Democracy and Civil Society in Early National Massachusetts.* Cambridge: Harvard University Press.

Newman, Simon P. 1997. *Parades and Politics of the Street: Festive Culture in the Early American Republic.* Philadelphia: University of Pennsylvania Press.

Nord, David Paul. 1991. "Newspapers and American Nationhood, 1776–1826." In *Three Hundred Years of the American Newspaper,* edited by John B. Hench, 391–405. Worcester: American Antiquarian Society.

——. 1995. "Religious Reading and Readers in Antebellum America." *Journal of the Early Republic* 15, no. 2 (Summer): 241–72.

Novak, William J. 1996. *The People's Welfare: Law and Regulation in Nineteenth-Century America.* Chapel Hill: University of North Carolina Press.

——. 2001. "The American Law of Association: The Legal-Political Construction of Civil Society." *Studies in American Political Development* 15 (Fall): 163–88.

Onuf, Nicholas, and Peter S. Onuf. 2006. *Nations, Markets, and War: Modern History and the American Civil War.* Charlottesville: University of Virginia Press.

Onuf, Peter S. 2000. *Jefferson's Empire: The Language of American Nationhood.* Charlottesville: University of Virginia Press.

Pasley, Jeffrey. 2001. *"The Tyranny of Printers": Newspaper Politics in the Early American Republic.* Charlottesville: University of Virginia Press.

Peterson, Merrill D. 1984. *Thomas Jefferson: Writings.* New York: Library of America.

Potter, David M. 1962. "The Historian's Use of Nationalism and Vice Versa." *American Historical Review* 67, no. 4 (July): 924–50.

——. 1976. *The Impending Crisis, 1848–1861.* New York: Harper Torchbooks.

Putnam, Robert D. 2000. *Bowling Alone: The Collapse and Revival of American Community.* New York: Simon and Schuster.

Putnam, Robert D., and Gerald Gamm. 1999. "The Growth of Voluntary Associations in America, 1840–1940." *Journal of Interdisciplinary History* 29, no. 4: 511–57.

Rhodehamel, John H. 1997. *George Washington: Writings.* New York: Library of America.

Robertson, Andrew W. 2001. "'Look on this Picture . . . And on This!' Nationalism, Localism, and Partisan Images of Otherness in the United States, 1780–1820." *American Historical Review* 106, no. 4 (October): 1263–80.

Rubin, Anne Sarah. 2005. *A Shattered Nation: The Rise and Fall of the Confederacy, 1861–1868.* Chapel Hill: University of North Carolina Press.

Ryan, Mary P. 1997. *Civic Wars: Democracy and Public Life in the American City during the Nineteenth Century.* Berkeley: University of California Press.

Schoen, Brian D. 2003. "Calculating the Price of Union: Republican Economic Nationalism and the Origins of Southern Sectionalism, 1790–1828." *Journal of the Early Republic* 32, no. 2 (Summer): 173–206.

——. 2004. "The Fragile Fabric of Union: The Cotton South, Federal Politics, and the Atlantic World, 1783–1861." PhD diss., University of Virginia.

Schudson, Michael. 1994. "The 'Public Sphere' and Its Problems: Bringing the State (Back) In." *Notre Dame Journal of Law, Ethics, and Public Policy* 8: 529–46.

——. 1998. *The Good Citizen: A History of American Civic Life.* New York: Free Press.

Scott, Donald. 1978. *From Office to Profession: The New England Ministry, 1750–1850.* Philadelphia: University of Pennsylvania Press.

Seavoy, Ronald E. 1982. *The Origins of the American Business Corporation, 1784–1855: Broadening the Concept of Public Service during Industrialization.* Westport, Conn.: Greenwood Press.

Shields, David S. 1997. *Civil Tongues and Polite Letters in British America.* Chapel Hill: University of North Carolina Press.

Silbey, Joel H. 1985. "'The Salt of the Nation': Political Parties in Antebellum America." In *The Partisan Imperative: The Dynamics of American Politics before the Civil War,* edited by Joel H. Silbey, 50–68. New York: Oxford University.

Silbey, Joel H., Allan G. Bogue, and William H. Flanigan, eds. 1978. *The History of American Electoral Behavior.* Princeton: Princeton University Press.

Skocpol, Theda. 2003. *Diminished Democracy: From Membership to Management in American Civic Life.* Norman: University of Oklahoma, 2003.

Skocpol, Theda, and Morris P. Fiorina, eds. 1999. *Civic Engagement in American Democracy.* Washington, D.C.: Brookings Institution Press.

Skocpol, Theda, Marshall Ganz, and Ziad Munson. 2000. "A Nation of Organizers: The Institutional Origins of Civic Voluntarism in the United States." *American Political Science Review* 94, no. 3 (September): 527–46.

Smith, H. Shelton. 1972. *In His Image, But . . . Racism in Southern Religion, 1780–1910.* Durham: Duke University Press.

Snay, Mitchell. 1993. *Gospel of Disunion: Religion and Separatism in the Antebellum South.* New York: Cambridge University Press.

Starr, Paul. 2004. *The Creation of the Media: Political Origins of Modern Communications.* New York: Basic Books.

Strong, William E. 1910. *The Story of the American Board: An Account of the First Hundred Years of the ABCFM.* Boston: Pilgrim Press.

Taylor, Charles. 1995. "Liberal Politics and the Public Sphere." In *New Communitarian Thinking: Persons, Virtues, Institutions, and Communities,* edited by Amitai Etzioni, 183–217. Charlottesville: University of Virginia Press.

———. 2003. "No Community, No Democracy, Part 1." *Responsive Community* 13, no. 4: 17–27.

Tocqueville, Alexis de. 2004. *Democracy in America.* Trans. Arthur Goldhammer. New York: Library of America.

Tomlins, Christopher L. 1993. *Law, Labor, and Ideology in the Early American Republic.* New York: Cambridge University Press.

Trees, Andy. 2000. "Private Correspondence for the Public Good: Thomas Jefferson to Elbridge Gerry, 26 January 1799." *Virginia Magazine of History and Biography* 108, no. 3: 217–54.

Verba, Sidney, Kay Lehman Schlozman, and Henry E. Brady. 1995. *Voice and Equality: Civic Voluntarism in American Politics.* Cambridge: Harvard University Press.

Waldstreicher, David. 1997. *In the Midst of Perpetual Fetes: The Making of American Nationalism, 1776–1820.* Chapel Hill: University of North Carolina Press.

Walters, Ronald G. 1978. *American Reformers, 1815–1860.* New York: Hill and Wang.

Warner, Michael. 1999. *The Letters of the Republic: Publication and the Public Sphere in Eighteenth-Century America.* Cambridge: Harvard University Press.

Watson, Harry L. 1990. *Liberty and Power: The Politics of Jacksonian America.* New York: Noonday.

Welter, Rush. 1975. *The Mind of America, 1829–1860.* New York: Columbia University Press.

Whitehead, John S. 1973. *The Separation of College and State: Columbia, Dartmouth, Harvard, and Yale, 1776–1876.* New Haven: Yale University Press.

Wiebe, Robert H. 1967. *The Search for Order, 1877–1920.* New York: Hill and Wang.

Wood, Gordon S. 1969. *Creation of the American Republic, 1776–1787.* Chapel Hill: University of North Carolina Press.

———. 1991. *Radicalism of the American Revolution.* New York: Vintage.

Wosh, Peter J. 1994. *Spreading the Word: The Bible Business in Nineteenth-Century America.* Ithaca: Cornell University Press.

Wright, Conrad Edick. 1992. *The Transformation of Charity in Postrevolutionary New England.* Boston: Northeastern University Press.

Wyllie, Irvin G. 1959. "The Search for an American Law of Charity." *Mississippi Valley Historical Review* 44, no. 2 (September): 203–21.

CHAPTER THREE

Steering the State: Government, Nonprofits, and the Making of Labor Knowledge in the New Era

Mark Hendrickson

In the late nineteenth and early twentieth centuries, leaders in government, business, and various nonprofit organizations struggled to determine how best to govern a growing nation and economy experiencing dramatic, wrenching, and often violent change. Between the 1880s and World War I, the U.S. gross national product grew from approximately $11 billion to $84 billion. As the economy expanded, the nation became more urban. By 1920 more than half of all Americans lived in cities, whereas in 1880 that number had been only 26 percent. As corporations came to dominate many sectors of the economy, the number of wage workers exploded from 5.3 million in 1860 to 17.4 million in 1900 and continued to rise to nearly 31 million by 1920. These wage workers found employment in highly capitalized industries often characterized by an anonymous relationship between employer and employee. By the outbreak of World War I, firms employing over 250 workers hired the majority of the nation's industrial workers. Ferocious economic and social instability accompanied this change, as competition between increasingly capitalized and unregulated firms drove down prices, forcing industrialists to slash wages and other costs. As the economy continued

I would like to thank Mary O. Furner, participants in the 2005 Social Science Research Council Capstone Conference on Philanthropy and the Nonprofit Sector, and the editors of this book for their help and advice. I would also like to thank the Social Science Research Council for its generous support.

to expand and businesses grew larger and larger, the costs of economic instability extended to nearly all segments of American society. Proprietary capitalists such as Andrew Carnegie recognized the fixed costs associated with modern industry and struggled to capture a greater share of the market; he was even sometimes willing to sell products at a loss rather than let plants stand idle. Such a strategy drove many competitors out of business, but it also contributed to increasing economic volatility. For industrial workers, this volatility manifested itself in constant insecurity arising from frequent unemployment, dangerous working conditions, long hours, and low wages. When industrial workers organized unions or struck for better working conditions, they often faced violent opposition and the threat of replacement by an army of unemployed workers desperate for work.

Solving the linked problems of social and labor instability brought on by economic change was made more difficult by a pronounced antistatist trend coming out of the nineteenth-century political and policy traditions (Furner 2005). By the late nineteenth century, however, it was clear to most observers that market forces alone were an insufficient means of stabilizing modern industry. In response, financiers such as J. P. Morgan led a turn-of-the-century merger movement, creating major corporations such as United States Steel. Modern vertically and horizontally integrated corporations aimed to bring greater stability to industry by capturing a larger share of the market, which allowed for the stabilization of prices and costs. On the shop room floor, mechanization and employers' victories over skilled workers, who had jealously guarded knowledge of the production process, shifted control over the process and pace of work from workers to managers and employers (Livingston 1987). The accompanying emergence of corporate capitalism in the Progressive Era led to increasing calls for the state to regulate industry. Before U.S. entry into World War I, the Wilson administration produced a number of important innovations in tax, tariff, labor, banking, and trust policy aimed at promoting a more just and stable economy. World War I itself spurred a more robust role for the state. Higher and more redistributive income taxes on business and wealthy individuals, the nationalization of the railroads, and the apparent success of government bodies in coordinating war production and controlling prices suggested to some progressives the efficacy of a more active federal government in economic and social matters.

By 1919 instability in race relations, the economy, and labor relations helped turn the tide against wartime statist policies and set the stage for a reinvigorated tradition of using nongovernment organizations to solve public problems. On the heels of World War I and President Wilson's bold effort to use statist means to reshape important aspects of American economic life and foreign policy, voters weary of war and reform turned to the Republican Party for leadership. The postwar transition away from a wartime economy produced social and economic upheavals reminiscent of the 1890s. With the end of hostilities, the federal government cancelled most of its wartime contracts and withdrew price controls implemented during the war. Initially, workers and employers benefited from high demand for consumer goods at home and a sustained increase in demand for U.S. goods in war-ravaged Europe, but the prosperity was short-lived and followed by a mix of inflation, unemployment, and labor and racial unrest. Just as veterans returned from the front, cancelled government contracts shrunk demand and the job supply. The loss of price controls and pent-up consumer demand, combined with a too-slow conversion to a consumer economy, led to prices that rose at an annual rate of 15 percent. As employers exercised their postwar leverage to cut wages and drive out unions, American workers walked off the job in unprecedented numbers. In 1919 alone, more than four million workers walked off the job in thirty-six hundred strikes. Workers turned on each other as well, as racial violence between white workers and African American workers, many of whom had recently migrated North in search of work and rights to escape the Jim Crow South or had returned from service in the war, broke out in dozens of American cities.

To make sense of the instability in American society, political leaders and the public increasingly turned to an emerging class of experts in nonprofit organizations. Among them, the Russell Sage Foundation, the National Urban League, and the National Bureau of Economic Research produced studies that educated the public and policymakers about issues ranging from race relations to the business cycle. Few people did more in the New Era to promote a partnership between nonprofits and government than Herbert Hoover. Though he flatly rejected many of the statist ideas embraced by Wilson and later by New Dealers, Secretary of Commerce (and later president) Hoover recognized fundamental inefficiencies in the organization of business and industry, and he advocated a partnership model for policymaking in which the federal government and nongovernmental institutions of economic inquiry would make these inefficiencies clear to industry leaders and help them formulate and implement solutions. Only in cases where the market clearly had failed or recalcitrant interests made inefficient decisions, Hoover believed, should the state intervene. In the 1920s, Hoover championed a tradition of voluntarism and associationalism that, going back to Tocqueville's time, had contended that by employing associations, Americans could solve public problems while protecting American liberty from dangerous intrusions by the state. The institutions and issue networks that supported Hoover's vision of an associative state and developed New Era economic thinking dramatically transformed the relationship among knowledge, policy, governance, nonprofits, civil society, and the state, and charted conceptual and policy directions that shaped labor policy in the public and private sectors throughout the twentieth century.

Not surprisingly, given the postwar unrest in labor and race relations, many of these emerging nonprofits turned their attention to aspects of the labor question. After World War I, a certain class of highly charged issues, among them the length of the workday in the steel industry and the nature and claims of black workers, was largely "spun off" by government and "taken up" by nonprofits. The results of this collaboration were mixed. Concerning the hours issue in the steel industry, engineering and economic experts turned a rights question into an efficiency issue, opening the controversy up to settlement by adoption of "best practices." A variety of experts, largely in nonprofits, created a body of expertise that persuasively argued for the benefits to company, worker, and the public of the elimination of the twelve-hour day. Thus, the nonprofit setting allowed for the avoidance of confrontation, court intervention, and federal-government-enforced labor standards. The second instance addresses the impact of labor expertise on racial stereotypes and understandings of race relations. Government investigations during World War I led by the Department of Labor's Division of Negro Economics produced findings that threatened racial stereotypes. The government—under pressure—backed away from its wartime engagement on black labor issues, and nonprofits had the courage and freedom to press the issue to a conclusion that undermined those stereotypes and pointed to white workers' responsibility for discrimination in the workplace.

These two examples bring into clearer focus a more integrated view of nonprofit, commercial, and government sectors that takes into account links in their historical development and relationship to governance issues. The fluid movement of individuals, findings, and ideas between these spheres speaks to the need for a model for understanding policymaking that more clearly integrates the state and nonprofits. In this period, labor efficiency and "Negro" labor experts moved easily and often between government institutions, nonprofits, and, in some cases, private industry. Even when issues were "spun off" from the government to the nonprofit sector, these were not clean breaks. Particularly in the steel industry, Hoover and his allies facilitated and legitimized a largely nonstate inquiry and used investigations by government and nonprofit organizations to rally public, labor, stockholder, and business support for dramatic changes in the organization of industry, without the assertion and expansion of the federal government's regulatory authority.

In addition to informing policymakers and shaping pubic opinion, these inquires into social and economic problems helped transform issues that previously had been private or regional concerns into matters of national public interest. In his pioneering 1927 work, *The Pubic and Its Problems,* John Dewey searched for the origins and functions of the modern state and redefined its role as a caretaker for public concerns. Dewey claimed that the public included groups and individuals affected by the consequences of policies and agreements that were negotiated without their involvement or consent.[1] The consequences of the Great Migration, racial violence, industrial unrest, and economic instability argued for an expanded role for government in stabilizing the economy, protecting the economic and civil rights of black Americans, and leveling to some degree the imbalance in power between workers and employers. However, the long history of dealing with issues of labor and race in the private sphere or at the state or local level combined with the voluntarist leanings of the Harding-Coolidge-Hoover years meant no one was clear on the precise role the federal government should play in solving what were becoming public problems. In the New Era, policymakers and reformers experimented with a number of means of solving industrial problems without dramatically expanding the regulatory power of the state. At this critical juncture, expertise-generating organizations working in combination with or outside of the state carved out an important role in shaping the understanding of policymakers and the public of what constitutes a public problem while, at times, proposing potential remedies.

---

1. Dewey defined the "public" to include "all those who are affected by the indirect consequences of transactions to such an extent that it is deemed necessary to have those consequences systematically cared for" (Dewey 1927, 15–16).

The increasing reliance on the nonprofit sector for expertise in the New Era has been scrutinized by historians such as Ellis Hawley, whose work makes clear that to understand the development of Hoover's "associational state" in the 1920s we *must* look outside of the state to these nonprofit organizations. Historian Guy Alchon has completed the most important work on the relationship between nonprofits and economic policy in the 1920s. Alchon describes cooperation between the National Bureau of Economic Research, philanthropic foundations, and the Department of Commerce as a "three-legged apparatus" designed by Herbert Hoover and his associates to "provide a 'middle way' between statist collectivism and laissez-faire individualism." Although Alchon's work provides historians with one of the most comprehensive views of 1920s policymaking to date, he privileges the National Bureau of Economic Research's work at the expense of many other government and nongovernment institutions that had equal or greater impact on economic inquiry and policy (Alchon 1985, 3; Hawley 1974; Barber 1985; Karl 1983; Donohue 2003, 144–52). Building on Hawley's and Alchon's analyses, historian David Hart has argued that Herbert Hoover's vision of an "associative state" in the 1920s, and not the New Deal, became the enduring blueprint for twentieth-century state and society building. According to Hart, Hoover sought to preserve republican virtue by promoting the "self-government" of industry through trade associations and by using the government to create information and expertise that would increase economic efficiency (Hart 1998). Hart's controversial article gets much of the story right; the 1920s need to be understood not as a "broken" decade whose retrograde character was revealed by the Great Depression and corrected by the New Deal. As the following examples suggest, in policy history the New Era is better understood as a unique period, incubating innovative and lasting policy paradigms, whose relevance to New Deal and post–New Deal policy history has too often been overlooked.

A Public Concern: The Workday in the Steel Industry

The labor experts in the 1920s who gave unprecedented attention to the relationship between hours worked and efficiency built on work done by previous generations of investigators. Investigations in the United States and Britain by Ira Stewart and Robert Owen in the mid-nineteenth century and, more recently, by Margaret Byington, Josephine Goldmark, and others, had publicized the relationship between efficiency and hours.[2] In 1905, the National Consumer League (NCL) took the lead in successfully defending Oregon's limits on hours for women workers in *Muller v. Oregon* (1908). The key to victory in *Muller* was the work of the NCL's Josephine Goldmark and Florence Kelly, who together did much of the research that made Louis Brandeis's brief to the Supreme Court so persuasive. The 113-page brief provided a short legal rationale for workplace protections for women and a lengthy discussion of the work of experts in the United States and abroad who had considered the hours question and found significant dangers in long hours for women workers. Following *Muller,* Goldmark completed pioneering research on worker fatigue, with funding from the Russell Sage Foundation. The result, Goldmark's *Fatigue and Efficiency* (1912), is emblematic of a larger shift among reformers who moved from defending hours legislation as a means of protecting the unique biological character of women workers to making the case for the benefits of labor standards to all workers, irrespective of gender.[3]

During and after World War I, Goldmark and other investigators further broadened the appeal of shorter hours by building up a body of knowledge demonstrating a link between increased efficiency and shorter shifts. During the summer of 1918, the U.S. Federal Public Health Service (FPHS), in cooperation with the National Research Council, brought together physiologists, chemists, and labor experts to conduct a two-year study of hours and fatigue that clearly demonstrated the advantages to employers and employees of a shorter workday. Goldmark joined Mary D. Hopkins in leading the study. The FPHS found a "steady maintenance of output" in the eight-hour day and a declin-

2. Margaret F. Byington, *Homestead: The Households of a Milltown* (New York: Russell Sage Foundation, 1910) 35, 171–72. For examples of Stewart's work, see Ira Stewart, "A Reduction of Hours an Increase of Wages," in *A Documentary History of American Industrial Society,* ed. John R. Commons et al. (Cleveland: Arthur H. Clark Company, 1910), 284–301; originally published in *Fincher's Trades' Review,* October 14, 1865. For an interesting summary of Stewart's conception of the relationship between workers, consumption, hours, and reform, see Dorothy Douglas, "Ira Stewart on Consumption and Unemployment," *Journal of Political Economy* 40 (August 1921): 532–43; John Rae, *Eight Hours for Work* (New York: Macmillan and Co., 1894); H. M. Vernon, *Industrial Fatigue and Efficiency* (New York: E. P. Dutton, 1921); Edgar L. Collis and Major Greenwood, *The Health of the Industrial Worker* (Philadelphia: P. Blakinston's Son & Co, 1921); Carter Goodrich, *The Miner's Freedom: A Study of the Working Life in a Changing Industry* (New York: Workers Education Bureau of America, 1925); and Charles S. Myers, *Industrial Psychology* (New York: People's Institution Publishing Co., 1925).

3. Josephine Goldmark, *Fatigue and Efficiency: A Study in Industry* (New York: Survey Associates, 1912). Goldmark also contributed to Felix Frankfurter, *The Case for the Shorter Work Day* (New York: National Consumer's League, 1916).

ing output in the ten-hour day. Other benefits of an eight-hour day included a decrease in industrial accidents, turnover, work stoppages, and
employee restrictions of output. FPHS investigators also examined the
efficiency of twelve-hour night-shift work and found "a progressive slow-
ing in the rate of production during the night" and an "abrupt fall of output in the last two hours" of the shift.[4]

Hours' research was aimed at a broad range of industries that would
benefit from a shorter workday and was intended to influence policymakers considering more statist solutions to the problem of long hours. In the
early part of the decade, many efficiency experts turned their attention
to the steel industry where they found a worthy adversary in Judge Gary
and US Steel, whose return to the two-shift system following World War I
provided a particularly scandalous example of the elimination of wartime gains in labor standards. Pressure on US Steel to institute the eight-
hour day mounted throughout World War I and reached a fever pitch in
1919, when more than three hundred thousand steelworkers unsuccessfully struck, demanding the eight-hour day, union recognition, and the
six-day work week. In May 1923, in response to public pressure and a
personal request by President Warren G. Harding, the American Iron
and Steel Institute, the research and political arm of the steel industry,
conducted an investigation into the viability of the eight-hour day in the
industry, which concluded that a tight labor market and a preference on
the part of employees for the twelve-hour day made any switch undesir-
able and unworkable.

The American Association for Labor Legislation (AALL) reported
that the American Iron and Steel Institute's actions "went dead against
the facts brought out in many competent, disinterested investigations."[5]

4. *Annual Report of the Surgeon General of the Public Health Service of the United States* (Washington, D.C.: GPO, 1919), 41–43; U.S. Public Health Service, "Comparison of an 8-Hour Plant and a
10-Hour Plant," *Public Health Bulletin* 106 (Washington, D.C.: 1920). The Public Health Service conducted other studies that focused more specifically on the chemical effects of industrial fatigue on workers. See "The Physiology of Fatigue," *Public Health Bulletin* 117 (Washington, D.C.: GPO, 1921); *Annual Report of the Surgeon General of the Public Health Service of the United States* (Washington, D.C.:
GPO, 1920), 37–38; *Annual Report of the Surgeon General of the Public Health Service of the United
States* (Washington, D.C.: GPO, 1921), 32; *Annual Report of the Surgeon General of the Public Health
Service of the United States* (Washington, D.C.: GPO, 1924), 26.

5. Frederick W. MacKenzie, "Steel Abandons the Twelve-Hour Day," *American Labor Legislation
Review* 13 (September 1923): 181. The AALL published two articles by Charles R. Walker, the editor
of the *Atlantic Monthly* and a former employee in the steel mills, detailing the conditions in the steelworks. Walker's articles made it clear that, contrary to Gary's assertions, workers did not prefer the
twelve-hour day and that lulls in the workday could hardly be considered relaxing, as Gary and the Institute had suggested. Charles R. Walker, "The Twelve-Hour Shift," *American Labor Legislation Review*

The task of convincing the steel trust and the public that the eight-hour day was possible and profitable fell to a number of efficiency experts, engineers, and public leaders, who combined publicity and expertise to make their case successfully. Commerce Secretary Herbert Hoover led the Harding administration's charge for the adoption of the shorter workday. Hoover arranged a White House dinner conference at which he came "armed with reports, studies, and statistics to justify the abandonment of the twelve-hour system" (Zieger 1969, 101). The conference failed to convince the steel industry, but the battle hardly ended there.

With the failure of the conference, Hoover partnered with various nonprofits to determine the merits of the steel industry's argument. The most important of these partners was the Federated American Engineering Societies (FAES), an organization of progressive-minded engineers. At Hoover's request the FAES conducted a Cabot Fund–financed report on the twelve-hour shift in industry that Hoover described as expressing the "unanimity of the whole engineering profession in their demonstration that from a technical point of view there is no difficulty with what was obviously necessary from a social point of view."[6] The study was led by Horace Drury, a former Ohio State University economist and member of the Industrial Relations Division of the U.S. Shipping Board who, through his investigations for the FAES, the Cabot Fund, and the Taylor Society, had established himself as a leading expert on the shift system. Drury found considerable evidence to suggest that a move to the three-shift system benefited both workers and employers. Blast furnace managers in three-shift plants "emphatically asserted" that "the higher grade of labor attracted by the shorter hours, the greater care and alertness, better work, and more skillful operation are all reflected in a saving in cost of production," Drury concluded.[7] Similarly, in the pig iron and rolling mills surveyed, investigators found that eight-hour shifts increased efficiency and decreased the costs of production.[8] After a survey of the twenty United States steel mills that had made the move to the three-shift day, Drury concluded, "If all the departments in a steel plant

---

13 (June 1923): 108–18; and Walker, *Steel: The Diary of a Furnace Worker* (Boston: Atlantic Monthly Press, 1922). For previous investigations of the steel industry, see Paul Kellogg, *The Pittsburgh Survey,* 6 vols. (New York: Charities Publication Committee, 1909–14), and Greenwald and Anderson 1996.

6. Hoover, quoted in Zieger, 103. The FAES report in question is "Committee on Work Periods in Continuous Industry of the Federated American Engineering Societies," in *The Twelve-Hour Shift in Industry* (New York: E. P. Dutton and Company, 1922).

7. *The Twelve-Hour Shift in Industry,* 18.

8. Ibid., 18–19.

were to be changed from two to three shifts, the increase in total cost for the finished rail, bar, or sheet could not on the average be more than 3 per cent."[9] Outside of steel production, Drury found that in "practically every major continuous-industry there are plants which have increased the quality of production per man up to as much as 25 per cent" after going to the three-shift system.[10] Nonferrous-metal industries had very similar smelting and refining processes to the steel industry, yet Drury found that in the western United States nonferrous companies had successfully moved to the three-shift system at the turn of the century; in the East and South, managers in these industries had made the switch during and shortly after World War I.[11]

Bradley Stoughton wrote the last third of the report, which described the costs and benefits of the three-shift system in the iron and steel industry and demonstrated how, with careful planning, the three-shift system would drive down costs and benefit the company. Stoughton had a long association with the industry including experience as a metallurgical engineer, associate professor at the School of Mines at Columbia University, vice-chairman of the Engineering Division of the National Research Council, and secretary of the American Institute of Mining and Metallurgical Engineers.[12] According to Stoughton, the hard physical labor of steel production meant that firms using the twelve-hour shift had to employ additional laborers on each shift in order to allow for periodic breaks, which sometimes amounted to 3.5 hours per shift. Additionally, at the end of the shifts, foremen in twelve-hour plants recognized that men were simply too tired to work and frequently postponed production until fresh men arrived for the next shift.[13] Three-shift plant managers also testified that they were able to recruit a "better class of labor" and a sufficient supply of appropriately skilled workers.[14] Finally, Stoughton

9. Horace B. Drury, "The Three-Shift System in the Steel Industry," *American Federationist* 38 (February 1921): 128.

10. *Twelve-Hour Shift in Industry,* 212–13.

11. Ibid., 56–58. Nonferrous includes metals such as copper, zinc, lead, nickel, and aluminum.

12. Stoughton had also served as the chief of costs in the Statistical Division at the American Steel and Wire Company. Stoughton, "The Iron and Steel Industry," in *The Twelve-Hour Shift in Industry,* 217.

13. Ibid., 221, 222, 228, 231, 270–72, and 274–76. For a summary of advantages of the three-shift system, see pages 290–93 of the report and L. W. Wallace, "The Twelve-Hour Shift in American Industry," *Proceedings of the National Conference of Social Work* (Chicago: University of Chicago, 1920), 142–45.

14. Stoughton, "The Iron and Steel Industry," 240–41. In the context of the report, a "better class of labor" implied a decrease in absenteeism, turnover, mistakes, and waste as well as an overall increase in efficiency and productivity. Stoughton also pointed to the need to incorporate new labor-saving devices that would increase productivity and decrease the number of workers needed. Ibid., 285–86.

pointed to the public relations advantages to employing an eight-hour day. During labor disputes, Stoughton advised, "the company which is working its men only eight hours a day enjoys much greater prestige with the public, whose influence in a labor dispute is always important."[15]

Religious organizations, labor legislation advocates, and even United States Steel stockholders joined in investigating the merits of the twelve-hour day. To Judge Gary's contention that the three-shift system was unworkable in a tight labor market, a report issued by the Federal Council of Churches of Christ in America, the National Catholic Welfare Council, and the Central Conference of American Rabbis responded that the "shortage of labor was not the reason for the failure to abolish the long day two years ago, when there was appalling unemployment, which could have been in large measure relieved in steel manufacturing districts by introducing the three-shift system in the steel industry."[16] An investigation ordered by the stockholders of the US Steel Corporation added that "a twelve-hour day of labor, followed continuously by any group of men for any considerable number of years means a decrease of the efficiency and lessening of the vigor and virility of such men."[17] In June 1922, the American Association for Labor Legislation began publishing a series of articles sharply critical of Gary and the steel companies that clung to the twelve-hour day. The AALL reported that at least twenty non–US Steel firms had adopted the eight-hour day.[18]

Expert advice and an informed public opinion mattered. On August 2,

15. Ibid., 291.

16. "Organized Religion Condemns Gary of Inhuman Twelve-Hour Day," *International Molder's Journal* 59 (July 1923): 390–91; "Churches Condemn Twelve-Hour Steel Day," *New York Times,* June 6, 1923, 23; "Long Working Hours Condemned by Rabbis," *New York Times,* June 29, 1923, 28; "Again the Twelve Hour Day," *New York Times,* June 9, 1923, 18; and Federal Council of Churches of Christ in America, *The Twelve Hour Day in the Steel Industry: Its Social Consequences and Practability of Its Abolition* (New York: Federal Council of the Churches of Christ in America, 1923).

17. "Organized Religion Condemns Gary," 390. John D. Rockefeller Jr. also came out publicly for the shorter day in the steel industry; see "Rockefeller Urges Fairness to Labor," *New York Times,* November 16, 1923, 1; and "Engineers Oppose Twelve Hour Day," *New York Times,* November 19, 1922, 44.

18. Frederick W. Mackenzie, "Steel Abandons the Twelve-Hour Day," *American Labor Legislation Review* 13 (September 1923): 183; *American Labor Legislation Review* 12 (June 1922): 121. For evidence of the how these investigations were used to persuade the public of the viability of the shorter workday, see Labor Bureau Inc., "Wage Theories and Arguments: No. 9—The Worth of the Worker," *Facts for Workers* 2 (June 1924): 1; "Twelve Hour Steel Day Must Go," *New York Times,* December 4, 1920, 17; "Billions Lost to Waste," *New York Times,* November 23, 1922, 6; "Engineers Oppose Twelve-Hour Day," *New York Times,* November 19, 1922, 44; "Finds Eight-Hour Day Aids Steel Mills," *New York Times,* June 7, 1923, 10; "The Twelve Hour Day," *New York Times,* September 20, 1922, 16; and "The Eight-Hour Shift in Continuous Industries," *New York Times,* June 18, 1923, 12.

1923, the American Iron and Steel Institute reversed its earlier decision and announced that it would eliminate the twelve-hour day as soon as possible. The AALL referred to the change as "one of the most remarkable demonstrations in the history of industrial progress of the power of the public to compel the repudiation by employers of indecent working standards."[19] After its introduction, even former opponents expressed surprise at the quality of work and ample supply of labor in the steelworks. The *Annalist,* a Washington, D.C., financial publication, stated that "there is no complaint whatever from the manufacturers of a shortage of available labor. . . . Curiously enough, the advertisement which the eight-hour day has received in the last month or so has attracted a considerable number of laborers to the mill centers, and the new laborers seem to be of a higher grade than the steel companies ordinarily have been able to attract."[20]

Bureau of Labor Statistics (BLS) investigations confirmed noticeable improvements in the steel industry following the industry's move to the eight-hour day. The BLS tracked a sudden decrease in average full-time hours per week after 1923 and noted an earlier increase in wages, particularly during the war and following the industry's recovery from the postwar downturn. In an examination of conditions between 1913 and 1926, the BLS concluded that "the long working hours in force in most of the departments in 1913 have been materially shortened and earnings, both per hour and per week, have increased greatly."[21] A survey of ten departments revealed that between 1913 and 1922 average weekly hours declined slightly from 66.1 to 63.2, but the significant drop came after US Steel started to eliminate the twelve-hour day and seven-day work week in August 1923. Between 1922 and 1926, the average weekly hours worked by steelworkers fell dramatically from 63.2 to 54.4 hours per week.[22] Though the BLS did not calculate real wages in its surveys,

19. Frederick W. Mackenzie, "Steel Abandons the Twelve-Hour Day," 180.

20. Quoted in "Eight Hour Day 'Surprises' Editor," *American Federation of Labor Weekly New Service* 13 (September 1923): 1. For a similar sentiment from business observers, see "Steel Plants Aided by Short Work Day," *American Federation of Labor: Weekly News Services* 13 (November 10, 1923): 1; "Steel Trust Accepts 8-Hour Theory," *AFL: Weekly News Services* 13 (March 8, 1924): 1; "Its Worth What It Costs," *New York Times,* February 28, 1924, 18; LBI, "The Five-Day Week," *Facts for Workers* 5 (November 1926): 1–2; "Short Day in Steel Mills Has Pleased All," *New York Times,* August 31, 1924, 28; other industries concurred that the shorter day worked well, see "Says Short Day Adds Oil," *New York Times,* January 31, 1923, p. 18.

21. Bureau of Labor Statistics, "Wages and Hours of Labor in the Iron and Steel Industry: 1907 to 1926," *Bulletin* 442 (Washington, D.C.: GPO, 1927), 4.

22. Ibid., 3.

its analysis of nominal wages suggested generally higher wages for iron and steel workers. Nominal weekly earnings for iron and steel workers in the ten departments surveyed increased from $18.89 in 1913 to $34.41 in 1926.[23]

Though the achievements of experts in reducing the workday should not be discounted, solving labor problems through expert nonprofit analysis rather than state, judicial, or union means left open the issue of enforcement. The federal government and the many nonprofits that contributed to resolving this complicated issue saw the work of the BLS as confirmation of their much-celebrated victory. Had they looked a little deeper into BLS data, they might have thought twice about the durability of that victory. For some steelworkers, the reduction in hours proved remarkably ephemeral. In six of ten occupational groups in the steel industry, the need to keep works operating continuously or nearly continuously with a smaller labor pool forced an increase in the number of employees who worked seven days a week. In 1914, 53 percent of steel employees in the blast furnace department worked seven days a week. By 1922, that number had fallen to 29 percent, but by 1926 it increased to 49 percent. Similarly, in blooming, standard rail, and plate mills a higher percentage of employees worked a seven-day week in 1924 than in any other year on record.[24]

Despite this backsliding in some though certainly not all steel occupations, public pressure and the efficiency argument had persuaded the steel industry to alter a policy that it had maintained in the face of a

23. Departments surveyed included blast furnace, Bessemer converters, open-hearth furnaces, puddling mills, blooming mills, plant mills, standard rail mills, bar mills, sheet mills, and tin-plate mills. The BLS investigations included data for select years going back to at least 1910 for all departments, except standard rail mills. "Wages and Hours of Labor in the Iron and Steel Industry," *Bulletin* 442 (Washington, D.C.: GPO, 1927), 1; Department of Labor, *Annual Report of the Secretary of Labor* (Washington, D.C.: GPO, 1927), 47–48; also see the following BLS Bulletins, "Wages and Hours of Labor in the Iron and Steel Industry: 1907 to 1920," *Bulletin* 305 (Washington, D.C.: GPO, 1922); "Wages and Hours of Labor in the Iron and Steel Industry: 1907 to 1922," *Bulletin* 353 (Washington, D.C.: GPO, 1924); "Wages and Hours of Labor in the Iron and Steel Industry: 1907–1924," *Bulletin* 381 (Washington, D.C.: GPO, 1925). For a summary of data on wages and hours between 1913 and 1926, see "Average Hours and Earnings in the Iron and Steel Industry, 1913–1926," *Monthly Labor Review* 24 (May 1927): 164–165; "Trend of Wages, 1907–1920," *Monthly Labor Review* 13 (December 1921): 81–89. For a summary of data concerning the decline of the twelve-hour day, seven-day work week, see "Hours of Labor and the 7-Day Work Week in the Iron and Steel Industry," *Monthly Labor Review* 30 (June 1930): 182–87; BLS, "Wages and Hours of Labor in the Iron and Steel Industry," *Bulletin* 513 (Washington, D.C.: GPO, 1930).

24. BLS, "Wages and Hours of Labor in the Iron and Steel Industry: 1907 to 1926," 10. The BLS found similar rates of seven-day work for employees in the open hearth and blast furnace occupations. The seven-day week was negligible in puddling, bar, sheet, and tin-plate mills.

strike of 350,000 of its workers just four years earlier. In the process, experts had moved the length of the workday in the steel industry from a private concern to a matter of public interest with ramifications for the public good, thereby successfully challenging management's jealously guarded interpretation of what historian Howell Harris has aptly termed "the right to manage" (Harris 1982). By making the benefits to industry of a reduction in the workday the focal point of their investigations, Goldmark, Hoover, Drury, Staughton, and others turned what labor unions had presented as rights issue into an issue of industrial efficiency, leaving the steel industry with a largely indefensible public position. The resolution of the hours problem in the steel industry demonstrated the potential of expertise to resolve contentious issues that previously had been fought out in the forums of courtrooms, state legislative chambers, and picket lines. However, as some steelworkers found out in subsequent years, the drawback to the voluntary, best-practices approach to solving labor problems was that, once the reform was instituted, no coercive mechanism existed to ensure that the industry did not return to old practices.

The "Negro Problem," the State, and the National Urban League

On race issues, the federal government's sporadic interest through the nineteenth and early twentieth centuries allowed nonprofits and philanthropic organizations to play a powerful shaping role in the nation's understanding of the "Negro Problem." As African American workers migrated to Northern cities in search of wartime employment, the federal government quickly mobilized its most experienced investigators to make sense of this unprecedented demographic shift and to attempt to coordinate wartime employment. To this end, the War Labor Administration established the Division of Negro Economics (DNE) within the Department of Labor (DOL) to answer pressing public concerns regarding dramatic changes in the black working class and to coordinate the placement of black workers in war industries. New government agencies with scarce resources and developing institutional capacity often turned to the nonprofit sector for assistance. For instance, the Women's Bureau looked to the National Consumers League and the Women's Trade Union League, not only for political support, but also for assistance in

conducting investigations (Hendrickson 2008). Similarly, the DNE drew
on political and social networks already in place and organized through
local branches of the National Urban League (NUL) to assist in important investigations aimed at explaining to concerned observers the character of the migration and the experiences of black workers in Northern
industries. Over the course of the decade, the work of the DNE, and later
the NUL, helped to undermine racial stereotypes and to transform the
"Negro problem" from an intractable regional concern that the federal
government could more or less ignore into a national issue and concern.

At its height, the DNE employed 134 examiners, 7 secretaries, and
15 state representatives. It had state branches in North Carolina, Virginia, Alabama, Kentucky, Mississippi, Florida, Georgia, California,
Ohio, Illinois, Pennsylvania, Michigan, New Jersey, and New York, as
well as a District of Columbia office. The DNE staffed its offices exclusively with black employees, many of whom had experience in other federal offices or the NUL, including Charles Hall and William Jennifer,
who moved from the Bureau of the Census and United States Employment Services to prominent positions in DNE offices in Ohio and Michigan respectively, and Forrest B. Washington of the Detroit NUL, who
served as the supervisor of Negro economics in Illinois.[25]

To lead the DNE, Secretary of Labor William B. Wilson appointed
George E. Haynes to the director's position. Between 1910 and 1916,
Haynes had helped found the NUL and served as its executive secretary, a post later held by Eugene Kinckle Jones. Haynes brought with
him a keen understanding of black migration and close connections to
the larger civil rights movement. Haynes was born in 1880 in Pine Bluff,
Arkansas, and educated at Fisk, from which he received a bachelor's degree in 1903, and then at Yale, where he studied under sociologist William Graham Sumner and completed his master's degree in sociology
in 1904. After four years of work with the Colored Department of the
International Committee of the Young Men's Christian Association,
Haynes returned to graduate school at the New York University School
of Philanthropy (later renamed the Columbia School of Social Work),
where in 1912 he completed his doctorate under economist Samuel Mc-

25. DNE, *The Negro at Work During the World War and Reconstruction; statistics, problems, and
policies relating to the greater inclusion of Negro wage earners in American industry and agriculture*
(Washington, D.C.: GPO, 1921; reprint, New York: Negro Universities Press, 1969), 68.

Cune Lindsay and became the first African American to receive a PhD from Columbia.[26]

DNE investigators were cautiously optimistic about black workers' status and future in Northern industries. During the war, DNE investigators found that black workers had gained a toehold in many unskilled and semiskilled industrial occupations, but in skilled occupations black workers gained access only to work in industries where they had previous experience, such as in steel and iron foundries. Although migrants found work chiefly in low-skilled positions, investigators pointed to black workers' experience in foundries as evidence that with time and experience these new industrial workers would rise through the ranks into the higher paying and more stable skilled positions.[27]

After the war, supporters of the DNE unsuccessfully petitioned Congress to make the division a permanent bureau, as it had the Woman-in-Industry Service, which became permanent as the Women's Bureau. The Hampton Institute's *Southern Workman* editorialized that African Americans "should have able representatives who may sit at the council tables and know what is going on and be in position to give some sane and timely advice."[28] By the time President Warren Harding took office in 1921, however, Haynes and his assistant, Karl Phillips, the only remaining DNE employees, were working part time with the BLS's Investigation and Inspection Service. Haynes continued to testify before the congressional appropriations committees through 1922 in hopes of reinstating funding for the DNE, but without success. At a 1921 appropriations hearing, Representative Walter W. Magee (D–NY) challenged Haynes on the need for the DNE, asking if there should be a "division of Italian economics, a division of Jewish economics, a division of Polish economics, a division of Indian economics, and so on down through all the races that make up this cosmopolitan people?" Haynes responded that the black population in the United States was "segregated from the

---

26. Haynes's dissertation published as George Edmund Haynes, *The Negro at Work in New York City: A Study in Economic Progress* (New York: Columbia University, Longman's, Green and Co., 1912; reprint, New York: Arno Press and the New York Times, 1968). For more on George Haynes, see Moore 1981, 42–59; Parris and Brooks 1971; Weiss 1974; Jessie Carney Smith, ed., *Notable Black American Men* (Detroit: Gale Research, 1999), 528–32; "In the Service of His People," *Journal of Negro History* 6 (April 1921): 107–8; and John A. Garraty and Mark C. Carnes, ed., *American National Bibliography,* s.v. "George E. Haynes."

27. DNE, *The Negro at Work During the World War and Reconstruction,* 42.

28. "Wise Federal Action," *Southern Workman* 48 (February 1919): 51–52.

white population . . . as no other group is." Magee's rejoinder was indicative of policymakers' willingness to close their eyes to the problems
that only two years earlier had erupted in some of the worst urban violence in American history: "There is no segregation up there so far as
I can see."[29]

In what amounted to an effort to replace the valuable work of the
DNE, Charles S. Johnson joined the National Urban League, where he
led an industrial research department funded with grants from the Laura
Spelman Rockefeller Memorial (LSRM) and the Carnegie Corporation.
By the early 1920s, Johnson had emerged as the decade's most important
investigator of black labor. As a lead investigator and an author of significant chapters of the Chicago Commission report on the 1919 race riots,
Johnson provided evidence of black workers' successful integration into
industrial occupations and identified white workers and middle managers as the chief obstacles to black workers' upward mobility.[30]

As the head of the NUL's Department of Research and Investigation,
Johnson worked to develop a body of expertise challenging an ideology
of black inferiority that dominated policymakers' understanding of the
"Negro Problem" and to keep the black labor question in play as a national political issue and public problem. To these ends, he led a number
of empirical studies of workplace race relations throughout the country. In these investigations he sharpened his critique of white workers as
the source of racial intolerance while continuing to draw attention to the
malleability of race relations.[31] In the process, he increasingly differenti-

29. Congress, House, House Committee on Appropriations, *Sundry Civil Appropriation Bill, 1921.
Part 2: Statement of Mr. George E. Haynes and Mr. Karl F. Phillips,* 66th Cong., 2nd sess., March 20,
1920, 2164. Phillips does not appear to have made any statements during the hearing.

30. Chicago Commission on Race Relations, *The Negro in Chicago* (Chicago: University of Chicago Press, 1922).

31. The NUL had a much more developed research department than the NAACP, which is why I
have chosen to focus on the NUL rather than the NAACP. In fact, my examination of NAACP papers
suggests that the NAACP relied on the DNE and NUL for information concerning black workers. For
example, see T. Arnold Hill, Executive Secretary of the Chicago Urban League, to Walter F. White,
Assistant Secretary NAACP, November 14, 1919, Reel 9, Group 1, Series C, Administrative File Cont.
Group 1, Box 319. File: General Labor, September 1919–December 1919, Papers of the NAACP: Part 10,
Peonage, Labor, and the New Deal, 1913–1939, Library of Congress. In this letter, Hill provides White
with detailed information on Northern black workers for a talk White would give later entitled "The Ne-
gro Migrant in the Industrial World in the North." White had similar correspondence with other NUL
branch offices. For a summary of the competition between the NUL's *Opportunity* and the NAACP's
Crisis, see Lewis 2000, 153–56. Lewis describes an internal evaluation of the *Crisis* by NAACP leader
Mary Ovington, who suggested that the *Crisis* had never produced a "good piece of research." She
contrasted the plight of the *Crisis* with *Opportunity,* which she described as "the magazine now in as-
cendant" (Lewis 2000, 155). L. Hollingsworth Wood to LSRM, December 17, 1918, Series 3, Box 99,

ated workplace interracial relations, which varied from friendly to antagonistic, from labor market interracial relations, which appeared to grow more and more antagonistic in the Northeast and Midwest. This tension became particularly acute as the labor market tightened after the war and employers increasingly recognized the ability of black workers to accomplish the same tasks as whites, often at a lower wage.

Johnson also functioned as editor of the NUL monthly *Opportunity*. Scholars have usually characterized *Opportunity* as a vehicle to publicize the achievements of Harlem Renaissance artists and, in Johnson's words, "to inculcate a disposition to see enough of interest and beauty in their own lives to rid themselves of the inferior feeling of being Negro." Significantly, the journal also served as an outlet for publicizing the work of the research department.[32] In the first edition of *Opportunity*, Eugene Kinckle Jones wrote that the journal would "try to set down interestingly but without sugar coating or generalizations the findings of careful scientific surveys and the facts gathered from research."[33] Reflecting on the mission of the monthly in 1928, Johnson wrote that "the policy of the magazine as it has developed has emphasized the objectives of making available for students, writers and speakers dependable data concerning the Negro and race relations for their discussions, with the thought that truth carries its own light, that accurate and demonstratable facts can correct inaccurate and slanderous assertions that have gone unchallenged."[34] After two years of publication, *Opportunity* had a monthly circulation of six thousand, which included more than one hun-

---

Folder 1005, LSRM Collection, Rockefeller Archive Center (hereafter RAC). A number of NUL employees assumed supervisory positions within the DNE. See "Appeal of the NATIONAL LEAGUE ON URBAN CONDITIONS AMONG NEGROES to the Laura Spelman Rockefeller Memorial," December 31, 1918, Series 3, Box 99, Folder NUL 1005, 1918–1922, LSRM Collection, RAC.

32. L. Hollingsworth Wood to Beardsley Ruml, Box 99, Folder 1006 NUL, 1923–1924, LSRM Collection, RAC; Charles S. Johnson, "The Rise of the Negro Magazine," *Journal of Negro History* 13 (January 1928): 18. For more on the journal and Johnson's role as a chronicler and advocate of the Harlem Renaissance see Lewis 1981, particularly 113–18, 179, 198–99. In the second volume of his biography of Du Bois, Lewis describes a sudden change in *Opportunity* as it "switched within a couple of issues from being a forum for the cutting-edge articles of distinguished social scientists and educators to become the premier review for literary and artistic effusion of the so-called New Negro." Lewis is correct to point to a shift in the periodical, but I find that in the biography—and in *When Harlem Was in Vogue*—Lewis overemphasizes the shift, not only in *Opportunity* but in Johnson's thinking as well. Though Johnson was one of the key players in the Harlem Renaissance, he also developed an equally important role as the leading expert on the "Negro labor question" in the 1920s. For Lewis's characterization of *Opportunity*, see Lewis (2000), 156.

33. Eugene Kinckle Jones, "'Cooperation' and 'Opportunity,'" *Opportunity* 1 (January 1923): 5. Also quoted in Lewis, *When Harlem Was in Vogue*, 95.

34. Charles S. Johnson, "The Rise of the Negro Magazine," *Opportunity*, 19.

dred public and university libraries. As a testament to the usefulness of the journal to social scientists, Jones reported "over forty classes in sociology use it for reference."[35]

The NUL relied on philanthropists for much of its funding, which left the organization open to the criticism that they were mere "Negro administers of white philanthropy," as Sterling Spero and Abram Harris suggested in their 1930 study, *The Black Worker*.[36] Indeed, foundation leaders did more than simply fund investigations. Through their funding choices and review of proposals, they played a key role in shaping the body of labor expertise concerning black workers and communities. A 1926 LSRM report conceded that "it should be borne in mind that the amount of work undertaken [by the NUL] has to a certain extent been determined by a deliberate Memorial policy."[37] But Harris and Spero go much too far in their dismissal of the NUL's work and their willingness to lump all recipients of philanthropic aid into one category. Where previous foundation-funded research and labor policy development had accommodated Southern racist traditions, the work of the NUL in the 1920s candidly analyzed and criticized impediments to black workers' upward mobility and assigned blame to a number of white-led organizations.[38] In fact, Johnson's analysis of the causes of black worker problems in industry resembled, in method and conclusions, W. E. B. Du Bois's

35. Kenneth Chorley to Beardsley Ruml, February 5, 1925, Series 3, Box 99, Folder 1007 NUL, 1925–1926, LSRM Collection, RAC. Eugene Kinckle Jones to Laura Spelman Rockefeller Memorial, January 15, 1925, Series 3, Box 99, Folder 1007 NUL, 1925–1926, LSRM Collection, RAC. See also "Race Relations and Negro Work, 1926–27," Series 3, Box 101, Folder 1021 Negro Problems 1927–1929, 4, LSRM Collection, RAC.

36. Sterling Spero and Abram Harris included interracial committees in this category as well. Sterling Spero and Abram Harris, *The Black Worker: The Negro and the Labor Movement* (New York: Columbia University Press, 1931), 464–65. An $8,000 grant by the Carnegie Foundation in 1923 provided the initial funding for the NUL's Department of Research and Investigation. In response to a 1924 plea from L. Hollingsworth Wood, the LSRM appropriated $5,000 as a "special contribution" in addition to its annual NUL appropriation for "research and investigations conducted by the League." By 1926 the NUL budgeted more than $23,500 toward research and investigation, making it by far the largest department in the NUL. Leonard Outhwaite to Hollingsworth Wood, June 4, 1926, Series 3, Box 99, Folder 1007 NUL, 1925–26, LSRM Collection, RAC.

37. "Race Relations and Negro Work, 1926–27," Series 3, Box 101, Folder 1021 Negro Problems 1927–1929, LSRM Collection, RAC. Eugene Kinckle Jones expressed a deep and personal gratitude for the aid provided by the LSRM and Rockefeller Foundation in general, and the Rockefeller family in particular. In a candid letter to John D. Rockefeller Jr., Jones wrote that he "like many other thousands of Negroes from the South had a deep-seated sense of appreciation of what" John D. Rockefeller Sr. had "done for us as a race." Eugene Kinckle Jones to John D. Rockefeller Jr., March 21, 1921, Series 3, Box 99, Folder 1005 NUL, 1918–1922, LSRM Collection, RAC.

38. For examinations of the relationship between philanthropists and the groups and organizations they funded, see Karl and Katz 1981, 1987; Critchlow 1993; Hammack 1999; Hammack and Wheeler 1994; O'Connor 2001; Smith 1990; and Lagemann 1999.

controversial labor analysis more than it did that of Booker T. Washington's, another important recipient of aid from foundations who was often charged with public appeasement of white worker and employer racism.

In the mid-1920s, a series of NUL studies stressed the socially constructed nature of racism and its many variations, while clearly assigning white workers the responsibility for restricting black workers to low-skilled and low-paid occupations. In Johnson's studies of workplace race relations in the Midwest, Northeast, and South, he found greater emphasis on de jure segregation in border states such as Missouri, Kentucky, and Maryland, where "the necessity has been felt for being explicit on absolute segregation in residential areas, enforcing the issue with an ordinance."[39] Johnson cited Allison Muir, personnel executive of the General Electric Company, who confirmed a hardening of racial divisions "the nearer you get to the Mason Dixon Line." According to Muir, in Birmingham you would find white workers who preferred to work with skilled black workers rather than "poor white trash," but in "Baltimore the white workers demand separation in everything."[40]

Johnson remained hopeful and committed to the Chicago model, which suggested interracial tension would diminish as white ethnic and black workers assimilated to the common mores of modern industrial society, but he made clear that white workers' willingness to work side by side with black workers and accept them as a legitimate part of the labor market was the decisive factor in the future of the color line. Johnson found that white workers maintained degrees of segregation through grassroots activism and institutional means that limited black workers' access to particular occupations. For instance, among barbers, motion picture operators, horseshoers, public accountants, and portable engineers, state examining boards exercised "a very rigid selection and by this means have been known to hold down the number of Negroes' licenses."[41] In other cases, white workers' militant refusal to work alongside black workers proved an adequate deterrent to the employment of black labor. In its work with employers, the NUL's Department of In-

39. Charles S. Johnson, "Negroes at Work in Baltimore, Md.: A Summary of the Report on the Industrial Survey of the Negro Population," *Opportunity* 1 (1923): 12–19.

40. Ibid., 12. See also, "Outline of Work and Activities of the Industrial Relations Department of the National Urban League, March 15th, 1925–May 31st, 1926," Series 3, Box 99, Folders NUL 1007, 1025–1926, LSRM Collection, RAC.

41. Charles S. Johnson, "Negroes at Work in Baltimore, Md.: A Summary of the Report on the Industrial Survey of the Negro Population," 12–19.

dustrial Relations found that the "almost invariable answer given by an employment manager to one seeking jobs for Negroes is 'Our white employees will not work with them.'"[42] In his study of Los Angeles, Johnson took great interest in examining how the addition of large numbers of Asian, Mexican, and Mexican American workers affected the color line. As in other cases, Johnson found the relationship between white, Mexican, and black workers varied radically across plants and firms. He reported that "white workers in one plant have demanded Mexicans and in another refused to work with them; insisted on separate lavatories in plants and accepted unsegregated ones in others; objected to Mexicans in one place and accepted Negroes in another."[43]

The struggle to establish a research arm in the civil rights movement demonstrates the importance that movement leaders and organizations placed on inquiry and expertise. Support for the DNE came from across the spectrum of civil rights movement organizations and included Tuskegee-style leaders in the South and more aggressive Northern urban leaders. In conducting their investigations, the DNE and NUL constructed an institutional and discursive space for rethinking the "Negro labor question" in the 1920s and gathered empirical evidence on a group of workers usually ignored by social scientists in academia and government agencies. Here, a new group of experts on the black labor question had unprecedented power, limited in some respects by a reliance on outside organizations for funding, to reconceptualize the "Negro problem," develop a language for discussing the problem, identify a mode of analysis, and formulate solutions to the "problem." As a result, these labor experts took large steps toward replacing pseudo-scientific notions of biological inferiority with a Chicago school assimilationist model suggesting the malleability of race relations. Further, the NUL's efforts to keep the black labor issue "in play" at a national level should not be dismissed. If black labor could be described as a Southern problem, it could easily be ignored by the federal government, but when it became a national problem it made federal government action on race relations more likely. By drawing attention to the national injustices visited upon African Amer-

    42. "Outline of Work and Activities of the Industrial Relations Department of the National Urban League, March 15th, 1925–May 31st, 1926," Series 3, Box 99, Folders NUL 1007, 1925–1926, LSRM Collection, RAC.
    43. Charles S. Johnson, "Negro Workers in Los Angeles Industries," *Opportunity* 6 (August 1928): 238. See also Charles S. Johnson, *Industrial Survey of the Negro Population of Los Angeles* (no publisher, 1926).

icans, this group of social scientists and their supporters established a tradition of publicizing the insupportable contradictions in American democracy and race relations that would culminate in Gunnar Myrdal's 1944 epic study of American race relations, *American Dilemma,* though Myrdal's study would not maintain the attention to political-economic issues so characteristic of the 1920s studies of black workers.

Conclusion

These two examples provide evidence of nonprofits' ability to pick up issues that were either designated for them to handle or that had been disregarded by the state. The first case supports the idea that nonprofit organizations should be considered as closely tied to the evolution of government and governance. Hoover and others had clearly defined the hours' issue as a public problem, but their commitment to an associational model of governance helped facilitate the development of nonprofit labor and economic research organizations. Their effective use of the policymaking expertise generated by these nonprofits further legitimized the research of these emerging institutions and underscored their effectiveness in solving what only years earlier appeared an intractable private conflict between employers and employees. In terms of altering the working conditions of American workers, the associational approach, which featured cooperation between the federal government and nonprofits with its reliance on expertise, could only be effective under certain circumstances. Nonprofit research organizations could increase public concern, but moral suasion and voluntary agreements did not bring with them the more durable effects of the force of law or the coercive power of a negotiated union-management labor agreement.

Further, the power of expertise to alter working conditions turned on investigators' ability to persuade industrial leaders, the public, and at times American workers that policy changes were in their and the nation's best interest. In the case of the twelve-hour day, investigators and government leaders employed all of these tactics. Engineers and public health experts combined to make the case to Judge Gary and US Steel that opposition to the eight-hour day on economic and efficiency grounds was unsound and in fact unhealthy for the industry and its employees. Such an understanding of the hours issue should not, of course, discount the crucial role that labor activism played in calling attention to issues related to working conditions, but it does suggest that expertise generated by progressive-minded nonprofits, when combined with support from the federal government and public opinion, could make previously private issues a public concern.

On civil rights issues, the absence of cooperation from the federal government and sympathetic public opinion made success much more difficult. The inability of the DNE and NUL to force the nation to address the problems of African American workers emerged from policymakers' lack of will or outright opposition to addressing issues of civil rights. Thus, the DNE-NUL example is more mixed and could be presented as the successful marginalization of an issue too incendiary for the federal government to address. It would be more accurate, however, to frame the NUL's work as a demonstration of the power of philanthropically funded organizations to keep alive controversial issues that legislators would just as soon have forgotten about and to cultivate a class of black social scientists whose empirical findings would be crucial to later analysis of race and citizenship in the United States. Though supporters of black labor inquiry would have certainly preferred and in many ways required a state bureau similar to the Women's Bureau, the DNE and the NUL reframed the "Negro Problem" as part of a larger urban, industrial labor problem and made it clear that civil rights issues were inexorably intertwined with class and labor issues.

The historically oriented chapters in this book suggest a larger ideological shift in nonprofit research organizations that spans U.S. history. The role assumed by associations and later nonprofits in addressing controversial public problems and helping to create a sense of national identity had its roots in the antebellum period, as described by Neem (chapter 2). As Alice O'Connor describes in chapter 5, in the post–World War II era new, more conservative nonprofits challenged the generally interventionist philosophy of pre–World War II nonprofit organizations. The New Era's contribution to the development of policy history rests on the nonprofits' effective efforts to bridge the gap between what the state could and would do to solve vexing problems. Nonprofit research organizations in the 1920s emerged as institutions willing to take on the most controversial issues of the time. Taking O'Connor's and my chapters together, we can identify a period wherein these nonprofits, from the early years of the century to midcentury, helped support a critique of the ideology of laissez-faire market capitalism, which seemed to many to have outlived its usefulness in the late nineteenth century. Looking ahead to O'Connor's work, we can observe how conservative nonprofits challenged this critique in the post–World War II era by helping to promote the slowly emerging "market-think" that flourished in the last quarter of the twentieth century.

References

Alchon, Guy. 1985. *The Invisible Hand of Planning: Capitalism, Social Science, and the State in the 1920s.* Princeton: Princeton University Press.

Barber, William J. 1985. *From New Era to New Deal: Herbert Hoover, the Economists, and American Economic Policy, 1921–1933.* Cambridge: Cambridge University Press.

Critchlow, David T. 1993. "Think Tanks, Antistatism, and Democracy: The Nonpartisan Ideal and Policy Research in the United States, 1913–1987." In *The State and Social Investigation in Britain and the United States,* ed. Mary O. Furner and Michael Lacey, 279–322. Cambridge: Cambridge University Press.

Dewey, John. 1927. *The Public and Its Problems.* Athens: Ohio University Press.

Donohue, Kathleen. 2003. *Freedom from Want: American Liberalism and the Idea of the Consumer.* Baltimore: Johns Hopkins University Press.

Furner, Mary. 2005. "Structure and Virtue in United States Political Economy." *Journal of the History of Economic Thought* 27: 1–27.

Greenwald, Maurine W., and Margo Anderson. 1996. *Pittsburgh Surveyed: Social Science and Social Reform in the Early Twentieth Century.* Pittsburgh: University of Pittsburgh Press.

Hammack, David C. 1999. "Foundations in the American Polity, 1900–1950." In *Philanthropic Foundations: New Scholarship, New Possibilities,* ed. Ellen Condliffe Lagemann, 43–68. Bloomington: Indiana University Press.

Hammack, David, and M. Stanton Wheeler. 1994. *Social Science in the Making: Essays on the Russell Sage Foundation, 1907–1972.* New York: Russell Sage Foundation.

Harris, Howell John. 1982. *The Right to Manage: Industrial Relations Policies of American Business in the 1940s.* Madison: University of Wisconsin Press.

Hart, David. 1998. "Herbert Hoover's Last Laugh: The Enduring Significance of the 'Associative State' in the United States." *Journal of Policy History* 10: 419–44.

Hawley, Ellis W. 1974. "Herbert Hoover, the Commerce Secretariat, and the Vision of an 'Associative State,'" 1921–1928." *Journal of American History* 61: 116–40.

Hendrickson, Mark. 2008. "Gender Research as Labor Activism: The Women's Bureau in the New Era." *Journal of Policy History* (Fall).

Karl, Barry Dean. 1983. *The Uneasy State: The United States from 1915 to 1945.* Chicago: University of Chicago Press.

Karl, Barry Dean, and Stanley Katz. 1981. "The American Private Philan-
    thropic Foundation and the Public Sphere, 1890–1930." *Minerva* 19 (Sum-
    mer): 236–70.
———. 1987. "Foundations and Ruling Class Elites." *Daedalus* 116 (March):
    1–40.
Lagemann, Ellen Condliffe, ed. 1999. *Philanthropic Foundations: New Scholar-
    ship, New Possibilities*. Bloomington: Indiana University Press.
Lewis, David Levering. 1981. *When Harlem Was in Vogue*. New York: Knopf.
———. 2000. *W. E. B. Du Bois: The Fight for Equality and the American Cen-
    tury, 1919–1963*. New York: Holt.
Livingston, James. 1987. "The Social Analysis of Economic History and Theory:
    Conjectures on Late Nineteenth-Century American Development." *Ameri-
    can Historical Review* 92 (February): 69–95.
Moore, Jesse Thomas, Jr. 1981. *A Search for Equality: The National Urban
    League, 1910–1961*. University Park: Pennsylvania State University Press.
O'Connor, Alice. 2001. *Poverty Knowledge: Social Science, Social Policy, and
    the Poor in Twentieth-Century U.S. History*. Princeton: Princeton University
    Press.
Parris, Guichard, and Lester Brooks. 1971. *Blacks in the City: A History of the
    National Urban League*. Boston: Little, Brown.
Smith, James. 1990. *The Idea Brokers: Think Tanks and the Rise of a New Policy
    Elite*. New York: Free Press.
Weiss, Nancy J. 1974. *The National Urban League, 1910–1940*. New York: Ox-
    ford University Press.
Zieger, Robert H. 1969. *Republicans and Labor, 1919–1929*. Lexington: Univer-
    sity of Kentucky Press.

CHAPTER FOUR

In the Shadow of the New Deal: Reconfiguring the Roles of Government and Charity, 1928–1940

Elisabeth S. Clemens

Four years into the Depression, President Herbert Hoover's commitment to voluntary relief was thoroughly discredited. Across the nation, private charities, religious organizations, and mutual associations had faltered in the face of the unprecedented calls for assistance. Thus, when Franklin Roosevelt took office in March 1933, policy took an abrupt turn toward federal funding and administration of relief. The Federal Emergency Relief Administration (FERA), under the leadership of Harry Hopkins, embodied this new approach. In his first regular order to state governments, Hopkins established that "grants of Federal emergency relief funds are to be administered by public agencies. . . . This ruling prohibits the turning over of Federal Emergency Relief funds to a private agency. The unemployed must apply to a public agency for relief, and this relief must be furnished direct to the applicant by a public agent" (Hopkins 1999, 83).

Overwhelmed by the magnitude of need, voluntary organizations were clearly not up to the task of taking care of the poor, a task that was elsewhere shifting to government with the establishment of modern welfare states (Cohen 1990, chap. 5).[1] This turn from private charity to pub-

I am grateful for support provided by the Rockefeller Archive Center and the research staff, particularly Thomas Rosenbaum and Mindy Gordon.

1. With respect to fraternalism, David Beito argues that there was as much retrenchment as collapse (Beito 2000, 222–28).

lic relief anticipated T. H. Marshall's progression from civil to political to social rights (Marshall 1964, 65–122). Yet, voluntary associations did not acquiesce, arguing that private charities constituted an impressive infrastructure for the delivery of publicly funded relief and were more attuned to fundamental American values (Hammack 2003, 269–70; Hopkins 1999, 83).[2] Stung by Hopkins's policy, Red Cross leaders advised lying low until government programs failed and they were again called upon to retake the lead in meeting the crisis.[3] Why should the government create some other infrastructure, when a national network of private charities was already in place and only in need of new funds to sustain their relief efforts?

There are a number of reasons why we might expect the response to the Depression to have taken the form of an extension—and intensification—of long-standing practices of public subsidy to private charities. Hopkins, after all, was himself very much a product of the world of private charities. He began his professional career in a New York settlement house, moved to the Association for Improving the Condition of the Poor, and, after a spell with New York's Bureau of Public Welfare, served for two years as the Gulf Coast regional director for the American Red Cross. In Congress, there were ample precedents for appropriating public funds for disaster relief (Landis 1997). In addition to providing supplies and funds for crises such as the San Francisco Earthquake of 1906 and the Mississippi River Flood of 1927, Congress had made major appropriations for foreign relief, notably in the aftermath of World War I and in response to the Soviet famine of 1921–22.[4] So why was this well-established model of appropriating public funds to

2. Mr. Cavin to Mr. Fieser, "Subject: 'The Future of the American Red Cross,'" May 6, 1933. NARA, RG 200, Box 78, Folder 102.

3. Don C. Smith to Mr. Fieser, "Subject: 'The Future of the American Red Cross,'" May 5, 1933. RG 200, Box 78, Folder 102. As one staff member argued in response to a memo circulated by James Fieser, "In my judgment public opinion will in due course swing away from large scale relief by public agencies and this may come sooner than we expect by the pyramiding of relief costs which will finally engulf the tax payer and cause reaction such as we have seen in the administration of veterans' benefits. When this happens, the private agencies which have stood their ground and have performed creditable work in contributing to the unemployment situation of the present day will find double favor in the eye of the public and because of this favor and also the fact that other private agencies have ceased to exist, will have little to fear in winning public support both financial and moral."

4. As secretary of commerce, Hoover had supported a $20 million congressional appropriation for food relief to the Soviet Union. This relief was managed by the American Relief Administration and by local authorities in the Soviet Union. These precedents were recited again and again during the congressional debates over drought relief in 1930 and 1931.

support the work of voluntary associations not adopted by the incoming Roosevelt administration?

The bright line that Hopkins drew between public funding and private organizations in 1933 reflected not only a history of struggle over the role of voluntary organizations in disaster response, but also the intense conflicts over the appropriate political response to the massive drought and surging unemployment of 1931 and 1932. The decision reflected a fierce politicization of charity as a site that articulated relationships between the well-off and the needy, between citizens and the state. In many respects, this moment exemplifies the classic conditions for institutional change: a once-dominant institutional logic overwhelmed and discredited;[5] a significant change in control of political power linked to advocacy of an alternative model. The conditions could scarcely be more favorable for asserting, in the words of Robert Penn Warren's populist demagogue Willie Stark, "Free. Not as charity, but as a right" (1960, 57).

Yet even this combination of delegitimated institutions, powerful exogenous shock, and entrepreneurial advocacy of an alternative was not enough to expunge private charity from the configurations of American governance and usher in Marshall's vision of social rights in a universal welfare state. Although the crisis would erode one strong categorical logic in which receipt of charity was antithetical to citizenship and the domain of rights, it would also open the possibilities of novel recombinations. The result was not a simple marginalization of voluntarism and charity from American governance, but a less-conflicted incorporation of voluntarism into the national project and the organization of governance. Thus, the encounter of the New Deal with the world of private charity was not one of progressive evolution or succession but rather an intensified contradiction followed by a novel synthesis that would develop into the nonprofit sector of the postwar decades, nurtured both by expanded tax exemptions and multiplying "partnerships" with government. Thus, the limits of the New Deal project of state-building established the foundations for a postwar regime in which a newly named "non-profit sector" would be deeply implicated in governance and individual philanthropy and volunteering would be central to the performance of good citizenship.

5. See Blyth 2002 (30–34) on "Knightian uncertainty."

Public versus Private Charities

Conflict over the role of public and private efforts in the relief of poverty is a durable feature of American history. In the wake of the Civil War, private charities mobilized opposition to the use of public funds for outdoor relief, which involved provision of aid to the poor in their own homes. These practices, it was charged, encouraged sloth and were instruments of political corruption. In their place, the poor would be forced to take whatever they could find in the labor market, to commit themselves to almshouses, or to request aid from private charities. Private benevolence, advocates argued, provided the personal attention and moral discipline required to inoculate recipients from the corrupting power of dependence. This discursive linking of economic independence and citizenship rights positioned relief and charity as key sites for struggles over political membership (Fitzgerald 2006, 87–93; Kurzman 1974, 45–49; Goldberg 2007).

Yet what appeared to be a sharply defined set of mutually exclusive categories was much muddier at the level of organizational practice. With respect to funding, personnel, and routines, the division of labor between publicly funded institutional care and privately controlled charity was far from exact. In response to outrage at the presence of children in public almshouses, there were efforts—most prominently in New York City—to move orphans and half-orphans from adult institutions into special institutions that were often funded by government subsidies (Crenson 1998; Fitzgerald 2006; Clemens 2006).[6] When the Panic of 1893 produced widespread unemployment and destitution, cities such as Chicago retreated from their insistence on individual responsibility and provided public-works jobs to those in need (Knight 2005, 283). Each disaster, each business downturn, put pressure on efforts to defend a bright line dividing public funds from private charity.

By the early twentieth century, the provision of relief in many American cities involved a diverse set of public agencies and private organizations. The latter group was often split by religious differences, with Protestant organizations and Catholic institutions championing quite different understandings of the nature of charity. Many Catholics rejected scientific charity with its demands for strict investigation of the needy, exchange of information (which would limit the ability of institutions to

---

6. Alexander Fleisher, "State Money and Privately Managed Charities," *Survey* 33 (October 31, 1914): 110–12.

protect the reputations of pregnant women), and prohibitions on the distribution of food or fuel to struggling families (Hopkins 1999, chap. 5; McKeown 1998, 148). The changing character of need in a rapidly industrializing and urbanizing nation created mounting pressure for—and objections to—greater public contributions to the provision of relief. As the magnitude of poor relief and unemployment tested the capabilities of private organizations, charities disagreed over the desirability of public funding and new forms of work relief. By 1914, prominent institutions such as New York City's Association for Improving the Condition of the Poor split with the equally prominent New York Charity Organization Society over the public provision of widow's pensions. The AICP advocated "'a complete welding in the power and prestige of the public agencies with the initiative and elasticity of private agencies.' The result of this 'welding process' would be the 'increased efficiency of both.' Most likely the agency saw hope for its survival in this position" (Hopkins 1999, 97–103).

Although conflicts over the relation of public and private relief persisted, there was a marked convergence between the organizational practices and personnel of private charity and public agencies. Careers crosscut the two sectors; growing requirements for incorporation and oversight of private organizations also generated pressures toward common understandings of what should be done and how. Most powerfully, the increasing professionalization of private social workers and the multiplying precedents for collaboration with government established what might have served as a framework for much more expansive collaboration in response to the challenge of the Depression (Lubove 1968, 8–9).[7] So why, instead, did the Hoover and then the Roosevelt administration draw bright—if rather different—lines between public funds and private organizations, reviving and reinforcing a categorical distinction that had been diminishing in force? And why, a few years later, was that line blurred in novel ways?

The Red Cross and the Politics of Drought Relief

Somewhat ironically, no organization was more central to the breakdown of relationships between government and charity than the charity that

---

7. On the tensions between professionals and volunteers within the Red Cross, see Dulles 1950, 237–38.

had long been closest to government: the American Red Cross. Founded in connection with efforts to promote U.S. adoption of the Treaty of Geneva,[8] the American Red Cross received a congressional charter in 1905 that specified a governance structure in which, ex officio, the U.S. president was the president of the Red Cross and a number of cabinet secretaries sat on the board. Prominent political figures from both parties, along with leading businessmen and philanthropists, populated the governing committees of the organization and chaired its annual appeals. This tight linkage of voluntary association to political elites was realized during World War I as the American Red Cross played a major role both in supporting troops and aiding in postwar relief efforts in Europe. As attention turned from fighting the war to caring for the survivors, the Red Cross sent teams to aid refugees and some in Congress identified the organization as the most preferred agent for food relief to Europe. Thus throughout Europe and Asia, the Red Cross—including both volunteers and professional staff—was the face of American relief.[9] In the decade after World War I, few organizations figured so prominently in the discussion of the relationship between private and public charity.

In the aftermath of the war and refugee crisis, the Red Cross took primary responsibility for continued service to veterans in their communities,[10] but also searched for new missions that would confirm its central place in American society. For a time, public health nursing was promoted as the new organizational mission, but declines in membership and finances continued (Dulles 1950, 243–55; Gilbo 1981, 95–97). Events in the late 1920s provided opportunities for the organization to shine once more in the field of disaster relief. Above all, the Mississippi River Flood of 1927 called forth an impressive mobilization of the re-

8. The International Committee of the Red Cross was established in 1863 and the First Geneva Convention issued in 1864. The American Red Cross, however, was not established until 1881, a year before the U.S. Senate ratified the Geneva Treaty.

9. The Depression-era Congress often looked backward to these precedents, quoting the House debate of 1919, albeit with some confusion as to whether $100 million to Europe or $20 million to Russia was at issue. "The one thought that inspired their intense activities at that time was that the distribution ought not to be made by the President, but that it ought to be made by the American National Red Cross. At that time the Red Cross never raised its voice against distributing Federal funds. It was willing, apparently, to take $25,000,000 of the money of the people of the United States and go across the sea and enter the soviet republics and administer to sufferers there the funds of the people of the United States." *Congressional Record,* February 3, 1931, 3854.

10. Note that one of the most time-consuming duties of Red Cross volunteers was to help veterans fill out the forms necessary to apply for government benefits.

lief services of the Red Cross and $17 million in voluntary contributions from across the nation and beyond (Dulles 1950, 270; Barry 1997, 272–86). Heading the federal response, Secretary of Commerce Herbert Hoover reinforced his reputation as the "great humanitarian" (earned for his role in food relief during and after World War I) and set the stage for his successful run for the Republican nomination and the presidency in 1928. After a decade of national prosperity, Hoover the engineer and humanitarian was in a position to enact his vision of a nation organized through volunteerism and collaboration between business and charity "convened" by government (Hawley 1998). But a few years after the floods, the stock market crashed and the rains stopped. Seized by a drought that would eventually afflict over twenty states as well as rapidly rising unemployment, the long-standing debate over the proper relationship of public funding to private charity took on new urgency.

At the beginning, of course, it was not clear that the combination of rising unemployment and drought in much of the rural South would become the Great Depression. Hoover's initial response relied on familiar recipes: gather businessmen to agree to voluntary measures to preserve employment and encourage state as well as local groups to raise the resources necessary for relief of the afflicted. Hoover pressured the Red Cross to move beyond its traditional mandates defined by war and natural disaster to address the destitution produced by severe drought. In this effort, he met with strong organizational resistance, securing only a special Red Cross drive for drought relief rather than a broad organizational commitment (Hawley 1998, 165–69; Hamilton 1982). The Red Cross leadership insisted that "help could only be given to those whose hunger resulted from a national disaster. In the plantation South, where the economy was based on a one-crop system, who could determine if farmers were starving because of an economic or a natural misfortune?" (Woodruff 1985, 9; Dulles 1950, 277–78). Even after beginning a relief effort, the Red Cross sought to minimize publicity, fearing that widespread knowledge of the effort would be self-defeating because it would create more demands from those who were afflicted by drought but might have made it through on their own resources.

Hoover also pursued a response to growing unemployment grounded in his philosophy of voluntarism. In the autumn of 1930, he established the President's Emergency Committee for Employment to address the problem of industrial unemployment and to forestall the growing demands for some sort of government intervention to relieve suffering and need, both in the nation's cities and in the drought regions. Hoover's actions, however, did not prevent the eruption of controversy in Washington. By December 1930, political conflict over relief broke out openly in Washington. President Hoover accused Congress of introducing $4.5 billion in relief measures (a figure arrived at by counting every reintroduction of measures) and of "playing politics at the expense of human misery." Congressional Democrats fired back, even as many of their Republican colleagues rose to the defense of a president who had consistently failed to consult them on policy and legislation.[11] Thus, as Hoover promoted an unprecedentedly expansive vision of voluntarism, the response was a more insistent articulation of the legitimate role of the federal government in relief.

As forces in Congress become increasingly disturbed about the lack of effective response to the drought and famine (not to mention industrial unemployment), a number of options were considered. Senator Hattie Wyatt Caraway (D–Arkansas) proposed that $15 million be appropriated for the Department of Agriculture to make loans for the purchase of food, while the House considered a joint resolution to appropriate $30 million to the American Red Cross "for the purchase of food and clothing for the purpose of relieving distress among the unemployed and in drought-stricken areas, and for other purposes."[12] As these debates intensified, they focused on a set of distinct issues. First, what were the resources available to the Red Cross and how were they being used? Members of Congress recited details of Red Cross finances: its assets, various endowments, the division of resources between the national organization and the local chapters.[13] Looking to the possibilities of public relief, senators and representatives considered how existing types of government programs—including loans and matching grants to the states for activities such as highway construction—could be adapted to the purpose of aiding drought victims.[14] The question of whether relief should be restricted to the victims of the drought or should also include the urban unemployed sparked sharp sectional differences. Finally, and most furiously, debate flared over the possibility of appropriating public funds to be spent by the Red Cross.

In many respects, this proposal should not have been controversial. In

---

11. "Men, Misery, and Mules," *Time,* December 22, 1930.
12. *Congressional Record,* January 9, 1931, 1754; January 9, 1931, 1899.
13. *Congressional Record,* January 14, 1931, 2152, 2154–57; January 15, 1931, 2249.
14. Senator David Walsh (D–Mass.), *Congressional Record,* January 19, 1931, 2553–54.

both World War I and in disasters such as the 1927 flood, Red Cross efforts were sustained by large quantities of supplies from the U.S. Army and other public agencies. But not all recipients and currencies are morally equivalent (Zelizer 1997). Throughout congressional debates and press coverage, the distribution of goods owned by the government—whether military tents for the homeless or surplus grain and cotton—appeared far less threatening to citizen virtue and to the organizational character of the Red Cross than did government money. Consequently, controversy focused on an amendment offered by Senator John Robinson (D–Arkansas) to appropriate $25 million from the U.S. Treasury to be given to the Red Cross to provide food relief.[15]

To preempt the Robinson proposal, Senator David Reed (R–Pennsylvania) offered an amendment (eventually defeated) to delay the decision on an appropriation until the outcome of the Red Cross $10 million fund drive was known. Playing defense for the administration, he argued that "the very integrity of the Red Cross is at stake, and I think we ought to postpone a Government contribution to give the Red Cross a chance to put through the drive which they themselves have started to fill up their funds by voluntary offerings."[16] But in the wake of much-heated debate and parliamentary maneuvering, on January 19 the amendment was passed by the Senate (56–27) with the support of Democrats as well as of a group of insurgent Republicans.[17]

The House, which was much more closely allied with the president than the Senate, then took up the issue with what many perceived as delaying tactics. Although highly unusual, the House held hearings on the amendment, which some of Robinson's allies suspected were intended only to ensure that a vote would not take place before the scheduled adjournment of Congress on March 4. Future U.S. Justice Hugo Black, then a Democratic senator from Alabama, questioned why "with the Red Cross announcing that it will be compelled in the drought-stricken areas alone to take care of 1,000,000 men, women, and children in order to keep them from starving, we find an investigation going on to see what will happen to the Red Cross."[18] There was also evidence of divi-

---

15. *Congressional Record,* January 15, 1931, 2219.

16. *Congressional Record,* January 19, 1931, 2534.

17. *Congressional Record,* January 19, 1931, 2563–64; "$25,000,000 Relief Passed in Senate," *New York Times,* January 22, 1931, 48.

18. *Congressional Record,* January 27, 1931, 3253–54. By contrasting administration support for a loan program that covered animal feed and seed with its opposition to federal support for food re-

sions within the Red Cross as the high politics of the national leadership allied with Hoover contrasted with calls from local leaders for government support for the relief effort. Under the banner of "Save the Red Cross!" the *Washington Daily News* explained that "we do not attack the Red Cross—the unselfish rank and file of members in the 3,500 chapters throughout the country which constitute that splendid relief organization. But we do challenge the judgment of those 11 board members who presumed to reverse the very purpose of the Red Cross and refused the duty laid upon the Red Cross by the congressional charter under which it operates."[19]

With consideration of the Robinson amendment slowed in the House, some senators began to warn of the need for a special session. Hoover responded with an extended message on drought relief in which he explicitly linked voluntarism to democracy: "My own conviction is strongly that if we break down this sense of responsibility of individual generosity to individual and mutual self-help in the county in times of national difficulty and if we start appropriations of this character we have not only impaired something infinitely valuable in the life of the American people but have struck at the roots of self-government."[20]

In the meantime, the Red Cross intensified its efforts to raise $10 million for drought relief, aided by public statements from Hoover and a committee formed of leading political and business figures. The high stakes—both humanitarian and political—in this fund drive led the Red Cross to adopt new procedures, including a decision in New York City to "depart radically from its policy of past campaigns for relief funds by dropping its traditional method of merely receiving contributions from those motivated by the spirit of generosity. Instead, it will begin the first personal canvass in its history in solicitation for funds."[21] For large do-

---

lief, Black's caustic commentary clarified how decisions about the methods for delivering relief had become aligned with distinct partisan positions: "We find the administration forces holding hearings to prove the soundness of philanthropy for the mule and parsimoniousness for the citizen . . . . [T]he recognized spokesmen and leaders of this allegedly great humanitarian administration appoint a committee of Sherlocks to prove that the governmental feeding of a mule is the quintessence of patriotism, while the governmental feeding of a hungry child will destroy the pillars of the Republic."

19. *Congressional Record*, January 30, 1931, 3578.

20. *Congressional Record*, February 3, 1931, 3857. See also "Hoover Acclaims Red Cross's Record as Vindicating Him," *New York Times*, April 14, 1931, 1. The moral valence of self-sufficiency was underscored by a *Washington Post* editorial that Senator Thomas Heflin (D–Alabama) excoriated as "ugly and vicious": "The willingness of States and cities to take charity from the Untied States Government is a reproach to the old American spirit. Several communities have brought shame upon themselves by asking." *Congressional Record*, January 19, 1931, 2547.

21. "Red Cross to Start Personal Canvass," *New York Times*, February 13, 1931, 2.

nors, the political implications were clear; John D. Rockefeller Sr. specified that his $250,000 contribution was contingent on Congress *not* ap-
proving a federal appropriation.[22] Early in February, a new compromise
ended the deadlock between the House, Senate, and White House with
the approval of an agreement to add $20 million to loan programs for
"agricultural rehabilitation." Although there was no specific mention of
using the loans for food, supporters of the Robinson amendment reassured themselves with the statement that one could not have agricultural
rehabilitation with dead farmers. The Red Cross fund drive continued
through February, passing the $10 million target only after the middle
of March and much concern over the slow rate at which contributions
arrived.[23]

Like so many episodes in congressional history, the controversy produced relatively little in policy and perhaps less in results. Ultimately,
many farmers were unable or unwilling to take up the terms of the agricultural loan program. Yet the arguments made during these two or three
months early in 1931 capture an important turning point in the politics
of public and private relief. By defending the voluntary character of the
Red Cross as moral and fundamental to American identity, congressional opponents of the Robinson amendment provoked a rethinking of the
meaning of charity in a democratic society. By staunchly opposing any
federal programs for drought or unemployment relief, Hoover firmly embedded voluntarism generally—and the Red Cross quite specifically—in
a highly partisan coalition.[24] The champions of the amendment responded with fierce arguments about the class-based nature of the opposition to federal relief for those suffering from drought and unemployment. This created an opening to rethink relief so that it could become

22. "Amer. Red Cross, Disaster Relief Contributions" (handwritten list July 1951) and Arthur W.
Packard to Mr. James G. Blaine (January 26, 1931). Rockefeller Archive Center (RAC), Office of the
Messrs. Rockefeller (OMR), Welfare Interests General, RG III, 2P, Box 2, Folders 19 and 19A.

23. "Red Cross Asks Aid for Lagging Drive," *New York Times,* March 2, 1931, 15; "Drought Fund
Past $10,000,000 Mark," *New York Times,* March 19, 1931, 4.

24. This politicization ran contrary to long-term Red Cross policy, which encouraged a rigorous
separation of its own members, and particularly leadership, from electoral politics. In separate memos
from the 1910s, 1920s, and 1940s, the national headquarters reiterated the recommendation that any local leader who ran for office should first resign their Red Cross position and Red Cross leaders should
be careful that any endorsement of candidates was understood to be strictly personal. In a response to
a younger Harry Hopkins, then working as director of the Gulf District, the national headquarters also
ruled out most forms of legislative lobbying, allowing only for the legitimate possibility that Red Cross
officials might appear in order to give expert testimony on matters central to the organization's own experience. H. J. Hughes to Harry L. Hopkins, January 19, 1920. National Archives and Records Administration, Records of the American National Red Cross, RG 200, Box 68, Folder 051.001, Legislation.

fully compatible with democratic citizenship. In seeking some way out of this deadlock between charity and "the government dole," politicians began to elaborate different understandings of the role of voluntarism and of the relationship of citizens and the federal government.

The Meanings of Voluntarism

These congressional debates over drought relief constituted a heated conversation about the appropriate relationship of voluntary aid to public funds. Hoover himself was the most prominent representative of the position that the first line of response to crisis should be voluntary and that only after voluntary, local, and state efforts had failed could federal aid even be considered. Yet he argued that the power of voluntarism was so great that this last resort would never be required:

> "I will accredit to those who advocate Federal charity a natural anxiety for the people of their States," the President said. "I am willing to pledge myself that if the time should ever come that the voluntary agencies of the country, together with the local and State governments, are unable to find resources with which to prevent hunger and suffering in my country, I will ask the aid of every resource of the Federal Government, because I could no more see starvation among our countrymen than would any Senator or Congressman. I have faith in the American people that such a day will not come."[25]

Some in Congress took up this model of federal aid as residual and offered variations on legislation that would make the spending of $25 million in federal funds contingent on the failure of the Red Cross and other private charities to meet the needs of the situation (this amendment was defeated in the House).[26] The mutually exclusive nature of public and private relief, it was argued by others, made even the discussion of such an arrangement dangerous to the efficacy of voluntarism or, from a more optimistic point of view, these debates might incite a

25. "Hoover Opens Way to End Drought Fund Deadlock as Congress Rift Widens," *New York Times*, February 4, 1931, 1. In the Senate, Arthur Vandenberg (R–Michigan) was a proponent of this argument. *Congressional Record*, January 19, 1931, 2540.

26. Throughout these discussions, some in Congress suspected delaying tactics because Congress was scheduled to recess on March 4, 1931, and not to meet again until December unless a special session was called. *Congressional Record*, January 19, 1931, 2542.

flurry of private charity to forestall government provision of relief. As Congress deadlocked,

> [New York City] Red Cross officials said many who were donating to the drive were doing so in order to prevent appropriation of the public funds by the Federal Government. A letter from a contributor of $100, which, according to the Red Cross was typical of this spirit, read:
>
> "I should have sent this check earlier had there been no talk of a large appropriation of the public moneys by Congress. It now looks as if the public moneys will not be used for this purpose unless private subscriptions prove inadequate. The American Red Cross has never yet failed to raise from private sources the money needed in an emergency like this. I hope it will not fail now. At any rate I want to do my part."[27]

For President Hoover and his allies, voluntarism was both central to what it meant to be American and antithetical to government intervention. In opposing the Robinson amendment, they invoked the distinctive character of the Red Cross and, by extension, of all voluntary associations: "The Red Cross obtains its funds through appeals to the Humanitarian instincts of the people. Any departure from this method would be disastrous to the organization."[28] Representative John Tilson, the Republican majority leader in the House, amplified this argument, asking, "Shall we stab [the Red Cross] to death and make it a cold, lifeless thing by substituting for it a governmental bureau, bound with red tape, administering a Federal dole?"

This line of argument could appear to give greater weight to the organizational integrity of the Red Cross than to the suffering of hungry farmers and the unemployed. But supporters of the Robinson amendment did not immediately dismiss claims for the distinctive quality of voluntary organizations; rather, they argued that the suffering of drought victims was greater than any damage that could come to the Red Cross from handling government funds. They minimized the corrosiveness of combining federal dollars with charitable activity by pointing to the many precedents for collaboration, which ranged from floods to foreign relief. But their attitude toward the organization became more hostile as

27. "$51,319 Needed Here in Red Cross Drive," *New York Times*, February 6, 1931, 2. A *New York Times* editorial making the same argument had been inserted in the *Congressional Record* two weeks earlier (January 17, 1931, 2429).

28. Rep. Allen Treadway of Massachusetts, *Congressional Record*, January 30, 1931, 3661.

Hoover's efforts to defeat the Robinson amendment intensified and the Red Cross came out with a statement that it would refuse federal aid if such were granted.

Advocates of drought relief condemned this apparent change in the position of the Red Cross on federal aid: from "we don't need it but we'll do whatever Congress asks of us" to a principled—or perhaps politically pressured—refusal to accept any federal funds for relief. In the judgment of Senator Caraway of Arkansas, the state most devastated by drought and famine, "this is a declaration of what a great number of us have suspected, that the Red Cross has ceased to be an independent organization, controlled and dedicated to the relief of human suffering everywhere, but is now the political screen behind which the President of the United States is undertaking to shirk his responsibility to see that those who are suffering and the starving in this country are relieved." Caraway portrayed the Red Cross as victim of Hoover's political machinations, castigating the unmanly action of the president toward "an organization founded by a woman" and declaring that "if the President himself wants to become the stark, naked oppressor of humanity, let him do it in his own name and not degrade this institution, which is known as the Red Cross and which is loved by millions of American citizens."[29] The sense of outrage in some supporters of the Robinson amendment resonated with disbelief from others, including Senator Royal Copeland, a Democrat from New York: "I can not believe that the Red Cross would deliberately take the action which has been mentioned here. . . . There must be some mistake about it; and if there is no mistake about it, it is time that those in our country who want to relieve human suffering should know what is the attitude of the Red Cross."[30] Increasingly, supporters of the Robinson amendment argued that the Red Cross—and with it the virtues of voluntarism—was being used as a defense against direct federal appropriations and, by extension, of the incomes of the rich that would be taxed to support direct relief.[31]

Whereas the president's allies posed a stark choice between private charity and a government dole, advocates of the $25 million appropriation to the Red Cross linked poverty to a societal failure to create the conditions for work and self-sufficiency. With loans for food off the ta-

---

29. *Congressional Record,* January 28, 1931, 3369–70.
30. *Congressional Record,* January 28, 1931, 3370.
31. *Congressional Record,* January 19, 1931, 2556.

ble in Congress, at least for a time, advocates of federal drought relief attacked the categories that underlay the opposition of voluntarism and direct government aid. In the House, Representative William Granfield (D–Massachusetts) argued that:

> the objectors to the appropriation of $25,000,000 characterize this appropriation as a "dole" and that it is socialistic meaning "state socialism"; I disagree with both arguments. To render assistance when an emergency exists is not a "dole," neither is it "state socialism." It is the response of humanity to the justifiable call for help, and the effort of the Government to assist its distressed people, performing a natural and proper duty.[32]

The specter of Bolshevism underscored how the struggle over the responsibilities of the Red Cross and its relationship to the government had become deeply embedded in a politics of class. In the context of a widespread economic downturn *and* a federal income tax that fell heavily on the rich, there was stiff political opposition to any program that would create a pipeline between the U.S. Treasury and direct relief. Senator Thomas Heflin (D–Alabama), a lame duck who had been defeated in the fall election, spelled out the connection:

> The administration is for exempting the large income-tax payers and the corporations of this country from paying increased taxes toward this relief. . . . To exempt the Federal Government means that you are going to place on the backs of the small property owners in every municipality and in every State the increased taxes for relief, not for this year, not for next year, but for several years. With their property depreciated, with themselves out of work, these people are to bear the entire burden! In a word, the poor must take care of the poor so far as the Federal Government is concerned.[33]

This connection between relief policy and the tax code would surface again late in the year when the U.S. Treasury announced that it expected that over $1 billion in deductions for charitable contributions would be taken on income tax returns.[34] Other advocates of the Robinson amend-

---

32. *Congressional Record,* January 30, 1931, 3667.

33. *Congressional Record,* January 14, 1931, 2157.

34. This compared to $518 million in charitable deductions in 1929. "Forecast a Record in Tax Deductions," *New York Times,* November 22, 1931, 54. A similar argument was made at length by Senator Hugo Black (D–Alabama), January 19, 1931, 2545–47.

ment pointed out the very different terms used to describe federal funds given to industry and to the needy. Heflin (D-Alabama) chimed in once more, arguing that "no one calls the huge donations to the railroad companies a dole. No one calls the millions donated to the shipping interests a dole. They have been granted by the hundreds of millions of dollars. But the very moment we ask for help for those who are weak and those who are destitute and those who are hungry, it becomes a dole."[35] Senator Caraway (D–Arkansas) underscored this attack on the categories that had organized debates over public and private charity for a century or more: "With unaccountable stupidity, this legislation was denounced as a dole and rejected; and everywhere we hear highbrows declaring their opposition to the dole, just as if a charity from the government is any more a dole than a charity through the Red Cross. Of course, Red Cross dole is not Government dole; but any form of charity is a dole."[36]

If the champions of voluntarism had one discourse about the morality of money, those in need of charity had others. Without diminishing the generosity of others, the sting of dependency was fierce. Speaking for his constituents in the state hit hardest by the drought, Senator Caraway (D–Arkansas) insisted that:

> no one down in my State . . . wants charity. We have lots of poor people, but they wanted to preserve their lives and their self respect if they might be allowed to do so. We asked that they might be permitted to borrow and were refused. That was killed by the influence of the administration. . . . They would rather have been allowed to borrow and to pay even exorbitant interest rather than to have to apply for charity. Lots of them will suffer before they will accept it. But this proposal is the only thing now before the Congress. We have to have it or get nothing.[37]

The words of one Arkansas farmer undercut every celebratory account of the Red Cross: "Asked why he had not applied for aid, he replied that he had known the Red Cross during the war overseas and 'God help me if I ever thought I'd have to ask them to feed me if I got home

---

35. *Congressional Record,* January 19, 1931, 2547.

36. *Congressional Record,* January 19, 1931, 2547, 2561.

37. *Congressional Record,* January 19, 1931, 2537. Various proposals for loans for food purchases had foundered on requirements that the government would have first claim on the borrowers' collateral—the land and future crops that were already burdened with the liens central to the tenant farming system of the South.

alive.' His wife suggested that maybe 'we have held our heads a little too high, but it's hard to get down in the class of the shiftless'" (Woodruff 1985, 106–7). In the pages of the *New York Times*,[38] an Arkansas state legislator drove home the point: "Our distressed people have been humiliated by men of national prominence, and it is up to us to take care of them." These "reckless, desperate citizens"[39] were not only humiliated, but they might prove dangerous to those very privileged interests that opposed federal direct relief and its demands on income tax revenues: "When they see their loved ones starving, sick, and dying, it is enough to make Bolshevists out of them; it might make communists out of them."[40] Senator Copeland (D–New York) warned that "we sit here so complacently, imagining that the social structure is safe; that the political structure is beyond danger!"[41]

Ironically, one of the sites of destabilization lay within the Red Cross itself. While the leadership, drawn from privileged circles and closely allied with President Hoover and major philanthropists, hewed closely to the categorical structure of benevolence with its bright line between government funds and charity, the membership and local volunteers had rather different understandings of the purpose of the organization. In part, this was to be expected, given the idiosyncratic character of a federally chartered voluntary association whose mandate was based on an international treaty. This legal form was not only unusual, but also deeply at odds with dominant models of voluntary association, exemplified by the Tocquevillian imagery of participatory membership. Informed by that cultural model, many of those attending the national meeting of the Red Cross in Washington, D.C., in April 1931, only shortly after the conflict over the Robinson amendment had come to an end, thought that they should have a say in Red Cross policy toward relief. To suppress this incipient rebellion, the national leadership went so far as to devote one of the keynote sessions to their legal adviser who lectured on the corporate nature of the American Red Cross, underscoring that the organizational charter was held by the national entity and that chapters operated only by charter from that entity.[42]

38. Read into the *Congressional Record,* January 30, 1931, 3577.

39. Heflin, *Congressional Record,* February 3, 1931, 3844.

40. Heflin, *Congressional Record,* January 28, 1931, 3375.

41. *Congressional Record,* January 19, 1931, 2548.

42. NARA, ARC, RG 2, Box 89, Folder 104.502. Address by H. J. Hughes, Legal Adviser, 4/15/1931, "Some Legal Aspects of the Red Cross."

The Red Cross, this lawyer made clear, was not a democratic, grass-roots organization but a *corporation*.[43] Consequently, relief was mapped onto the hierarchical models that aligned more easily with relations of charity and benevolence, rather than the reciprocal relationships of mutualism that also had strong bona fides in American political culture. In the wake of the Robinson amendment, the Red Cross was ever more securely embedded in a system of categories in which relief mapped onto charity and was contrasted with independence as well as full citizenship.

Public Money, Public Administration

So what could be done to help those in need? Although robust intervention would wait until Roosevelt's inauguration in 1933, the arguments over drought relief challenged the cultural categories that made moral distinctions between public and private relief. In the words of Senator David Walsh (D–Massachusetts), "two things about this [Robinson] amendment are objectionable: First, to take money from the public funds and give it to a private agency; and, secondly, to let the private agency administer the fund when we have Government officials in every section of the country and whose activities will not cost us a dollar."[44] By rejecting claims for the superior moral virtue of private relief, those opposing strong claims for voluntarism prepared the ground for direct forms of federal relief for those in need.

But the case for federal relief was not totally bereft of moral grounding. Among the arguments for the Robinson amendment there also emerged an alternative to the philanthropic model of benevolence and gratitude, a case for reciprocity between citizens and states. As articulated by Congressman Edward Eslick (D–Tennessee):

> These very families in distress contributed their sons to the American Army as offerings on the western front to save the civilization of the world. The folks back home, of their means and through their taxes, contributed to the $100,000,000 appropriated February 25, 1919, as a revolving fund for furnish-

43. This confusion between "corporate" and "Federationist" arrangements has proved to be a durable feature of American discussions of voluntary associations.

44. *Congressional Record,* January 19, 1931, 2554–55.

ing foodstuffs to the hungry people of Europe. . . . [W]e who have seen the generosity of the Nation shown to the hungry people of the Old World wonder why it is that our women and children, without fault on their part, come with outstretched hands to the Congress of the United States and say, "We are hungry and need your help," get the answer that we can not feed you because it means to adopt the dole system in the United States.[45]

Here, paying taxes, making voluntary contributions, and sending sons to war are all treated as important manifestations of citizen generosity. These acts of generosity could then legitimately be reciprocated by public help in times of distress without undermining the status of recipients as full citizens. But for this emergent understanding to take institutional form, the political conditions would have to change. And that did not happen during 1931.

Although Congress adjourned as scheduled in March 1931, the Depression continued and with it efforts to provide relief through public or private means. In June, Governor Gifford Pinchot of Pennsylvania, a progressive Republican, called on the Red Cross to aid the hungry children of miners, arguing that the state had exhausted its funds. The chairman of the Red Cross, Judge Barton Payne, denied the request, explaining that the "organization deals only with emergencies,"[46] emergencies that by definition could not be prevented by the responsible behavior of moral individuals. Anticipating a new wave of demands for relief in the winter of 1931–32, President Hoover appointed Walter S. Gifford, chairman of American Telephone and Telegraph, to organize a national committee to coordinate relief efforts. Localities followed in preemptively mobilizing fund-raising drives to meet the winter's needs. In New York City, both old-line charities such as the Association for the Improvement of the Condition of the Poor and Depression creations such as the Emergency Unemployment Relief Committee joined in helping thousands of individuals and families.[47]

But this intensification of voluntarism was a last gasp, even for the Hoover administration. During the next congressional session, the Red Cross figured only marginally, as a vehicle for the distribution of large

45. *Congressional Record,* January 30, 1931, 3664–65.

46. "Holds Red Cross Cannot Aid Miners," *New York Times,* July 9, 1931, 48.

47. "Gibson Committee to Disband September 30," *New York Times,* June 5, 1933, 1; "Vast Food Supply Aided Needy Here," *New York Times,* August 8, 1933, 6.

quantities of government-owned crops and cotton to the needy.[48] Looming larger was the creation of the Reconstruction Finance Corporation, which would make loans to the states for public works that would generate employment. But although private charity had proven inadequate to the need and inappropriate for citizens, the question of whether public money could be a legitimate source of relief remained.

Relief as a Right

In the aftermath of the fight over the Red Cross and drought relief, voluntarism had been firmly linked to the Republican Party. In the process, long-standing arguments for the propriety and virtue of private charity became starkly opposed to an emerging discourse of relief as a democratic entitlement. To legitimate the precursor of the Federal Emergency Relief Administration in New York State (TERA or the Temporary Emergency Relief Administration), then-governor Franklin Roosevelt took "this opportunity to urge all who have such hesitancy about applying for home relief to realize that home relief is in no sense charity. Home relief is being given to individuals to whom *society will have failed in its obligations* if it allows them to suffer through *no fault of their own.*"[49]

To secure this reconstruction of the category of relief, major organizational changes were required. With the creation of the FERA shortly after FDR's inauguration in March 1933, Harry Hopkins moved rapidly to consolidate the dominance of public agencies and their independence from the infrastructure of private charity. This required much political arm-twisting to get state governments to appropriate the required matching grants, but it also required an institutionally complex procedure of extracting the core relationships of relief—among the needy, the caseworkers, politicians, and local elites—and realigning them with federal policies and programs. Emergency relief blasted through categorical identities that legitimated special claims to assistance (e.g., for military veterans) and abolished exclusions including the long-standing practice of denying relief to strikers. In Hopkins's vision, all Americans in need

---

48. The Red Cross, however, would remember its role in commodity distribution as a tremendous success given the technical difficulties of milling grain and transforming surplus cotton into cloth and clothing.

49. Emphasis added. Quoted in Hopkins 1999, 72.

would apply to the same program for relief.[50] Following up on his first order that federal funds could only be expended by public agencies, by early summer he signaled that personnel would have to shift from private agencies to be sworn in as public officials before August 1, 1933.[51] Hopkins was committed to a model of relief fully located in the public domain.

By the winter of 1933–34, the dominance of public aid was clear. In New York City, which had long had the strongest system of private charities in the nation, these organizations were distributing more than twice as much in 1934 as they had in 1929, but this had dropped from over 25 percent of total relief spending to less than 4 percent (see table 4.1). Public funds (not including the "semi-official" sources) had increased from over $7 million to more than $157 million and now constituted over 95 percent of the total expenditures for relief in New York City. With impressive rapidity, both funding and personnel shifted to the public sector. From this vantage point, the establishment of a public system of social provision would seem to be an accomplished fact. Why then, did conflicts over the relationship of relief and citizenship persist?

Looking at the Depression from the vantage point of the 1920s, the question was why the Roosevelt administration did not build upon the existing infrastructure of public and private collaboration to construct an expansive system of relief on well-established foundations. Viewed from the middle of the 1930s, however, the puzzle is how this ascendance of public provision failed to inaugurate a fully public system, one consistent with Marshall's understanding of social rights. Even building an overwhelmingly public system of economic relief was not enough to establish that government services, in the words of Willie Stark, should be "Free. Not as charity, but as a right." This short-circuiting of progress toward an expansive understanding of universal citizenship rights underscores the complex interactions of a new "logic of appropriateness"

50. In this sense, FERA represents a "found counterfactual" to the standard argument about the source of racial and gender exclusions to the core New Deal programs. Whereas such arguments often point to the blocking role of Southern Democrats (Amenta 1998, 20–22; Mettler 1998, 20; Quadagno 1988, 115–16), FERA was implemented so quickly that we can trace how inclusiveness at the level of policy encountered a social world full of ascriptive inequalities.

51. "Bars Private Groups Handling Federal Aid," *New York Times,* June 27, 1933, 6; "Broad Policy Set on Federal Relief," *New York Times,* July 14, 1933, 8. For an example of implementation, Eric H. Biddle, Executive Director, Pennsylvania State Emergency Relief Board, July 27, 1933. NARA RG 69, WPA FERA Central Files, 1933–36, Box 250, PC 37, Entry 10.

TABLE 4.1. **Public and private relief spending in New York City, 1929–1934**

	1929	1930	1931	1932	1933	1934
Private Agencies[a]	2,549,881	5,289,771	15,354,435	18,821,275	13,211,332	6,016,099
Semi-Official Agencies[b]	n/a	361,451	2,135,606	3,689,018	2,643,250	1,850,406
Public Agencies[c]	7,493,412	9,021,041	28,768,074	57,673,506	93,427,242	157,161,233
Total	10,043,293	14,672,263	46,258,115	80,183,799	109,281,824	165,027,738
Private as percent of Total	25.4	36.1	33.2	23.5	12.1	3.6
Public as percent of Total	74.6	61.5	62.2	71.9	85.5	95.2

Source: "Private and Public Agencies' Relief Outlays for 5-Year Period," *New York Times*, July 28, 1935, N2.[1]

a. Includes the American Red Cross (NYC and Brooklyn), the Salvation Army, various professional, charitable, and family service agencies.

b. Includes the mayor's relief committee and the School Relief Fund of the Board of Education.

c. Includes state work projects, city work relief, Home Relief Division, Department of Public Welfare, and the Board of Child Welfare.

1. As the caption explains, the table presents "the figures on unemployment relief expenditures by private and public agencies for the years 1929 to 1934 inclusive. They do not include the cost of administration of relief or institutional relief expenditures by the city and private agencies, such as those involved in the operation of the municipal lodging houses and shelters by the Salvation Army."

in a social world already full of entrenched institutions and embodied systems of distinction. How, then, was the Roosevelt administration reconciled—willingly or no—with the world of private charity and what would come to be known as the nonprofit sector?

Making New Rights Work

With strong endorsements from the president on down, Harry Hopkins set out to implement economic relief understood as a right, not as charity. Yet this new understanding needed to be accomplished, not simply proclaimed. Operating in fields of discourse and organizational practices premised on very different understandings—of both relief and citizenship—the proponents of this new model faced a complex practical project of implementing a new right of citizenship that would displace traditional models of charity, models often deeply held by both those in need and those charged with providing aid.

The conflict over the Robinson amendment had begun this work, dramatizing new equations of "the dole" with all forms of government aid and elaborating new understandings of reciprocity between citizen service and federal relief. But to implement anything like this would require reordering practices and relationships on the ground, in each community where those in need might potentially receive relief. To accomplish this, Hopkins turned to the same individuals who had been central to the private regime of charity: volunteers and, even more importantly, professional social workers.

But appointment as a public official did not instantly transform individuals. Even those social workers who supported the new policy carried with them many of the assumptions and practices of the pre-Depression world of social work and social relations. Many of them held strong assumptions of status inequality that were at odds with Roosevelt's appeal for those in need to apply for relief without fear to their standing as citizens. As former journalist Lorena Hickok toured the country in 1933 and 1934, acting as the eyes and ears of Harry Hopkins, she repeatedly noted how relief administrators made special efforts to preserve the dignity of their white relief applicants and, above all, their white white-collar relief cases. When possible, these formerly white-collar citizens would be given cash relief, rather than grocery orders, and social workers took what care they could to protect these people from the indignities of "intake" offices and home visits.[52]

To realize a right to relief also demanded considerable forbearance for the political standing of recipients, an acceptance of grievances that would be damning evidence of ingratitude within a system of charity or benevolence. According to FERA policy, if "clients" "wish to join labor unions, or the leagues or councils of the unemployed, we have assumed they have a right, as American citizens, to do so. This hold [sic] also for workers employed on the staff in the states and localities."[53]

But if social work methods were to be harnessed to government programs, this needed to be a government of rational bureaucracy and civil service, not of patronage politics. Just as the administration of relief was not to marginalize citizens in hierarchical relations of dependence, it was not to demand partisan political loyalty of government staff. As Aubrey Williams, assistant administrator of FERA, explained to the director of the Philadelphia County Relief Board:

> Our position is simply this: That no one gives up his right as a citizen when he becomes an employee of the Federal Emergency Relief Administration. Employees have all the rights which go with citizenship in this country, such as the right to organize, right of assemblage, right of free speech, etc. They have the right to criticize and express opinions. Obviously, however, this must not take the form of sabotage. We are justified when that occurs, in dismissing anyone.[54]

This insistence on the status of recipients—and officials—as full citizens could crosscut other progressive commitments of New Deal administrators. In 1930s America, where some citizens were in practice more

---

52. This transposition of social work methods and personnel to the public domain, however, opened up new lines of challenge. Businessmen, for example, sought access to relief rolls in order to verify credit applications. Absolute confidentiality, they argued, was not warranted because "this is no longer a matter of the social worker supplied with private charity funds who can deal more effectively with a relatively few problem cases if working in secrecy. Relief recipients are getting public monies, tax money, in hundreds of millions. To have this whole matter clouded in secrecy certainly gives a wonderful opportunity for abuse and corruption." G. I. Chadwick, Manager, Carlisle [Pennsylvania] Credit Exchange to Harry Hopkins. August 7, 1935. NARA RG 69, FERA Central Files, 1933–36, Box 249, PC 37, Entry 10.

53. Aubrey Williams to Dorothy Kahn, October 12, 1935. NARA RG 69, FERA Central Files, 1933–36, Box 249, PC 37, Entry 10.

54. Williams to Dorothy Kahn. October 12, 1935. NARA RG 69, FERA Central Files, 1933–36, Box 249, PC 37, Entry 10.

equal than others, local officials were ever aware of (and often sympathetic to) the dangers involved in a program that was to serve needy citizens, both whites (particularly those who had lost white-collar jobs) and "thousands of Mexican and Negro families" along with American Indians. As one Texas official told Lorena Hickok, "If it's a choice between a white man and a Negro, we're taking the white man. . . . We've got to, because of the mental attitude of the whites. We've been threatened with riots here." In her letters to Hopkins, Hickok herself repeatedly returned to the central dilemma of how to implement a right to relief in a society marked by stark inequalities of race and class (some of which she herself assumed). She pondered whether government should keep nonwhites, particularly domestic and agricultural workers, "out of peonage and on relief, thereby, unless we spend a whole lot more money, actually forcing the white man's standard of living down to that of Negro and Mexican labor?" While setting different standards for different types of recipients (a standard practice in the earlier world of private charity) might circumvent the problem, Hickok didn't "see how the Federal Government could go in for that sort of discrimination."[55] Nor would many whites submit to the standard social workers' tool of individualized assessment of need rather than reliance on categorical discrimination. From Salt Lake City, Hickok reported the assessment of one veteran social worker that relief clients "seem to mind most being 'regimented.' They hate like poison having certain days set when they may visit their case worker in her office. They loathe being investigated all the time. They want to be 'on their own' with wages. However little, to spend as they see fit."[56]

Thus, efforts to relocate relief fully within the category of citizen rights ran into two seemingly insuperable obstacles. If these efforts took the form of government social work, they were deeply resented by citizens who might retaliate with their votes. In Fresno, California, for example, the Unemployed Citizens' Council successfully operated as a political club, using the electoral leverage of three thousand votes to se-

---

55. Lowitt and Beasley 1981, 228, 231. Such a system of differentiated relief was used in some locales; Hickok provides a particularly detailed description of the arrangements in Tucson, Arizona (240–42), where relief applicants were discretely put into one of four classes on the basis of a combination of occupational skills, social status, and race. Each group had a separate intake system, "no mixing." The most privileged group ("engineers, teachers, lawyers, contractors, a few former businessmen, architects, and some chemists who used to be connected with the mines") received not only the largest amount of relief ($50 per month) but also the largest proportion in cash (50%). In Class D, the almost fifteen hundred "low class Mexican, Spanish-American, and Indian families" received $10 a month, all in kind.

56. Lowitt and Beasley 1981, 322.

cure "reorganization of the relief setup in the county, and a work program." Hickok reported that these politically organized unemployed people were "happy and reasonably contented. There have been no riots, either." Was the Fresno group, she wondered, "any worse than—say, the sugar lobby or the lobby of the American Federation of Labor in Washington"?[57] Yet if relief were delivered to all in need in a manner that did not damage the dignity of citizens, it would offend those many Americans committed to various forms of racial and class inequality— and bankrupt the government at the same time. Thus, even as relief was relocated within the jurisdiction of government, a sense that it was not consistent with full citizenship persisted.[58]

Here, then, was the conundrum. Receiving government aid was no longer understood to taint support for those in need; public provision of relief was basically legitimated, although avoided out of personal dignity and still shadowed by charges of political corruption and bureaucratic inefficiency. But the relationship of a right to relief and democratic citizenship was still fraught. A social right entails some commitment to treat all citizens equally, and this impulse would shatter on both the complex inequalities of American society and the limited political as well as fiscal reserves of the Roosevelt administration. Early public opinion polls captured this moment of ambivalence and flux. Government and relief were no longer antithetical; in 1939, only 7 percent agreed that "all relief should again be the sole responsibility of private charity," with all others supporting state or federal relief programs on the same or a somewhat reduced scale. Government old-age pensions received overwhelming support from 89 percent of respondents, but of these three-fourths felt that pensions should be for the "needy only" rather than for all. Seventy percent approved of the new federal food stamp program for those on relief and, of all respondents, 60 percent were inclined to allow poor but nonrelief families to qualify for food stamps.[59]

These results confirm an important realignment of the categories of charity and government. The experience of Depression-era relief had largely erased the boundary that separated the federal govern-

---

57. Lowitt and Beasley 1981, 311.

58. The stark opposition of dependence and citizenship had been overcome, however. In a 1938 poll, only 19 percent of respondents agreed with the suggestion that "persons on relief should not be allowed to vote" (1938–0132).

59. From Roper Polling Center Archives (which include many Gallup polls). Roper 1939–0145; Gallup 1939–0176; Gallup 1939–0167.

ment from care of the needy. But it was still far from accepted that there could be something like a general citizen entitlement to certain kinds of social support such as old age pensions. The Gallup polls addressed specific entitlement proposals such as the Townsend plan and another California-based proposal for old age pensions, "Ham and Eggs." In both cases, support for general public pensions was much lower than that recorded for old age pensions for the "needy alone," and substantial proportions agreed that such plans would bankrupt government.[60] Consequently, by the end of the decade, and certainly by the close of World War II, the United States had returned to a system built on complex collaboration between public and private agencies, complex mixes of public and private resources. But the character of this collaboration reflected important changes in the world of private charity or, as it was increasingly called, of non-proprietary, not-for-profit, or nonprofit organizations.

A New Division of Labor

In the wake of the 1931–32 struggle over relief linked to drought and unemployment, the tensions between government programs and private charities gradually diminished. Yet rather than a simple process of "crowding out" or displacing private agencies from their traditional activities, the mid-1930s saw a more complex repositioning and renegotiation of relationships between public programs and private charities. The Red Cross retreated from direct relief and instead reinvigorated the concern for public health evident in its initiatives from the 1920s, but reframed these efforts under the rubric of "safety." Workplace safety, water safety, highway safety, first aid—all these gained prominence in the organization's roster of activities. The head-to-head combat between public and private relief deescalated as private charities distanced themselves from the core policy concerns of the New Deal. At least some personnel who remained with private organizations also determined to approach the new regime as an opportunity rather than a defeat. As one

60. A 1938 poll investigated support for a plan to provide $30 a week "to every person 50 or over not employed." Of those with an opinion, 66 percent were opposed; 60 percent thought it would bankrupt the state (1938–0135). By 1939, 69 percent were opposed and of those supporting such a plan, almost one-fifth were unwilling to pay additional taxes to support it (1939–0175). The Townsend plan elicited a similar response. Of those with an opinion, 61 percent were opposed and 86 percent did not think that the government could afford such a pension program (1939–0146).

Red Cross staffer proclaimed, "We should not bury ourselves in the rut of our own Red Cross experience, for a rut, after all, is nothing more than an elongated grave."[61] Nor did Roosevelt seek to vanquish private charity. Instead, the administration successively redefined the role of the Red Cross in relation to governmental activities. In the winter of 1934–35, FDR encouraged giving to private charity, which would lighten "as far as possible the relief drain on the Federal, State, and local governments."[62]

This image of charity taking up a portion of the same load carried by government was overshadowed by calls for a distinctive new division of labor. Initially, it was stunningly clear that private organizations were very junior partners—cataloguing the varieties of cooperation with the federal government, the Red Cross paid great attention to its efforts to teach first aid to those enrolled in various public programs.[63] In New York City, an alliance of charity organizations explicitly addressed the question of "what do the private agencies do that government can't?" and followed with a list of individualized services and support central to a new "therapeutic mission" for private charity.[64] Consequently, the mandate of private organizations needed rethinking. As Harry Hopkins explained in his address to a national symposium on the administration of relief:

> I believe voluntary efforts in behalf of community social welfare need to be strengthened and projected along new frontiers. In my opinion the immediate future holds out tremendous opportunities and responsibilities for private organizations in connection with rehabilitating individuals and families long denied the privilege of employment and normal existence.
>
> The bulk of public assistance probably will be financed from tax funds, but numerous opportunities will be open to private organizations to provide intensive family service of the type which citizens are not yet ready to accept as a public responsibility.[65]

With this speech, Hopkins endorsed a new functional division of labor between charity and government, but also foreshadowed how private

61. Mr. Baker to Mr. Bondy, "Organization problems in relationship to present day events" (July 17, 1934). NARA, RG 200, Box 69, Folder 102.

62. "President Urges Aid for Charities," *New York Times*, October 23, 1934, 1.

63. It is telling that in the official "timeline" for the American Red Cross, no events are listed between the 1932 distribution of surplus cotton and wheat and the onset of World War II.

64. "A Job Taxes Won't Do," Citizens Family Welfare Committee of New York City, RAC, OMR II 2F, Box 22, Folder 204.

65. "Private Charity Is Held Essential," *New York Times*, October 21, 1935, 5.

foundations and the "nonprofit sector" would come to understand their relationship to government in the post–World War II period as innovators and experimenters whose successful programs would then be models for public policy.

This realignment was not without political dangers. As with the conflict over the Robinson amendment, claims to charity, philanthropy, and benevolence were threatened by overly close partisan alliances. Opponents of the New Deal continued to invoke the Red Cross, arguing "that the Federal Government in its distribution of relief should have more widely availed of the voluntary services of this agency of its own, which was, during and following the World War, the most extensive and efficient instrument of mercy that humanity has ever known." Conservative critics of Social Security held up the Red Cross as a model of "appropriate financial responsibility."[66] For Roosevelt, therefore, an independent and oppositional population of private charities posed a potential political threat, a threat described with unusual bluntness by one state administrator of the Works Progress Administration who "blasted enemies of the New Deal," asserting that "when I say that these economic parasites had regimented all their forces to 'gang up' on President Roosevelt, *I mean all their forces,* including the forces of servile organized charity—that brand of organized charity which is twin brother of organized greed."[67]

By contrast, new alliances with private charities both augmented the capacity of the federal government to intervene on social problems and multiplied the channels available for mobilizing public support. Even the pinnacle of public social provision, the Social Security Act, created new channels for the expenditure of public funds by private organizations, notably new funding for care of the disabled and elderly in nursing homes, including nonprofit organizations (Hammack 2003, 269–70). Although this change was important as a precedent for the flow of federal funds to nonprofit organizations that would swell in the decades after the war, a shift in the tax code had more immediate consequences. In the wide-ranging revisions of 1935, business deductions to charity became tax deductible. This provision also legitimated long-standing practices that had been contested by shareholders who sought to deny

66. "The Ever-Ready Red Cross," *New York Times,* October 22, 1934, 14; "Social Act Perils Security of All, Says W. W. Aldrich," *New York Times,* July 11, 1936, 1.

67. Address delivered by Edward N. Jones, WPA administrator for Pennsylvania, December 14, 1935. NARA RG 69, WPA FERA Central Files, 1933–36, Box 249, PC 37, Entry 10.

management the right to divert profits from dividend checks to charities of their own choosing. With this new source of revenues, private organizations began to regroup, positioning themselves to take up needs that could not be addressed by expanding programs based on citizenship rights: programs for the poor who were excluded from meaningfully complete citizenship and particular programs for the privileged who, despite their needs or circumstances, would resist being treated in accord with the standards applied to the poor.

Conservative opponents of government expansion along with advocates of philanthropy also recognized that the battle lines had shifted. In a 1938 speech to the opening rally of the Greater New York Fund, John D. Rockefeller Jr. listed the reasons that the seven-man leadership was once again taking up the cause of charitable fund-raising. He first listed concern for health, then support for the ecumenical character of the effort:

> The third reason why we are so profoundly interested in this movement is because failure to support adequately these privately operated health and welfare agencies may mean ultimately the taking over by government of their functions—an eventuality to be avoided at all costs. There is only one thing that I have ever envied my father—not his wealth, nor his power, nor his position, nor his ability; nor even his indominatable [*sic*] courage, his infinite patience and his boundless human sympathy. The one thing I have always envied him is the fact that he made his own way in the world and, as a result, developed the ability to meet any situation, withstand any hardship, overcome any difficulties. This country was developed by men who toiled unremittingly and uncomplainingly, took no account of hardship and disregarded danger. Hardy, self-reliant, resourceful men, prizing liberty above all things. How they would have scorned the thought of bartering liberty for security! Very different is the present attitude. Typical of it is the belief that "society owes every man a living," rather than "man shall live by the sweat of his brow." Constantly is the question asked, "what is there in it for me," rather than "how much can I put into it of value"? While the query, "why should I go back to work so long as the government is willing to keep me on relief?" is heard on every hand. The manhood of the nation is being sapped. That spirit of pride and self-respect that formerly would have led men to starve rather than accept relief, is rapidly dying out. A great national asset—self-reliance—is being dissipated. While, admittedly, as we have been passing through difficult

times and men must not be allowed to go hungry, direct governmental administration of relief, even as a temporary measure, is inevitably accompanied by countless abuses, needless waste and the loss of self-respect on the part of the recipients, from which privately administered relief is relatively free. It is, therefore, of the first importance that our privately organized health and welfare societies should not only be adequately maintained, but that they should be greatly strengthened so that they may be able at the earliest moment to take over, as it assumes less abnormal proportions, the relief now administered by government and address themselves to the vital task of so handling the problem of relief as to reawaken in mankind a just pride in work and a renewed sense of the individual's responsibility for self-support.[68]

This gradual reorientation on the part of private organizations helped to take up the mandates that were not included in Roosevelt's social security state—whether excluded by political resistance, fiscal limits, or the president's own discomfort with greatly expanded government responsibility. Roosevelt reinforced this new understanding: "Community leaders have met the challenge of changing conditions. They are not looking backward with resentment against the government. They have welcomed the acts of their government as a liberation of their efforts, as an opportunity to move forward on the front of social progress."[69] In endorsing the 1938 Mobilization for Human Needs (the national fund drive of the community chests), Roosevelt used the language of "adjustment" to define these new jurisdictional boundaries:[70]

Direct relief is aimed at many problems of human misfortune—adjusting maladjusted families, taking care of the sick, tiding over a great number of kinds of crises in family life. Work relief is aimed at the problem of getting jobs for normal people who can give useful work to the country, and seeking adjustment of a maladjusted society rather than an adjustment of maladjusted individuals.[71]

68. RAC, OMR, JOHN D. ROCKEFELLER, JR. PERSONAL SPEECHES, "Cooperation and Stewardship," 02/24/1938, 111 2 Z, B4, F166. "Address introducing the Mayor at the opening rally of The Greater New York Fund in the Center Theater, Thursday evening, February 24, 1938."

69. "President Hails Private Agencies as Essential to Effective Relief," *New York Times*, October 15, 1938, 19.

70. I am grateful to Andrew Abbott for identifying the implications of this language.

71. Franklin Delano Roosevelt, "Radio Address for the Mobilization for Human Needs, Washington, D.C.," March 11, 1938 (www.presidency.ucsb.edu).

Charity as Good Citizenship

In addition to realigning the division of labor between private charity
and government programs, the Roosevelt administration also encouraged a nationalization of charitable sensibilities, a highly generalized
reciprocity among citizens in contrast to the emphasis on local community control, which had been a key element in Hoover's vision of voluntarism. Disaster response rather than relief of the poor was central to the
project. As FDR explained in his message supporting the 1935 appeal:
"The American Red Cross is an institution which our people in every
walk of life and in every section of the nation can unite in a common tie
of brotherhood. It knows no distinction of race, creed or color. There are
no boundary lines, either State or national, in its never-ending mission
of mercy for those who are in distress."[72] Reports of fund-raising created
imagery of a diverse nation unified in charitable giving:

> Funds continued to pour in from the most varied sources. Ninety North Car-
> olina road gang prisoners sent $10.60 from their small funds ordinarily used
> for smoking supplies and other necessities. From the Eskimo village of Gam-
> bell in Alaska came $60.50 obtained through the sale of ivory carvings by the
> village's arts and crafts association.
>   A check for $26 came from a foreman and twenty-two men working on a
> WPA project in Kentucky. In Rochester a Polish woman who had no funds
> to contribute raised $2.52 for the relief agency by selling lilies of the valley
> picked from her garden.

Even without going beyond the boundaries of New York City to find
"convicts and Eskimos," reporters listed donations of seventy-seven pen-
nies from one man, a "small contribution" from a blind woman, "$20
of my hard-earned money working as a waitress" from a Scandinavian
woman, and then contributions in the hundreds and thousands of dollars from wealthier individuals and corporations. Lacking funds to give,
patients in hospitals did their bit by sewing.[73] Even when nondiscrimi-

72. "Roosevelt Issues Red Cross Appeal," *New York Times,* November 12, 1935, 17. This connection is also clear in the records of the Committee to Celebrate the President's Birthday, the forerunner
of the March of Dimes.
     73. "Red Cross Fund Reaches $6,591,000; Convicts and Eskimos Among Contributors to War Re-
lief," *New York Times,* June 5, 1940, 17; "War Relief Funds Stress Need of Aid," *New York Times,*
May 27, 1940, 7; "Patients in Hospital Sew for Red Cross," *New York Times,* July 15, 1940, 19.

nation had been embraced by relief officials, it had met resistance, but this expanded terrain of citizen philanthropy allowed for a new kind of "unity in diversity."

This was particularly true of the Red Cross, with the president as the ex officio head of the organization holding the power of appointing the chairman and a number of the board. Roosevelt recognized that the Red Cross could provide a mechanism for transforming the moral understanding of citizenship. In numerous messages and speeches, he endorsed the linkage of voluntarism and citizenship that had been a signature theme of Herbert Hoover (Karl 1998, 248). Charities themselves adopted the same linkage of voluntarism and citizenship: "It is one of the true romances of a democracy that a whole people can unite in such a common expression of human brotherhood. . . . The small sum asked from each citizen is as a self-imposed poll tax which every man, woman and every child . . . should be happy to pay, because it gives every one, whatever the amount, a share in showing human kindness which is, after all, the best thing in the world with all its hardships and bitternesses and despairs."[74]

Alongside this discursive linkage of the Red Cross and voluntarism to good citizenship, new working relationships were established between public and private agencies. Some were quite mundane, with the Red Cross offering safety classes to workers in the WPA (Works Progress Administration), the CCC (Civilian Conservation Corps), and the NYA (National Youth Authority). A heightened collaboration in the provision of services was forged in a series of devastating floods in the late 1930s. Only a few years after the Red Cross and the federal government had been posed as mutually exclusive sources of drought and unemployment relief, reporters described

a system of improvised and complicated, yet surprisingly close-fitting, gear meshes. All the services that have to do with the labor and mechanical processes of lessening and curbing the flood mesh in with the regular army engi-

74. "The Ever-Ready Red Cross," *New York Times*, November 13, 1937, 18. This linkage of giving as a social good (rather than as an expression of individual religious or moral commitments) was taken still further by Edward Stettinius Jr., chairman of the 1938 Red Cross roll call in New York and future director of the wartime lend-lease program, secretary of state, and U.S. ambassador to the United Nations: "Viewing the purposes of the organization in a larger sense, contributions to the Red Cross are not charity, but 'part of the social overhead required for maintaining the morale of the nation and its people.'" "Stettinius Urges Aid to Red Cross," *New York Times*, November 10, 1938, 29.

neers' expert direction of flood control activities. All the services capable of lending a hand to relieve human suffering mesh in with the Red Cross. Both the major cogs of the army engineers and the Red Cross mesh in with the master cog at the White House.[75]

Tens of thousands of WPA and CCC workers were reassigned to levee and flood protection projects. The Red Cross called in boats from the Navy, the Coast Guard, and other public services as well as using CCC trucks (driven by employees of the WPA) to CCC camps to house those made homeless by the floods.

If floods had demonstrated the closely meshed relief machinery of government and charity working together, Roosevelt also used the Red Cross as a vehicle for conducting politics by other means. This was particularly evident in the domain of foreign policy, where the nationalization of charitable sensibilities, reinforced in each annual Red Cross roll call or Mobilization for Human Needs, underscored an identification of private voluntary gifts with national purpose. Constrained by an isolationist Congress, Roosevelt repeatedly used charitable relief as a method for projecting U.S. support for foreign countries. The president endorsed a $1 million drive for civilian relief in China—a drive that admittedly fell short and closed after raising only $250,000 (which was augmented by $200,000 from the Red Cross general fund).[76]

The fusing of voluntary relief and government effort culminated in 1940. Eight years before, the Red Cross (urged on by President Hoover) had declared that it would not accept a $25 million appropriation from Congress to aid in drought relief. But, with the onset of war in Europe and the mobilization of Red Cross activities to raise funds for refugees, Roosevelt resurrected the possibility of congressional appropriations as gifts to charitable organizations:

> Many millions of dollars have been given to the Red Cross for relief purposes in Europe, but I feel that the government itself should greatly add to the assistance that is now being given.
>
> In the pending Relief Bill before the Congress we are making possible ex-

---

75. "Relief Machinery Runs Smoothly," *New York Times,* January 31, 1937, 65. See also "President Hails Private Agencies as Essential to Effective Relief," *New York Times,* October 15, 1938, 19; "California Floods Spreading Wide," *New York Times,* February 12, 1938, 19.

76. "Roosevelt Praises Appeal for Chinese," *New York Times,* May 15, 1938, 9; "China Relief Drive Ended," *New York Times,* June 16, 1938, 9.

penditure of over $1,000,000,000 for the relief of the needy unemployed in the United States. And in addition to this, large further sums are being spent from day to day by States and municipalities for the care of the needy who cannot be given employment on work-relief projects.

In view of these large sums spent at home, I feel that the Congress would receive nationwide support if it were to add an appropriation to the Relief Bill in the sum of at least $50,000,000 as a token of our deep-seated desire to help not only Americans but people who are destitute in other lands.[77]

And Congress agreed. In contrast to the fierce fight over the Robinson amendment to appropriate $25 million to give to the Red Cross for drought relief, Roosevelt's proposal for a congressional "gift" of $50 million was approved rapidly. In stark contrast to the 1931 debate, the congressional appropriation was not portrayed as antithetical to voluntarism. Instead, coverage made clear that the situation required *both* government and charitable funds. Red Cross chair Norman Davis emphasized that the $50 million "will not lighten the burdens which the Red Cross already has assumed in furnishing clothing, medicines and ambulances to the war wounded and needy." By late July, arrangements were being put in place to administer the aid through the Department of Agriculture and then the Red Cross; at the same time, the Red Cross announced that it had pulled within $176,000 of its fund-raising goal of $20 million, almost double the $10 million collected when the president had called for the congressional appropriation six weeks earlier.[78] The preparation for war thus cemented a new working partnership between the federal government and private charities or, to use the term that would gain prominence in the following decades, the nonprofit sector.

For those who had championed the public provision of social support, these developments represented a defeat. As one veteran policy activist lamented, "Virtually unchallenged and undebated, the principle established with the first large-scale federal welfare program, the Federal Emergency Welfare Administration [*sic*], that public funds should only be expended by public agencies, was quietly repudiated."[79] But whereas this reversal is often associated with the expansion of federal social pro-

77. "Asks $50,000,000 to Aid Refugees," *New York Times,* June 12, 1940, 25; "Roosevelt Moves to Help Red Cross Aid the Refugees," *New York Times,* July 28, 1940, 1.

78. "Red Cross Aid Seen in Roosevelt Plea," *New York Times,* June 13, 1940, 19; "Roosevelt Sets Up Machinery to Aid Europe's War Victims," *Washington Post,* July 28, 1940, 1.

79. Elizabeth Wickenden, quoted in Morris 2004, 275.

grams during the 1960s War on Poverty programs (Smith and Lipsky 1993), the turn to new forms of collaboration between the federal government and nonprofit organizations had begun in the very shadow of the New Deal.

References

Amenta, Edwin. 1998. *Bold Relief: Institutional Politics and the Origins of Modern American Social Policy.* Princeton: Princeton University Press.

Barry, John M. 1997. *Rising Tide: The Great Mississippi Flood of 1927 and How It Changed America.* New York: Simon and Schuster.

Beito, David. 2000. *From Mutual Aid to the Welfare State: Fraternal Societies and Social Services, 1890–1967.* Chapel Hill: University of North Carolina Press.

Blyth, Mark. 2002. *Great Transformations: Economic Ideas and Institutional Change in the Twentieth Century.* New York: Cambridge University Press.

Clemens, Elisabeth S. 2006. "Lineages of the Rube Goldberg State: Building and Blurring Public Programs, 1900–1940." In *Rethinking Political Institutions: The Art of the State,* edited by Ian Shapiro, Stephen Skowronek, and Daniel Galvin. New York: New York University Press.

Cohen, Lizabeth. 1990. *Making a New Deal: Industrial Workers in Chicago, 1919–1939.* Chicago: University of Chicago Press.

Crenson, Matthew A. 1998. *Building the Invisible Orphanage: The Prehistory of the American Welfare System.* Cambridge: Harvard University Press.

Dulles, Foster Rhea. 1950. *The American Red Cross.* New York: Harper and Brothers.

Fitzgerald, Maureen. 2006. *Habits of Compassion: Irish Catholic Nuns and the Origins of New York's Welfare System, 1830–1920.* Urbana: University of Illinois Press.

Gilbo, Patrick F. 1981. *The American Red Cross: The First Century.* New York: Harper and Row.

Goldberg, Chad Alan. 2007. *Citizens and Paupers: Relief, Rights, and Race in the Development of the American Welfare State.* Chicago: University of Chicago Press.

Hamilton, David E. 1982. "Herbert Hoover and the Great Drought of 1930." *Journal of American History* 68, no. 4: 853–55.

Hammack, David C. 2003. "Failure and Resilience: Pushing the Limits in Depression and Wartime." In *Charity, Philanthropy, and Civility in American History,* edited by Lawrence Friedman and Mark McGarvie. New York: Cambridge University Press.

Hawley, Ellis W. 1998. "Herbert Hoover, Associationalism, and the Great Depression Relief Crisis of 1930–1933." In *With Us Always: A History of Private Charity and Public Welfare,* edited by Donald T. Critchlow and Charles H. Parker. Lanham, Md.: Rowman and Littlefield.

Hopkins, June. 1999. *Harry Hopkins: Sudden Hero, Brash Reformer.* New York: St. Martin's Press.

Karl, Barry D. 1998. "Volunteers and Professionals: Many Histories, Many Meanings." In *Private Action and the Public Good,* edited by W. W. Powell and E. S. Clemens. New Haven: Yale University Press.

Knight, Louise. 2005. *Citizen: Jane Addams and the Struggle for Democracy.* Chicago: University of Chicago Press.

Kurzman, Paul A. 1974. *Harry Hopkins and the New Deal.* Fair Lawn, N.J.: R. E. Burdick.

Landis, Michele L. 1997. "Let Me Next Time Be 'Tried by Fire': Disaster Relief and the Origins of the American Welfare State, 1789–1874." *Northwestern University Law Review* 92 (Spring): 967–1034.

Lowitt, Richard, and Maurine Beasley, eds. 1981. *One Third of a Nation: Lorena Hickock Reports on the Great Depression.* Chicago: University of Illinois Press.

Lubove, Roy. 1968. *The Struggle for Social Security, 1900–1930.* Cambridge: Harvard University Press.

Marshall, T. H. 1964 [1949]. "Citizenship and Social Class." In his *Class, Citizenship, and Social Development.* Garden City, N.Y.: Doubleday.

McKeown, Elizabeth. 1998. "Claiming the Poor." In *With Us Always: A History of Private Charity and Public Relief,* edited by Donald T. Critchlow and Charles H. Parker. Lanham, Md.: Rowman and Littlefield.

Mettler, Suzanne. 1998. *Dividing Citizens: Gender and Federalism in New Deal Public Policy.* Ithaca: Cornell University Press.

Morris, Andrew. 2004. "The Voluntary Sector's War on Poverty." *Journal of Policy History* 16, no. 4: 275–305.

Quadagno, Jill. 1988. *The Transformation of Old Age Security: Class and Politics in the American Welfare State.* Chicago: University of Chicago Press.

Sills, David L. 1957. *The Volunteers: Means and Ends in a National Voluntary Association.* Glencoe, Ill.: Free Press.

Smith, Steven Rathgeb, and Michael Lipsky. 1993. *Nonprofits for Hire: The Welfare State in the Age of Contracting.* Cambridge: Harvard University Press.

Warren, Robert Penn. 1960. *All the King's Men.* New York: Random House.

Woodruff, Nan Elizabeth. 1985. *As Rare as Rain: Federal Relief in the Great Southern Drought of 1930–31.* Urbana: University of Illinois Press.

Zelizer, Viviana A. 1997. *The Social Meaning of Money: Pin Money, Paychecks, Poor Relief, and Other Currencies.* Princeton: Princeton University Press.

PART II

Nonprofits in a World of Markets

Traditionally, the world of charity and nonprofits has been defined by its differences from the world of markets. Charity was directed at those who were unable to support themselves through work for some legitimate reason such as age or infirmity. The principle of "less eligibility" was championed specifically to prevent charity from becoming more desirable than self-sufficiency through participation in the labor market. The world of voluntarism and mutual benefit societies rested on a vision of cooperation and self-provisioning that could insulate individuals and communities from the risks presented by the capitalist system as well as the natural world. And, finally, large-scale philanthropy provided public goods—libraries, museums, colleges—that could not be profitably supplied in response to pure market demand.

This conventional view obscures a much more complex history of the relationship between nonprofits and markets, both as institutional arrangements and as political ideals. As Alice O'Connor documents, the very idea of a distinct "third" or "independent" sector was itself the product of the postwar decades. This claim to the independence of foundations, however, was itself already problematic. During this period, foundations adopted a model of change that involved a division of labor between philanthropy as a sponsor of experiments and government as the means to take those experiments "to scale" as full social programs. From the late 1960s and 1970s onward, conservative critics of mainstream foundations sought to redirect their philanthropy to renew the nation's commitment to the values and practices of free enterprise. This project included a sustained effort to disrupt the linkage of philanthropic experiments to national social programs; instead, by supporting programs such as school vouchers, this emerging cohort of conservative philanthropists sought to displace government programs with market-based—or at least market-like—social provision. In this vision, philanthropy would not create shelters from markets but rather would sustain the wellsprings of entrepreneurialism.

Yet the distance between the logic of markets and the activities sustained within nonprofit organizations or foundations was not simply the product of the hegemony of a liberal elite friendly to the expansion of the welfare state. Rather, the distinctive legal character and financial foundation of the nonprofit form provided leverage for acting upon markets as well as some insulation from their uncertainties. Thus James Evans's contribution on nonprofit scientific research institutes provides a telling counterpoint to the agenda of those conservative philanthropists described by Alice O'Connor. Although in many cases these institutes were founded either to compete directly with for-profit industrial research facilities or to supplement the markets in areas (such as agriculture in developing nations) where the promise of returns on research investment were uncertain, since the 1960s these organizations have come increasingly to resemble "universities without students" rather than "companies without products." Market-oriented behavior is sustained not only by an ideological commitment to free enterprise, but also by specific networks of relationships with other organizations and constituencies. Given their unusual location in between universities, firms, and markets, scientists in nonprofit research institutes have turned toward those who appear "most like them"—research scientists in academic settings.

But if scientists have repositioned their nonprofit institutes in closer alignment with universities than with industry, many American corporations are actively involved in the world of philanthropy. Drawing on a national sample of firms, Doug Guthrie explores which firms give how much to which causes. The results illuminate how philanthropic giving reflects not only the characteristics of the firm but how firms respond to the level of unionization, the intensity of taxation, and moments of national crisis. These findings reframe philanthropy as an expression not only of corporate values but also of corporate strategy. In contrast to O'Connor's conservative foundation leaders who sought to use philanthropy to reinvigorate markets in general, patterns of corporate philanthropy suggest that firms enact their interests through giving as well as through market-based competition.

In place of that traditional categorical distinction between profit and not-for-profit, these chapters combine to underline the porous and contested boundaries between the worlds of markets and of philanthropy. Whereas the first half of the twentieth century saw an extended debate over the relationship of voluntary associations and nonprofit organizations to public programs, in recent decades much more energy has focused on the ability of philanthropy to create markets and the possibilities for firms to pursue their interests through philanthropic activity.

CHAPTER FIVE

Bringing the Market Back In: Philanthropic Activism and Conservative Reform

Alice O'Connor

In January 1977 front-page headlines announced news guaranteed to shake the foundation world. Henry Ford II was resigning from the board of the Ford Foundation after thirty-three years of service, severing the one official tie that—in the wake of the foundation's earlier divestment of Ford Motor Company stock—remained to bind the largest tax-exempt foundation in the United States to the family and corporate enterprise that had given it both fortune and name.[1] Though played down in the tempered press statements of foundation president McGeorge Bundy, the resignation came as one more in a series of headline-making blows that had marked the former national security advisor's decade-plus tenure at the foundation. It was a tenure, according to contemporary observers, most notable for its considerable expansion of foundation engagement in public policy and public affairs, and for Bundy's unprecedented commitment to making the foundation a bold and independent "third force" for change—independent, that is, of both the state and the market—in areas hitherto treated with extreme caution, if at all, by the big establishment foundations: race, civil rights, the environment, and poverty (Nielsen 1972, 78–98; Bird 1998, 376–95).[2] Though criti-

---

1. Maurice Carroll, "Henry Ford 2d Quits Foundation, Urges Appreciation of Capitalism," *New York Times,* January 12, 1977, A1.
2. Irwin Ross, "McGeorge Bundy and the New Foundation Style," *Fortune,* April 1968, 105.

cized by many a movement activist for its lingering caution and ultra-establishment profile, the Ford Foundation under Bundy had come to be seen as the leading edge of a philanthropic activism that aimed to put the nation's big foundations at the forefront of social reform, and that would keep them at the helm of the Great Society's unfinished agenda even as the political tide was turning against it. Coming, as it did, after more than a decade of controversial, high-visibility initiatives—school decentralization experiments in New York City, voter registration drives in Cleveland's African American neighborhoods, funding for civil rights and public interest law, environmentalism, public television—Ford's resignation seemed to repudiate Bundy's willingness to make the foundation a "change agent," and to put it on what program officers had come to refer to as the urban "firing line" (O'Connor 1999, 169–94; Lagemann 1989, 216–52).[3]

But Henry Ford's resignation was not really, or not only, a repudiation of Bundy's record or the activism his tenure had encouraged. Indeed, Ford himself had earlier defended the foundation against conservative organizers who, threatening massive consumer boycotts, had tried to pressure him into wresting control from the "leftists" who were squandering the fruits of Ford Motor Company enterprise on a wide range of "subversive" causes.[4] And in his own letter of resignation, he had faulted foundation staff for growing self-satisfied if not risk-averse, for backing away from what he invoked as an earlier willingness to experiment, and for developing something of a "fortress" mentality. Instead, as his widely reprinted letter would assure, Ford's resignation offered a broader indictment of the kind of "third force" that modern, large-scale philanthropy had come to represent. Underlying his own growing sense of "disengagement" from staff programming and trustee deliberation was what Ford had come to see as the foundation's own disengagement from the very system of "competitive enterprise" that had made its existence possible. "In effect," he wrote to board chairman Alexander Heard, "the Foundation is a creature of capitalism—a statement that, I'm sure, would be shocking to many professional staff people in the field of philanthropy." And yet, he went on, it had become "hard to discern recognition of this fact in anything the foundation does. It is even more difficult

3. "Ford Foundation: Charity Begins at Home," *Economist,* January 22, 1977, 26.
4. F.O.R.D. (Families Opposing Revolutionary Donations) pamphlet, included as attachment in Report # 012797, New York: Ford Foundation Archives.

to find an understanding of this in many of the institutions, particularly the universities, that are the beneficiaries of the Foundation's grant programs."[5] Henry Ford was not, he insisted in the portion of the letter that provided the *New York Times* with its quote of the day, "playing the role of the hard-headed tycoon who thinks all philanthropoids are socialists and all university professors are communists." Nevertheless, he did think it time "to examine the question of our obligations to our economic system and to consider how the Foundation as one of the system's most prominent offspring, might act most wisely to strengthen and improve its progenitor."[6]

It is with this broader indictment in mind, echoed and discussed as it was on the editorial pages of the *Wall Street Journal,* in newsletters of the U.S. Chamber of Commerce, and in newly organizing lobbying groups such as the Business Roundtable, that I use Henry Ford's resignation as an entry point to a discussion of a distinct phase of philanthropic activism in the United States, in which a small but growing and synchronized group of conservative foundations set out not merely to celebrate but to revive the market as the dominant force in American governance, political culture, and civic life. Notably, the emergence of conservative movement philanthropy in the late 1970s coincided with a kind of beginning-of-the-end of an extended period of more state-centered philanthropic activism, in which leading liberal foundations such as Ford, Carnegie, and Rockefeller positioned themselves as "change agents" working to catalyze and shape what they expected would, and should, become federal government interventions to realize such high-minded but deeply contested goals as equal opportunity, educational equity, worldwide economic development, human rights, and international cooperation. As if to circumvent the political struggles attending such goals, the ethos these foundations cultivated was one of "cool-headed," above-the-fray professionalism and (seemingly) apolitical expert-driven reform. The change they envisioned would take place at the level of processes, institutions, attitudes, social knowledge, and human capital rather than in more overt shifts in political power. Education, litigation, policy advocacy, applied research, and evaluated social experimentation would be the tools of the trade. Foundations would work in "partnership" with government and with an expanding array of nongovernmental

5. Henry Ford II to Alexander Heard, December 11, 1976, Ford Foundation Archives.
6. *New York Times,* January 12, 1977, A1.

agencies rather than in electoral or otherwise political coalitions. They would represent no constituency or particular interest; none other, that is, than the broader "public interest" their independence from both state and market enabled them to represent (O'Connor 1999; Marris and Rein 1967). Nevertheless, the market—whether understood as a source of revenue, a commitment to capitalism, or a disciplinary force—was even for the most liberal foundations never far from view. Moreover, by the time of Henry Ford's resignation, the big foundations were feeling battered by the degree of controversy, public scrutiny, resistance, and outright conflict their presumably apolitical activism had provoked, and they had already moved to temper their claims as change agents—a move hastened, to be sure, by the chastisement they had received in the form of federal regulations passed in the Tax Reform Act of 1969, and their own diminished resources brought on by the combination of stock market declines, economic slowdown, and the oil shocks of the early 1970s.[7] And yet, far more than the end of an era, Henry Ford's resignation would come to signal a turning point in the era of philanthropic activism. Whether he meant it to or not, Ford's letter was used as a kind of rallying cry for an increasingly energized and aggressive mobilization of private philanthropic wealth on the right.

The objective of this mobilization was, in the most immediate sense, to marshal philanthropic resources not as some presumably disinterested "third force" but as a decidedly interested countervailing force—"counter," that is to the pervasive influence of what conservatives memorably envisioned as an all-powerful liberal establishment that, through its interlocking hold on the centers of power in American government, academia, media, civil society, and even some quarters of the business community, was leading the country down F. A. Hayek's fabled "road to serfdom" and was now threatening to undermine what remained of capitalist enterprise.[8] With Ford, Carnegie, Rockefeller, and other "liberal establishment" foundations as visible stalking horses, conservative activists and intellectuals organized to create and energize an alternative foundation establishment even as they continued to depict themselves as outsiders and renegades. Indeed, well after the conservative ascendancy in politics had taken hold, they continued to define their mission as an end-

7. See, for one aptly titled expression of the shift in mood, Tom Alexander, "The Social Engineers Retreat under Fire," *Fortune*, October 1972, 132–48.

8. On the concept of the postwar establishment and its genesis, see Fraser 2005, 512–16; Bird 1992, 1998; Silk and Silk 1980; Hayek 1944.

less battle against the left-liberal stranglehold on American politics and culture and on behalf of limited government, free enterprise, individualism, and "traditional" morality. Their strategy emphasized funding for conservative individuals, institutions, and liberal-convention-smashing books and ideas. But it also consciously emulated the activist approach of McGeorge Bundy's Ford Foundation, taking especially from the examples of public interest law, public policy advocacy, and, to a lesser extent, community-based social experimentation a lesson in the power of the putatively apolitical nonprofit or "independent" sector to effect political change. Especially significant for the purposes of this chapter, conservative movement philanthropy cultivated an ethos of antiregulatory, antibureaucratic entrepreneurship as the basis of a reconfigured, decidedly more market-friendly and antistatist philanthropic and nonprofit sector. And it drew on the considerable but still comparatively limited coffers of then little-known family foundations, including the Smith-Richardson, Sarah Scaife, Coors, J. M., and the two featured in this chapter, the Lynde and Harry Bradley and the John M. Olin foundations. Even more than the deep pockets of these and like-minded foundations, however, conservative movement philanthropy relied on the self-styled counter-revolutionaries—intellectuals, policy analysts, lawyers, program officers, lobbyists—who occupied key positions in emerging nonprofit association networks.

In focusing here on the late twentieth-century rise of conservative philanthropic activism, I hope to contribute to our broader discussion of "politics and partnerships" in several ways.

First, the story of conservative movement philanthropy can contribute to the ongoing revision of the notion that nonprofit organizations, and philanthropy specifically, should be understood as part of a blurrily bounded "third" or "independent" sector that is somehow above particularism, politics, ideology, or identifiable "interests" other than the "public interest" or the "common good." Indeed, the dramatic shift in the direction of philanthropic activism starting in the late 1970s helps us to historicize the language of the "third force" or "independent sector" by recognizing it as a construction of the very institutions that, under attack for their liberal establishment leanings, staked their claim to legitimacy on their ideological as well as political neutrality. Meanwhile, right-wing critics of these "liberal establishment" foundations had long seen such language as a political cover for the drift toward welfare statist collectivism. More significant, conservative philanthropic activism rested on the

notion that philanthropy *should* be both ideological and politically interested: interested, that is, in protecting the "free enterprise" capitalism that made it possible. Hence the conservative construction, also in
the 1970s, of a properly functioning civil society by hearkening back to
a bygone era of Tocquevillian voluntary associations, charities, religious
organizations, and other "mediating institutions" that had presumably
been overrun by the welfare state.

Second, I hope at the same time to complicate what has to date been
a rather state-centered revision of both the "third/independent sector"
and the Tocquevillian narrative, by focusing on a set of nonprofit institutions that defined themselves, their missions, and their partnerships
with reference to the market rather than to the state. While the state-
centered revision has rightly drawn our attention to the degree to which
the "third" sector has long relied on a substantial public subsidy or "partnership" as a source of financial, infrastructural, but most especially of
ideological and philosophical legitimation, these increasingly influential
right-wing nonprofit institutions found legitimation by positioning themselves as defenders of the virtues of profit and the rights of private property, as part and parcel of their efforts to remake political economy and
civil society along market lines.

Third, I would suggest that the rise and extraordinary success of conservative philanthropic activism offers a way of reframing the narrative
of privatization in the nonprofit sector as more than simply a reaction to
government devolution or the demise of the liberal New Deal welfare
state. Rather, our frameworks need to acknowledge the degree to which
the "privatization" of the nonprofit sector—like the conservative philanthropic activism that helped to spawn it—is part of a broader movement
to reassert the authority of the unregulated market in American governance, political economy, and civil society and indeed for some as the
basis of a remoralized society.

Finally, I hope to raise questions about how we might think about
"bringing the market back in" to our own understanding of the nonprofit
sector by recognizing how it has historically been intertwined as much
with the interests, changing shape, and fortunes of market capitalism as
it has with the changing size, scope, and fortunes of the state. The market, that is, and the changing political economy of capitalism, is an ongoing if not inevitable point of reference for organized philanthropy and for
the broader nonprofit sector: as a source of funds, to be sure, but also a
source of the shifting norms, standards of effectiveness, institutional im-

peratives, and, as we shall see, the varying political agendas that animate foundations over time. Bringing the market back in to our analysis, then, does not necessarily suggest a return to celebratory visions of an associationalist nonprofit sector as a bulwark against the state. Instead, it points us to an understanding of the nonprofit sector as part of a broader reconfiguration in the relationship between states, markets, and key segments of civil society in the historical reconstruction of political economy, and to the oft-contested balance between public and private in that process. Thus, even as conservative activists began in the late 1970s and '80s to reinvent philanthropy as the "creature of capitalism" Henry Ford said it should be, they were also supplying the intellectual, ideological, and a substantial portion of the political capital for restructuring political economy along market-friendly lines. The state, though ideologically devalued, figured importantly in this restructuring as well, with policies that favored wealth accumulation, global free trade, and the primacy of private property rights, among others. By the same token, the twentieth-century nonprofit sector, or significant segments of it, can be understood as a "creature of capitalism" even within the context of the expanding welfare state. As historical research on the extensive role of the private (albeit heavily subsidized) sector in U.S. social welfare provision has shown, the nonprofit sector has been as much an invention of welfare capitalist efforts to expand employer-provided benefits and stave off state expansion as it has been a branch of the state (Klein 2003; Hacker 2002).

McGeorge Bundy's "Third Force"

Henry Ford II was by no means the first to suggest that the philanthropic sector had lost sight of its capitalist roots. That charge, indeed, had been haunting Ford, Carnegie, Rockefeller, and other major foundations since at least the early 1950s, when widely showcased McCarthy-era congressional hearings had asked whether they were acting as "enemies of the capitalistic system" with their grants to such suspect causes as civil liberties, internationalism, racial integration, and social scientific research (O'Connor 2006).[9] Nor was he the first or only prominent business ex-

---

9. *Final Report of the Select Committee to Investigate Foundations and Other Organizations,* U.S. House of Representatives, 82nd Congress, 2nd Session, Report No. 2514 (Washington, D.C.: U.S. Government Printing Office, 1953), 21.

ecutive to call upon corporate capitalists to channel philanthropic dollars toward the defense of free enterprise (Fones-Wolf 1994). But among
the many factors that gave Ford's indictment more than symbolic significance for conservative activists at the time was their own recognition of
philanthropy's potential as a "change agent"—spurred, in no small part,
by the liberal philanthropic activism they were trying to combat.

That activism, though most widely associated with Bundy's Ford
Foundation, had earlier and more widespread institutional roots, coming
to fruition most prominently, and proudly, in the absorption of the Ford
Foundation's "Gray Areas" and, later, community development corporation models of urban reform into the Johnson administration's War on
Poverty. Emboldened by the apparent success of these demonstration
projects, Ford Foundation president Henry Heald—known more for his
cautious traditionalism than his activism—had already taken steps to seal
and systematize the special relationship that Ford, like other major foundations, was forging with government officials by the time Bundy took
over in 1966. But it was Bundy who, for would-be conservative critics,
became the emblem of all that was wrong—and all that was possible—
with philanthropic activism. Most notable to them was its role—as incuba-
tor of ideas, seeder of institutions, and financier of social movements—in
carrying out what they saw as an increasingly radical, if not "revolutionary," liberal reform agenda. It was this activism that conservative philanthropies would emulate in setting out to turn the tide against liberal
reform.

For all the talk about "social revolution," however, there were distinct limitations to liberal philanthropic activism and its capacity to act,
as Bundy had put it, as a "third force for change, apart from the power
centers of government and business."[10] Although foundations may have
tried to keep themselves apart from the state, their activism relied for
its success—indeed, even its measure of success—on not simply a neutral "partnership" but on actual political alliances with government officials and agencies. Indeed, the real power behind their change agenda
rested in the state, in its capacity to assume and institutionalize the ideas
and interventions that foundations were initiating on a smaller scale. A
second limitation was their heavy reliance on a naively apolitical—or,
perhaps, safely apolitical—"demonstration" model of reform, in which
ideas and institutional innovations would be tested, assessed, and, if

10. Bundy quoted in Ross, "McGeorge Bundy," 105.

found effective, adopted on a large scale. Despite the countless instances in which this model proved ineffective or was thwarted by any number of political forces, it remained at the core of the "change agency" embraced by the foundation mainstream.

Third, while focusing attention on various catalyzing interventions, liberal foundations did little to cultivate, develop, and build support for the underlying ideas and ideological commitments their interventions presumed. Instead, they turned to more "applied," presumably neutral forms of policy research such as cost-benefit analysis, outcomes-oriented evaluation, and statistical modeling. Fourth, despite the suspicions of foundation watchers on the right, the big powerhouses of liberal philanthropy were careful to keep an arm's distance from movement politics, and to avoid grants that could be construed as movement-building.

Finally, as Bundy, his program officers, and anyone privy to the composition of major philanthropic boards were well aware, even the most liberal of the big foundations were operating squarely within the parameters of the mildly welfare-statist capitalism their own programming helped to prop up. Radical though it may have appeared to the Right, their reform agenda was bound as much by their allegiance to capitalism as to expanding the capacity of the state. Among their signature programs, after all, were community-based initiatives—including nonprofit corporations—designed to promote local enterprise, draw private-sector investors and employers to low-income neighborhoods, and provide job training services, all of which was hardly a recipe for ghetto "revolt."[11] Ford also prided itself on having launched a decadelong, multimillion-dollar program to modernize and professionalize business education in the United States starting in 1956, by introducing more rigorous analytic and case-study teaching methods, among other things (Magat 1979, 102–4). Ford and other large liberal philanthropies had also been instrumental in various aspects of the "cultural" cold war in Europe and the developing world, as well as in the transfer of rational choice techniques perfected at the Rand Corporation to public policy, all considered essential to the defense and ultimate triumph of "democratic capitalism" (Amadae 2003; Berghahn 2001). Moreover, from their corporate managerial style to their increasingly global reach, the most prominent postwar foundations exhibited much of the cultural and organizational as

11. For more on these types of interventions, see Halpern 1995; McKee 2008; O'Connor 1995, 23–63; Ferguson 2007.

well as the financial hubris of American capitalism. By the mid-1970s, however, the Ford Foundation was suffering the consequences of what many feared was American capitalism's imminent decline. In a startling message opening the 1974 Annual Report, Bundy confirmed what many grantees already knew. Faced with the "stark fact" of assets cut nearly in half (from $3.1 to $1.7 billion), the foundation was drastically reducing its program budgets, "in order to conserve its long-term strength." Bundy pointed to "bad weather" in capital markets brought on by persistent recession and the oil crisis, but clearly more was at stake. This was indeed the end of an era: after decades of spending from capital under assumptions of endless growth, the Ford Foundation, like American capitalism, had to learn to live within its means.[12]

For all the soul searching it caused behind the scenes at the foundation, Henry Ford's resignation was thus not the only reason one reporter found it in a "mid-life crisis" several months afterward.[13] Nevertheless, Bundy was firm in his official response to these internal woes. The Ford Foundation was here to stay; its "distinctive contribution" as a source of professional knowledge and "trained intelligence" was more important than ever in a complex and interconnected world; its role was to complement other institutions, "especially governments," in the business of meeting needs that could benefit from its "technical assistance as well as timely grants."[14] Nor was Ford's resignation reason to reconsider the studied independence from private enterprise that the foundation had worked hard to maintain. In this, Bundy would be echoed by the findings of the Commission on Private Philanthropy and Public Need, at the time just finishing its work. Created by John D. Rockefeller Jr. and headed by John H. Filer of the Aetna Corporation, the commission was a response to the broader malaise that had been gripping philanthropy since at least the passage of the Tax Reform Act of 1969, which subjected private foundations to the most extensive regulatory norms and restrictions they had ever experienced under federal law—and to an extended period of political scrutiny that had punctured the image of selfless public beneficence they had worked hard to maintain (O'Connor 2006, 242–45). Among the commission's central recommendations, alongside measures to encour-

---

12. Ford Foundation, *Annual Report* (1974), v–vii.

13. Carey Winfrey, "In Its Forties, Ford Foundation Faces Change," *New York Times*, May 11, 1977, B1.

14. Ford Foundation, *Annual Report* (1974), vi.

age greater pluralism, accountability, and even a voice for grantees, was the creation of an organization to represent the interests of philanthropy and its nonprofit affiliates as part of a socially necessary "third" sector in between more identifiably "private" and "public" realms. The resulting organization, established during a time of challenge and questioning from all sides, would come to be known as Independent Sector.[15]

Funding a Market Counterrevolution

As treasury secretary (1975–77), William E. Simon had been broadly supportive of the Filer Commission and its efforts to shore up organized philanthropy. But that didn't stop him from issuing a sweeping attack on the philanthropic establishment in his 1978 manifesto for limited government and unfettered capitalism, *A Time for Truth*. In it, the famously abrasive Wall Street executive and one-time energy czar launched a broadside against modern liberalism and the reigning "philosophy" of economic regulation, welfare statism, and "egalitarianism" it had ushered in. Although few escaped his ire, he reserved special animus for the wide-ranging liberal "intelligentsia" that had made this effectively silent revolution possible. The nation's leading foundations, along with the major media, universities, and other centers of intellectual and cultural life, had allowed themselves to be taken over by a liberal elite dedicated to dethroning free market capitalism as the nation's "dominant orthodoxy." Simon pointed to Henry Ford's resignation as a "textbook case" of how far the "infiltration" had gone. In their naive efforts to tolerate voices of dissent, he and other titans of industry had inadvertently been underwriting their own philosophical enemies. Now, as Henry Ford tacitly acknowledged, it was too late to reform the likes of the liberal establishment foundations from within. Instead, with evidence of liberalism's excesses and delusions all around, the time was ripe for a new kind of foundation, "imbued with the philosophy of freedom," opposed to "appeasing" its enemies, and devoted to restoring capitalism to its rightful position of dominance "not just in government and in the marketplace but in our universities as well." Philanthropy, Simon thought, could and

15. For an in-depth discussion of the Filer and the similarly constituted Peterson Commission, see Brilliant 2000.

should be a force for the market by launching a concerted effort to build a conservative "counterintelligentsia" as a first step in a "crusade" for political and economic freedom (Simon 1978, 230–31).

Although certainly among the most alarmist, Simon's was not the only or the first voice pointing out the need for a conservative counterintelligentsia—and a broader counterestablishment to unseat the proverbially left-liberal political and cultural elite (Blumenthal 1988). In a now well-known, widely credited 1971 memorandum to the U.S. Chamber of Commerce, lawyer and soon-to-be Supreme Court Justice Lewis Powell called on the nation's leading business organization to cease its own policy of de facto "appeasement" by cultivating a procapitalist "faculty of scholars" and academic programs (see also Hollinger 2000; Houck 1984).[16] "Free enterprise" became the rallying cry for a number of parallel efforts to introduce the virtues of capitalism into college curricula—and to win the hearts and minds of a post-1960s generation of college students in search of a cause (Moreton 2008). And neoconservative gadfly Irving Kristol had been using his *Wall Street Journal* columns to warn business about the dangers of an increasingly influential "new class"—defined broadly to include teachers, lawyers, scientists, social workers, journalists, media executives, government bureaucrats, foundation program officers, and other assorted professionals and intellectuals. He maintained that they harbored a kind of inbred hostility to capitalism and were aiming at no less than "the power to shape our civilization—a power which, in a capitalist system, is supposed to reside in the free market."[17] Kristol himself would come to play a key role in forming at least one part of the counterintelligentsia, as the reputed "godfather" of neoconservatism, founding editor of the more and more right-leaning social science journal the *Public Interest,* and erstwhile emissary to the free-market corporate elite; Simon quoted extensively from his columns in *A Time for Truth,* and singled him out as an exemplar of the rare intellectual who appreciated the importance of capitalism.[18] Certainly Kristol shared Simon's disdain for the program of-

16. Lewis F. Powell, Jr., "Confidential Memorandum, Attack on Free Enterprise System," August 23, 1971, reprinted in the Chamber of Commerce *Washington Report,* and at http://www.mediatransparency .org.

17. Irving Kristol, "Business and the New Class," *Wall Street Journal,* May 19, 1975. On the genesis of the "new class" concept and its use in conservative polemic, see O'Connor 2007, 124–26; Ehrenreich 1990; Lind 1996, 146–51.

18. "Irving Kristol: Patron Saint of the New Right," *New York Times Magazine,* December 6, 1981, 90. On neoconservatism, see Steinfels 1979; Hodgson 1996; Kristol 1995.

ficers at the Ford Foundation, with their "elitist" pretensions to representing "the 'public interest,' as distinct from all the private interests of a free society."[19] In a *Wall Street Journal* column prompted by news of Henry Ford's resignation, he warned corporate philanthropists to steer clear of such pretensions in order to keep "the longer-term interests of the corporation" in view. "Corporate philanthropy should not be, cannot be, disinterested."[20] Ford's departure provided added fodder for *Journal* editorialists. It was a sign, they noted, not only of "the estrangement between business and that intellectual-academic-artistic community the Ford Foundation has done so much to subsidize and foster," but of the pervasive power and influence of the anticapitalist "new class."[21]

Although framed as counteroffensives against the "excesses" of 1960s liberalism, the counterculture, and Ralph Nader–style public interest movements—and to the accompanying feeling that capitalism was under siege—these various calls to arms in fact picked up on and mobilized around themes that had been cultivated since the New Deal by a small cadre of such free-market funders as the Foundation for Economic Education, the Earhart, W. H. Brady, and Volker foundations, and Sun Oil tycoon J. Howard Pew. Inspired by Austrian émigré economists Friedrich Hayek and Joseph Schumpeter and, in the United States, by Milton Friedman and his colleagues at the University of Chicago, they aimed to create an intellectual bulwark against the Keynesian revolution, the postwar welfare state, organized labor, and the "creeping socialism" they associated with the New Deal order more generally (Nash 1998, 1–29). Through international networks sustained by annual gatherings of the Mont Pelerin Society, they joined with British financier Anthony Fisher and other leading free-market activists to begin laying the institutional and ideological groundwork for what only later would come to be known as a "neoliberal" insurgency, with reference to its grounding in eighteenth and nineteenth century classical, or "laissez-faire," liberalism.[22] To be sure, even at their most orthodox, the free market foundations were after more than "free markets" alone. To conservative funders such as J. Howard Pew, capitalism was the lifeblood of a wider range of "traditional," often Christian, values that they associated with

19. Kristol, "Business and the New Class."

20. Irving Kristol, "On Corporate Philanthropy," *Wall Street Journal,* March 21, 1977, 18.

21. Editorial, "Grants and Groans," *Wall Street Journal,* January 14, 1977, 10.

22. For recent discussions setting neoliberalism in international context, see Prasad (2006) and Harvey (2005).

the "American" way of life. By the 1970s, their ranks were rapidly expanding, joined by the Koch Family, Adolph Coors, Smith Richardson, Scaife, De Vos, and J.M. as well as the Olin and, later, the Bradley foundations. So, too, were the number of free-market oriented think tanks and public policy institutes that would play a central role in shaping economic priorities and policy debates and, equally important, in housing and sustaining the momentum of the conservative counterintelligentsia for decades to come.

Simon's call for a battle of ideas notwithstanding, the newly resurgent free-market philanthropy of the 1970s and '80s was not about mobilizing intellect alone. As Lewis Powell had anticipated in his famous memo, it was about creating a broader associational infrastructure of market-friendly legal institutes, think tanks, advocacy groups, educational organizations, and media outlets to rival and ultimately to replace liberalism's stronghold in civil society. In a strategy later widely known as "defunding the left," conservative foundations were very much engaged in monitoring with the aim ultimately of reconstituting the nonprofit sector.[23] In this, free market philanthropy was very much in convergence, and in conversation, with the other vectors feeding into conservative movement politics. Over time, it would come more consciously to serve broader conservative movement purposes, not only by funding the nonprofit outposts of the conservative counterestablishment but by using the nonprofit sector as a staging ground for what emboldened movement activists were embracing as a full-scale counterrevolution in politics and public philosophy writ large.[24]

Indeed, more than any single factor, more even than its forthright market orientation, it was this growing integration into movement politics that most clearly distinguished the resurgent free market foundations from their predecessors as well as from their liberal counterparts.

23. As an effort specifically to cut off or limit federal government funding for the nonprofit sector starting in the early 1980s, "defunding the left" centered on a combination of obscure budgetary regulations and proposed legislation that severely restricted allowable tax-exempt activity. Neither formally succeeded, in part due to vociferous opposition from a broad spectrum of nonprofit organizations, though commentators referred to the "chilling" effect of the increased vigilance these efforts signaled. Here I use the term more broadly to include those nonofficial, and arguably more successful, efforts to maintain vigilance, undertaken by such organizations as the Capitol Research Center and the American Conservative Union as well as leading right-wing think tanks such as the Heritage Foundation and the Cato Institute. For further discussion of the regulatory/legislative strategies, see Paget (1999) and Berry and Arons (2003), 81–92.

24. On the "revolutionary" aspirations of conservative movement activists, see Hodgson (1996) and O'Connor (2007), 73–79.

This movement orientation would in turn be reflected in a conceptualization of the role of private philanthropy and the nonprofit sector that was markedly different from the independent "third force" embraced by the philanthropic establishment. Thus, while Bundy and the Filer Commission had argued for the necessity of "trained intelligence" dedicated expressly to the "common good," conservative philanthropic activists saw the imperative of building a conservative "new class" to work in alliance with capital. Conservative movement foundations also prided themselves on their distinctive approach to knowledge, which engaged them far more in promoting ideas and core values, and especially in challenging liberal narratives and conventional wisdom, than in the more applied, empirical, options-weighing analysis that had become the signature of a more neutralized philanthropic approach (O'Connor 2007).

Free market aims would shape the way movement philanthropists approached other functions traditionally associated with the nonprofit sector as well. Although the trend toward "contracting out" had already begun to transform public social service delivery, conservative foundations used it as an opportunity to promote larger-scale "privatization," to promote the values of market choice and agency competition as well as "faith-based" interventions, and more generally for blurring the lines between for-profit and nonprofit providers (Smith and Lipsky 1993; Katz 2001, 130–70). Taking a page from the Left, conservative movement foundations sponsored community-based demonstration projects to advocate and organize local support for market-based reforms in health, welfare, and especially in education. In these and other areas of social provision, the "turn" to the market and away from the state, and, not coincidentally, away from unionized public sector employment, came to define the essential meaning of conservative philanthropic reform. Even charity, that most traditional of nonprofit, voluntary sector functions, would be construed as an expression of the special virtues of private, marketized over public, socialized provision. Only private charity could prevent the "culture of dependence on the government," according to a report sponsored by the Bradley Foundation. Private charity alone was able to recognize the roots of so-called social problems in individual behavior, and to "help people learn to behave properly and live virtuously."[25] Philanthropy, in this as in the corporate functions Kristol

---

25. National Commission on Philanthropy and Civic Renewal, "Giving Better, Giving Smarter" (National Commission on Philanthropy and Civic Renewal, 1997), 17.

and Simon had articulated, had no business claiming the "public interest" as its constituency.

Of course, as no less a luminary than Hayek had acknowledged, the
"return" of the market would require active and ongoing intervention
from the state, not only to undo the shackles of New Deal-style regulation
and redistribution but to sustain the legal, legislative, and policy environment within which "free" markets would thrive. No one was more aware
of this than William E. Simon, who as Nixon's energy czar had waged a
futile battle from within the bureaucracy to lift rather than impose further regulations on the market in response to the oil crisis (Jacobs 2008,
193–209). Back in New York, and on Wall Street, after President Jimmy
Carter's election, he would find other, friendlier venues for free market
activism in the nonprofit sector. In 1977 he became the president of the
John M. Olin Foundation, and with the full endorsement of its founder,
moved to put it at the forefront of conservative movement philanthropy.[26]

Foundations of Free-Market Reform

Simon and Olin came from very different generational and business
perspectives. John M. Olin was born in 1892 and headed a Midwestern
family-owned weapons and munitions manufacturer that subsequently
diversified and doubled in size after merging with the Mathieson Chemical Corporation in 1954.[27] Simon, born in 1927 to family wealth diminished by the Great Depression, had made his subsequent fortune on
Wall Street and would go on to huge success in the leveraged buyout
boom of the 1980s. Still, the two men shared what observers considered
the near evangelical conviction that the time was ripe to save free enterprise from the "creeping stranglehold" of liberal collectivism. Olin had
made this his chief philanthropic mission a few years earlier, channeling more of his traditionally educational and good-works philanthropy
into conservative public policy institutes.[28] Simon brought added politi-

26. On the relationship between Simon and Olin, and Olin's aspirations for the foundation, see
Miller (2006), 32–59, and Anne Crittenden, "Simon: Preaching the Word for Olin," *New York Times,*
July 16, 1978, F1. Author interview with James Piereson, Olin Foundation Offices, New York, Febru-
ary 2004.

27. Leslie Lenkowsky, "John M. Olin," in Robert T. Grimm, ed., *Notable American Philanthropists*
(Westport, Conn.: Greenwood Press, 2002), 224–28; *New York Times,* September 10, 1982, D16.

28. Olin quote reported in *New York Times* obituary, September 10, 1982, D16.

cal celebrity to the effort, and made sure to mention Olin's newly invigorated free market philanthropy while on the lecture circuit for *A Time for Truth*. He also stepped up spending levels considerably, and solidified ties between Olin's traditional free market conservatism and neoconservatism by bringing Irving Kristol in as a regular consultant, and drawing on Kristol's extensive networks for key staff positions as well as for links to potential grantees. Kristol protégé Michael Joyce was hired as the Olin Foundation's executive director in 1979, joined soon after by James Piereson, a one-time colleague of Irving Kristol's son, William, at the University of Pennsylvania. Piereson would go on to direct the foundation when Joyce moved on to head the Lynde and Harry Bradley Foundation in 1985.[29]

No single factor would be more important to the success of the conservative foundations and their programs, however, than the political sea change ushered in by the election of President Ronald Reagan in 1980, which opened up an extended period of access and influence comparable only to the "smooth running time" liberal foundations had enjoyed at the height of cold war and Great Society liberalism in the 1960s (O'Connor 1999, 189).[30] With the free market and religious right in power in Washington, Olin's massive investment in the counterintelligentsia had far greater chances of paying off: if not in the form of a transformed nonprofit sector, then in its capacity to influence the policies and politics shaping the relationship between the market and the state. Thus, early efforts to persuade major corporations to stop funding "liberal" causes with their charitable donations met with little success, a failure conservatives attributed to corporate concerns about public relations. Corporate giving, according to a 1989 study by the Olin-funded right-wing Capital Research Center, continued to provide support for "the enemy." In pursuing a philanthropy based on "trendy" notions of public interest and "social responsibility," the report claimed, corporate funders were supporting groups—pro-regulatory, environmentalist, feminist, antinuke—that were fundamentally opposed to free enterprise.[31] On the other hand, Olin's support for the Law and Economics movement—with major university endowments and start-up funds for the conservative Federalist

---

29. Miller, 2006, 52–59; Piereson interview.

30. This was the language used by Ford Foundation program officer Paul Ylvisaker to describe the foundation's relationship with the Kennedy administration.

31. Stanley J. Modic, "Corporate Giving Aids 'The Enemy': Liberals Win Big Philanthropic Dollars," *Industry Week*, March 6, 1989, 51.

Society, among other organizations—found a far more receptive outlet in the judicial appointments and litigation strategies that helped reestablish private property rights and other free market principles as prevailing values in the judiciary (Miller 2006, 83–102; Teles 2008; Rosen 2008). Key to this success, as would be the case in other areas of law and public policy, was the broader associational infrastructure of think tanks, property-interest law firms, advocacy organizations, and publications Olin and others underwrote in the nonprofit sector. Here and elsewhere, ironically, foundation movement activists were consciously borrowing from "what McGeorge Bundy did at Ford," as Olin's James Piereson would later recall: orchestrate political change through all those "hidden," nongovernmental channels of elite advocacy, strategizing, and constituency building the Right had too long ignored.[32]

The Olin Foundation was more peripherally involved in the thoroughgoing effort to bring the market into one of the last remaining public sector preserves—thoroughgoing, that is, in its willingness to deploy all the tools of philanthropic activism for the purposes of market-based reform. That was the (still-ongoing) school choice "movement," as its advocates call it, which since the mid-1980s has aggressively promoted publicly funded vouchers as the key to educational turnaround. Among the central players in the movement was the Milwaukee, Wisconsin-based Lynde and Harry Bradley Foundation. Thanks in no small part to its efforts, the city historically known for its socialist mayors and progressive reform past is today widely recognized as the launch pad for private school vouchers as well as a series of workfare experiments that would pave the way to the official "end" of federal welfare in 1996.

The genesis of the Lynde and Harry Bradley Foundation was itself a reflection of conservative movement philanthropy at work. Endowed by the earnings of the Bradley family-run Allen-Bradley Company, a diversified electronics manufacturer, major employer, and power broker in Milwaukee, the foundation remained traditionally charitable and locally oriented for the three decades after its creation in 1953, with major grants for the arts, education, hospitals, and youth organizations. The company profile, on the other hand, had long been aggressively conservative and antiunion, and would remain so well after both Lynde (1942) and Harry (1965) had died. The Bradley brothers were "unpretentious but unrepentant capitalists," according to the company's official biographer John Gurda, with a management team equally well known for its hard-right Republican affinities (Gurda 1992, 160). "Liberals in Allen-Bradley's management were as scarce as atheists in the Vatican," Gurda wrote; throughout the 1950s and '60s, Bradley executives backed the stalwarts of conservative politics, including the John Birch Society and William F. Buckley's *National Review,* as well as a wide range of anti-New Deal, anticommunist and antiunion causes. Company-sponsored political action training classes were credited with swelling the ranks of Robert Taft and Barry Goldwater Republicanism in the Midwest (Gurda 1992, 114–18). In the mid-1980s, with a huge windfall after the company's sale to Rockwell International, the foundation followed suit, joining up with and very quickly assuming a leading position in the rapidly growing movement of free enterprise funders. By then, the newly flush Bradley Foundation had networks to draw on and models to emulate. Board member W. H. Brady, himself a leading funder of conservative ideas, joined company chief executive officer Andrew "Tiny" Rader in recruiting Olin's Michael Joyce for the directorship, reportedly telling him that their ambition was to create "Olin West."[33] For Joyce, this represented "the chance to double [Olin's] impact, more than double our impact," by putting ideas Olin had supported "on a theoretical level" into action "in a manageable-sized city."[34] The first big opportunity came up when Republican governor Tommy Thompson proposed a sweeping voucher program for all of Milwaukee County in 1988, including religious as well as nonsectarian schools in the range of options. The subsequent compromise whittled the measure down to a far more limited demonstration program, open to a smaller number of low-income families in the city and to nonreligious private schools (a restriction subsequent legislation would eliminate). In a twist on an age-old progressive tradition, Milwaukee would become an urban "laboratory" for free market reform (Witte 2000, 43–46).[35]

In entering the school reform thicket, Bradley and other conservative foundations were entering into well-trod philanthropic territory. Despite setbacks in the struggle for integration and the debacle of the New York

---

33. Miller 2003, 36; author interview with Michael Joyce, Olin Foundation Offices, New York, May 2004.

34. Joyce interview.

35. For more on conservative urban reform efforts, see O'Connor 2008.

City school decentralization experiment, Ford and other leading foundations continued to invest heavily throughout the 1970s in litigation, advocacy, demonstration, and legislative strategies aimed at making public school education both more equitable and more responsive to community needs.[36] At the time school choice was gaining momentum in Milwaukee in the late 1980s and early 1990s, neighboring Chicago was in the midst of a widely watched decentralization and community governance reform in which the MacArthur, Joyce, and Spencer foundations figured prominently, and privatization was deliberately off the table. By then, however, the entire reform conversation had changed, galvanized by the alarmist conclusions of President Reagan's National Commission on Excellence in Education. According to *A Nation at Risk,* the commission's extraordinarily influential 1983 report, the central problem in education was not equity but "mediocrity," and the threat to global economic competitiveness that declining standards portended.[37] *A Nation at Risk* would continue to figure prominently in the case for market-based school reform, as activists promoted vouchers as a way of exposing public schools to the discipline of competition, empowering parents to exert consumer demand, and giving students the "freedom" to, in effect, take their business elsewhere by making it possible to exit the public school system altogether.

From the standpoint of movement philanthropy, the school choice issue tapped into deeper currents—and opened new possibilities—in free market politics. This was increasingly apparent to those who, like Michael Joyce, were beginning to work at the state and local as well as the national level to build free-market-friendly reform agendas. Bradley's interventions built on this potential in what, from a movement perspective, would turn out to be strategic ways. Embracing vouchers, of course, would consolidate ties to the older conservative intellectual vanguard and to its penchant for core values and ideas. Milton Friedman, as choice proponents never tired of pointing out, was widely credited with having originated the idea of treating education as a marketplace and using parental vouchers as a way of breaking the "monopoly" controlled by state bureaucrats and teachers' unions. In 1996, along with his wife and frequent coauthor, he created the Milton and Rose D. Friedman Founda-

---

36. For an overview of the state of school equity reforms in the 1990s, see Gittell 1998.

37. The National Commission on Excellence in Education, *A Nation at Risk* (Cambridge, Mass.: USA Research, 1984).

tion specifically to promote school choice and to back, among other measures, unsuccessful state ballot initiatives in California and Michigan.[38] But Bradley and other school choice proponents also began investing in more applied research, in what would prove controversial, widely contested efforts to make the case on empirical grounds. As an added dividend, the "opening gambit" for vouchers in think tank circles came from Bradley and Olin-funded scholars at the once stalwartly liberal Brookings Institution.[39] Meantime, Bradley-supported intellectuals were also using school reform to build the case that market choice was compatible with, rather than corrosive of, a whole host of "civic values" they deemed essential to democratic society, let alone to educational success: not only individual freedom, but self-discipline, parental responsibility, community engagement, religious freedom and, to the astonishment of those who recalled post–*Brown v. Board of Education* attempts to use vouchers to evade desegregation orders in the South, racial justice and tolerance.[40] Such arguments figured prominently in Bradley's local activism for school choice, which focused heavily on policy advocacy, issue framing, and community-based organizing to bring low-income African Americans and neighborhood groups into the reform coalition. In these efforts in particular, movement activists framed the struggle over proposed voucher measures as a veritable David and Goliath battle pitting the beleaguered forces of parental free choice and community "empowerment" against the overwhelming and well-funded resistance of the educational "establishment." Bradley funds also proved critical in defending Milwaukee's voucher program in the lengthy constitutional challenges that held up the program's implementation and planned expansion at various stages. In August 1995, faced with a Wisconsin Supreme Court injunction as the school year was about to start, Joyce made a

38. Friedman first proposed the idea in an article in the 1950s, and then expanded on it in *Capitalism and Freedom* (1962). Milton Friedman, "Prologue: A Personal Retrospective," vii–x, in Enlow and Ealy 2006.

39. Chubb and Moe, 1990. On Bradley's funding for research, and its strategic role in the movement, see Michael S. Joyce, "Harmonizing Sentiments: Philanthropy and the American Political Imagination," presentation to the Waldemar A. Nielsen Seminar Series, Georgetown University, March 28, 2003. On Bradley and Olin, see Miller 2003 and 2006, 126–28. On disagreements and conflicts over contracted evaluation research and its use, see Witte 2000, 132–34; Carnoy 2001; Ladd 2002; "School Vouchers: Publicly Funded Programs in Cleveland and Milwaukee," (Washington, D.C.: U.S. General Accounting Office, 2001).

40. See, for example, essays by Jay P. Greene and Abigail Thernstrom, both scholars affiliated with the Bradley-supported Manhattan Institute, in Enloe and Ealy 2006. For an extensive examination of African Americans and school choice in Milwaukee, see Pedroni 2007.

dramatic announcement at what a *New York Times* reporter called a "revival-like gathering" at an African American congregation in Milwaukee. Bradley was donating $1 million to the emergency fund of a group it had started called Parents Advancing Values in Education (PAVE), Joyce told the congregants, and would be organizing other donors to step in with private replacement vouchers.[41] Especially important in the legal phase of the extended "war," the foundation subsidized the legal strategies and litigation that would eventuate in favorable court decisions for school vouchers, first in Wisconsin and later in the precedent-setting 2002 U.S. Supreme Court decision in *Zelman v. Simmons-Harris,* that would uphold Cleveland's voucher program, which included religious schools.[42] By then the school choice movement had truly taken off, propelled by a massive influx of conservative foundation and individual donor dollars in states and cities across the country, a host of dedicated advocacy organizations such as the aptly acronymed CEO (for Children's Educational Opportunities), and essential support from state and local as well as federal legislative reform coalitions.

Reforming Nonprofits

Even as they became more engaged in direct public policy advocacy and reform, Bradley, Olin, and other conservative foundations stepped up their criticisms of liberal efforts to "change the world," aided by groups such as the Capital Research Center, a conservative watchdog group started by activist Terrence Scanlon in 1984 to monitor nonprofit organizations "that promote the growth of government" and to advocate private, voluntary alternatives.[43] That same year, Olin and other prominent conservative foundations formally broke with the Council on Foundations, nominally in a refusal to adhere to the Council's proposed "Principles and Practices" for grantmakers (which included guidelines regarding staff and board diversity) but more fundamentally in objection to what Michael Joyce considered its insistence "that each foundation must serve

---

41. Peter Applebome, "Milwaukee Forces Debate on Vouchers," *New York Times,* September 1, 1995; Joyce, "Harmonizing Sentiments."

42. Bolick (2003) and "How We Won the Choice Case," *Wisconsin Interest* (Fall–Winter 1998): 43–53.

43. http://www.capitalresearch.org/about/.

the public interest." "Foundations are private, not public, institutions," he wrote in a letter explaining Olin's decision; to assert otherwise was to conflate their interests with those of the state (Miller 2006, 131–32). A few years later, Olin, Bradley, and others took steps to institutionalize their alternative vision of philanthropy by establishing a kind of trade organization of their own. Known as the Philanthropy Roundtable, this organization was an outgrowth of the more informal meetings of conservative grantmakers dating back to the 1970s. Formalized in 1991 with a one-time Olin program officer as its first director, it now sponsors a magazine, annual meetings, issue-oriented affinity groups, and publications dedicated to the philosophy and how-to's of conservative philanthropy, urging "strategic grantmaking" to promote market values in policy areas such as education and the environment, and pointing prospective philanthropists to free market reform-minded grantees.[44]

Two themes run prominently throughout Roundtable literature and in its ongoing efforts to realign the interests of philanthropy. One is a strict constructionist adherence to the doctrine of "donor intent," explained by no less an authority than one-time Supreme Court nominee Robert H. Bork as a moral rather than a readily enforceable legal obligation—and one that had been routinely violated by "activist foundation officials" operating in the name of "the public interest."[45] The other is that philanthropy is itself a market-based institution, reliant on the "free enterprise system" for both its values and its wealth.[46] These themes are in turn anchored in a more widely shared historical narrative, expanded on by conservative intellectuals Marvin Olasky in *The Tragedy of American Compassion* (1992), Heather MacDonald in *The Burden of Bad Ideas* (2000), Joel Schwartz in *Fighting Poverty with Virtue* (2000), and Martin Morse Wooster in publications with titles such as *Return to Charity?* (2000), *By Their Bootstraps* (2003), and *Great Philanthropic Mistakes* (2006), which points to the early twentieth-century emergence of so-called root cause, social reform–oriented philanthropy as the original betrayal of philan-

---

44. Among the issue guides published by the Philanthropy Roundtable are Brian C. Anderson, *A Donor's Guide to School Choice;* Thomas J. Bray, *Soaring High: New Strategies for Environmental Giving;* and Michael E. Hartmann, *Helping People to Help Themselves.*

45. Robert H. Bork, "Donor Intent: Interpreting the Founder's Vision," *Philanthropic Prospect* (Washington, D.C.: Philanthropy Roundtable, 1993).

46. Richard B. McKenzie, "The Market Foundations of Philanthropy," *Philanthropic Prospect* (Washington, D.C.: Philanthropy Roundtable, 1994).

thropy's moral obligation to uphold the principles of individual responsibility and limited government. Nevertheless, and despite its own imprimaturs against expanding public over private power, the Roundtable has not shied away from urging donors to leverage the power of the state, and electoral politics, in the name of market-strengthening reforms. Among the "imperatives" listed in the Roundtable's Donor's Guide to School Choice: "Get Political," with funding for legislative lobbying and school board candidates; and "Be Prepared to Battle in the Courts." Moreover, with the George W. Bush administration in office, the guide noted, there were opportunities to leverage federal power as well. Despite having dropped voucher provisions in order to gain Democratic support, the No Child Left Behind Act had included obscure measures that opened the door to federal remedial education dollars in private, religious schools. The Bush administration's Department of Education also embraced school choice, both as part of the administration's larger emphasis on public funding for "faith-based" social provision and in its own efforts to encourage "innovation" in the states. A 2007 report issued by the Department of Education's Office of Non-Public Education featured vouchers or voucherlike programs in thirteen states and the District of Columbia as examples of innovative programs that expand educational options for primary and secondary school children.[47]

Movement foundations also proved willing to forge a partnership with the state, and specifically with the George W. Bush administration, in their most concerted effort to make philanthropy a force for a decidedly privatized, "faith-based," and antistatist vision of the nonprofit sector. In September 1996 the Bradley Foundation established the National Commission on Philanthropy and Civic Renewal, chaired by the one-time Republican presidential candidate and former Tennessee governor Lamar Alexander and joined by leading figures in conservative philanthropic politics as well as representatives from community-based religious charities. Launched in the immediate wake of the historic 1996 welfare-"ending" legislation Bradley had done so much to promote, the Commission sought to capitalize on the heightened emphasis on indi-

---

47. Anderson, *A Donor's Guide to School Choice*, 64–70. "Education Options in the States: State Programs that Provide Financial Assistance for Attendance at Private Elementary or Secondary Schools" (Washington, DC: Office of Non-Public Education, U.S. Department of Education, 2007). For an expression of Department of Education and White House support for faith-based educational programs during the Bush administration, see the proceedings from an administration-sponsored educational summit at http://www.whitehouse.gov/infocus/education/whschoolsummit/index.html.

vidual redemption prompted by such provisions as the local "charitable choice" option—giving states the leeway to fund religious providers—included in the nation's new poor law. It also grew out of a concept Joyce and other foundation officials had begun to refer to as the "New Citizenship" in the course of local school choice and welfare reform battles, a concept, as Joyce would later describe it, linking free market individualism to religious faith. "We understood and acted upon the principle that when the self interest of people is rightly understood and encouraged, they are naturally inclined toward family, community, and religion—where virtue is most effectively nurtured," he wrote.[48] The Commission report, issued in 1997, reiterated the historical narrative of a "philanthropy establishment" that had lost sight of the virtues of charitable giving and had come to "act like government" instead, and offered guidelines for "redirecting American giving" that advised donors to promote individual self-sufficiency, to invest in local faith-based initiatives, and especially to "avoid and resist government's embrace."[49] Despite such imprimaturs, the Commission's vision would become the basis of an intensive, controversial lobbying effort headed up by Michael Joyce himself, not long after President Bush had announced the creation of the White House Office of Faith-Based and Community Initiatives in early 2001 and reportedly at the invitation of the White House political strategist Karl Rove. Recently retired from the Bradley Foundation, Joyce had by then inherited the "godfather" soubriquet from his own mentor Irving Kristol, who dubbed him "the godfather of modern philanthropy." The appraisal was echoed by *National Review* columnist Neal B. Freeman, who called him the "chief operating officer of the conservative movement" for the way he had been able to "maximize" his position at Bradley. Now operating from a new platform called Americans for Community and Faith-Centered Enterprise (and an accompanying foundation), Joyce set out to push the administration's legislative and administrative agenda, and more generally "to make Charitable Choice a cornerstone of national social policy." The Bush White House was focused, he insisted, "not on reinventing government but on rediscovering charity."[50]

48. Joyce, "Harmonizing Sentiments," 3.

49. *Giving Better, Giving Smarter: Renewing Philanthropy in America* (National Commission on Philanthropy and Civic Renewal, 1997).

50. Mike Allen, "Bush Aims to Get Faith Initiative Back on Track," *Washington Post,* June 25, 2001, A2.

Movement Philanthropy

As Joyce and other Charitable Choice proponents would soon discover, their attempts to "reinvent" the nonprofit sector would prove in some respects more elusive than even the movement's most ambitious goals. Efforts to make Charitable Choice a transformative edge in areas of social provision beyond welfare met with resistance in Congress as well as among religious and nonreligious-affiliated service providers alike. A number of faith-based organizations, it seems, were as concerned about maintaining church/state separation as they were about the distinction between public services and private charity. School voucher initiatives began to lose steam, despite having gained unexpectedly widespread traction, in the face of evidence that "choice" and "competition" reforms were expensive, limited in reach, and not translating into the systemic gains they promised.[51] And ironically enough, right-wing philanthropic activism has proved far more successful at doing what conservatives accused liberal foundations of doing, bringing about the kind of sweeping reforms and institutional changes that now continue to redefine the relationship between individuals, government, and the market—welfare reform, judicial "counterrevolution," financial and environmental deregulation, the logic of "supply-side" economics—than it has in the more circumscribed goal of restoring institutionalized philanthropy to its so-called original intent. There remains, as conservatives see it, a pervasive liberal anticapitalist bias in the mainstream foundation world as much as in the academic world. The financiers of counterrevolution, it appeared, had still to convince those creatures of capitalism that the true responsibility of philanthropic wealth—very much like that of government—was to their private shareholders. Meantime, Henry Ford's 1977 resignation continues to serve as a tremendously symbolic moment on the right, far more momentous, it turns out, than any changes it prompted at the Ford Foundation, as if to prove the point. So wrote Michael Joyce, echoing many a conservative commentator, in 2003: "Ford's resignation failed to reform Ford, but it sounded an alarm that rang in John Olin's ears and set in motion a chain of events that marked the ascendancy of a new conservative philanthropy."[52]

---

51. For a recent controversy among "choice" advocates on these issues, see Sol Stern, "School Choice Isn't Enough," *City Journal* 18, no. 1 (Winter 2008); http://www.city-journal.org/2008/18_1_instructional_reform.html.

52. Joyce, "Harmonizing Sentiments," 6.

Perhaps for those very reasons, reforming the broader "philanthropy establishment" was not a goal conservatives pursued with great fervor—convinced as they were of the deeply entrenched liberalism of the sector as a whole. There is also a degree to which, in a movement that thrives on its sense of being embattled by a pervasive "enemy," the so-called liberal bias of philanthropy (like the so-called liberal bias in the media and academia) remains a convenient foil and rallying point. Nor can we necessarily conclude that conservative activism has had no impact on the "liberal" philanthropic mainstream, which has, on such defining issues as welfare reform, consistently acceded to the conservative reformulation of the terms of debate, if not to the very goals of conservative reform. While still operating in the name of the "public interest" and the "common good," even the most established foundations have come under pressure to act more like the market than the state.[53]

More important for this immediate discussion, however, conservative activists have redefined and rechanneled philanthropic activism in fundamental ways, turning it from a state- to a market-centered enterprise and in the process making it a far more powerful "change agent" than its liberal counterpart has ever been. Along with the emphasis on core ideas and ideology, persistent organizing, and ties to movement culture that have been recognized as conservative trademarks, I would highlight two others as especially significant for our understanding of how "politics and partnerships" continue to shape and reshape the nonprofit sector. One is the unbending commitment among right-wing philanthropic activists to the pursuit of radical reform in the name of "traditional" aims. The other is their use of that historically most powerful of change agents, the market, in bringing it about.

References

Amadae, S. M. 2003. *Rationalizing Capitalist Democracy: The Cold War Origins of Rational Choice Liberalism.* Chicago: University of Chicago Press.

Berghahn, Volker R. 2001. *America and the Intellectual Cold Wars in Europe.* Princeton: Princeton University Press.

53. In perhaps the most telling indicator, the Ford Foundation in 2007 named a new president, Luis A. Ubinas, who had made his career in the management consulting firm McKinsey and Company. Stephanie Strom, "Ford Foundation Selects Its New Leader from Outside the Philanthropic World," *New York Times*, August 14, 2007.

Berry, Jeffrey M., and Daniel F. Arons. 2003. *A Voice for Nonprofits*. Washington, D.C.: Brookings Institution Press.

Bird, Kai. 1992. *The Chairman: John J. McCloy—The Making of an American Establishment*. New York: Simon and Schuster.

———. 1998. *The Color of Truth, McGeorge Bundy and William Bundy: Brothers in Arms*. New York: Simon and Schuster.

Blumenthal, Sidney. 1988. *The Rise of the Counter Establishment: From Conservative Ideology to Political Power*. New York: HarperCollins.

Bolick, Clint. 2003. *Voucher Wars: Waging the Legal Battle over School Choice*. Washington, D.C.: Cato Institute.

Brilliant, Eleanor L. 2000. *Private Charity and Public Inquiry: A History of the Filer and Peterson Commissions*. Bloomington: Indiana University Press.

Carnoy, Martin. 2001. "Do School Vouchers Improve Student Performance?" *American Prospect* (January): 42–45.

Chubb, John, and Terry Moe. 1990. *Politics, Markets, and American Schools*. Washington, D.C.: Brookings Institution Press.

Ehrenreich, Barbara. 1990. *Fear of Falling: The Inner Life of the Middle Class*. New York: Perennial.

Enlow, Robert C., and Lenore T. Ealy, eds. 2006. *Liberty and Learning: Milton Friedman's Voucher Idea at Fifty*. Washington, D.C.: Cato Institute.

Ferguson, Karen. 2007. "Organizing the Ghetto: The Ford Foundation, CORE, and White Power in the Black Power Era, 1967–1969." *Journal of Urban History* 34 (July): 67–100.

Fones-Wolf, Elizabeth. 1994. *Selling Free Enterprise: The Business Assault on Labor and Liberalism 1945–60*. Urbana: University of Illinois Press.

Fraser, Steve. 2005. *Every Man a Speculator: A History of Wall Street in American Life*. New York: HarperCollins.

Gittell, Marilyn, ed. 1998. *Strategies for School Equity: Creating Productive Schools in a Just Society*. New Haven: Yale University Press.

Gurda, John. 1992. *The Bradley Legacy: Lynde and Harry Bradley, Their Company, and Their Foundation*. Milwaukee: Bradley Foundation.

Hacker, Jacob. 2002. *The Divided Welfare State: The Battle over Public and Private Social Benefits in the United States*. New York: Cambridge University Press.

Halpern, Robert. 1995. *Rebuilding the Inner City: A History of Neighborhood Initiatives to Address Poverty in the United States*. New York: Columbia University Press.

Harvey, David. 2005. *A Brief History of Neoliberalism*. New York: Oxford University Press.

Hayek, F. A. 1944. *The Road to Serfdom*. Chicago: University of Chicago Press.

Hodgson, Godfrey. 1996. *The World Turned Rightside Up*. New York: Houghton and Mifflin.

Hollinger, David A. 2000. "Money and Academic Freedom a Half-Century after McCarthyism: Universities amid the Force Fields of Capital." In *Unfettered Expression: Freedom in American Intellectual Life*, ed. Peggie J. Hollingsworth, 161–84. Ann Arbor: University of Michigan Press.

Houck, Oliver A. 1984. "With Charity for All." *Yale Law Journal* 93, no. 8 (July): 1457–60.

Jacobs, Meg. 2008. "The Conservative Struggle and the Energy Crisis." In *Rightward Bound: Making America Conservative in the 1970s*, ed. Bruce J. Schulman and Julian E. Zelizer, 193–209. Cambridge: Harvard University Press.

Katz, Michael B. 2001. *The Price of Citizenship: Redefining the American Welfare State*. New York: Henry Holt.

Klein, Jennifer. 2003. *For All These Rights: Business, Labor, and the Shaping of America's Public-Private Welfare State*. Princeton: Princeton University Press.

Kristol, Irving. 1995. *Neoconservatism: The Autobiography of an Idea*. New York: Free Press.

Ladd, Helen F. 2002. "School Vouchers: A Critical Review." *Journal of Economic Perspectives* 16, no. 4 (Fall): 3–24.

Lagemann, Ellen Condliffe. 1989. *The Politics of Knowledge: The Carnegie Corporation, Philanthropy, and Public Policy*. Chicago: University of Chicago Press.

Lind, Michael. 1996. *Up From Conservatism: Why the Right Is Wrong for America*. New York: Free Press.

Magat, Richard. 1979. *The Ford Foundation at Work*. New York: Plenum Press.

Marris, Peter, and Martin Rein. 1967. *The Dilemmas of Social Reform: Poverty and Community Action in the United States*. New York: Atherton Press.

McKee, Guian. A. 2008. *The Problem of Jobs: Liberalism, Race, and Deindustrialization in Philadelphia*. Chicago: University of Chicago Press.

Miller, John J. 2003. *Strategic Investment in Ideas: How Two Foundations Reshaped America*. Washington, D.C.: Philanthropy Roundtable.

———. 2006. *A Gift of Freedom: How the John M. Olin Foundation Changed America*. San Francisco: Encounter Books.

Moreton, Bethany. 2008. "Make Payroll, Not War." In *Rightward Bound: Making America Conservative in the 1970s*, ed. Bruce J. Schulman and Julian E. Zelizer, 52–70. Cambridge: Harvard University Press.

Nash, George H. 1998. *The Conservative Intellectual Movement in America since 1945*. Wilmington, Del.: Intercollegiate Studies Institute.

Nielsen, Waldemar. 1972. *The Big Foundations*. New York: Columbia University Press.

O'Connor, Alice. 1995. "Evaluating Comprehensive Community Initiatives: A View from History." In *New Approaches to Evaluating Community Initiatives: Concepts, Methods, and Contexts*, ed. James P. Connell, Anne C. Kubisch, Lisbeth B. Schorr, and Carol H. Weiss, 23–63. Washington, D.C.: Aspen Institute.

———. 1999. "The Ford Foundation and Philanthropic Activism in the 1960s." In *Philanthropic Foundations: New Scholarship, New Possibilities*, ed. Ellen Condliffe Lagemann. Bloomington: Indiana University Press.

———. 2006. "The Politics of Rich and Rich: Postwar Investigations of Foundations and the Rise of the Philanthropic Right." In *American Capitalism: So-*

cial Thought and Political Economy in the Twentieth Century, ed. Nelson Lichtenstein, 228–48. Philadelphia: University of Pennsylvania Press.

———. 2007. *Social Science for What? Philanthropy and the Social Question in a World Turned Rightside Up.* New York: Russell Sage Foundation.

———. 2008. "The Privatized City: The Manhattan Institute, the Urban Crisis, and the Conservative Counterrevolution in New York." *Journal of Urban History* (January).

Paget, Karen. 1999. "The Big Chill: Foundations and Political Passion." *American Prospect* 10, no. 44 (May–June).

Pedroni, Thomas C. 2007. *Market Movements: African American Involvement in School Voucher Reform.* New York: Routledge.

Prasad, Monica. 2006. *The Politics of Free Markets: The Rise of Neoliberal Economic Policies in Britain, France, Germany, and the United States.* Chicago: University of Chicago Press.

Rosen, Jeffrey. 2008. "Supreme Court, Inc." *New York Times Magazine* (March 16).

Silk, Leonard, and Mark Silk. 1980. *The American Establishment.* New York: Basic Books.

Simon, William E. 1978. *A Time for Truth.* New York: Reader's Digest Press.

Smith, Stephen Rathgeb, and Michael Lipsky. 1993. *Nonprofits for Hire: The Welfare State in the Age of Contracting.* Cambridge: Harvard University Press.

Steinfels, Peter. 1979. *The Neoconservatives: The Men Who Are Changing American Politics.* New York: Simon and Schuster.

Teles, Steven M. 2008. *The Rise of the Conservative Legal Movement: The Battle for Control of the Law.* Princeton: Princeton University Press.

Witte, John F. 2000. *The Market Approach to Education: An Analysis of America's First Voucher Program.* Princeton: Princeton University Press.

CHAPTER SIX

Nonprofit Research Institutes: From Companies without Products to Universities without Students

James A. Evans

A dam Smith's *Wealth of Nations* claimed economic productivity and expansion as the state's central purpose, while recommending the state do very little to tamper with it. Besides providing national defense and justice, government should only compensate for one market failure—the provision of "public works" such as roads and canals essential to market growth for which no private investor could expect a timely return on investment (Smith 1976, 245.) Although Smith neither anticipated nor would have welcomed it, scientific and technological innovation has subsequently been framed as just such a market-expanding public work. Private "underinvestment" is expected in research and development (R&D) not because returns are small but because they are unpredictable. Moreover, ideas are so easy to share that they become hard to sell. Philanthropists have strategically founded science and technology nonprofits to remedy these so-called market failures—and to help govern prosperity—by spanning the supply of research and the demands of the marketplace. This chapter illustrates, however, that these founding purposes do not constrain the position of nonprofits within the national system of innovation (Nelson 1993a). A "spanning" position is an unstable one, and interactions between nonprofits and their environment play a greater role in determining what these nonprofits do and become.

In this chapter, I trace the twentieth-century history of nonprofit research institutes (NRIs) and document their shift from developing technology in the 1940s to performing basic science at the turn of the twenty-first century—from appearing like "companies without products" to "universities without students." Their founding purpose was to enrich the market and yet they retreated from it. In asking why, I show that nonprofits' increasing financial independence fueled this shift, and argue that complex interactions with their environment directed it. Nonprofits selected their new activity and environs, in part, by following public and nonprofit universities just as their scientifically trained personnel emulated academic peers. And yet I argue that their mission and activities themselves engaged with the environment and reinforced this shift. By responding to the precise feedback received from research and the limited feedback from development activities, nonprofits drifted closer to universities and further from the market and the problems they were founded to solve.

The Ecology of U.S. Innovation and the Role of Nonprofits

Beginning in 1743, with Benjamin Franklin's founding of the American Philosophical Society, the American colonies and later the republic would promote science as both an essential humanity and as an instrument to solve human problems through private organization. Though the society's activities encompassed both research and development, the interplay between the frontiers of science and technology was minimal. Even by the turn of the nineteenth century, fifteen decades later, most inventions that relied on the physical sciences built on a rudimentary understanding of principles formalized a hundred years earlier (Rosenberg 1982). If anything, the second industrial revolution reversed scholars' perceptions about the influence of science on technology. With the mass production of power, steel, and chemicals, academic fields like electrical engineering, metallurgy (now material science), and chemical engineering sprang into existence at entrepreneurial universities such as Cornell and MIT. The new sciences sought principles to govern the new processes; they also pursued fresh sources of support (Rosenberg 1985, 2000; Thakray 1982).

Half a century later, World War II forced a union of science and invention as the United States put university scientists and corporate engineers together in government projects for the rapid invention of radar, nuclear weapons, and other defense technologies. Many prominent scientists have argued that this period represented a dearth of theoretical innovation. Historians of science, however, point to numerous ways in which the fields forced together by war came to fertilize each other with new methods and sensibilities (Gallison 1997; Stokes 1997). Following the war, Vannevar Bush presented a report, *Science—The Endless Frontier*, to President Roosevelt in 1945 that would have a lasting impact on U.S. science policy. Basic science—a phrase Bush coined—was the source of ideas that would trickle unexpectedly into useful technologies. But Bush argued that time and patience were required. The orientations underlying science and technology were different and required separation. Bush hoped, with much of the scientific elite, that science would return to the theoretical concerns—and control—of elite scientists (Kleinman 1995). With the postwar expansion of the National Institute of Health in 1948 and the founding of the Atomic Energy Commission, the Office of Naval Research, and the Joint Research and Development Board in 1946, followed by Bush's brainchild, the National Science Foundation in 1950, the organizational ecology of science and invention was irreversibly altered. Most of these agencies funded research in their own government labs and sponsored science and outreach in universities, research institutes, and other public and nonprofit institutions.

Nonprofit institutions played a number of roles in the new postwar innovation system. First, science foundations, many formed at the turn of the century, continued to fund science through the postwar period. Foundations had been extremely consequential for 1920s academic science, but their influence was attenuated by restrictions imposed by new tax legislation in the 1950s and 1960s (Simon 1987). Their scientific contributions were also eclipsed by funds from new government agencies in many of the subfields they had previously dominated (Nelson 1993b).

Second, nonprofits continued in the calling embraced by Franklin's American Philosophical Society. "Scientific communicators"[1] facilitated the association of scientists and the sharing of scientific ideas—usually through conferences, journals, and newsletters.[2] Some, such as

---

1. The National Science Foundation, through its Division of Science Resource Statistics, has collected data on the different types of science-related organizations since the foundation's birth in 1950. It classifies nonprofits (excluding nonprofit universities) according to their functional role, their broad research focus, and their specific sources of government funds. In this section of the chapter, the use of quotation marks indicates an NSF functional classification.

2. Some of the scientific communications organizations *only* produce journals, though most are associated with a more integrated association.

the American Philosophical Society, the American Academy of Arts and Sciences, and the National Academy of Sciences (later Academies of Science)[3], functioned as exclusive, self-perpetuating fraternities in which membership was the culminating honor of a career of scientific achievement. Other "communicators," like the American Association for the Advancement of Science (AAAS) and the state- and regional-level affiliates of the National Academy, functioned as open societies facilitating communication between scientists, but also advancing the public image of science and lobbying for its political support. In contrast, nonprofit "science exhibitors"—museums, zoos, botanical gardens—focused outward by translating scientific insight into demonstrations that engaged the public in the humanity of science and its ideals. Finally, trade associations and industrial consortia played a role parallel to "communicators" in technology-intensive industries by facilitating scientific and technological communication between companies.[4] Internationally, many governments have directly sponsored scientific communication, but in the United States "scientific communicators" have almost universally organized as nonprofits.[5]

Third, private nonprofit universities represent a sizeable fraction of the nation's higher education and research system. With the Morrill Act of 1862 and federal support for state agricultural and mechanical universities (A&Ms), public universities had come to outnumber and outsize the private nonprofits by midcentury, but not to displace them in research eminence. Both public and private universities relied on government grants and student enrollment for income. State legislatures offered public institutions a layer of critical oversight unknown to privates, but the most politically powerful fought off government impositions in their competition for professors and students (Nelson 1993b).[6] With most of the same constituents, nonprofit universities faced many of the same

3. The National Academies of Science (NAS) eventually emerged as the leading voice for elite science. Signed into incorporation by President Lincoln at the height of the Civil War, NAS was formed with the express mandate to advise Congress on matters of national importance.

4. Trade associations were not considered "charitable" for purposes of legal identity and tax status—they worked only in their affiliates' interests and rarely published findings beyond their membership. These organizational guilds, however, inspired collaborative research that broadened existing markets and "spilled over" into public, noncommercial uses.

5. By "science communicators," I do not also include "exhibitors" here, which federal and state governments have frequently sponsored.

6. For example, some public institutions—such as the University of Michigan—built endowments large enough to enable substantial independence from the imposed budgets of legislatures.

pressures experienced by publics, making their approaches to scientific research and education virtually indistinguishable (Nelson 1993b).[7]

Fourth, research hospitals expanded with the emergence of scientific medicine in the first half of the twentieth century, punctuated by the development of penicillin and other pharmaceuticals during World War II. These sought scientific insight into health and the development and medical deployment of diagnostics and therapies. Although many of the most prominent nonprofit research hospitals maintained ties to universities, others drew their funds and mission from religious or local communities.

Finally, nonprofit laboratories or research institutes formed a new feature of the scientific landscape. Nonprofit research institutes, almost all of which were formed after 1940 and were treated by tax law as operating foundations (Science 1956), initially focused on the translation of scientific research into technological applications. Following on the war's spectacular creation of nuclear weapons, radar, and other science-directed advances, research institutes sought to bridge the gap between science and the needs of the military, consumers, and the disadvantaged. At the same time, competing government and commercial research labs were organized to fill the same role.

This diversity of science nonprofits—like all U.S. nonprofits—are organized to forward diverse private interests that claim to advance the public good. Within the U.S. system of innovation, these interests have specifically meant spanning institutionally divided parties and activities. Private individuals and groups founded science nonprofits between other institutions, facilitating the communication of science and its translation into desired applications. In this way, U.S. nonprofits form part of the connective tissue between scientists, between science-based companies, and between science, students, and the public and practical problems of the world. Some of these nonprofit forms, however, span more distance than others.

Nonprofit "science communicators" span the minimal distance between similar agents. "Communicators" justify their privileged tax status and subsidies by facilitating association between scientists at conferences or science-based firms in trade associations. These gatherings,

---

7. As a reflection of this fact and to politically avoid comparison of their allocations to public versus private entities, NSF science resource statistics have chosen to ignore the distinction between public and private universities in their statistical evaluations and refer to nonprofits only as a residual category of all non-university not-for-profit research organizations.

and the conversations, coordination, and publications that result, constitute collective goods that members contribute to and draw upon. In this way, communicators remain true to their purpose because their organizational identity is stably bound to the uniform professional identity of their members.

Nonprofit science educators, hospitals, and exhibitors, on the other hand, typically span a vast distance from scientifically refined staff to scientifically uncivilized student, patient, and museum-going customers. These nonprofits justify their tax status by partnering with the state in the provision of social services. Following Henry Hansmann's classic argument (1980), they ameliorate market failures when consumers have poor information relative to providers about the quality of a service. By foregoing their ability to profit from these opaque transactions, universities, hospitals, and exhibitors earn the trust of students, patients (Sloan 1998), and the museum-going public.[8] Though the distance between parties spanned by these nonprofits is considerable, the asymmetric framing of the exchange between them suggests that producers and not consumers drive nonprofit activities. Education, health care, and exhibitions are generally conceived to be a function of "scientific advance" and not the tastes or preferences of those partaking of them. As a result, their organizational identities and position are stably tied to the identities and practices of those who produce these services.

Moreover, because U.S. citizens and their legislative representatives have increasingly chosen to publicly support the educational services of universities, the health care services of hospitals, and the cultural services of museums, it seems natural to support nonprofits in these sectors. As such, large university, hospital, and museum communities have grown up, composed of both public and nonprofit forms. This allows nonprofits in these sectors a different kind of stability—one that comes from being centered within a group of similar institutions that look to each other as referents.

Nonprofit research institutes span more real distance than other types of science nonprofit organization. They were initially founded to occupy an important but unstable position within the U.S. system of innovation. Research institutes and the research missions of universities and hospitals receive public support for their contribution to the creation of sci-

---

8. This trust signal does not depend on its underlying accuracy, and can operate whether or not nonprofit services actually deserve that trust (Weisbrod and Schlesinger 1986).

entific and technological public goods. These goods claim to enrich human happiness, and in the process stimulate the economy. In the 1950s
and '60s, when many nonprofit research institutes were founded, economists argued that the difficulty of forecasting the utility of basic discoveries and appropriating rents from them (Nelson 1959; Arrow 1962) led
to less than optimal investment in basic science. Science yielded technology, but rarely at the times and in the ways predicted. Moreover, once a
technology is conceived, it is often difficult to sell. Markets depend on
complete information for efficiency, but to advertise an idea is to give it
away. The creation of intellectual property represents one policy attempt
to solve this problem, but companies that produce products or process
innovations are much more likely to forsake the market for ideas than to
patent them. They tend to prefer secrecy and compete only in the market
for finished goods (Cohen, Nelson, and Walsh 2000).

Public support for research and development was seen as one way to
counterbalance this trend. Nonprofits in this role served not only the long-
term desires of consumers but applied science to needs that didn't have a
traditional voice in the market: some invented products for the military,
others designed agricultural and engineering innovations for the developing world, and still others developed treatments for neglected diseases.
Research institutes thus span the theories of science and the demands of
the marketplace.[9] Unlike the service mission of hospitals, colleges, and
museums, where producers determine the form of service, the coupling
of science with technology, and technology with human needs, must be
snug, taking the shape and size of each equally into account. Moreover,
research institutes are the newest type of science nonprofit—born out of

---

9. The recent entry of companies into these basic research areas, increasingly allowing the publication of their research (Powell and Owen-Smith 1998), might be understood to beg a further justification
for nonprofit privilege (Weisbrod 1998). If the growth of science-based firms signals improvement in the
ability to forecast the uses of science and to appropriate them, then the market failure for basic research
may be correcting itself in some areas. Not all basic science, however, has commercial application, just
as not all basic science can contribute value to the general social welfare or to the disadvantaged. Thus,
what may appear like a correction may, in fact, be systematically partial, leaving understudied many potential avenues of basic science. This leaves open the potential for nonprofits—universities, research institutes, and hospitals—to make important, if less easily appreciated, contributions as they work more
closely beside private companies. Richard Nelson generalizes this argument (1981). He argues that a
field populated with multiple forms of organization, collaborating and competing over the same research, will give rise to more novel discoveries and technologies than a field settled exclusively with organizations pursuing profit. This outcome could result from the scientific and social-welfare-oriented
logics contributed by public and nonprofit organizations, as Nelson suggests. The "creative abrasion" of
different organizational forms interacting with one another (Powell, Koput, and Smith-Doerr 1996) and
the environmental selection of best practices from a broader pool of organizational repertoires could
also contribute to the same outcome.

a World War II technological imagination—and they represent a much smaller organizational community than hospitals, universities, or museums. Research institutes are thus unstable for a second reason, because their peers are much less numerous than universities performing basic research upstream and companies producing goods downstream. Taken together, these dual instabilities suggest the difficulty that research institutes face in staying true to their founding mission. And if they forsake that mission, will they turn from science or the market?

At the birth of modern science in the seventeenth century, its practice was the province of private actors such as gentlemen Robert Boyle and Isaac Newton, who had no interest in profits (Shapin 1994). From the second half of the nineteenth century, governments increasingly sponsored research, and science thereafter became marked by both public and non-profit institutions. The market, on the other hand, is populated almost exclusively with profit-seeking firms. With this contrast, it should be no surprise to see nonprofits drifting toward the public sector of science.

Scientists and engineers that staff NRIs have other reasons to follow science and retreat from the market. Institute personnel receive their training from universities. Midcentury research on scientists in industry (Marcson 1960; Kornhauser 1962) portrays them as resenting managerial oversight and longing for the freedom of science in the academy. Moreover, because university science is a public enterprise, findings are publicly presented and printed, facilitating collaboration among organizations. Industry science is more commonly secret (Cohen, Nelson, and Walsh 2000), making such relationships uncommon. With more opportunities to both copy and cooperate in fundamental scientific research, it should be no surprise if institute researchers trail science.

I argue, however, that there is one other important reason that makes research institutes unstable; there are forces beyond homophily that turn them from applications to ideas. In his 1993 examination of the role of nonprofit organizations in technological innovation, Richard Nelson argues that interactions with the environment drive stable identities and activities within an organizational community. For universities, he argues that "who pays" constitutes the primary feature. From "the fact that public monies are now important to all universities . . . it [is] inevitable that private and public universities will behave and be governed in quite similar ways" (1993b). After direct market forces, Nelson acknowledges the influence that overlapping university "constituencies"—students, donors, trustees—exert to circumscribe public and private university behavior. In emphasizing feedback from suppliers and customers, however, Nelson ignores the influence of peers.

Harrison White, in his sociological treatment of art markets, argues that artistic producers often know very little about those with whom they exchange. They know a great deal, however, about artists like them. As a result, they search for information about how to successfully serve customers by orienting themselves toward, and mimicking, peers. The result is a "self-perpetuating role structure" as producers and consumers compare, compete with, and conform to their peers in creating a market (White 2001). DiMaggio and Powell, who speak more specifically about organizational conformity, describe organizational mimicry as occurring within "organizational fields" that comprise all organizations interacting, responding, and orienting themselves toward each other (1983).[10] Although binary comparison processes like conformity (i.e., you do or don't share an activity or feature) may operate in broad organizational fields, more refined ordinal comparisons like status operate only on the more local level of organizational populations or communities composed of only one *type* of organization (Podolny 1993). These ordered assessments may become cardinal when organizations are close enough to specify the precise quality of their peers' output (e.g., biochemistry departments evaluating the quality of each others' publications) or when "expert" evaluations are used (e.g., article citation counts as an expert indicator of quality publications). The more similar peer organizations are, the more refined the comparison process, the more feedback organizations will receive to reinforce or undermine aspects of their identity (i.e., their behavior, performance, structure, and so on). Talcott Parsons notes the same thing in a very different context (1970): the more precise a medium of exchange, the more information it communicates, the more likely it is to be heeded.[11] In this way, feedback focuses organizations' at-

---

10. DiMaggio and Powell emphasize three forces that drive organizational conformity: coercion, normative pressures, and mimicry. The first two can be seen to ally with Nelson's "who pays" and the pressure imposed by constituencies. Those "who pay" have the power to threaten and coerce conformity; peers and constituents can apply normative pressure on organizations to follow conventions, and an organization, lacking direction, may seek to mimic the behavior of others. In this scheme, coercion and normative pressure are viewed as externally imposed influences, while mimicry is conceived as internal motivation. I do not deny the possibility of externally applied coercive or normative power, but emphasize the way in which market power and normative pressure can be understood to inspire mimicry through the provision of feedback and organizational attention.

11. Parsons uses money as a "theoretical model" for other, less precise, symbolic media of exchange such as votes (1959) and status and value-commitments (1970) because its precision more cleanly exhibits the inflationary and deflationary dynamics that peg the media to its underlying value. As such, the

tention on some aspects of themselves and away from others (March and Simon 1958).[12] And in attending to those aspects and not others, organizations change.

Nelson's economic perspective combines with White's sociological one to create an ordering of the types of feedback in terms of precision. Discrete exchanges with suppliers and customers or expert evaluations of peer quality generate precise forms of cardinal feedback such as dollars or publication citations. Comparisons in organizational communities by peers and constituents generate less precise ordinal feedback in the form of a status ranking. Comparisons in organizational fields generate a still more vague form of binary feedback, conformity. These considerations lead me to expect that organizations will be more attentive to feedback from peers than from suppliers or customers (1) to the degree that peers are more similar than transactors, and (2) to the degree that communicating and transacting is difficult or expensive.[13] Moreover, it suggests that organizations will be more attentive to feedback that is more precise than that which is less.

Nonprofit "science communicators" receive multiple and precise feedback from *exchanges* with their members: subscriptions and citations to their journals and attendance at their meetings provide clear feedback regarding performance. Nonprofit science educators, universities, and science exhibitors are different from their customers, and transactions are complicated and extended (e.g., four years of biology classes paid for by installment). As a result, universities and museums will orient themselves primarily toward precise evaluations of their peers and what they are doing.

Application-oriented nonprofit research institutes arguably have a harder time finding stabilizing feedback. Their potential customers—government agencies, commercial firms, and impoverished populations—are each increasingly different from themselves. More determinative, however, is that the process of technological development is *usually* ex-

---

more precise a medium of exchange, the more attuned its users are to its value, and the more likely they are to respond to it.

12. It may also be possible to make a case for a psychological craving for feedback. Research associated with Hackman and Oldham's job characteristics theory (1980) suggests that workers find jobs with more proximate feedback more satisfying. More research is required to understand the precise nature of this relationship, and the degree to which it scales to an organizational level.

13. Williamson (1975) emphasizes these "transaction costs" as determining the size and shape of commercial organizations. I view them as an extension of the degree to which transacting organizations are similar and the ease with which they communicate.

pensive and capricious. Because markets for not-yet existent technology don't yet exist, firms are often wary to purchase the ideas and prototypes developed at a price that would cover invention. Furthermore, when the populations being served by anticipated technologies are impoverished, feedback (in the form of a price) will be vague and nearly silent.

Following this line of reasoning, Nelson (1993b) is pessimistic about the prospects of independent research institutes, whether public, nonprofit, or commercial, for generating useful products. Nelson argues that successful development involves experimentation by users as well as by scientists and engineers. Following this premise, he predicts that technological development undertaken by firms that produce and market their technologies will outperform development by labs without such proximate market feedback. Rosenberg and Nelson reinforce the importance of feedback in American medical research by demonstrating how the concerns of U.S. medicine have evolved as they have responded to feedback from exchanges between doctors and patients, rather than researchers (1994). In short, research institutes may find it difficult to be technically successful *and* to know whether and what parts of themselves are successful. As a result, they may attend to and "drift" toward organizational communities where they receive such feedback.[14] This process is suggested by the shift of research labs from firms without products to universities without students—from applied to basic science.

Research Institutes: 1940–1997

At the end of World War II, a field of research institutes—government, nonprofit, and commercial—emerged out of the remnants of scientific organization assembled by the government during the war. Nonprofit labs found funding in federal grants as well as gifts from wartime fortunes, fueled by the promise of wartime technical advances in aerospace, nuclear physics, medical pathology, and other applied fields. Nearly every nonprofit research institute operating in 1950 was formed after 1940 (Science 1956). Like the government and industrial labs beside them, nonprofits were founded to focus on the translation of scientific research into

---

14. Taken to its logical conclusion, this would suggest that larger organizational communities (such as universities), which have had to elaborate detailed ranking procedures, will be more likely to inspire involvement than will smaller communities.

technological applications. Though some nonprofit labs concentrated on the development of noncommercial applications, such as the International Maize and Wheat Improvement Center (CIMMYT), which was founded in 1943 by the Rockefeller Foundation as an agent of international development, others—such as MITRE (Missile Test and Readiness Equipment) and the RAND Corporation, which consulted with the Air Force about its early development—worked in direct competition with for-profit labs in the early postwar period. In fact, a 1953 survey of nonprofit and industrial labs conducted by the Maxwell Research Center at Syracuse University indicated that "there is little significant difference between the research and development programs of the two types of organizations. In general, both types have been established to provide scientific services to industry and are oriented toward solving specific practical problems" (Science 1956). If anything, the report suggested that nonprofits were more applied than industry. In 1953, commercial laboratories spent $35 million on research, with $4 million (11%) going toward basic research. Nonprofits, in contrast, spent $50 million on research, with only $3 million (6%) funding basic investigations.

In a protest to nonprofit competition, scientists and administrators from private laboratories drew on the political resources of cold war McCarthyism to level an anticommunist critique at the nonprofit ethos. David Charleton, founder of Charleton Laboratories, wrote that "the vague term 'socially useful' has been used in explaining what we regard as socialist practices [in justifying the support of nonprofit research efforts]" (1964). C. Burton Smith, president of a division of the American Council of Independent Laboratories, asked "Who is going to pay the taxes to run the government now [after private industry is supplanted with 'nonprofit institutes']? Well, there's still a chemical industry? And if that and others fall too? . . . [I]f we're going to live under socialism, at least let us vote on it" (1964). These were not the only accusations that nonprofits were anti-American because they were against "free enterprise" (Langer 1966), but nonprofit labs, institutes, and consultancies continued to play a role in translating science into technologies and practices for public and private ends.

By the 1970s, political currents had turned, as had the fortunes of independent commercial labs. Anticipated by Joseph Schumpeter in *Capitalism, Socialism and Democracy* (1950), large firms built and extended their own research divisions and succeeded in driving many independent commercial labs out of business. Although many corporate research

TABLE 6.1. **Nonprofit (NPO) R&D by source of funds and character of work: 1973, 1996, and 1997 (in millions of 2004 dollars)**[1]

Source of funds and character of work	Intramural R&D expenditures			Character of work as percentage of total R&D			
	1973	1996	1997	1953	1973	1996	1997
Total R&D	3,344	8,504	8,649	100.0	100.0	100.0	100.0
Federal	2,063	4,503	4,365				
Nonfederal	1,281	4,001	4,284				
Basic research	1,353	4,727	4,712	6.2	40.5	55.6	54.5
Federal	796	2,457	2,412				
Nonfederal	557	2,269	2,301				
Applied research	1,408	2,479	2,592		42.1	29.1	30.0
Federal	898	1,401	1,421				
Nonfederal	511	1,078	1,171				
Development	583	1,299	1,345		17.4	15.3	15.6
Federal	370	645	532				
Nonfederal	213	655	813				
Applied research or development	1,991	3,778	3,937	93.8	59.5	44.4	45.6

[1] Adapted from the National Science Foundation/Division of Science Resources Studies, R&D Activities of Independent Nonprofit Institutions, 1973, and Survey of R&D Funding & Performance by Nonprofit Organizations, 1996 and 1997. Data exclude R&D performed by nonprofit-administered Federally Funded Research and Development Centers.

divisions were later closed when companies found it difficult to transfer knowledge to operating divisions,[15] it was apparently *less* difficult to transfer knowledge across divisions than it was to transfer knowledge through transactions with an external lab, sustaining Nelson's hypothesis. At the same time, nonprofit research institutes continued to receive government aid to perform applied projects (NSF 1974–80). In spite of many of their explicit application-oriented missions, however, many NRIs began to deploy their own funds elsewhere. These NRIs were usually composed of scientists who had previously published, and they began to drift from the lonely organizational niche of applied research—between science and technology—toward the much larger field of basic research performed predominantly by universities.

By 1973, nonprofit research institutes represented only 1.6 percent of national R&D expenditures, the equivalent of two billion 2004 dollars. Their allocation of funds across research priorities was dramatically different from 1953, as documented in table 6.1. In 1953 nonuniver-

15. There were two waves of corporate research division closings: one following the merger wave in the late 1980s and a second following the NASDAQ crash of 2000.

sity nonprofits had only spent 6 percent on basic research; by 1973 this
had grown to 40 percent, or the equivalent of 1.3 billion in 2004 dollars
(318 million 1974 dollars). Although applied research (42%) still eclipsed
basic research, nonprofits were performing basic research more than
twice as much as they were developing technologies (17.4%).

Table 6.2 reveals that the highest priority of nonprofits in the early
'70s was agricultural science. The term *green revolution* had entered
popular parlance in the mid-1960s to suggest the modern, high-yielding
varieties of rice and wheat developed by NRIs for distribution in Latin
America and Asia and the increased use of modern agronomic techniques including nitrogen fertilizer, herbicides and pesticides, irrigation,
and heavy machinery (Evenson and Gollin 2002).

Following agriculture, nonprofits were most clustered in biology, engineering, the social sciences, and then the physical sciences. Table 6.3
indicates the sources from which NRIs in 1973 funded their activities.
Following federal grants, industry made up the second largest source,
followed by "other sources"—mostly their own operating funds[16]—and
other nonprofits. Returning to table 6.1, federal government dollars received by nonprofits were 5 percent more likely to go toward applied
than basic research. Nonfederal sources—the largest being the combination of nonprofits' own funds with those from other nonprofit funders—
were now 5 percent more likely to go to basic research. The strong postwar economy had grown foundation and research institute endowments.
Along with retained earnings, nonprofits were increasingly in a position
to direct their own research. With minimal external accountability, a
lack of commercial peers in applied research (although government labs
remained concentrated there), and attention-getting feedback from the
publication process, NRIs had quickly moved from development organizations—from companies without products—to research organizations—
universities without students.

NRIs were not following dollars as they moved away from their
founding mission to translate science into technology; they directed the
applied-to-basic shift with their own money. They may have been more
uniquely suited to research than development: being a company without products may have been a liability for technological development

---

16. A 1996 conference with many of the executives of the surveyed nonprofits revealed that most of
these "other sources" are none other than their own war chests, supplemented with the fruits of their
own donor-level fund-raising activities.

TABLE 6.2. **NPO R&D by type of NPO and field of science and engineering: 1973 (in millions of 2004 dollars)**[1]

Type of NPO	Total[2]	Life sciences			Psychology	Environ-mental/earth sciences	Physical sciences	Mathematics and computer sciences	Engineering	Social sciences	Other sciences
		Biological sciences	Agricultural sciences	Medical and health sciences							
Total	3,344	689	711	111	128	81	306	157	579	553	21
Research institutes	2,072	442	187	47	77	38	213	145	417	481	21
Hospitals	693	170	417	26	21	0	21	9	9	26	—
Private foundations	60	21	4	—	—	9	9	0	0	9	0
Other nonprofit organizations	519	60	102	38	26	34	68	0	149	38	0
Professional or technical societies	264	21	72	17	—	21	55	—	64	9	0
Trade associations	111	9	0	0	0	4	9	—	85	4	0
Science exhibitors	34	17	—	0	—	9	4	0	0	9	0
Residual nonprofit organizations[3]	111	13	30	21	26	0	0	—	17	—	—

[1] Adapted from the National Science Foundation/Division of Science Resources Studies, Survey of R&D Funding & Performance by Nonprofit Organizations, 1973; inflation adjusted with CPI for urban consumers.

[2] The original NSF table indicated "because of rounding, detail may not add to totals." Some of these errors were exacerbated when I transformed the amounts into 2009 dollars (e.g., Psychology).

[3] Residual nonprofit organizations include academies of science or engineering, academic and industrial consortia.

TABLE 6.3. **NPO R&D by type of NPO and source of funds: 1973 (in millions)**[1]

Type of NPO	Total	Federal government	State and local government	Nonprofit organizations[2]	Universities and colleges	Industry	Other sources[3]
Total	3,344	2,063	72	213	n.a.	421	570
Research institutes	2,072	1,319	51	106	n.a.	336	260
Hospitals	693	451	13	60	n.a.	17	153
Private foundations	60	9	–	–	n.a.	–	47
Other nonprofit organizations	519	285	4	43	n.a.	68	115
Professional or technical societies	264	187	4	13	n.a.	9	47
Trade associations	111	34	–	–	n.a.	60	21
Science exhibitors	34	9	–	4	n.a.	–	17
Residual nonprofit organizations	111	55	–	26	n.a.	–	30

[1] Adapted from the National Science Foundation/Division of Science Resources Studies, R&D Activities of Independent Nonprofit Institutions, 1973; inflation adjusted with CPI for urban consumers.

[2] In the 1973 survey, the only nonprofit funder organizations listed on the survey form were foundations and voluntary health agencies.

[3] Other sources of funds include organizations' own funds, gifts, grants, or contracts received from private individuals, and all foreign sources.

(Nelson 2003), while being a university without students may have been a benefit for basic research. Such an efficiency argument, however, relies on the presence of competitive pressures, and there is no indication that such pressures existed for nonprofits in this period. It seems more plausible that this small organizational population, situated between universities and businesses in a market yielding minimal identity-affirming feedback, attended to the precise feedback of the "publication market" by mimicking the research allocations of universities. NRIs could be confident in their public perception as succeeding in basic research. They were also entering a sector rich in established public support, where they could avoid charges from industry of unfair competition. Having chosen this new path, their competitive advantage likely became salient. Without the liabilities of inexperienced students and the tax of teaching, nonprofit research institutes could increasingly lure talented scientists, committed to their research, from the academy.

Over the course of the next twenty-five years the trends continued. The size of the nonuniversity nonprofit sector more than doubled (see table 6.1), as did the size of other institutions in the national system, representing 3 percent of U.S. R&D in both 1973 and 1997 (NSF 1997). Nonprofits shifted further toward basic research in these years, with basic allocations reaching 55 percent of their total budgets. It is interesting to note that applied research dropped substantially during this period, from 42 percent in 1973 to 30 percent in 1997, but that development remained steady. This reflects a trend in a number of key scientific areas, most notably the life sciences, where the distance between basic research and technological development narrowed substantially.

The rise of molecular biology in the 1970s spawned the ability to manipulate the genetic content of cells, the key insight of the 1980 Cohen-Boyer patent, which allowed scientists to enlist bacteria as factories in the mass production of organic chemicals. The patent, held jointly by Stanford and Berkeley, was used by virtually every institution doing basic biology in this period. It was licensed to nearly five hundred companies and acted as the general-purpose tool of the fledgling biotechnology industry. Subsequent discoveries of gene and protein function were much quicker to enter products—health diagnostics, therapeutics, and, in the case of plants and animals, eugenics. Although this erosion of the distinction between basic and applied research is most notable in the life sciences, the life sciences themselves became more important, representing an increasing proportion of the total funds to national R&D in

general and to nonprofits in particular. Tables 6.2, 6.4, and 6.5 illustrate
the explosive rise in the nonprofit medical and health sciences, from
$111 million in 1973 to $5.2 billion in 1997 (in inflation-adjusted 2004
dollars), a sixty-six-fold increase. Nonprofit investment in the physical
sciences, in contrast, stayed the same.[17] An increased commitment by
the federal government to health research, begun with President Nixon
declaring "war on cancer" in 1971, accounts for the rise in basic research
funding from federal sources listed in table 6.1.

Although federal funding more than doubled for research over this
period in real dollars (see tables 6.6 and 6.7), NRIs relied more on "other
sources"—primarily their own funds—which rose from $260 million
to $1.8 billion in real dollars, a seven-fold increase. The proportion of
NRI funding from federal sources dropped by more than 18 percent.
This tracks the much publicized relative decline in federal and state
funding for science, generally. In 1988, industry allocations to health-
related R&D exceeded federal ones (Powell and Owen-Smith 1998).
These trends, along with the recent ability to patent the results of federally funded research[18] and a general rise in patent protection, have influenced public and nonprofit universities to derive more funds from industry (Press and Washburn 2000). Note, however, in table 6.7, that for
NRIs, industry funds increased even less than federal sources, drop-
ping slightly as a proportion of operating funds between 1973 and 1997.
It is thus unlikely that NRIs were following the dollars into industry.
Moreover, they are not magnifying their university-industry spanning
role, though many were founded for that purpose. As universities became slightly more commercial over the last quarter century, nonprofit
research institutes became slightly less so. Universities and research institutes met in the middle, as an increasingly undifferentiated basic research community.

I attempted to trace these later developments precisely by assembling a list of U.S. nonprofits and matching them to the articles and U.S.
patents they produced between 1965 and 2000. The methodological

17. A 1997 survey of nonprofit foundations indicated that those fostering R&D in the biological sciences were much more likely to fund nonprofits than those supporting activity in the physical sciences.
This suggests not only that nonprofits have multiplied in the health sciences but that they have shrunk as
a percentage of the organizational population engaged in physical science research.

18. The Bayh-Dole Act, ratified in 1981, allowed universities, NRIs, and anyone else receiving federal funds to patent the results of their federally funded research. It may not have driven the shift in
university patenting, but this act represents a broader set of commercializing trends that have done so
(Mowery et al. 2004).

TABLE 6.4. **NPO R&D by type of NPO and field of science and engineering: 1997 (in millions of 2004 dollars)**[1]

| Type of NPO | Total | Life sciences | | | Psychology | Environmental/earth sciences | Physical sciences | Mathematics and computer sciences | Engineering | Social sciences | Other sciences |
		Biological sciences	Agricultural sciences	Medical and health sciences							
Total	8,649	1,005	26	5,194	82	273	300	317	577	383	493
Research institutes	5,695	934	13	3,081	77	114	173	310	539	359	98
Hospitals	1,681	24	0	1,657	—	0	0	1	0	0	0
University-affiliated hospitals	546	0	0	545	0	0	0	1	0	0	0
Other voluntary nonprofit hospitals	1,136	24	0	1,112	—	0	0	0	0	0	0
Private foundations	539	33	13	454	5	2	13	4	—	12	2
Other nonprofit organizations[2]	734	15	1	2	0	157	114	2	38	12	393

[1] Adapted from the National Science Foundation/Division of Science Resources Studies, Survey of R&D Funding & Performance by Nonprofit Organizations, 1996 and 1997; inflation adjusted with CPI for urban consumers.

[2] Other nonprofit organizations include professional and technical societies, academies of science or engineering, science exhibitors, academic consortia, industrial consortia, and trade associations.

TABLE 6.5. **NPO R&D by type of NPO and field of science and engineering: Growth as proportion of 1973's budget in 1997**[1]

| Type of NPO | Total | Life sciences | | | | Environmental/earth sciences | Physical sciences | Mathematics and computer sciences | Engineering | Social sciences | Other sciences |
		Biological sciences	Agricultural sciences	Medical and health sciences	Psychology						
Total	2.59	1.46	0.04	46.95	0.65	3.38	0.98	2.01	1.00	0.69	23.18
Research institutes	2.75	2.11	0.07	65.84	1.00	2.98	0.81	2.14	1.29	0.75	4.59
Hospitals	9.05	1.55	3.04	—	—	0.28	1.52	—	—	1.38	—
Private foundations	2.19	0.40	0.00	29.05	—	0.00	0.00	—	0.00	0.00	—
Other nonprofit organizations	2.59	1.46	0.04	46.95	0.65	3.38	0.98	2.01	1.00	0.69	23.18

[1] Adapted from the National Science Foundation/Division of Science Resources Studies, Survey of R&D Funding & Performance by Nonprofit Organizations, 1973; inflation adjusted with CPI for urban consumers.

[2] Residual nonprofit organizations include academies of science or engineering, academic and industrial consortia.

TABLE 6.6. **NPO R&D by type of NPO and source of funds: 1997 (in millions of 2004 dollars)**[1]

Type of NPO	Total	Federal government	State and local government	Nonprofit organizations	Universities and colleges	Industry	Other sources[2]
Total	8,649	4,364	204	484	56	969	2,570
Research institutes	5,695	2,866	148	288	21	539	1,833
Hospitals, subtotal	1,681	917	32	135	34	364	199
University-affiliated hospitals	546	319	20	34	1	84	88
Other voluntary nonprofit hospitals	1,136	598	12	101	33	280	111
Private foundations	539	300	22	56	—	49	111
Other nonprofit organizations[3]	734	281	1	4	1	16	430

[1] Adapted from the National Science Foundation/Division of Science Resources Studies, Survey of R&D Funding & Performance by Nonprofit Organizations, 1996 and 1997; inflation adjusted with CPI for urban consumers.

[2] Other sources of funds include organizations' own funds, gifts, grants, or contracts received from private individuals, and all foreign sources.

[3] Other nonprofit organizations include professional and technical societies, academies of science or engineering, science exhibitors, academic consortia, industrial consortia, and trade associations.

TABLE 6.7. **NPO R&D by type of NPO and source of funds: Growth as proportion of 1973's budget in 1997[1]**

Type of NPO	Total	Federal government	State and local government	Nonprofit organizations[2]	Universities and colleges	Industry	Other sources[3]
Total	2.59	2.11	2.82	2.27	n.a.	2.30	4.51
Research institutes	2.75	2.17	2.90	2.71	n.a.	1.60	7.06
Hospitals	0.41	0.49	0.40	0.44	n.a.	0.05	0.77
Private foundations	9.05	35.27	—	—	n.a.	—	2.36
Other nonprofit organizations	1.41	0.99	0.28	0.08	n.a.	0.24	3.74

[1] Adapted from the National Science Foundation/Division of Science Resources Studies, R&D Activities of Independent Nonprofit Institutions, 1973; inflation adjusted with CPI for urban consumers.

[2] In the 1973 survey, the only nonprofit funder organizations listed on the survey form were foundations and voluntary health agencies.

[3] Other sources of funds include organizations' own funds, gifts, grants, or contracts received from private individuals, and all foreign sources.

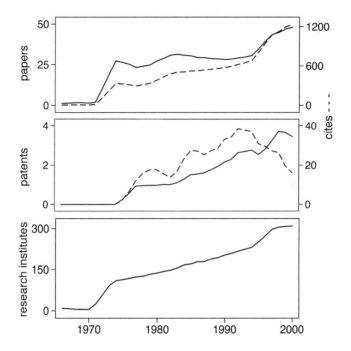

FIGURE 6.1.

appendix describes the derivation of this sample and the document-matching procedures in detail. The resulting sample contains 415 non-profit institutions, which produced 197,022 articles and secured 14,330 patents that, in turn, received over 4 million paper citations and 130,000 patent references by 2006.

The top panel of figure 6.1 captures the general publication trend by tracing the average number of articles and citations that articles received over time. The figure's bottom panel indicates the number of research institutes publishing or patenting in each year. What is immediately obvious is that while articles per institute have grown from the mid-1960s to the present, citations per article have grown more dramatically. It is not the slope of the growth lines that matters—these depend only on the scale of the graph—but that article growth is concave while citation growth is convex. This increased attention reflects the enlarging role of high-quality science in research institute activities. Although part of this change is driven by the remarkable success of the few most academically successful institutes listed in table 6.8—for example, the 1,559 papers

TABLE 6.8. **Top ten most visible institutions in molecular biology and genetics: 1988–1992**[1]

Institution	Cites per publication	Number of papers
Salk Institute[2]	41.6	403
Cold Spring Harbor Labs	40.8	359
Whitehead Institute	39.7	392
Genentech	33.1	225
Chiron	32.8	200
Institute Chemie Biologique	31.8	261
Fred Hutchinson Cancer Center	27.1	413
MIT	25.8	1,060
Princeton	24.0	369
MRC Lab Molecular Biology	23.7	430

[1] Powell, Koput, and Smith-Doerr 1996, 141.
[2] Titles in bold indicate nonprofit research institutes.

generated by the Mayo Clinic in 2000 generated 38,399 cites by the end of 2003—the same is true, to a lesser extent, for median nonprofits. The second panel of figure 6.1 illustrates the growth of patents and patent future citations. Institutes secure more patents just as they author more articles over time, but the rise in patent citations is directly proportional to the rise in patents.[19] Ironically, this rise in patenting trails growth in academic publishing and the decline in institute funds dedicated to applied research and development. The rise betrays several influences: the Bayh-Dole Act of 1980, which enabled institutes to patent results from federally funded research (Mowery et al. 2001); strengthened intellectual property rights for basic discoveries such as genes and organisms (*Diamond v. Chakrabarty* 1980, U.S. Supreme Court 447 U.S. 303); and the increasingly immediate utility of insight gained from basic research, especially in the molecular life sciences. When academic life scientists publish a flurry of papers surrounding a new finding, they will often simultaneously file for patents (Azoulay, Ding, and Stuart 2006).[20] Although nonprofits are patenting more today, the growth reflects no more applied orientation than exhibited by a comparable sample of universities.

In order to identify the locus of these trends, I dissect research output for nonprofits with expertise in the biological and physical sciences—those fixed on problems of medicine and agriculture versus engineering.

19. The drop in patent citations after 1990 simply reflects right censoring: patent citations reference patents that are roughly five years older than referenced articles, and these citations were only accrued through 2005.

20. This is likely different for life scientists in most European countries, where patents granted require that no publication precede them.

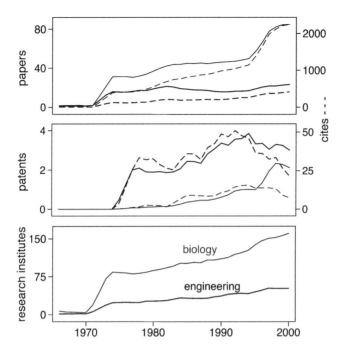

FIGURE 6.2.

Figure 6.2 shows that the patterns described above hold for both types of nonprofits. Both biological and engineering institutes experienced a jump in articles in the early 1970s, and citations for both rose faster and at an accelerating rate. This figure also traces the rise of biological nonprofits as research powerhouses, whose articles increase through 2000. Engineering nonprofits have not, on average, produced more articles since the early 1970s, but their articles have garnered more citations, likely reflecting an increase in quality. In 1972, papers from engineering nonprofits attracted, on average, five citations per paper; in 2002, they attracted twenty-two. The rise in biological articles is similar, from eleven citations per paper in 1972 to twenty-eight in 2002.

Figure 6.3 splits the paper and patent data by founding cohorts to show that research institute activities have changed, as I have argued.[21]

21. The founding dates of research institutes were gathered in two ways. First, archival research, including the probing of research institute web pages, was used to directly identify founding dates. Second, for those still unidentified, the first date of an article or patent was used to *infer* the decade in which that institute was founded.

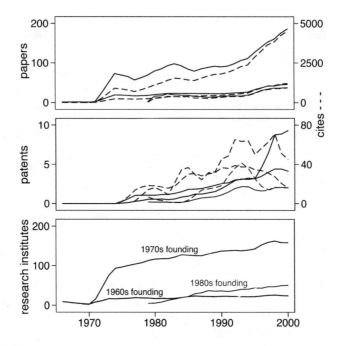

FIGURE 6.3.

This puts to rest any concern that nonpublishing institutes from the early years have merely been replaced by publishing ones in later years. Research institutes born before the end of the 1960s exhibit the most dramatic increase in rate of articles produced. This suggests that older institutes have grown larger, but also that institutes have shifted the locus of their activities. Newer, smaller institutes founded in the 1970s, 1980s, and 1990s have increased their production of academic articles at a similar rate, although they have not yet caught up with the earlier institutes. The convexity of citation growth is true for all eras of nonprofits, but it is most pronounced for those founded by the 1960s. As with articles, patents also increase over time for all cohorts, but for the first twenty years—from 1976 until 1996—research institutes founded in the 1970s produced more, per institute, than those founded earlier. This suggests that the mix of applied research and development activities common to institutes in the earliest period is not identical to those in later ones. In particular, in the mid-1990s the spike in patents from nonprofits founded by the end of the 1960s tracks with the spike in biology nonprofit patenting from figure 6.2, and reflects a rise in the commercial relevance of basic biology.

These trends demonstrate that NRIs have not only become accepted in the community of basic research, they have excelled and achieved considerable status. Table 6.8 lists the ten most visible research organizations in molecular biology and genetics in terms of citation impact (Powell, Koput, and Smith-Doerr 1996). Paper citations represent not only popularity, but fundamental discoveries applied across a range of applications. The top three of these institutions, and half of the top ten overall, are nonprofit research institutes. Although the stature of NRIs is not so striking in all areas of science, NRIs have come to be viewed as universities without students to elite young scientists intent on establishing their careers—and fame—in basic science. Although some NRIs, like the agricultural labs supported by the Rockefeller Foundation or the myriad small "upstream" institutes founded by companies, are still doing applied and development work, most NRIs are now themselves upstream, a virtually indistinguishable branch of the academic community.

Conclusion

Nonprofit organizations play many diverse roles within the U.S. innovation system. As "communicators," facilitating information exchange between scientists and between science-based companies, their identity is recognizably not-for-profit. These organizations are not trying to make money; participants volunteer a substantial amount of time and effort to achieve broadly shared benefits. Nonprofits involved in education, research, and development, on the other hand, represent only part of the membership involved in these organizational communities. Public and commercial organizations work beside them. Though legally diverse, these organizations appear remarkably similar. Similar organizations result from similar contexts: similar funding, peers, and customers inspire (and constrain) conformity. Public and private universities, competing for the same grants and the same students, behave very much the same.

The retreat of nonprofit research institutes from the market—from an applied, development orientation to one fixed on basic research—illustrates how interactions with the broader environment can dislodge organizations from the philanthropic "purposes" that founded them. Moreover, this case illuminates forces that influence how organizations select between organizational communities within a broader field. Competence probably matters: research institutes were probably better as universities without students than as companies without products. And yet this more likely answers the question of why NRIs succeeded in their identity shift than why they initiated it. In this chapter, I argued that organizations and individuals likely seek peers similar to themselves—that "birds of a feather flock together." Reinforcing this homophilic motive, organizations attend to socially proximate and precise feedback, which market peers and market transactors provide for them. In this way, markets stabilize organizational communities and the identities they inscribe. Moreover, organizations will gravitate toward markets where they can find stronger feedback, and, in responding to it, achieve the credit and status that culturally reinforces them.

More detailed research is required to tease out subtle distinctions in the content of nonprofit research to determine the existence or absence of a unique nonprofit contribution, but in terms of the applied or fundamental character of research, NRIs looked like commercial and government labs in the 1950s and like preeminent universities at the turn of the twentieth century. They continue to stoke the economy by generating new ideas, but less directly—at a greater distance from the market. What may be the most unique nonprofit contribution of research institutes is that while midcentury commercial labs went out of business, and government labs remained applied, nonprofit labs changed. They moved from one organizational community to another. The Howard Hughes Medical Institute shifted its entire endowment from supporting applied to basic research between 1973 and 1997 (Burk 2001). U.S. nonprofits have more freedom from administrative oversight than government labs, and more freedom from economic constraint than commercial ones. This flexibility, allowing nonprofits to reinvent themselves, may also facilitate the transfer of practices from one area to another. Perhaps their remarkable success in basic research is not simply a freedom from students but an application of the focused, organized approach to research pioneered by independent labs in the postwar years. If so, NRIs may indeed have fulfilled their mandate to span basic and applied research, if not quite in the way they had intended.

Methodological Appendix

In order to trace the intellectual output of NRIs, I gathered data on the scientific articles published from 1960 to 2003 and the technology patents granted from 1976 to 2003 to U.S. nonprofits. To locate the position of those outputs within the broader system of U.S. innovation, I also gathered the citations these articles and patents received from subsequent articles and patents. The number and scientific importance of papers suggest the degree to which research institutes focus their resources on academic outputs. The number and importance of patents conversely hint at their focus on translating science into applications.

I began by assembling an extensive list of nonprofits, which started with the complete list of nonprofit research institutes that received any allocation of federal funds in 2000 (NSF 2000). I supplemented this list with all of the nonprofits surveyed in the 1953 and 1996–97 NSF surveys of nonprofit research institute activity.[22] I also performed an independent search for other, unmentioned research institutes that were prominent publishers or patenters at any point in the postwar period. This process yielded 415 distinct nonprofit research institutes. Of these, 237 were rooted in biology, supporting the concerns of medicine and agriculture, while 129 were based in the physical sciences, concerned primarily with engineering. The remaining forty-nine dealt with social science issues or their expertise could not be identified. The names of these institutes were then matched to the institutional affiliation of scientists authoring scientific articles in the Science Citation Index (SCI), an extensive database containing more than five thousand of the most cited scientific journals—and more than thirty million articles—from 1945 to 2003. I also matched the institute names against the assignee field of the U.S. Patent Database, from 1976 to 2004.[23] Both of these databases contain citations to these papers and patents from all subsequent SCI papers and all U.S. patents, respectively. In total, my sample of U.S. research institutes produced 197,022 articles, which subsequently attracted 4,190,599 citations, and secured 14,339 patents, which drew 130,973 cites. In all figures, I graph numbers of articles, patents and their forward citations, or the citations that those articles or patents received over the entire period observed. For example, if twenty articles and one hundred citations are noted in 1993, this suggests that in 1993 nonprofits produced on average twenty articles that attracted one hundred citations in total by 2003.

---

22. Although the list of nonprofits surveyed in 1973 was not retained by the NSF organization that performed the survey (the Division of Science Resources Statistics), they believed that most of them were present in the 2000, 1996, and 1953 lists.

23. I used a fuzzy string-matching algorithm to make gross institution matches, and then affirmed or refined the accuracy of those matches by hand.

180 JAMES A. EVANS

References

Arrow, Kenneth J. 1962. "Economic Welfare and the Allocation of Resources for Inventions." In *The Rate and Direction of Inventive Activity: Economic and Social Factors*, edited by R. R. Nelson. Princeton: Princeton University Press.

Azoulay, Pierre, Waverly Ding, and Toby Stuart. 2006. "The Impact of Academic Patenting on the Rate, Quality and Direction of (Public) Research Output." *NBER Working Paper 11917.*

Burk, Mary V. 2001. "Nonprofit Sector's R&D Grows over Past Quarter Century." In Data Brief, Division of Science Resources Studies: National Science Foundation. NSF-01-318, February 15. http://www.nsf.gov/sbe/srs/databrf/sdb01318.html.

Bush, Vannevar. 1945. *Science—The Endless Frontier: A Report to the President by Vannevar Bush, Director of the Office of Scientific Research and Development, July 1945.* Washington, D.C.: U.S. Government Printing Office.

Charleton, David B. 1964. "Letter to Science." *Science* 144, no. 3624 (June 12): 1293.

Cohen, Wesley M., Richard R. Nelson, and John P. Walsh. 2000. "Protecting Their Intellectual Assets: Appropriability Conditions and Why U.S. Manufacturing Firms Patent (or Not)." *NBER Working Paper 7552.*

DiMaggio, Paul, and Walter Powell. 1983. "The Iron Cage Revisited: Institutional Isomorphism and Collective Rationality in Organizational Fields." *American Sociological Review* 48: 147–60.

Evenson, Robert E., and Douglas Gollin. 2002. "The Green Revolution: An End Century Perspective." Working paper, available from Doug Gollin, Economics Department, Williams College.

Galison, Peter. 1997. *Image and Logic: A Material Culture of Microphysics.* Chicago: University of Chicago Press.

Hackman, J. Richard, and Greg R. Oldham. 1980. *Work Redesign.* Reading, Mass.: Addison-Wesley.

Hansmann, Henry B. 1980. "The Role of Nonprofit Enterprise." *Yale Law Journal* 89: 835–901.

Kleinman, Daniel Lee. 1995. *Politics on the Endless Frontier: Postwar Research Policy in the United States.* Durham, N.C.: Duke University Press.

Kornhauser, William. 1962. *Scientists in Industry: Conflict and Accommodation.* Berkeley: University of California Press.

Langer, Elinore. 1966. "Nonprofits: Air Force Says We Can't Do Without Them." *Science,* n.s. 152, no 3723 (May 6): 734–36.

March, James G., and Herbert A. Simon. 1958. *Organizations.* New York: Wiley.

Marcson, Simon. 1960. *The Scientist in American Industry.* New York: Harper and Row.

Maxwell Research Center, Syracuse University. 1953. *Research and Development by Nonprofit Research Institutes and Commercial Laboratories, 1953.* National Science Foundation (NSF 56-15).

Mowery, David C., Richard R. Nelson, Bhaven N. Sampat, and Arvids A. Zie-
donis. 2001. "The Growth of Patenting and Licensing by U.S. Universities:
An Assessment of the Effects of the Bayh-Dole Act of 1980." *Research Policy* 30: 99–119.

———. 2004. *Ivory Tower and Industrial Innovation: University-Industry Technology Transfer before and after the Bayh-Dole Act in the United States.*
Stanford: Stanford Business Books.

Nelson, Richard R. 1959. "The Simple Economics of Basic Scientific Research."
Journal of Political Economy 67: 297–306.

———. 1981. "Assessing Private Enterprise: An Exegesis of Tangled Doctrine."
Bell Journal of Economics 12: 93–111.

———, ed. 1993a. *National Innovation Systems: A Comparative Perspective.* New
York: Oxford University Press.

———. 1993b. "Technological Innovation: The Role of Nonprofit Organizations."
In *Nonprofit Organizations in a Market Economy: Understanding New Roles,
Issues, and Trends,* edited by David Hammack and Dennis Young. San Fran-
cisco: Jossey-Bass.

———. 2003. "On the Uneven Evolution of Human Know-How." *Research Policy* 32: 909–22.

NSF (National Science Foundation), Division of Science Resources Statistics.
1973. *Survey of R&D Funding and Performance by Nonprofit Organizations,
1973.*

———. 1974–80. *Federal Science and Engineering Support to Universities, Colleges, and Nonprofit Institutions.*

———. 1997. *Survey of R&D Funding and Performance by Nonprofit Organizations, 1996 and 1997.*

———. 2000. *Federal Science and Engineering Support to Universities, Colleges,
and Nonprofit Institutions: Fiscal Year 2000.*

Parsons, Talcott. 1959. "'Voting' and the Equilibrium of the American Political
System." In *American Voting Behavior,* edited by Eugene Burdick and Arthur Brodbeck. New York: Free Press.

———. 1970. "On the Concept of Value-Commitments." *Sociological Inquiry* 38:
135–60.

Podolny, Joel M. 1993. "A Status-Based Model of Market Competition." *American Journal of Sociology* 98: 829–72.

Powell, Walter W., Kenneth W. Koput, and Laurel Smith-Doerr. 1996. "Interorganizational Collaboration and the Locus of Innovation: Networks of Learning in Biotechnology." *Administrative Science Quarterly* 41: 116.

Powell, Walter W., and Jason Owen-Smith. 1998. "Universities and the Market
for Intellectual Property in the Life Sciences." *Journal of Policy Analysis and
Management* 17: 253–77.

Press, Eyal, and Jennifer Washburn. 2000. "The Kept University." *Atlantic
Monthly* 285: 39–54.

Rosenberg, Nathan. 1982. "The Growing Role of Science in the Innovation Process." In *Science, Technology and Society at the Time of Alfred Nobel,* edited
by Carl Gustaf Bernhard. Oxford: Pergamon Press.

———. 1985. "The Commercial Exploitation of Science by American Industry." In *The Uneasy Alliance: Managing Productivity and Technology Dilemma,* edited by K. B. Clark, R. H. Hayas, and C. Lorenz. Boston: Harvard University Press.

———. 2000. "American University-Industry Interfaces: 1945–2000." Manuscript, Stanford Institute for Economic Policy Research, Stanford University.

Rosenberg, Nathan, and Richard R. Nelson. 1994. "American Universities and Technical Advance in Industry." *Research Policy* 23: 323–48.

Schumpeter, Joseph. 1950. *Capitalism, Socialism, and Democracy.* New York: HarperCollins.

Science. 1956. "New Series," 124, no. 3227 (November 2): 882.

Shapin, Steven. 1994. *Social History of Truth: Science and Civility in Seventeenth-Century England.* Chicago: University of Chicago Press.

Simon, John. 1987. "The Tax Treatment of Nonprofit Organizations: A Review of Federal and State Policies." In *The Nonprofit Sector: A Research Handbook,* edited by Walter W. Powell. New Haven: Yale University Press.

Sloan, Frank A. 1998. "Commercialism in Nonprofit Hospitals." In *To Profit or Not to Profit: The Commercial Transformation of the Nonprofit Sector,* edited by Burton A. Weisbrod. Cambridge: Cambridge University Press.

Smith, Adam. [1776] 1976. *An Inquiry into the Nature and Causes of the Wealth of Nations.* Chicago: University of Chicago Press.

Smith, C. Burton. 1964. "Nonprofit R&D and the Free Enterprise System." *Science,* n.s. 144, no. 3624 (June 12): 1293.

Stokes, Ronald. 1997. *Pasteur's Quadrant: Basic Science and Technological Innovation.* Washington, D.C.: Brookings Institution Press.

Thakray, A. 1982. "University-Industry Connections and Chemical Research: A Historical Perspective." In *University-Industry Research Relationship,* a report by the National Science Board. Washington, D.C.: National Science Board.

Weisbrod, Burton A. 1998. "The Nonprofit Mission and Its Financing: Growing Links between Nonprofits and the Rest of the Economy." In *To Profit or Not to Profit: The Commercial Transformation of the Nonprofit Sector,* edited by Burton A. Weisbrod, 1–22. Cambridge: Cambridge University Press.

Weisbrod, Burton A., and Mark Schlesinger. 1986. "Ownership and Regulation in Markets with Assymetric Information: Theory and Empirical Application to the Nursing Home Industry." In *The Economics of Non-profit Institutions: Studies in Structures and Policy,* edited by Susan Rose-Ackerman, 133–51. New York: Oxford University Press.

White, Harrison. 2001. *Markets from Networks: Socioeconomic Models of Production.* Princeton: Princeton University Press.

Williamson, Oliver. 1975. *Markets and Hierarchies: Analysis and Antitrust Implications.* New York: Free Press.

CHAPTER SEVEN

Corporate Philanthropy in the United States: What Causes Do Corporations Back?

Doug Guthrie

In the last three decades, the field of corporate social responsibility (CSR) has evolved from a primary focus on philanthropic activity to a much broader focus on corporate practices that touch the lives of workers, communities, the broad array of stakeholders within a corporation's sphere, the environment, and many other aspects of community and social life. However, despite this broadly defined view of CSR, philanthropy itself still remains an important part of how corporations engage with the communities in which they are embedded. The level of philanthropic commitments by corporations has risen steadily since the middle of the twentieth century, and in 2000 the Fortune 100 group donated over $2 billion in cash gifts.[1] Spread evenly across the nonprofit sector, the amount of money coming from the corporate sector would not be all that significant—indeed, nonprofit revenues from the corporate sector is a relatively small percentage of total revenues for this sector. And the amount of money we are talking about in comparison to public funding is an insignificant amount, compared to, say, funding from govern-

Research for this paper was funded through a grant from the Ford Foundation, with additional support provided by the Social Science Research Council. Send inquiries to Doug Guthrie, Department of Management, Stern School of Business, 44 W. 4th St., 7th Floor, New York, NY 10012; doug.guthrie@nyu.edu.

1. *Chronicle of Philanthropy* 13, no. 19, July 26, 2001.

mental sources.[2] However, this source of funding is *not* spread evenly, and, as such, the corporate sector is a very significant source of revenue for some organizations. Further, with the ways in which public-private partnerships have changed the flow of corporate dollars (as discussed by Michael McQuarrie in chapter 9, for example), the amounts can have a significant impact.[3] The question of what corporations do with their charitable donations becomes an important issue to explore in CSR research. This chapter illuminates exactly what corporations have done in recent years with their charitable donations. My focus here is on the question of the funding priorities of corporate philanthropic giving and, in the multivariate analysis, how these priorities are shaped by contextual and legal constraints.

Statutory law relating to corporate philanthropy first emerged at the state level in 1917, a time when individual states began to pass legislation allowing corporations to give to charity. The next significant change in the institutional environment came in 1935, when Congress created the first set of incentives for philanthropic action by corporations, allowing corporations to write off up to 5 percent of net income.[4] This amount was raised to 10 percent of taxable earnings during the Reagan administration as a provision of the Economic Recovery Act of 1981. Corporations are not mandated to give, and some scholars have interpreted such practices in economic, profit-maximizing, or self-interested terms.[5] Ron Burt has argued that corporate philanthropy is actually little more than a public relations or marketing tool: to the extent that corporations reside in industries that provide incentives for them to institutionalize close ties with consumers, philanthropy becomes a useful tool for that end.[6] Though tightly focused around assumptions of a rational profit-maximizing framework for corporate expenditures, Burt's analysis of corporate philanthropy across industrial sectors is among the most systematic to date and therefore must be taken seriously as a starting

---

2. "Governmental" is more specific than "public sources"; the latter can include anything that an individual or an organization can apply for (usually for which there is a formal and open application process, which is often competitive). Private sources are amounts of money given by an individual or organization to a selected individual or organization that are not open or accessible to the general public.

3. As McQuarrie (2007) and Guthrie and McQuarrie (2005, 2007) have argued, concentrated corporate giving in community development significantly shifted the flow of resources into low-income housing development.

4. Fremont-Smith 1972.

5. Fry, Keim, and Meiners 1982; Navarro 1988; Piliavin and Charng 1990.

6. Burt 1983a, 1983b.

point for understanding corporate motivations to give back to the community. Joe Galaskiewicz's work has been among the most systematic at interrogating the local commitments of corporations.[7] Anchoring his research in the Twin Cities of Minneapolis and St. Paul, Galaskiewicz and his collaborators systematically examined corporate philanthropic giving. Based on a 1981–82 survey of the population of publicly owned corporations headquartered in Minneapolis and St. Paul, Galaskiewicz conceives of the urban grants economy as a network of collective action, where, for a variety of reasons, normative pressure from within the community shapes corporate pressure to give.[8]

Despite these and a few other exemplary studies, we still have relatively little systematic data on corporate philanthropy. And we have almost no data that compare the practices of corporations across a variety of size ranges and across the country. Drawing on one of the largest systematic studies conducted on corporate philanthropic giving in recent years, this chapter explores corporate giving practices. Although, with the data I employ here, it is not possible to develop a truly dynamic sense of the ways in which corporate funding shapes nonprofit organizations themselves, it is nevertheless still useful to develop a clear sense of where corporations direct their charitable donations. I first lay out benchmarks on a variety of practices in the area of corporate philanthropy, and then go deeper in the analysis, focusing on three key areas in which corporations have given in significant ways in recent years. My goal is to look beyond *what* corporations do to attempt to answer *why* they do what they do in the area of corporate philanthropy.[9]

Selected Results of the Corporate-Community Relations Study

We live in an era of receding governmental funding for societal goods and a growing reliance on private sources across social sectors. Philanthropic donations have been on the rise since the middle of the century, and for the quarter century from 1975 to 2000, the rise was especially rapid, with philanthropic activity increasing by over 1,200 percent overall—nearly 400 percent in inflation-adjusted dollars. Private foun-

7. Galaskiewicz 1979, 1985a, 1985b, 1989, 1991, 1997.
8. A follow-up survey was conducted in 1989 to give temporal dimension to the study (Galaskiewicz 1997).
9. Details of the Corporate-Community Relations Study can be found in the appendix.

dations have become a significant force in this distribution of resources.[10] Behind the rise in the availability of private resources for public goods, we have seen a dramatic growth in population of foundations in the United States, as they grew from 21,877 in 1975 to more than fifty thousand by the end of the century.[11]

Somewhat less well known, however, is the role of the business community and specifically corporations in this growing trend. Indeed, we know not only less about corporate philanthropic activity—and what the norms around these practices are and should be—but we know little about the ways that corporations form relationships with local governments, local nonprofit communities, and the priorities they assign to the philanthropic practices on which they engage. The issue is especially significant, given the power of the corporation in modern society. Among Global 500 corporations (that is, the largest five hundred corporations in the world), the collective revenues, profits, and assets of these institutions are $14 trillion, $667 billion, $45 trillion, respectively, and they employ forty-five million employees (the corresponding figures for Fortune 500 companies are $7 trillion, $443 billion, $17 trillion, and $24 million). Such control over resources and person power is surpassed only by nation-states in today's global economy. In addition, the growing emphasis within the corporate community on CSR further highlights the role of the corporation in social sectors.

Corporate Practices in Corporate Philanthropy

The philanthropic giving patterns among corporations must first be viewed from the national level. Over 85 percent of all corporations nationwide engage in some kind of philanthropic or charitable activity, and among large organizations the figure is above 90 percent. In other words, most corporations give. The question then becomes what they give, how much, and why they give what they do. The first and most obvious fact of corporate philanthropy is that it varies significantly with the size of the giving corporation: virtually all large corporations engage in some kind of philanthropic or charitable activity, and they tend to have a di-

---

10. Private foundations include corporate and individual private foundations (the latter category being much larger). The latter category includes the Ford Foundation; the corporate foundation is the Ford Motor Corporation Foundation.

11. *Foundation Yearbook* (2001), the Foundation Center.

verse portfolio, from cash and in-kind gifts to programs of awards and grants, and a variety of other ways of engaging the communities to which they contribute. Smaller corporations, on the other hand, tend to donate cash and in-kind gifts and are much less likely to award grants or have a portfolio that extends to other types of giving. This is not too surprising, given that awards and grants and, more generally, a diverse portfolio of community investment tends to be the province of organizations that have formal community relations offices or corporate foundations, institutions that also track closely with the size of the organization. For example, the formalization of philanthropic activity plays an important role: corporations were asked to identify whether there is a specific office for handling philanthropic projects and activities. Some 28 percent of corporations in the country have a department that is dedicated solely to the corporation's philanthropic and charitable activity. For those less institutionalized organizations, other offices are in charge of this area of work, with human resources (42.73%) and marketing departments (20.26%) being the most common homes for decision making in this area.

In addition, about 44 percent of U.S. corporations have a formal policy on charitable giving. In formal econometric analyses, controlling for size, having a formal office directing philanthropic activities is associated with higher levels of giving: those that have a formal office, on average, give over $2.1 million more than those that do not have a formal office to direct giving and other community-related activities. Instead of designating internal departments for philanthropic activities, some corporations set up corporate foundations or funds to manage them. Over 39 percent of corporations in the United States own such institutions. Among them, almost 63 percent fund projects for the underprivileged, 46 percent fund arts projects, and around 40 percent donate to health-related programs. Other foundations focus on other purposes such as special events (36%), infrastructure (34%) and research projects (29%). About 21 percent have also established foundations that are separate from the parent corporations' earnings. As private foundations, the underprivileged (51%), the arts (39%), and public health (30%) are the most popular areas of giving among foundations. Most of both types of foundations are either small in scale with both annual budget and total endowment under $1 million (40% and 30%, respectively), or large scale with endowments and annual funding of at least $10 million (25% and 27%).

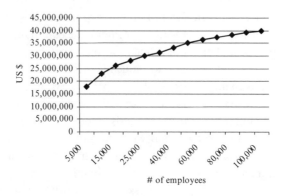

FIGURE 7.1. Philanthropic giving among Global 500 companies.

Overall Giving: How Much?

Corporate giving varies significantly with size—large corporations giving significantly more than small corporations. Levels of giving increase
from an average of a few thousand dollars for small corporations to an
average of between $8 and $9 million for large corporations (figure 7.1).
On average, 77 percent of the available funds for corporate charitable
activities go to the local metropolitan areas of each corporation. Also,
the average largest single donation of corporations averages well over
$1 million, with over 80 percent of the corporations claiming that, in any
given year, the largest single donation has gone to the local community.
The rates indicate high levels of commitment to the local communities
where corporations reside. Contributing to local projects serves as a ges-
ture of appreciation for the local efforts in developing an area's economy
and society, which in turn benefit the corporations. Many of the individuals we interviewed in greater depth for this study spoke of the local norms of "giving back" to the communities in which they are embedded. There also may be tax cuts and financial benefits tied to their
respective metropolitan areas. Finally, corporations benefit from publicity and goodwill with the local community through donations or supporting nonprofits and schools in the area.

However, corporate orientation toward the local community is in-
versely proportional to size: as corporations grow larger, even though
their overall rates of giving increase, the percentage of those gifts directed toward the local community decrease (figure 7.2). As corpora-

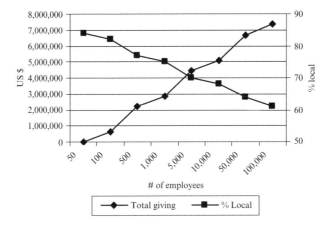

FIGURE 7.2. Total giving and percent of total directed to local Metropolitan Statistical Area.

tions rise in size from fifty to one hundred thousand employees, the proportion of their gifts directed locally drops from 84 to 61 percent. There are a variety of reasons for this decline. Large firms are much more likely to seek markets beyond their local metropolitan area, and inasmuch as philanthropic and charitable activities are tied to image and marketing, corporations seeking national and international markets push their resources in these directions. In addition, large firms are more likely to have foundations that are set up by their founders, and these foundations often take over for the local philanthropic activity where the corporate foundations leave off. For example, the Woodruff family's commitment to Atlanta is highly localized, while the Coca-Cola Corporate Foundation sends a good deal of its resource support to other communities.

Over the same size distribution, the value of corporate contributions, on average, rises from very small amounts for small firms to about $7.5 million for large corporations. Regarding the overall size of average gifts, there is an important caveat to keep in mind, however: Fortune and Global 500 companies, which are under a higher level of scrutiny than those that do not have such a public profile, give at significantly higher levels than firms that are not placed on these elite lists. As firms in this category increase from small to large, the average levels of giving increase from about $15.5 million to about $40 million. The range of giving for these corporations tops out at a much higher level than these results depict, with the largest companies, such as Wal-Mart, giving at levels of over $100 million per year.

Donations from corporations each year also depend on available funds. This reflects the financial health of the companies in the previous year, and that of the economy in general. In 2000, the average amount of charitable gifts from corporations nationally was around $3.36 million, rising to $3.53 million in 2001 and declining to $3.21 million in 2002. These trends reflect economic swings during these time periods, and as corporations on the whole had better financial performance, more funding was available for philanthropic activities.

Priorities

The priority areas for giving among U.S. corporations include contributions to nonprofit organizations (87%), schools (69%), donations to specific events (56%), and the arts (50%). Other major donation recipients include sports teams (37%) and local government projects (18%).

Although corporations give more to nonprofit organizations than to schools, even the nonprofit organizations they support are heavily oriented toward education. When asked about their "giving focus," the number-one category named by corporations was education (75%), followed by health-related causes (60%). These are followed by concerns for the arts (51%), social inequality (51%), environmental protection (40%) and economic development (25%). When asked to name their "single highest priority" in philanthropic activity, education was ranked first (33%), health second (12%), and environment, arts, and social inequality all statistically equal at below 10 percent (~5–7%).

As in giving focus, most corporations have their largest single gift activities designated to nonprofit organizations (49%) and schools (20%). Around 11% and 6% of them also provide grants as largest single gifts to nonprofits and schools, respectively. Education was the largest single gift area (34%), once again showing the special interest in this category by American corporations. Health came second (28.87%), and social inequality third. On average, large corporations report being involved in more than twenty charitable activities for schools during the year. To fill out our understanding of corporate-school relations, we asked corporations to identify the types of schools to which they typically contribute. The highest rate of contribution is to elementary schools (69%), followed by high schools (65%), and middle schools (54%). Corporate donations also go to local universities (46%) and community colleges (33%).

Many philanthropic programs are not initiated by corporations or corporate foundations alone but as joint projects with other nonprofit organizations or local government agencies. Corporations active in philanthropy have frequent and close contacts with local nonprofit organizations. Nonprofits, in turn, also often consider private corporations as possible sources of funding. Over 89 percent of the corporations reported that they receive requests from local nonprofit organizations. About 47 percent have received enquiries from local government agencies about possibilities for funding and cooperation. Joint projects between corporations and the government often include signing of government contracts in development ventures; 37 percent of the corporations have had such cooperation with the government, of which 61 percent was with state governments and 53 percent was with local governments.

Over two-thirds of the nation's corporations have engaged in community development projects. Most of them have funded and supported local projects that are cause-related (71%), directly devoted to donations (64%), or designated to the disabled (46%). Corporations also play significant roles in developing local programs for sports (36%), schools (20%), housing (13%), and improving local roads (4.9%). On average, corporations in America cooperate with forty-eight local civic organizations and 6.3 local government departments by supporting local programs (72%), sponsoring events (50%), subsidizing local developments (29%), and funding federal programs (13%).

In-Depth Analyses of Corporate Giving: Getting behind the Numbers

I turn now to a deeper analysis of corporate giving in the United States, looking beyond the descriptive data on what corporations give to assess why they do what they do. I focus on three aspects of corporate giving—corporate giving locally, corporate giving internationally, and corporate giving in response to the September 11 attacks. I choose these three areas of giving because they loosely represent different orientations of corporate philanthropic programs. Corporate giving locally versus internationally indicates something about how much a corporation is oriented toward the local community in which it is embedded. This is an important question because, as I noted above, how corporations define the "communities" to which they are responsible is an ever changing question in the era of increasing global integration. How corporations respond to crises is important for understanding the overall profile of corporate philanthropy today.

Local versus International Giving

The means, standard deviations, and definitions for the variables included in this part of the chapter are in table 7.1.[12] First, I look at the total philanthropic giving of a corporation. In the Corporate-Community Relations Study, we also asked corporations what percentage of their philanthropic activity is directed to the local metropolitan area in which the corporation resides, so I analyze the determinants of this issue as well.[13] Third, I look at specific causes that corporations name as their philanthropic priorities. Here I look at whether a corporation gives to international causes and whether they made donations in response to the September 11 tragedies.[14]

At the organizational level, I control for the size of the organization. I use the natural log transformation of this variable, as I assume that the effect of size increases at a diminishing rate. I include dummy variables for whether the corporation is publicly traded, whether it is a multinational corporation, and whether the corporation is unionized. I also include dummy variables for whether the organization has an official policy articulating goals and practices surrounding corporate-community relations and whether it has an office that is "devoted solely to [philan-

12. As noted above, I include poststratification probability weights so that the sample population is approximately representative of the universe from which the sample was drawn, that is, business organizations in the United States.

13. For this outcome, we look at the actual percentage as an outcome. However, as a significant number of the cases are clustered within the range of 90–100 percent, we also look at this variable as a dichotomous outcome—those firms that directed greater than 90 percent of their philanthropic contributions to the local metropolitan areas in which they are headquartered, and those that direct 90 percent or less to causes outside of their area.

14. Serendipity and tragedy came together to create the unique data for this part of the study. After over a year of workup in the development of this corporate survey, our survey team was set to begin data collection on September 15, 2001. The events of September 11 caused an immediate shift in the landscape of corporate philanthropy. As a result of these events, we altered the survey, inserting two key questions in an attempt to understand the ways in which the September 11 events would change corporate philanthropic practices for the fiscal year 2001. The first question was "Has your company given any monetary gifts or donations in response to the September 11th tragedies at the World Trade Center and the Pentagon?" The second question was "What was the amount of those gifts or donations?" The answers to these questions are the dependent variables this study seeks to examine.

TABLE 7.1. **Determinants of Corporate Giving, Representative Sample of U.S. Corporations, 2002**

	Model I: Total Giving 2001 B/(SE)	Model II: Total Giving 2002 B/(SE)	Model III: % Local B/(SE)	Model IV: International B/(SE)	Model V: Sept. 11 B/(SE)
Size (ln)	519,389.25 (368,700.14)	814,578.85 * (344,153.57)	−1.17 (.92)	.31 *** (.07)	.26 *** (.07)
Multi-est.	1,037,727.38 (689,099.63)	879,601.07 (643,618.92)	6.99 *** (1.74)	−.08 (.15)	−.37 *** (.12)
Public	1,421,526.37 * (717,034.11)	1,345,071.51 * (675,576.93)	−2.90 (1.82)	.15 (.16)	.38 *** (.13)
Union	−3,028,701.68 * (1,271,905.71)	−2,717,625.25 * (1,235,395.47)	3.48 (3.30)	−.76 * (.38)	−.30 (.24)
Formal Office	7,313,134.30 * (888,201.39)	6,908,013.62 *** (829,684.82)	−3.79 (2.26)	1.06 *** (.17)	1.27 *** (.18)
Formal Policy	536,184.06 (703,053.98)	879,701.86 (669,471.11)	−3.22 (1.82)	.25 (.16)	.64 *** (.13)
Female-CEO	1,204,463.56 (1,927,819.32)	910,341.89 (1,871,726.62)	15.82 *** (5.24)	.13 (.49)	−1.32 *** (.40)
Fin. Svcs.	718,895.35 (1,600,289.21)	501,602.26 (1,355,530.06)	6.36 (3.75)	−.70 * (.30)	.28 (.27)
Manufacturing	1,661,323.98 * (784,187.72)	988,953.90 (736,858.81)	−3.03 (1.94)	−.64 *** (.17)	−.47 *** (.13)
Prof. Svcs.	−1,122,176.62 (1,059,850.44)	−1,570,839.55 (966,092.91)	−1.96 (2.51)	.05 (.20)	.13 (.17)
Retail	−1,676,061.03 (991,606.64)	−2,007,157.25 * (941,736.81)	4.30 (2.43)	−1.48 *** (.27)	−.10 (.16)
Union Density	124,813.63 * (49,955.63)	90,778.11 * (47,659.44)	0.10 (.12)	.01 (.01)	
Tax Rate		501,672.57 *** (107,302.47)	−1.07 *** (.28)	.10 *** (.03)	
Tristate					.81 *** (.18)
Constant	−5,245,722.02 *** (2,059,906.71)	−8,767,662.71 *** (1,988,200.23)	90.42 *** (5.30)	−3.87 *** (.43)	−1.25 *** (.38)
N	2,776	2,776	2,776	2,776	2,776 ***
R^2	.23	.37	.20		
Chi-square				178.36 ***	263.75

$*p < .05, **p < .01, ***p < .001$

thropic] activities." In the models presented below, I also control for sector based on 2-digit standard industrial classification codes; I include dummy controls for a corporation's location in manufacturing, wholesale and retail trade, and finance sectors.[15] I also expect that institutional environments shape corporate philanthropic practices, so I operation-

15. We also include dummy variables for the three oversampled cities as added controls to capture additional effects of this oversampling process.

alize variables relating to the institutional environment in three ways. First, one key way that states vary with respect to governance of the corporate sector is through local taxation: some states, such as Washington, have no corporate tax, while others levy corporate taxes (in New York, of more than 9 percent). I include a continuous variable ranging from 0–9.99 to capture the effects of the corporate tax rate of the state in which a corporation is headquartered. Second, I look at the union presence in the area that the corporation is headquartered. I measure this variable as union density (the percentage of full-time employees that are members of a union) in the metropolitan area. Third, for the September 11 model, I look at whether a corporation is headquartered in the tristate area.

Table 7.1 presents the results of these analyses, giving us a deeper sense of the characteristics that shape corporate giving, the percentage of giving directed toward a corporation's local metropolitan area, the probability that a corporation gives to international charities, and the probability that a corporation gave to September 11 causes.[16] Statistical significance in the models is designated by an asterisk, with additional asterisks representing higher levels of statistical significance.[17] The models are all multivariate models, meaning that when I discuss each effect, I am viewing the effect, holding all other variables in the model constant. Models I and II represent overall giving in 2001 and 2002, respectively. I will limit my discussion here to Model II, as it has most recent data, and the model also includes the local tax variable (though Model I is included here as comparative data on what corporations did in the previous year). There is a statistically significant relationship between organizational size and the amount a corporation gives. This is not a surprising finding: larger corporations have larger revenues, a higher profile, and they deal with larger sectors of society. Thus, the larger corporations are, the greater the burden of giving to the community becomes. This is not a linear effect, however: With each 1-point increase on a natural log scale, corporate philanthropic donations rise by a little over $800,000. In other words, as corporations grow from about 150 to 400 employees (5 and 6,

16. For the continuous variables I model these outcomes with the use of ordinary least squares analysis; for binary outcome variables, I employ logistic regression analysis.

17. The lowest statistical designation used here is the cutoff of 95% likelihood. In other words, with regard to the effects I discuss here, we can be at least 95% confident that this association is representative of the population from which the sample was drawn, that is, the population of business organizations in the United States.

respectively, on a natural log scale), their philanthropic budget will increase by about $800,000; as they grow from about 400 to 1,100 employees (6 and 7 on a natural log scale), another $800,000 is added to their budget; 1,100 to 3,000 (7 and 8, natural log scale), another $800,000; and so on. Holding other variables constant, publicly traded corporations have significantly larger philanthropic budgets than their privately held counterparts. In other words, comparing public and private corporations of the same size, same sector, same location, and so forth, the public corporation will have a philanthropic budget that is about $1.3 million larger than the private firm. Among the variables analyzed here, having a formal office that is devoted to the organization of a corporation's philanthropic activity has the single largest effect on corporate philanthropy: all other things being equal, corporations with philanthropy or CSR offices give $7 million more than their counterparts without formal offices. Corporations in the retail sector give about $2 million less than similar firms in other sectors.

Union density and the state corporate tax rate effects illuminate relationships between corporate philanthropic practices and the places in which they are headquartered. All other things being equal, union density increases the philanthropic practices by a small but nevertheless significant amount. For each percentage increase in union density in a given metropolitan area, corporations headquartered in that area will devote about $90,000 more to philanthropy. For example, comparing identical corporations (same size, sector, formal office, and so forth) in Atlanta (7.1% union density in 2001) and Chicago (17.9% union density in 2001), the Chicago corporation will devote about $1 million more in philanthropic resources than the identical corporation in Atlanta. The reasons behind this association are likely complex. A number of scholars have suggested that corporate philanthropy is largely a public relations phenomenon, as corporations seek to ingratiate themselves to the public through their charitable work.[18] In other work, I have extended this argument to speculate on the association between union density and philanthropic activity, arguing that corporations employ the philanthropic PR strategy as a defense against other community pressures. One very concrete community pressure that can be costly to corporations is the pressure from local unions for union contracts. Thus, corporations in highly unionized areas may be more aggressive about their philanthropic activ-

18. Many scholars have made this argument. See, for example, Burt 1983a.

ity than their counterparts in less unionized areas as a signal to the community that they are good citizens.

If the union density effects present somewhat of a puzzle, the effects of state corporate tax rates fit well with other research on philanthropic giving. As Model II shows, net of other effects, higher state corporate tax rates increase the overall levels of corporate philanthropy. Conventional wisdom often asserts that a reduction in taxes will lead to an increase in philanthropic and charitable giving.[19] The argument here is that a reduction in taxes (and thus a removal of the state from the allocation of resources for public goods) will free up resources for "grass-roots and community-based" fulfillment of the social contract. However, this view of the trade-off between taxes and charitable donations, while popular, is not supported by research. Indeed, a number of studies have shown that as taxation declines, so does philanthropic giving.[20] The argument most commonly advanced for this association is simple: with taxes, potential givers—individuals or corporations—have incentives to give because of tax write-offs; without taxes, there is no opportunity for write-offs and thus no incentive to give. As we see here, all other things being equal, corporate taxation has a significant and positive effect on corporate philanthropy, increasing the level of philanthropy by over $500,000 for each percentage increase in corporate tax. In other words, a corporation headquartered in New York, where the state corporate tax is 9.99 percent, will have a philanthropic budget about $5 million larger than an identical corporation (same size, sector, and so forth) in Washington, where there is no state corporate tax.

Turning now to Model III, I address the question of which factors are significant in the percentage of resources that a corporation directs locally, that is, to philanthropic activity in the metropolitan area in which the corporation is headquartered. All other things equal, organizations with multiple establishments in the same metropolitan area direct 7 per-

19. In his famous "1,000 Points of Light" statement, President George Bush (1989) declared that public goods should be fulfilled by a "readiness and ability of every individual and every institution in America to initiate action as 'a point of light'; meaningful one-to-one engagement in the lives of others is now required to overcome our most serious national problems." Arguing that charitable action and the fulfillment of public goods should be individual and community based rather than federally funded, Bush called for "a movement that is grassroots and community-based rather than devised in and imposed from Washington, a movement that does not compensate people with federal dollars for what should be an obligation of citizenship."

20. Burt 1983a; Levy and Shatto 1978; Bennett and Johnson 1980; Schwartz 1966; Bakija and Slemrod 1996, 2001; Bakija and Steuerle 1994; Bakija, Gale, and Slemrod 2003; Bakija and Gale 2003.

cent more of their total philanthropic budgets to their local areas than their counterparts with a single establishment. One of the most interesting findings that comes out of Model III is that corporations with a woman at the helm (including both female-owned businesses and public corporations with female CEOs) are significantly more oriented toward their local areas than firms run by men. Comparing corporations that are identical on all other fronts, the ones guided by women divide the philanthropic pie differently, directing resources locally at a rate 15 percent higher than identical corporations run by men. The other important finding that comes out of Model III is what I call the paradox of state activism in the area of corporate philanthropy. As we noted above, higher state corporate tax rates increase corporate philanthropy overall. However, those same tax rates also push corporations to direct their philanthropic resources elsewhere. So comparing again our imaginary identical corporations in New York and Washington, the New York corporation will have a philanthropic budget of about $5 million more than the Washington corporation, but of its overall budget it will devote about 10 percent less of its resources to the local area in which it is headquartered. In these extreme cases, the net effect for New York charities is still positive; however, in places that are not at opposite ends of the spectrum (as New York and Washington are), the trade-offs for the local community are less clear.

Model IV presents results from the analysis of international giving. Here we are dealing with the likelihood that a corporation will have international charities as part of their philanthropic portfolio.[21] All other things being equal, the larger a corporation is, the more likely it will be to give to international causes. For corporations that are average in every other category,[22] those of about 150 employees have only a 13 percent likelihood of being involved in international causes; corporations of 400 employees have a 17 percent likelihood; and so on. Even a large-scale multinational corporation of 150,000 has only about a 50 percent likelihood of having international charities as part of the philanthropic causes they support. Unions have a significant negative effect on giving to international causes: the average nonunionized corporation has about a 14.6 percent likelihood of giving to international causes, while

---

21. The numbers presented in Models IV and V are log-odds probabilities (or "logits") so they are not immediately interpretable as probabilities.

22. That is, varying size while all other values are constrained at the means.

the identical unionized organization has only about a 7.5 percent likelihood of supporting causes overseas. Similar to the union density effect introduced above, the likely logic behind this association is that unions pressure organizations to think first about their local communities before thinking about charitable causes elsewhere. Having a formal office devoted to charitable causes, on the other hand, significantly increases the likelihood of international engagement, moving organizations from 12 to 28 percent likelihood of charity in this area. Finally, fitting with the argument above about the implications of local corporate tax rates for local focus, as corporate tax rates rise, corporations are more likely to direct their resources elsewhere. Returning again to our imaginary identical corporations in New York and Washington, those in New York are more than twice as likely (19.7%) to support international causes than those in Washington (8.6%).

Finally, Model V shows the results of an analysis of corporate giving in response to the September 11 terrorist attacks. Because of the attacks, 2001 became a special year for philanthropy. More than half of corporations nationwide (67.52%) responded to the incident by giving donations to various foundations and organizations related to or affected by the attacks. Most of the $1.88 billion that flowed in following the attacks came from individual donations, with more than $1.5 billion pouring in before the end of 2001 alone. Corporate philanthropy generated about $410 million in the same period.[23] Organizational size, once again, had a statistically significant positive effect on giving in this area. All other things being equal, 62 percent of small corporations of about 150 employees contributed, while likelihoods rose steadily from there. Large-scale multinationals had about a 90 percent likelihood of giving something in response to the attacks. Publicly traded corporations gave at a rate of almost 70 percent, while an otherwise identical privately held corporation was about 60 percent likely to contribute. Having a formal office devoted to managing philanthropy increased the probability from 57 to 83 percent. Interestingly, again, female-led organizations were significantly less likely to contribute to 9/11 funds than their male-led counterparts (44% compared to 63%). One of the strongest predictors of giving in this area was location in the tristate area, which increased the probability of giving from 61 to 77 percent.

23. Carpenter 2002; Meadow 2005.

Conclusions

In this chapter, I have attempted to give a sense of the basic priorities and trends that guided corporate philanthropy in the early 2000s. As important as CSR is, especially in the era of the receding welfare state, quality data on the practices of corporations in this area are somewhat thin. Although some datasets on the practices of large-scale firms exist, such as the KLD dataset, these studies do not allow for a comparative sense of the differences between large-, medium-, and small-scale corporations. Drawing on data gathered in the Ford Foundation-funded Corporate-Community Relations Study, this chapter lays out the basic decisions of corporations of all sizes in this area. It is a representative sample and therefore, within a small margin of error (±2.7), a representative picture of corporate philanthropy in the United States today.

To be sure, corporate philanthropy is but one small part of the world of CSR. As we have attempted to show with this book, CSR covers many sets of practices and decisions that corporations make, and only a broad definition of CSR can truly place all of the facets of what it means to be a good corporate citizen on the agenda for corporations. From philanthropy and environmentalism to labor practices and accounting decisions, all are part of the CSR realm. Nevertheless, corporate philanthropy has long been a mainstay of the ways in which corporations conceive of their CSR practices. Accordingly, this chapter attempts to benchmark those practices for corporations of various sizes across the country.

In terms of the absolute and relative sizes of what corporations are giving, the amounts are actually quite small. As a percentage of profits, philanthropy represents a small portion of corporate earnings. For U.S. corporations, corporate giving represents less than 1 percent of profits; among the top 100 U.S. corporations, the largest percentages of profits given to philanthropic causes are Philip Morris (7.7%), State Farm (5.9%), Merck (2.9%), Wal-Mart (1.7%), and Sears (1.6%). All other top-100 U.S. corporations fell below the 1 percent threshold in 2002. And while some corporations are giving away in excess of $100 million a year, corporate philanthropy is dwarfed by governmental spending on social services. Nevertheless, corporate philanthropy can have a catalytic effect on specific social causes. As Michael McQuarrie's research on Cleveland shows, organizations such as Cleveland Tomorrow, which brought together corporate leaders from Cleveland to direct Cleveland corporations and foundations to focus on saving the city through investing in community development, have changed the social structure of that city. In Cleveland and nationally, corporate investment in communities did not transform inner cities across the United States, but it did change the risk structure enough that organizations such as Bank of America would eventually see these markets as profit opportunities as opposed to risks. In 1999, Bank of America committed itself to provide $750 billion over ten years to low-income communities. This commitment was a business decision, and it was not based on corporate philanthropy. However, corporate targeting of these areas certainly played a role in helping these communities to be viewed as more attractive investment opportunities. Another example might be the targeted corporate dollars that flowed into the arts over the course of the twentieth century and then were shifted toward other causes in the late 1990s. For decades, organizations such as the Metropolitan Opera relied on the stream of corporate dollars that supported the organization and then had to fundamentally shift their business model to find new sources of support.[24] In this case, declining corporate support put the institution itself at risk of survival. The main point here is that corporate philanthropy cannot replace public goods, but it can shift the balance in targeted areas. What corporations do with their philanthropic agendas can certainly have an impact on specific causes and specific organizations. In this chapter, I have simply attempted to explore what those philanthropic agendas are.

Appendix: Details of the Corporate-Community Relations Survey

In 2002, with funding from the Ford Foundation, the Social Science Research Council, and the University of California at Berkeley, the Survey Research Center surveyed three thousand corporations on their decisions and practices in the areas of social investment, the ways they align themselves with and support local governments and nonprofit organizations and, more generally, corporate social responsibility. The result was a unique, nationally representative social scientific survey on the prac-

24. Freedman 2003a, 2003b, 2003c.

tices of corporations in this area.[25] The Survey of Corporate-Community Relations examined the ways corporations interact with their local communities. With a goal of better understanding the role of the corporate sector in society, the study looked at charitable giving and philanthropy as the primary means of community involvement, but we also looked at the ways that corporations build alliances with local governments, the ways in which they have created new types of government-business partnerships in the area of low-income housing, and the ways in which they have helped transform the inner cities in which they are headquartered. Data collected in this study provided insight into how corporations see their roles in the community. After the survey was completed, over 150 individuals from nonprofit organizations, governmental agencies, and corporations were interviewed to give us a deeper sense of the ways that corporations and the organizations they fund make decisions surrounding these important issues. This body of in-depth qualitative data complements and guides our interpretations of the survey data.

In addition to the national sample, the survey focused in on three cities with diverse histories and economies: Cleveland, Seattle, and Atlanta. Companies from those three cities made up three-fourths of the sample we interviewed. The remaining one-fourth of the sample was drawn from the population of medium- and large-scale organizations in the fifty largest urban areas in the United States; the samples were drawn from Metropolitan Statistical Areas (MSAs). This sampling strategy allowed us to combine national patterns of corporate-community relations across the United States with an in-depth understanding of how corporations, nonprofit organizations, and governmental agencies in specific MSAs interact in the current era.[26]

Through telephone interviews with senior officials in charge of corporate decisions surrounding community relations and corporate social

---

25. The principal investigator for the study was Doug Guthrie. The project was funded by a grant from the Ford Foundation and supported administratively by the SSRC. The survey itself was carried out in collaboration with the Survey Research Center at the University of California, Berkeley, one of the premier survey research institutes in the country.

26. The sample was drawn from the Dun and Bradstreet Database of U.S. Organizations, with the sampling frame consisting of for-profit organizations of fifty or more employees in the fifty largest MSAs in the United States. The sample was stratified by size and by sector; the sector stratification approach was used to ensure a representation of organizations from a variety of important sectors, as defined by the 2-digit Standard Industrial Classification (SIC). Stratification by size was a little more complicated: it is likely that the practices of larger corporations have a greater impact than the practices of smaller corporations in the area of corporate giving, and it is likely that this relationship does not vary monotonically with size, so the survey also oversampled larger corporations.

TABLE 7A.1. **Means, standard deviations, and variable definitions**

	Mean	SD	Definition
Size (ln)	5.18	.87	Natural log of company size
Public	.29	.46	Company is publicly traded (yes = 1)
Union	.21	.41	Company has a union (yes = 1)
Female CEO	.91	.30	Company has a female CEO (yes = 1)
Business	.11	.32	Located in business services sector (yes = 1)
Professional	.20	.40	Located in professional services sector yes = 1)
Legal	.02	.15	Located in legal sector (yes = 1)
Financial	.06	.24	Located in financial services sector (yes = 1)
Retail	.16	.37	Located in retail sector (yes = 1)
Manuf./const.	.29	.45	Located in manufacturing/construction sector (yes = 1)
Union			
Density	14.80	6.48	Union density at the MSA level
Tax Rate	5.85	2.70	Corporate tax rate at the state level (range 0–9.99)
Tristate	.09	.29	Company is located in the tristate area (yes = 1)
Giving			
Structure			
Office	.18	.39	Company has separate office for giving (yes = 1)
Policy	.35	.48	Company has formal policy for giving (yes = 1)
Foundation	.29	.45	Company has separate giving foundation (yes = 1)
Donations '01	$1,394,949	$9,661,288	Total amount given in 2001
Donations '02	$1,599,685	$10,731,957	Total amount given in 2002
Sept. 11	.61	.49	Made donation to 9/11 (yes = 1)
9/11 Donation	$298,588	$1,203,254	Total amount given to 9/11 fund

investment, we asked a wide range of questions about company involvement in the community. Any involvement at all, or even an absence of involvement, was of interest. Much of the survey focused on corporate philanthropic activities and charitable giving, though there are many other questions about corporate ties to nonprofit sectors and governmental agencies. The demographic section of the survey asked for data describing the company: size, revenues, nature of the business, growth history, age of company, union status, and labor force. These data were supplemented with accounting data on each corporation compiled by the accounting firm of Dun and Bradstreet. The sampling procedures and probabilistic weighting techniques allow us to illuminate trends in corporate practices across the country and within the specific areas surveyed to within ±2.7 percent.[27] Our sample is representative of the population of medium- and large-scale corporations in the United States. This

27. The margin of error, which is based on the sample size and the sampling technique employed, applies primarily to percentages reported herein. Where data are not reported percentages but actual

full population of corporations is a group of some 380,000 business organizations that employ at least fifty workers. In the study we discuss here, we sampled heavily on larger organizations, but then weighted the data such that the population we are describing is representative of the whole. The results I present here give us an in-depth picture of how this population of organizations shape and are shaped by the communities in which they are embedded.

Table 7A.1 presents the means and standard deviations of the variables used in the multivariate analysis.

References

Bakija, Jon, and William Gale. 2003. "Effects of Estate Tax Reform on Charitable Giving." *Tax Notes,* June 23, 1841.

Bakija, Jon, William Gale, and Joel Slemrod. 2003. "Charitable Bequests and Taxes on Inheritances and Estates: Aggregate Evidence from across States and Time." *American Economic Review Papers and Proceedings.*

Bakija, Jon, and Joel Slemrod. 1996. *Taxing Ourselves: A Citizen's Guide to the Debate over Taxes.* Cambridge: MIT Press.

———. 2001. "Growing Inequality and Decreased Tax Progressivity." In *Inequality and Tax Policy,* edited by Kevin Hassett and R. Glenn Hubbard. Washington, D.C.: American Enterprise Institute.

Bakija, Jon, and Eugene Steuerle. 1994. *Retooling Social Security for the 21st Century.* Washington, D.C.: Urban Institute.

Bennett, J. R., and M. H. Johnson. 1980. "Corporate Contributions: Some Additional Considerations." *Public Choice* 35, no. 2: 137–45.

Burt, Ronald. 1983a. "Corporate Philanthropy as a Cooptive Relation." *Social Forces* 62, no. 2: 419–49.

———. 1983b. *Corporate Profits and Cooptation: Networks of Market Constraints and Directorate Ties in the American Economy.* New York: Academic Press.

Fremont-Smith, Marion. 1972. *Philanthropy and the Business Corporation.* New York: Russell Sage Foundation.

Fry, L. W., G. Keim, and R. Meiners. 1982. "Corporate Contributions: Altruistic or For Profit?" *Academy of Management Journal* 25, no. 1: 94–106.

Galaskiewicz, Joseph. 1979. *Exchange Networks and Community Politics.* Beverly Hills: Sage.

———. 1985a. *Social Organization of an Urban Grants Economy: A Study of Business Philanthropy and Nonprofit Organizations 1981.* Orlando, Fla.: Academic Press.

---

projections of trend data based on relationships among variables (for example, the relationship between size and level of giving), the results rely on more advanced econometric analyses.

———. 1985b. "Professional Networks and the Institutionalization of a Single Mindset." *American Sociological Review* 50, no. 5: 639–58.

———. 1989. "Corporate Contributions to Charity: Nothing More than a Marketing Strategy?" *Philanthropic Giving: Studies in Varieties and Goals,* edited by Richard Magat, 246–60. New York: Oxford University Press.

———. 1991. "Making Corporate Actors Accountable: Institution Building in Minneapolis-St. Paul." In *The New Institutionalism in Organizational Analysis,* edited by Walter Powell and Paul DiMaggio, 293–310. Chicago: University of Chicago Press.

———. 1997. "An Urban Grants Economy Revisited: Corporate Charitable Contributions in the Twin Cities, 1979–1981, 1987–89." *Administrative Science Quarterly* 42: 445–71.

Levy, F. K., and G. M. Shatto. 1978. "The Evaluation of Corporate Contributions." *Public Choice* 33, no. 1: 9–27.

Schwartz, R. A. 1966. "Corporate Philanthropic Contributions." *Journal of Finance* 23: 479–97.

PART III

Boundary Crossing: Contemporary Recombinations of Markets, States, and Nonprofit Organizing

Whether one views nonprofit organizations through the lens of government relations or market influences, the picture reveals ongoing conflicts over the appropriate boundaries between different forms of social organization. These challenges and experiments involve not only the location of these boundaries—is this a legitimately not-for-profit and therefore tax-exempt organization?—but also their porosity. To what extent can nonprofit organizations engage in politics? How far can corporations and business leaders go in imposing market logics on the nonprofit sector? What new possibilities can be realized by activists and entrepreneurs weaving together different organizational capacities and resources?

In recent decades, these ambiguous categories of market, state, and nonprofit domain have become still more unsettled by a fundamental change in the philosophy of governing at the federal level. The great expansion of federal participation in social provision during the 1960s did not conform to the model of building explicitly public institutions supported by explicitly public funds. Instead, as Nicole Marwell details, much of the War on Poverty was carried out by channeling federal funds to local agencies. By privileging a new kind of organization—the Community Action Agency—this federal policy shift decoupled the local delivery of public services from elected officials at the state, county, and municipal levels. The resulting backlash from elected officials then

worked its way through the heightened commitment to privatization and
devolution that was central to the Reagan Revolution and the ensuing
conservative shift in the social welfare politics of the 1990s. The result
has been a new opportunity to forge exchange relationships among beneficiaries, nonprofit organizations, and elected officials that echoes the
earlier arrangements of patronage politics criticized by Progressive reformers at the beginning of the century.

Local politicians have not been alone in discovering the opportunities afforded by these increasingly fragmented and porous boundaries
between government, markets, and nonprofit organizations. The privatization and devolution of social provision analyzed by Marwell have been
accompanied by the creation of new roles for business to participate in
publicly supported programs for the poor and working poor. Focusing
on the development of low-income housing programs in Cleveland, Michael McQuarrie illuminates the role of nonprofit organizations within
"heterarchic governance," or systems that operate by linking together
institutions with very different practices and goals. Just as Lyndon Johnson's War on Poverty created new local actors as partners (the Community Action Agencies), so Cleveland's business elites discovered a de-
tour around the city council through the establishment of community
development corporations. In a process of innovation and improvisation spanning decades, these CDCs transformed one of their seemingly
worthless assets—tax credits held by a not-for-profit organization—into
a market for corporate investment that fueled construction of low- and
moderate-income housing and also sustained important alliances between the CDCs and local politicians.

Taken together, the chapters by Marwell and McQuarrie underscore
the promise of replacing the framework of "the nonprofit sector" as a
distinct domain governed by its own rules and logics of appropriateness
with greater attention to the role of nonprofit organizations as mediating
among a variety of different actors and institutions. The final two chapters expand this theme, demonstrating how nonprofit organizations or
partnerships may have the capacity of crosscutting major social divides or
meeting crises with flexibility and improvisation that cannot be matched
by the entrenched institutions of government, business, or even established nonprofit organizations. In part, this flexibility reflects the capacity of the nonprofit form to be infused with different cultural themes, notably those drawn from religion. In Knoxville, Tennessee, for example, a
prosperous, suburban, predominantly white megachurch partnered with

a new, urban, predominantly African American congregation committed to community building. Omri Elisha explores how the template of "sister churches" sustained a financial partnership in housing construction while also cloaking many divisions of race and class through a language of "accountability," both Christian and financial.

For Alyshia Gálvez, this capacity to improvise and mediate—to *resolver*—is central to understanding the ability of a Catholic religious confraternity to emerge as a key link between undocumented workers and the collapse of the World Trade Center towers on September 11, 2001. Until that moment, Asociación Tepeyac had been one of many small, struggling, nonprofit groups that responded to the multiple needs of the diverse immigrant communities in New York City. In the aftermath of September 11, however, they became a central node attempting to link an unacknowledged group of victims—the undocumented workers in the towers—to the streams of relief available from larger charities and government agencies. But whereas the recipients of public services described by Marwell could leverage their status as voters, Asociación Tepeyac worked to secure the standing of noncitizens and undocumented workers, of widows without marriage licenses seeking death certificates for vanished husbands.

Across these four different settings and diverse policy concerns, these chapters document the potential for nonprofit organizations to mediate between different modes of social organization and fragmented constituencies. In the process, the nonprofit organizations themselves are often transformed as they acquire new sources of support and possibly lose older constituencies, as they shift from the improvisational tactics of outsider challengers to elaborating the routines required for managing regular relationships with major government institutions, firms, and foundations. Thus, nonprofit organizations appear as sites of change, agents of change, and objects of change, providing a lens through which we can view the ongoing transformation of social institutions.

CHAPTER EIGHT

Privatizing the Welfare State: Nonprofit Community-Based Organizations as Political Actors

Nicole P. Marwell

Most current sociological theory about public social provision is built on studies of income transfers from governments to individuals, and focuses on the factors affecting how nations and subnational governments set income transfer *policy* (Amenta 1993). This research has answered important questions about how much public money is devoted to income-based social provision, what categories of people have access to public income support, why amounts and access change over time, and so on.[1] Because these studies do not account for the large amounts of public money devoted to direct services, however (e.g., Bradley et al. 2003, 199), they are incomplete guides to understanding the profile of present-day social provision.

This is especially true if we are concerned with the social welfare of our poorest citizens. The poor receive only a small proportion of income transfers (Ellwood 1988; Katz 1989), and these are usually of the relatively small, means-tested kind. As such, services represent an especially important part of the social benefit package for the post-transfer poor, who in the United States constitute 15 percent of the total population—the largest proportion in all the industrialized democracies (Moller et al.

---

1. Amenta 1998; Amenta and Halfmann 2000; Bradley et al. 2003; Cauthen and Amenta 1996; Esping-Andersen 1990; Heclo 1974; Hicks and Misra 1993; Huber, Ragin, and Stephens 1993; Korpi 1983; Orloff and Skocpol 1984; Pierson 1995; Piven and Cloward 1971; Skocpol 1992; Soss et al. 2001; Soule and Zylan 1997; Stephens 1979; Weir, Orloff, and Skocpol 1988; Winston 2002; Zylan and Soule 2000.

2003). With the five-year time limits on cash assistance imposed by the 1996 welfare reform, the importance of social provision services to the poor in the United States will continue to rise.

Government is not the primary provider of state-sponsored social provision services in the United States. Rather, private, nonprofit organizations (NPOs) under contract to government deliver the majority of these services (Hodgkinson and Weitzman 1986; Katz 1996; Salamon 1995; Smith and Lipsky 1993). Until very recently, however, studies of the welfare state rarely addressed the role of NPOs in social provision. There are two principal reasons for this. First, service-delivery NPOs have little to do with the formation or implementation of policies on income transfers, the principal object of analysis for most social provision studies. Second, most studies of the U.S. welfare state focus on historical periods in which large-scale delivery of public services via NPOs did not exist: the turn of the twentieth century (Clemens 1997; Orloff and Skocpol 1984; Skocpol 1992) and the New Deal (Amenta, Dunleavy, and Bernstein 1994; Cauthen and Amenta 1996; Gilbert and Howe 1991; Liska et al. 1999).

Recent U.S. trends in social provision policy, however, make it necessary to add a consideration of publicly funded direct services to the current focus on income transfers. Beginning with Reagan-era efforts to shrink the size of the federal government, two far-reaching national policy shifts—so-called privatization and devolution—have greatly altered the face of social provision, especially for the poor. *Privatization* refers to the contracting out of public service provision to private third parties. *Devolution* is the transfer of decisions over the details of spending public funds from the federal government to states, counties, and municipalities.

Privatization largely has been ignored in studies of the U.S. welfare state because income transfers—the basis of most extant work—have not been privatized. In contrast, devolution *has* received attention in recent welfare state analyses, primarily in studies of welfare reform. A number of recent studies have examined state-level policy responses to the 1996 Personal Responsibility and Work Opportunities Reconciliation Act, using it as a new opportunity to examine welfare-state-policy formation in comparative context (Breaux et al. 2002; Meyers, Gornick, and Peck 2002; Rogers-Dillon and Skrentny 1999; Soule and Zylan 1997; Zylan and Soule 2000). Again, however, the focus of these studies has been on how social provision *policy* about *income transfers* is made, rather than examining the *allocative* processes that are essential to understanding state-sponsored *direct services*.

Privatization and devolution have had significant effects on the delivery of social provision services to the poor. The move to privatization has driven a sharp rise in government spending on NPOs. For example, from 1974 to 1995 federal public support to NPOs increased from $23 billion to $175 billion (Johns Hopkins Nonprofit Sector Project 2000; Salamon 1995). There has been a concomitant rise in the size of the nonprofit sector: the most recent figures (Johns Hopkins Nonprofit Sector Project 2000, 1995 data) show NPOs account for $567 billion in annual revenues (about 7 percent of national GDP) and employ 8.6 million full-time workers (nearly half the size of the public sector workforce). For its part, devolution has relocated the site of decisions about how to spend these enormous funds. As the federal government increasingly relies on block grants to the states, state- and municipal-level officials have increased responsibility for deciding how to spend these dollars, including which NPOs receive government support (Bishop 2006; Caputo 1994; Conlan 1998; Fellowes and Rowe 2004; Gainsborough 2003; Lambright and Allard 2004; Winston 2002).

Understanding service-based social provision thus requires consideration of theoretical questions and analytical problems different from those faced by analyses of income transfers. Cash transfer policies are based on standardized eligibility rules, have been classified as entitlements, and come directly to individuals in the form of automatic payments. In contrast, the delivery of direct services is a zero-sum game, and very often the relationship between government and citizens is indirect. Government agencies have fixed sums available to support services, regardless of the level of citizen need, and citizens' ability to access services depends not only on their eligibility but also on the location of service providers and the ability of individuals to find providers. Thus, a key object of analysis in any study of service-based social provision must be the bureaucratic process of *service allocation,* not just the political process of *policy formation* (see Austin 2003; Bockmeyer 2003; Gronbjerg 2001; Longoria 1999; McConnell et al. 2003; Provan and Milward 1994, 1995; Smith 1996).

The Rise of Community-Based Organizations in U.S. Social Provision

U.S. social provision has long been a joint public-private enterprise, with oscillations over time in the availability of assistance via each of these sectors (Katz 1996). For much of U.S. history, according with prevailing ideas about the divided responsibilities of federalism, public funds to private (usually nonprofit) service providers came from state and local governments—not the federal government (Hall 1992; Salamon 1995; Smith and Lipsky 1993). By the early 1960s, however, the visibly growing poverty and segregation of African American and Latino urban ghettos spurred President Lyndon Johnson to search for policy solutions to the era's rising race-based inequality. The Economic Opportunity Act of 1964 (also known as the War on Poverty) was Johnson's effort to use federal power to challenge state and local foot-dragging around this issue.

Much has been written about the accidental, contradictory, and problematic aspects of Title II of the War on Poverty: the Community Action Program. In an unusual move, the federal government declined to send Community Action dollars to the states as grants-in-aid. Instead, these funds were allocated to newly established, independent Community Action Agencies (CAAs), which operated at the municipal or county level. CAAs took different legal forms, including public-private corporations and public agencies, but the majority were established as independent, nonprofit organizations run by volunteer boards of directors (Clark 2000, 27). CAA boards set antipoverty policy for their local areas, and then sent funds to lower-level nonprofit organizations—for example, at the neighborhood level in cities—to implement antipoverty programs (Clark 2000; Levitan 1969; Vanecko 1969). While the CAA boards usually contained key stakeholders from government and the old-line charitable sector, representatives of each locality's poor population also served. The Community Action Program thus had both policy and political purposes.

The federal charge to the CAAs was to attack poverty on two levels: by *delivering services* that would help poor people improve their socioeconomic circumstances; and by *organizing the poor* to demand greater attention to their needs from government and the private sector. The service delivery component meant that public dollars would bypass the usual state and municipal channels in favor of the independent CAAs, thereby reaching underserved populations—usually African Americans, Mexican Americans, and Puerto Ricans. In the political arena, Community Action meant using federal expenditures bequeathed by a Democratic administration to leverage political support from ghetto residents (Clark 2000; Gillette 1996; Piven and Cloward 1971; Sundquist 1969).

To the consternation of the architects of the War on Poverty, however, the Community Action Program quickly became a lesson in the difficulties of controlling state and local politics from Washington, D.C. Governors and mayors bristled at the growing organizing successes of neighborhood organizations funded by the CAAs, and feared being thrown out of office by newly mobilized, mostly poor and minority voters (Andrews 2001; Gillette 1996; Quadagno 1994). After three years of federally sponsored critique of and protests against city and state government practices, mayors, governors, and state and municipal legislators had finally had enough. Working with their congressional representatives, the lower levels of the system struck a crippling blow to the federal program. In 1967, Congress passed the Green amendment to the Economic Opportunity Act of 1964, requiring that Community Action funds only be released to CAAs that had been approved by the elected heads of local government. This meant that CAAs with radical or critical agendas—especially those that sought to fundamentally reshape the workings of public agencies or private corporations—would not be certified as eligible to receive federal funds (Clark 2000; Eisinger 1969).

The political scientist Charles Hamilton has argued that the disconnection of the CAAs from electoral politics left them vulnerable to the Green Amendment and other changes in the policy and funding parameters of the Community Action Program (Hamilton 1979). Unlike the nineteenth-century political machine, whose patron-client relationships established a strong link between service provision and electoral mobilization (Banfield and Wilson 1963; Gosnell 1937; Merton 1967; Riordan 1948), Hamilton argued that the CAAs developed only a "patron-recipient" relationship with local residents, distributing benefits that were not contingent on any reciprocal behavior. This was the fatal flaw of the Community Action Program, he argues, as "a political strategy that fails to concentrate heavily on the stakes of the electoral process means that groups not involved electorally will always be in demand-making, benefit-seeking, and invariably subordinated positions" (Hamilton 1979, 226).

Government controls public resource allocation, and elected officials are the decision makers within government. Without representation at that table—which might have been won through electoral organizing—Community Action groups were unable to participate in the governmental bargaining process. Instead, their main tool for influencing resource allocation decisions was popular protest directed toward government (Moynihan 1969; Quadagno 1994), and this proved to be a short-lived strategy for success. By the end of the 1960s, Congress cut Community Action funds dramatically, and soon ended the program completely. Despite its demise, however, the Community Action Program left an important lasting legacy: a set of nonprofit community-based organizations (CBOs) capitalized by public (largely federal) funds, and ready to continue work on behalf of the poor.

I use the term "CBO" to refer to nonprofit groups organized around a particular geographic place ("community"), such as an urban neighborhood. CBOs aim to increase attention to the needs of disadvantaged residents of their geographic place—i.e., "community members"—who are understood to be receiving insufficient resources and consideration from government and market entities. They are characterized by the significant participation of "community members" in the organizations' daily activities, e.g., as staff, volunteers, or members of the board of directors.[2]

In the remainder of this chapter, I demonstrate how trends toward privatization and devolution have made CBOs a new option for the exchange of service provision and electoral activity that was performed so well by the political machine, but did not occur in the Community Action Program. The machine built its reliable voting constituencies through the mechanisms of patronage and party organization, usually via a set of local political clubs (Erie 1988; Gosnell 1937; Wilson 1962). The present-day context of a weak or absent machine, however, makes the task of creating identifiable, reliable constituencies at the local level much more difficult (Freedman 1994; Guterbock 1980; Ware 1985). I argue that today's nonprofit CBOs are structurally positioned to fill the gap left by defunct political party organizations in poor neighborhoods. Their cultivation of electoral strength results in the generation of additional government financial support, which is vital to CBO survival and expansion.

Data and Methods

Despite the importance of CBOs to social provision in the United States, we know very little about how public dollars actually end up in these

---

2. For a more detailed definition of CBOs, see Marwell (2004b).

organizations. Answering such questions is done most convincingly by looking closely at how such processes operate on the ground, as in participant observation.[3] I use this method to examine the work of CBOs that are providing publicly funded direct services to needy citizens.

The evidence presented here is drawn from a field study conducted from May 1997 until September 2000 in a low-income, majority-Latino area of New York City (Marwell 2004b, 2007). The study area's population was about 65 percent Latino and about 35 percent poor. The first fifteen months of the study involved intensive participant observation at eight local CBOs. I worked as a volunteer in each of the organizations for a half day each week. Volunteer work was staggered over the fifteen months, such that I volunteered continuously in each CBO for a period of six to nine months. I also attended a wide variety of neighborhood events, community meetings, and family gatherings, in addition to accompanying staff and participants of the CBOs on trips and events outside the study area.

At the conclusion of the intensive fieldwork period, I carried out a series of eighty network data interviews with staff members and clients of the eight study organizations. During the four months it took to complete the interviews, I checked in with the study organizations on a regular basis and continued to attend neighborhood events and gatherings. I then largely withdrew from the field for approximately eight months, although I did maintain occasional contact with most of the study organizations. I returned to the field in September 1999 as part of a separate research project,[4] and resumed data collection until September 2000.

Community-Based Organizations and Electoral Politics: The Triadic Exchange

In previous work, I have discussed the wide range of activities carried out by CBOs in the study area (Marwell 2004b, 2007). Here, I focus on the aspect of CBO work that is most relevant to the themes of this book: how CBOs are structurally positioned to operate in the electoral

3. See Gans (1999) for an important methodological discussion of participant observation and other qualitative methods often grouped under the umbrella term "ethnography."
4. The Second Generation in Metropolitan New York Project, a study of young adults from the second generation of the "new" immigration (Kasinitz, Mollenkopf, and Waters 2004; Marwell 2004a).

arena and how they have clear incentives to do so in order to fulfill their service-provision missions. Almost no existing research addresses CBOs and elections, focusing instead on the service provision and community-building activities of these groups (Chaskin 2001; De Souza Briggs, Mueller, and Sullivan 1997; Gronbjerg 2001; Halpern 1995; Hodgkinson and Weitzman 1986; Leavitt and Saegert 1990; Portney and Berry 1997; Saegert, Thompson, and Warren 2001; Salamon 1995; Smith and Lipsky 1993; Von Hassell 1996). The primary reason for this gap is that the nonprofit law *explicitly prohibits* CBOs from engaging in most forms of politics, especially partisan electoral politics. Without violating this law, however, CBOs can in fact conduct activities that have electoral impacts, and they do so in order to influence the politics of public resource allocation for social provision.[5]

Public agencies charged with allocating government contracts for various social provision services usually fall under the direct control of the executive—e.g., mayor, governor—which means executives have the capacity to control contract decisions. Powerful legislators also may influence these decisions as part of their bargaining with the executive to pass policy changes or other legislation. Politicians need to win elections in order to stay in office. By engaging in electoral organizing and by producing reliable voting constituencies, CBOs can pressure these political actors to make favorable contract allocation decisions.

The political machine organized voters by distributing patronage through a direct exchange between voter and party. CBOs, however, are explicitly prohibited from engaging in this kind of exchange, which would entail fusing the CBO with the political party, thus jeopardizing the CBO's legal nonprofit status. Data from my research show that CBOs can engage in a more complicated—and technically legal—resources-for-votes exchange. This is a three-way, indirect exchange among CBO, client/voter, and elected official (see figure 8.1).

In this exchange triad, the CBO serves as the fulcrum through which patronage resources are distributed and client/voters are organized. The CBO is a necessary component of the primary exchange between the

---

5. CBO electoral political activity is distinct from policy advocacy or protest movements, both of which are legally permitted by CBOs under section 501(c)4 of the Internal Revenue Code, and represent the participation of CBOs in more generalized processes of political voice than the electoral organizing discussed here (see, e.g., Goetz 1993; Portney and Berry 1997; Saegert, Thompson, and Warren 2001; Warren 2001).

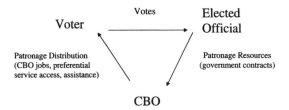

FIGURE 8.1. Triadic Exchange.

political entity—the elected official—and the individual client/voter. To-day's elected officials, unlike their predecessors from the political machine period, no longer control significant divisible benefits that can be distributed to client/voters, such as patronage jobs. In the triadic exchange, the CBO holds and distributes benefits to client/voters, but the elected official is the conduit through which resources for distribution—government contracts—come to the CBO. In essence, CBOs are structurally positioned to replace political party organizations.

This replacement has been partly the result of the dramatic decline in resources that are controlled by political parties. For example, civil service reform has significantly reduced the number of jobs under the direct control of party organizations (Erie 1988; Freedman 1994; Moynihan and Wilson 1964). The concomitant decline of party organizations—usually linked to resource depletion—has been well documented (Erie 1988; Guterbock 1980; Jones-Correa 1998; Ware 1985). In contrast, CBOs have seen the resources under their control expand with the increasing privatization of public services (Salamon 1995). CBO patronage resources now include jobs in the CBO itself and in its related efforts, preferential access to CBO services, and other kinds of assistance, including help with navigating public service bureaucracies.

The proposed model of CBOs as practitioners of a new machine politics must be understood within a wider set of political and organizational practices, illustrated in figure 8.2. The bottom half of figure 8.2 captures the local system of relationships and practices between the CBO and its individual client/voters. The triadic exchange only becomes complete, however, when it connects to the top half of figure 8.2—via the relationship between CBO and elected official.

This completion of the triadic exchange activates the processes described in the top half of figure 8.2. It should be noted that not all CBOs

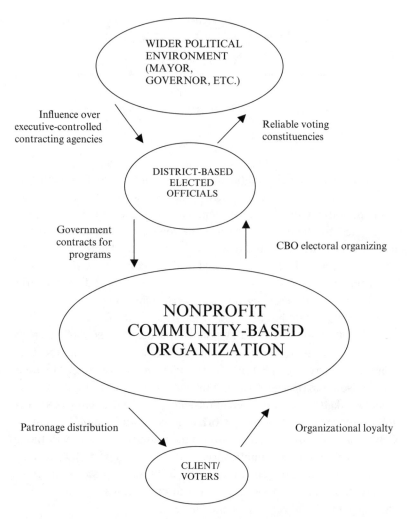

FIGURE 8.2. Triadic exchange.

choose to complete the triadic exchange. In those cases, there is no link to processes represented in the top half of figure 8.2: the broader political system in which the triadic exchange is embedded. Here, the lower-level electoral districts in which CBOs are located (e.g., city council, state Assembly, state Senate districts) connect to higher, aggregated levels of the polity (e.g., city, state, nation). The top half of figure 8.2 includes the position of each of the constituent elements in this process and specifies the exchange relations that link them.

The Triadic Exchange in Operation

Successfully engaging the triadic exchange depends upon a CBO's ability to cultivate, maintain, and turn out a reliable voting constituency in elections. Of the eight CBOs I studied in north Brooklyn, only one has chosen to engage in the kind of constituency work that the triadic exchange requires: the Ridgewood-Bushwick Senior Citizens Council (hereafter Ridgewood-Bushwick). The key elected official in this process is New York State assemblymember Vito Lopez, who founded Ridgewood-Bushwick in 1976. When Lopez was elected to the Assembly in 1984, he resigned from Ridgewood-Bushwick, but he has maintained his position as de facto head of the organization up until the present day. Lopez also is the head of Ridgewood-Bushwick's "shadow" political institution—the Bushwick Democratic Club—under whose auspices the most direct of Ridgewood-Bushwick's electoral politics work is performed.

Through its service provision and employment activities, Ridgewood-Bushwick has placed Lopez at the head of a reliable voting constituency with considerable appeal in the wider political environment. First, it is a relatively large group of voters as voter networks go. In most elections, Lopez's political club can deliver about three thousand votes in a district of the city that usually turns out only about five thousand voters. Although this may seem like a small absolute number of votes for a citywide or statewide contest, the number should be seen in the context of a severely diminished capacity for delivering blocs of voters at all. The increasing disconnection of voters from party or other political organizations, combined with the importance of media-based voting appeals, has rendered constituencies such as Lopez's fairly uncommon. Thus, there is added value to capturing even these relatively small-number constituencies.

In addition, the political context of New York City in the 1990s made these constituencies even more valuable, given that the city's mayor, Rudolph Giuliani, was a Republican in a heavily Democratic city. In both his election (1993) and reelection (1997) campaigns, Giuliani's margins of victory were relatively small. Delivering otherwise Democratic voters to a Republican candidate—even in small numbers—thus represented an important contribution, for which rewards were forthcoming. Lopez was the first major Democratic elected official to cross party lines and endorse Giuliani for reelection. Lopez maintained a good relationship with the mayor throughout his tenure.

Lopez's reliable voting constituency also is of interest to citywide, statewide, and national officials because of its ethnic composition. Lopez's voters are primarily members of minority groups, particularly Latinos—mostly of Puerto Rican and Dominican descent. With the rapid growth of the Latino population, the "Latino vote" has recently become a voting segment of much interest to politicians both in New York and nationwide (DeSipio 1996). Lopez certainly recognizes this interest, and, in partnership with Ridgewood-Bushwick, has organized a group called Brooklyn Unidos (Brooklyn United), which he bills as "the largest group of Latino leaders in New York City." This organization represents a clear public announcement that his constituency is a Latino one. Brooklyn Unidos operates under the nonprofit umbrella of Ridgewood-Bushwick.

Educating Client/Voters

Engaging the triadic exchange begins in the bottom half of figure 8.2: in the relationship between the CBO and its client/voters. Ridgewood-Bushwick has two sets of client/voters: organizational staff members and organizational clients. Ridgewood-Bushwick operates some fifty separate programs and organizations, offering cradle-to-grave services. To deliver them all, Ridgewood-Bushwick employs over fifteen hundred people. Ridgewood-Bushwick uses its job opportunities to involve local residents in its operations, and to cultivate and reward their loyalty. These jobs span a wide range, including superintendents at Ridgewood-Bushwick-managed buildings, tenant organizers, GED teachers, receptionists, social workers, home attendants, and others.

Many of these employees also are local residents. This is key to transforming organizational staff into reliable voters: if a Ridgewood-Bushwick employee cannot vote in local district elections, the job is wasted patronage. There is strong recognition of this fact, such that if an employee moves out of the area, he or she often maintains voter registration at the address of a family member who lives in the old neighborhood.[6] In addition to counting on staff members' own votes, Ridgewood-

6. Not all Ridgewood-Bushwick employees are local residents. Many professional jobs—housing development, legal assistance, accounting, social work—are filled by outsiders. It is important for Ridgewood-Bushwick that qualified workers fill these jobs because organizational competence is a necessity for CBOs if they want to continue receiving government contracts. I myself—a relatively unknown quantity, but, as a graduate student, identified as someone with a high level of education—was of-

Bushwick relies on staff to help with the arduous tasks of grassroots campaigning, including creating lists of reliable voters,[7] calling voters before Election Day, and turning out voters on Election Day.

For a large core group of Ridgewood-Bushwick staff, the relationship between working at Ridgewood-Bushwick and participating in the organization's electoral politics efforts is well understood. Explicit electoral activities cannot take place on Ridgewood-Bushwick premises or on Ridgewood-Bushwick time: nonprofit law prohibits this. Instead, the Bushwick Democratic Club, whose members are nearly all affiliated with Ridgewood-Bushwick (either as employees or clients), performs the electoral piece of the triadic exchange. Ridgewood-Bushwick is officially closed on Election Days, and many staff members instead congregate at the political club. There is a strong expectation of this behavior, as noted in this excerpt from my fieldnotes:

> [About three weeks before the 1997 mayoral election], I ask [one of the Ridgewood-Bushwick employees] what employees from Ridgewood-Bushwick will be doing on Election Day. He says that of course they'll be at the political club [Bushwick Democratic Club], working there. I ask "that's not required, is it?" and he smiles, says ironically, "of course not." The implication is clearly that employees are expected to show up and work. I ask what would happen if someone didn't go. He says he wouldn't necessarily lose his job, but it certainly wouldn't help him hold onto it. Again, he has the ironic smile, though the implication is a bit less clear. [This employee] is always careful not to give me any directly damning quotations when I talk to him. (*Author's field notes, October 18, 1997*)

Fieldwork on this and several other Election Days confirmed that many Ridgewood-Bushwick employees—on this day in the role of members of the Bushwick Democratic Club—spent upward of twelve hours going door-to-door throughout the neighborhood to pull out voters for favored candidates. Many of the doors they knocked at belong to people

---

fered jobs at Ridgewood-Bushwick numerous times. The number of jobs filled by outsiders is relatively small, however, and some Ridgewood-Bushwick professionals are also local residents.

7. Most political campaigns in New York City purchase these lists, which identify registered voters who have voted in recent primary and general elections. Campaigns usually target these voters, rather than the general public, through mailings and phone calls before Election Day and door knocking on Election Day itself. The Bushwick Democratic Club compiles and maintains these lists itself, rather than purchasing them.

who also are Ridgewood-Bushwick clients, and the value to the triadic exchange of staff members' role ambiguity on this day is clear.

Ridgewood-Bushwick staff have multiple opportunities to learn about the relationship between engaging in electoral politics and securing government contracts to fund organizational activities. Their daily job tasks are embedded within a continual discourse about government funding and the political processes that affect contract allocations. Ridgewood-Bushwick clients receive similar messages about the connections between political activity and service availability, but usually in more public forums, such as gatherings to commemorate new Ridgewood-Bushwick services or coverage of Ridgewood-Bushwick's work in its community newspaper, the *Bushwick Observer.*

During the fieldwork period, I observed numerous events to celebrate the opening of new Ridgewood-Bushwick services. These events always featured Assemblyman Lopez as keynote speaker, and frequently attracted actors from the wider political environment. Ridgewood-Bushwick organizational leaders and Assemblyman Lopez always made sure to point out to the assembled client/voters how political activity played a role in service delivery. The following excerpt from my field notes marks the presence of several key political figures at the well-attended ribbon-cutting ceremony for a new housing development built by Ridgewood-Bushwick:

> There is a large tent set up on Bleecker Street in front of the new building, Plaza de los Ancianos, with balloons tied to many of the tent poles and floating around inside. There are about 200 senior citizens sitting in chairs under the tent, and about 50 more people standing around outside. At the front of the crowd is Angela [Battagglia, director of the Ridgewood-Bushwick Housing Office], flanked by [Assemblyman] Vito [Lopez], U.S. Senator Alfonse D'Amato, Brooklyn Borough President Howard Golden, and two City Council representatives. Vito speaks first, says Angela deserves so much credit for the new building, but that all of the elected officials there helped, too, and he's happy to work with them to bring things into the community. (*Author's field notes, July 2, 1997*)

Events such as these represent one opportunity for Ridgewood-Bushwick client/voters to make the connection between services and politics. In the monthly Ridgewood-Bushwick community newspaper, the *Bushwick Observer* (circulation: ten thousand free copies), these connections often are made more explicit. An analysis of the *Observer* from April 1997 to December 1999 found that the newspaper's articles fall into three main groups. The first and smallest category covers items of general community interest. The second group—about 47 percent of all articles—covers the programs and services provided by Ridgewood-Bushwick. The third category of articles—about 28 percent—covers Assemblyman Lopez. This latter category communicates the important role that Lopez plays in bringing benefits to Bushwick residents, as well as the political clout he wields. For example, the cover story of the March 1998 issue begins: "On February 4, 1998, history was made in Bushwick as [New York State] Gov. George E. Pataki made an unprecedented visit and tour of the community. The Governor, who was invited to visit and tour the area by Assemblyman Vito Lopez, arrived with many of his top commissioners" (1). This and similar stories are part of the client/voter education process employed by Ridgewood-Bushwick as it works to turn its staff and clients into reliable voters.

Displaying the Constituency

A second key piece of Ridgewood-Bushwick's electoral politics work is displaying its voting constituency to public officials who make decisions about government service contract allocations. This practice communicates that Assemblyman Lopez has a responsive—and large—set of potential voters. The public events Ridgewood-Bushwick utilizes for client/voter education also double as opportunities for constituent display. Perhaps the most important of these events during the course of the year is the annual retreat of Ridgewood-Bushwick's Brooklyn Unidos organization. It is here that the embeddedness of the triadic exchange in the wider political environment can be most clearly viewed.

Brooklyn Unidos is a coalition of some 350 neighborhood leaders from north Brooklyn, including members of tenant associations, block associations, low-income cooperatives, parent-teacher associations, and local CBOs. Brooklyn Unidos operates under the nonprofit umbrella of Ridgewood-Bushwick, but, in another example of role fluidity at Ridgewood-Bushwick, is organized by staff members at Assemblyman Lopez's district office. In addition to monthly meetings at which high-ranking city and state political figures regularly make appearances, the highlight of the year is the annual three-day retreat, held at a nonprofit conference center in upstate New York.

The formal goal of the retreat is to allow Brooklyn Unidos leaders to have concentrated interaction with government officials in charge of service programs that affect people's lives in north Brooklyn. The informal goal of the retreat is for Assemblyman Lopez to put his voting constituency on display for these officials, who certainly report on the retreat to their respective executives. The retreat helps facilitate the triadic exchange: client/voters receive patronage benefits; Lopez displays his constituency; and government officials connect Lopez's political strength to their future decisions about government contract allocations.

Two types of events held during the retreat contribute to this process. During the day on Saturday and Sunday, Brooklyn Unidos members attend workshops that address issues of concern to their neighborhood work, such as affordable housing, welfare reform, or domestic violence. Each of the workshops features a panel of speakers, a mix of high-ranking public agency officials and representatives of study area CBOs. Lopez himself moderates each panel, and makes sure to comment on the significance of the gathering for both panelists and Brooklyn Unidos members. An excerpt from my field notes on the first session from the 1998 retreat illustrates this:

> By 10:00 a.m., all the workshop panelists are seated, including Vito [Assemblyman Lopez], the moderator. The room is mostly full [with about 160 people]. Vito stands up and begins the session. First, he introduces the panelists: Veronica White, CEO of the New York City Housing Partnership; Richard Roberts, Commissioner of New York City's Department of Housing Preservation and Development; Joseph Lynch, Acting Commissioner of New York State's Division of Housing and Community Renewal; Bill Traylor, Vice President of the Local Initiative Support Corporation [a major syndicator of tax credits for subsidized low-income housing programs]; and Cece Tkaczyk, Executive Director of the Neighborhood Preservation Coalition of New York State. He points out to the Brooklyn Unidos members that *they're important enough for all these important people to give up their Saturday for them,* and Joe Lynch even brought his wife, who Vito also introduces. (*Author's field notes, January 10, 1998; emphasis added*)

The triadic exchange is in clear view here. Ridgewood-Bushwick has organized a group of nearly two hundred local leaders who have sufficient commitment to their work to give up their Saturday—and Sunday—to the retreat. Lopez presents this constituency of client/

voters—designated as community leaders—to the public officials who represent the mayor, governor, and other relevant political players. Lopez's remarks make clear that he is responsible for the organization of these client/voters—and of many more who answer to these leaders. The Brooklyn Unidos members see how Lopez has brought top-level government officials to meet with them, thereby demonstrating his connections to the decision makers who provide the government contracts underwriting CBO jobs and services. Furthermore, Lopez's speeches remind the client/voters of the role that voting plays in delivering these resources.

The workshops are a key feature of the conference because they embody the triadic resources-for-votes exchange. At the same time, the conference continues to distribute patronage to client/voters, reinforcing their loyalties to Ridgewood-Bushwick and to Lopez. The main benefits of the conference are its leisure activities. First, there is the simple fact of a free weekend in the country for a group of people who have few opportunities for such activities. Lopez pays for the entire cost of the retreat—conference rooms, lodging, food, transportation, and so forth—out of his Assembly "member-item" budget.[8] In addition, the Brooklyn Unidos conference is well known for its parties. There are four parties during the weekend: one on each of the bus trips to and from the conference center, one on Friday night, and one on Saturday night. On the bus trips, Brooklyn Unidos members share food they have made and mix drinks from an impromptu bar set up in the bus aisle. The Friday and Saturday parties feature a disc jockey brought along from Brooklyn, flashing lights, drinking, and lots of dancing. Both parties go on until the wee hours of the morning, but people always make it to the workshops the next day.

The Brooklyn Unidos retreat is a highly illustrative example of the ways in which Ridgewood-Bushwick and Assemblyman Lopez work to-

---

8. Each member of the New York State Legislature receives a quantity of public funds to distribute to nonprofit organizations in his or her district. Assemblyman Lopez spends the majority of his member-item funds on the annual Brooklyn Unidos retreat. At the 2000 retreat, for example, Lopez stated that he had spent $40,000 for the weekend (author's field notes, February 19, 2000). The importance of member-item funds to legislators who seek to build machine-politics CBOs like Ridgewood-Bushwick is underlined by an ongoing political battle in New York State. In 2001, state Senator Pedro Espada (Bronx) switched his party affiliation from Democrat to Republican. His publicly stated reason was that since the Republicans control the state Senate his member item would increase significantly by switching parties (Perez-Peña 2002). Afterwards, it was found that Espada had channeled over $400,000 in member-item funds to a CBO of which he serves as the executive director. Public outcry led to the funds being returned, but Espada remains embroiled in a legal fight over his party switch. He continues to maintain that he wants to be a Republican because of the additional resources it brings into his district.

gether to organize client/voters and then parlay that voting constituency into influence within the wider political environment. Top elected officials not only send their agency leaders to the retreat but also make appearances at Ridgewood-Bushwick events and facilities on a regular basis. During their election campaigns, for example, Mayor Giuliani appeared at the Ridgewood-Bushwick senior citizen picnic at a state park on Long Island, Governor Pataki traveled to the Ridgewood-Bushwick senior center to speak about his health policy proposals, and former U.S. senator Alfonse D'Amato was the featured speaker at the opening of a new subsidized housing development built by Ridgewood-Bushwick. Clearly, Ridgewood-Bushwick and Lopez have the attention of important players in the wider political environment.

Winning Elections

The final piece of Ridgewood-Bushwick's electoral politics work involves converting the promising display of client/voters into actual electoral victories. During the fieldwork period, Assemblyman Lopez's political club was recognized as a contributor to one citywide electoral victory—Mayor Rudolph Giuliani's 1997 reelection—and also as the winner of three critical district-level elections—a 1999 state judicial election, a 2000 state district leader (a post that entitles its holder to vote on party nominations) election, and a 2001 city council election. At a meeting of Brooklyn Unidos two days after the 1999 judicial election, which pitted Lopez's candidate against a candidate backed by the district's Hasidic Jewish population, Lopez drove home the importance of his organization's win:

> Vito says that [Election Day] was a "very, very successful day" for the organization [Brooklyn Unidos/Ridgewood-Bushwick/Bushiwck Democratic Club]. The Hasidim lost, and they lost badly. . . . He says that the victory is only the beginning of a larger struggle, in which they have to find out who their friends are. Candidates have to choose sides, and if they want the support of one of the more impressive Democratic organizations in the city [i.e., Brooklyn Unidos], they [the candidates] are going to have to play with [Lopez and his organization]. . . . He says that you can't expect things to move your way without understanding the politics of what's going on. A political favor means that when there are two hundred requests for public money, and only two get funded, the people who are owed a favor get one of those two. At work today, he had three high-level people from the Mayor's office call to talk to him

about what Bushwick needs. He says he's not sure if he wants to take that step [of getting so close to the Republican mayor, Rudolph Giuliani], since it's a little scary, but this is the kind of recognition the organization is getting now. (*Author's field notes, November 4, 1999*)

Rewards of the Triadic Exchange

Ridgewood-Bushwick completes the triadic exchange by pursuing these three types of electoral politics work. The result is a steady flow of government contracts to the organization. During the fieldwork period, Ridgewood-Bushwick received millions of dollars in contract revenues for a wide variety of projects. These included the organization's third federally funded Section 202 supportive housing building for senior citizens. Most neighborhoods are lucky to win one of these highly competitive contracts, but Ridgewood-Bushwick opened its third such building in 1997. In 2000, Ridgewood-Bushwick won an extremely unusual, $26 million contract to build and operate a 216-bed nursing home in Bushwick. This contract was facilitated by Governor Pataki, who allowed it to be funded through the New York State Dormitory Authority. Also in 2000, Ridgewood-Bushwick won a new contract to operate its own legal assistance program for low-income individuals who need help with civil cases. These three important new contracts were in addition to the ongoing contracts that fund over 90 percent of Ridgewood-Bushwick's regular $7 million budget.

Although the focus of this chapter has been on explicating a model of the social provision work of CBOs, it is important to ask why only Ridgewood-Bushwick, among the eight CBOs I studied, pursues the triadic exchange as part of its social provision strategy. A combination of individual-, organizational-, and neighborhood-level factors are required to explain this, and a full discussion is beyond the scope of this chapter. At the individual level, the amount of interest in, and ideological orientation toward, politics among CBO leadership, staff, and clients is critical. So, for example, Ridgewood-Bushwick leaders have shaped strong interest in and acceptance of political activity among both staff and clients through the organization's political education work, described above. Almost no efforts of this nature—particularly around the specific issue of the relationship between voting and winning contracts—are found at any of the other seven study organizations. It is important to note that

Ridgewood-Bushwick's electoral efforts are limited to influencing contract allocation decisions; the organization has minimal interest in creating policy change.[9]

At the organizational level, both political history and primary service type affect CBO participation in electoral politics. For example, one of the other CBOs in this study very nearly collapsed in the 1980s after a staff member was elected to the city council and then convicted for taking bribes. This experience led the CBO to assiduously avoid involvement in electoral politics, even though some of its staff members are independently involved in political activism. Another CBO in the study avoids electoral politics because it receives one large contract from city government to support its services, and there is no additional public support available. As such, electoral organizing provides no benefit to this organization.

Finally, there are neighborhood-level factors affecting CBO involvement with electoral politics. Given that politics is a district-level game in New York, there is an important effect from the structure of local political opportunity. Actors at higher levels of the wider political environment (see figure 8.2) seek to identify and pull together reliable, identifiable voting constituencies from the lower levels of the system. It is more efficient for the higher levels of the system to have clear winners within lower-level districts, as this makes the identification and organization of multiple, discrete, lower-level constituencies easier. Ridgewood-Bushwick has become the clear winner in this competition within the section of Brooklyn where it is located. This means there are very limited opportunities for other local CBOs to gain from becoming involved in electoral politics. This pattern of one politically dominant CBO emerging in low-income neighborhoods with larger CBO populations can be observed in other areas of New York City as well.[10]

Conclusion

Nonprofit community-based organizations (CBOs) are key players in an expanding arena of public social provision: privately delivered direct ser-

9. This is an important distinction between the machine politics CBO and social movement organizations, which generally focus on policy issues.

10. Newspaper accounts and my own observations show the existence of at least several other New York City CBOs that are in a similar position vis-à-vis other local CBOs and the wider political environment.

vices. Devolution has actually *decreased* the total public dollars being spent on these services (Conlan 1998), but privatization has rapidly *increased* the amounts being funneled through government service contracts to CBOs (Johns Hopkins Nonprofit Sector Project 2000; Salamon 1995). Together, these two national policy shifts have greatly altered the face of social provision to the poor. Current sociological theories of public social provision, with their focus on income support, miss out on this important component of the social benefit package. More and more, the well-being of our poorest citizens depends on state- and local-level decisions about how to allocate public service contracts.

Although services increasingly are provided by CBOs, contract allocation decisions remain a function of government. Those governmental decisions, as always, are affected by political concerns. The model of economic and political exchanges within which nonprofit CBOs are embedded (figure 8.2) illustrates the mechanisms by which CBOs can influence governmental decisions about contract allocation. Importantly, however, many CBOs do *not* engage in this strategy. Instead, like seven of the eight CBOs I studied, they remain within more traditional CBO activity arenas: service provision and community building (see Marwell 2004b).

This latter group of CBOs focuses on practices internal to the communities in which they operate. They do not orient their actions toward a critical external institution that has significant control over their ability to pursue their missions: the broader political processes that affect government contracting decisions. Ethnographic studies that examine only CBO service provision and community-building work similarly overlook the importance of these organizations' engagement with institutions beyond the boundaries of their neighborhoods. The present study incorporates that broader perspective, linking highly local events to broader social, political, and institutional processes (see also Abu-Lughod and others 1994; Duneier 2000; Gregory 1998; Rabrenovic 1996; Venkatesh 2000).

Thus, a CBO that pursues the triadic exchange can be understood as opting into a key component of democratic decision making: electing the representatives who make governmental choices, including decisions about how to distribute resources for public service provision. The foregoing discussion of Ridgewood-Bushwick demonstrates that it is legally and practically possible for CBOs to add electoral politics work to the more traditional service provision and community building activities, thereby producing what is essentially a new version of machine politics.

The distinction between political machines and machine politics (Sayre and Kaufman 1960) is important here. Political parties created political machines by exerting strict discipline over their component parts throughout the polity (e.g., city, state). Indeed, the very notion of a political *machine* is that it aggregates the work of otherwise independent organizations for the benefit of a larger entity. As the data presented here show, however, Ridgewood-Bushwick currently practices only the *exchange function* of machine politics, using the resultant political power only within its immediate neighborhood. There is no effort to link Ridgewood-Bushwick's nonprofit-political operation to similar units of organization across the polity (e.g., city, state) in order to control larger processes. The potential for CBOs to attempt such an approach certainly exists, but empirical evidence shows no such activity at this time.

The machine politics CBO thus represents a *particular* kind of political enfranchisement for the poor. Client/voters who participate in this type of organization have partially demystified the processes by which government allocates public resources, and can claim to be part of an ongoing—albeit highly localized—political pressure group. CBOs that take alternative approaches to creating political voice among the poor exist alongside machine politics CBOs (Ferman 1996; Goetz 1993; Jones-Correa 2001; Purcell 2002). CBOs of this former type will decline, however, if they consistently prove less adept at meeting the social provision needs and preferences of the poor than the machine politics CBO. In other words, as with the political machine, the machine politics CBO likely will suppress political contention in poor neighborhoods, though very possibly in exchange for tangible benefits for its constituents.

The discussion of the machine politics CBO illustrates that informal organizational means of controlling public resource allocation continue to exist in cities, despite the advent of civil service reform, program proposal merit ratings, and other bureaucratic procedures designed to eliminate particularistic treatment. Larger policy shifts of privatization and devolution provided an institutional opening for the machine politics CBO to emerge. As social provision policy continues to change in the United States—time-limited welfare benefits, privatization of Social Security, public education vouchers, and discussion of expanded government-sponsored health insurance, and so forth—sociologists need to pay more attention to the state- and local-level processes that shape citizens' access to service-based social provision.

References

Abu-Lughod, Janet. 1994. *From Urban Village to East Village: The Battle for New York's Lower East Side.* Cambridge, Mass.: Blackwell.

Amenta, Edwin. 1993. "The State of the Art in Welfare State Research on Social Spending Efforts in Capitalist Democracies since 1960." *American Journal of Sociology* 99: 750–63.

———. 1998. *Bold Relief: Institutional Politics and the Origins of Modern American Social Policy.* Princeton: Princeton University Press.

Amenta, Edwin, Kathleen Dunleavy, and Mary Bernstein. 1994. "Stolen Thunder? Huey Long's 'Share Our Wealth,' Political Mediation, and the Second New Deal." *American Sociological Review* 59: 678–702.

Amenta, Edwin, and Drew Halfmann. 2000. "Wage Wars: Institutional Politics, the WPA, and the Struggle for U.S. Social Policy." *American Sociological Review* 64: 506–28.

Andrews, Kenneth T. 2001. "Social Movements and Policy Implementation: The Mississippi Civil Rights Movement and the War on Poverty, 1965 to 1971." *American Sociological Review* 66: 71–95.

Austin, Michael J. 2003. "The Changing Relationship between Nonprofit Organizations and Public Social Service Agencies in the Era of Welfare Reform." *Nonprofit and Voluntary Sector Quarterly* 32: 97–114.

Banfield, Edward C., and James Q. Wilson. 1963. *City Politics.* Cambridge: Harvard University Press.

Bishop, S. W. 2006. "Nonprofit Federalism and the CSBG Program: Serving the Needs of the Working Poor in the Post-TANF Era." *Administration & Society* 37: 695–718.

Bockmeyer, J. L. 2003. "Devolution and the Transformation of Community Housing Activism." *Social Science Journal* 40: 175–88.

Bradley, David, Evelyn Huber, Stephanie Moller, François Nielsen, and John D. Stephens. 2003. "Distribution and Redistribution in Postindustrial Democracies." *World Politics* 55: 193–228.

Breaux, David A., Christopher M. Duncan, C. Denise Keller, and John C. Morris. 2002. "Welfare Reform, Mississippi Style: Temporary Assistance for Needy Families and the Search for Accountability." *Public Administration Review* 62: 92–103.

Briggs, Xavier N. De Souza, Elizabeth J. Mueller, and Mercer L. Sullivan. 1997. *From Neighborhood to Community: Evidence on the Social Effects of Community Development.* New York: Community Development Research Center, Graduate School of Management and Urban Policy, New School for Social Research.

Caputo, Richard K. 1994. *Welfare and Freedom American Style: The Role of the Federal Government, 1941–1980.* Lanham, Md.: University Press of America.

Cauthen, Nancy K., and Edwin Amenta. 1996. "Not for Widows Only: Institutional Politics and the Formative Years of Aid to Dependent Children." *American Sociological Review* 61: 427–48.

Chaskin, Robert J. 2001. *Building Community Capacity.* New York: Aldine de Gruyter.

Clark, Robert F. 2000. *Maximum Feasible Success: A History of the Community Action Program.* Washington, D.C.: National Association of Community Action Agencies.

Clemens, Elizabeth S. 1997. *The People's Lobby: Organizational Innovation and the Rise of Interest Group Politics in the United States, 1890–1925.* Chicago: University of Chicago Press.

Conlan, Timothy. 1998. *From New Federalism to Devolution: Twenty-Five Years of Intergovernmental Reform.* Washington, D.C.: Brookings Institution.

DeSipio, Louis. 1996. *Counting on the Latino Vote: Latinos as a New Electorate.* Charlottesville: University Press of Virginia.

Duneier, Mitchell. 2000. *Sidewalk.* New York: Viking.

Eisinger, Peter K. 1969. "The Anti-Poverty Community Action Group as a Political Force in the Ghetto." Unpublished manuscript, Political Science, Yale University.

Ellwood, David T. 1988. *Poor Support: Poverty in the American Family.* New York: Basic Books.

Erie, Steven P. 1988. *Rainbow's End: Irish-Americans and the Dilemmas of Urban Machine Politics, 1840–1985.* Berkeley: University of California Press.

Esping-Andersen, Gosta. 1990. *Three Worlds of Welfare Capitalism.* London: Polity Press.

Fellowes, M. C., and G. Rowe. 2004. "Politics and the New American Welfare States." *American Journal of Political Science* 48: 362–73.

Ferman, Barbara. 1996. *Challenging the Growth Machine: Neighborhood Politics in Chicago and Pittsburgh.* Lawrence: University Press of Kansas.

Freedman, Anne E. 1994. *Patronage: An American Tradition.* Chicago: Nelson-Hall.

Gainsborough, J. F. 2003. "To Devolve or Not to Devolve? Welfare Reform in the States." *Policy Studies Journal* 31: 603–23.

Gans, Herbert J. 1999. "Participant Observation in the Era of 'Ethnography.'" *Journal of Contemporary Ethnography* 28: 540–48.

Gilbert, Jess, and Carolyn Howe. 1991. "Beyond State vs. Society: Theories of the State and New Deal Agricultural Policies." *American Sociological Review* 56: 204–20.

Gillette, Michael L. 1996. *Launching the War on Poverty: An Oral History.* New York: Twayne.

Goetz, Edward G. 1993. *Shelter Burden: Local Politics and Progressive Housing Policy.* Philadelphia: Temple University Press.

Gosnell, Harold Foote. 1937. *Machine Politics: Chicago Model.* Chicago: University of Chicago Press.

Gregory, Steven. 1998. *Black Corona: Race and the Politics of Place in an Urban Community.* Princeton: Princeton University Press.

Gronbjerg, Kristin A. 2001. "The U.S. Nonprofit Human Service Sector: A Creeping Revolution." *Nonprofit and Voluntary Sector Quarterly* 30: 276–97.

Guterbock, Thomas M. 1980. *Machine Politics in Transition: Party and Community in Chicago.* Chicago: University of Chicago Press.

Hall, Peter Dobkin. 1992. *Inventing the Nonprofit Sector and Other Essays on Philanthropy, Voluntarism, and Nonprofit Organizations.* Baltimore: Johns Hopkins University Press.

Halpern, Robert. 1995. *Rebuilding the Inner City: A History of Neighborhood Initiatives to Address Poverty in the United States.* New York: Columbia University Press.

Hamilton, Charles V. 1979. "Patron-Recipient Relationship and Minority Politics in New York City." *Political Science Quarterly* 94: 211–27.

Heclo, Hugh. 1974. *Modern Social Politics in Britain and Sweden.* New Haven: Yale University Press.

Hicks, Alexander, and Joya Misra. 1993. "Political Resources and the Growth of Welfare in Affluent Capitalist Democracies, 1960–1982." *American Journal of Sociology* 99: 668–710.

Hodgkinson, Virginia Ann, and Murray S. Weitzman. 1986. "Dimensions of the Independent Sector: A Statistical Profile." Washington, D.C.: Independent Sector.

Huber, Evelyne, Charles Ragin, and John D. Stephens. 1993. "Social Democracy, Christian Democracy, Constitutional Structure, and the Welfare-State." *American Journal of Sociology* 99: 711–49.

Johns Hopkins Nonprofit Sector Project. 2000. "United States Nonprofit Sector at a Glance, 1995 (table)." http://www.jhu.edu/~cnp/pdf/us.pdf.

Jones-Correa, Michael. 1998. *Between Two Nations: The Political Predicament of Latinos in New York City.* Ithaca: Cornell University Press.

———. 2001. "Structural Shifts and Institutional Capacity: Possibilities for Ethnic Cooperation and Conflict in Urban Settings." In *Governing American Cities: Interethnic Coalitions, Competitions, and Conflict,* edited by M. Jones-Correa. New York: Russell Sage Foundation.

Kasinitz, Philip, John H. Mollenkopf, and Mary Waters. 2004. "Becoming New Yorkers: Ethnographies of the Second Generation." New York: Russell Sage Foundation.

Katz, Michael B. 1989. *The Undeserving Poor: From the War on Poverty to the War on Welfare.* New York: Pantheon Books.

———. 1996. *In the Shadow of the Poorhouse: A Social History of Welfare in America.* New York: Basic Books.

Korpi, Walter. 1983. *The Democratic Class Struggle.* London: Routledge and Kegan Paul.

Lambright, K. T., and S. W. Allard. 2004. "Making Trade-offs in Federal Block Grant Programs: Understanding the Interplay between SSBG and TANF." *Publius: The Journal of Federalism* 34: 131–54.

Leavitt, Jacqueline, and Susan Saegert. 1990. *From Abandonment to Hope: Community-Households in Harlem.* New York: Columbia University Press.

Levitan, Sar A. 1969. "The Community Action Program: A Strategy to Fight Poverty." *Annals of the American Academy of Political and Social Science* 385: 63–75.

Liska, Allen E., Fred E. Markowitz, Rachel Bridges Whaley, and Paul Bellair. 1999. "Modeling the Relationship between the Criminal Justice and Mental Health Systems." *American Journal of Sociology* 104: 1744–75.

Longoria, T. 1999. "The Distribution of Public-Private Partnerships: Targeting of Voluntary Efforts to Improve Urban Education." *Nonprofit and Voluntary Sector Quarterly* 28: 315–29.

Marwell, Nicole P. 2004a. "Ethnic and Postethnic Politics: The Dominican Second Generation in New York City." In *Becoming New Yorkers: Ethnographies of the Second Generation,* edited by P. Kasinitz, J. H. Mollenkopf, and M. Waters, 257–84. New York: Russell Sage.

———. 2004b. "Privatizing the Welfare State: Nonprofit Community Based Organizations as Political Actors." *American Sociological Review* 69: 265–91.

———. 2007. *Bargaining for Brooklyn: Community Organizations in the Entrepreneurial City.* Chicago: University of Chicago Press.

McConnell, Sheena, Andrew Burwick, Irma Perez-Johnson, and Pamela Winston. 2003. "Privatization in Practice: Case Studies of Contracting for TANF Case Management, Final Report." U.S. Department of Health and Human Services, Washington, D.C.

Merton, Robert King. 1967. *On Theoretical Sociology: Five Essays, Old and New.* New York: Free Press.

Meyers, Marcia K., Janet C. Gornick, and Laura R. Peck. 2002. "More, Less, or More of the Same? Trends in State Social Welfare Policy in the 1990s." *Publius: The Journal of Federalism* 32: 91–108.

Moller, Stephanie, David Bradley, Evelyne Huber, François Nielsen, and John D. Stephens. 2003. "Determinants of Relative Poverty in Advanced Capitalist Democracies." *American Sociological Review* 68: 22–52.

Moynihan, Daniel Patrick. 1969. *Maximum Feasible Misunderstanding: Community Action in the War on Poverty.* New York: Free Press.

Moynihan, Daniel Patrick, and James Q. Wilson. 1964. "Patronage in New York State, 1955–1959." *American Political Science Review* 58: 286–301.

Orloff, Ann Shola, and Theda Skocpol. 1984. "Why Not Equal Protection? Explaining the Politics of Public Social Welfare in Britain and the United States, 1880s–1920s." *American Sociological Review* 49: 726–750.

Perez-Peña, Richard. 2002. "Senator Wins State Grants for Group He Heads, but Albany Objects." *New York Times,* B1.

Pierson, Paul. 1995. "Fragmented Welfare States: Federal Institutions and the Development of Social Policy." *Governance: An International Journal of Policy and Administration* 8: 449–78.

Piven, Frances Fox, and Richard A. Cloward. 1971. *Regulating the Poor: The Functions of Public Welfare.* New York: Pantheon Books.

Portney, K. E., and J. M. Berry. 1997. "Mobilizing Minority Communities: Social Capital and Participation in Urban Neighborhoods." *American Behavioral Scientist* 40: 632–44.

Provan, Keith G., and H. Brinton Milward. 1994. "Integration of Community-Based Services for the Severely Mentally Ill and the Structure of Public

Funding: A Comparison of Four Systems." *Journal of Health Politics, Policy, and Law* 19: 865–94.

———. 1995. "A Preliminary Theory of Interorganizational Network Effectiveness: A Comparative Study of Four Community Mental Health Systems." *Administrative Science Quarterly* 40: 1–33.

Purcell, M. 2002. "Politics in Global Cities: Los Angeles Charter Reform and the New Social Movements." *Environment and Planning A* 34: 23–42.

Quadagno, Jill. 1994. *The Color of Welfare: How Racism Undermined the War on Poverty.* New York: Oxford University Press.

Rabrenovic, Gordana. 1996. *Community Builders: A Tale of Neighborhood Mobilization in Two Cities.* Philadelphia: Temple University Press.

Riordan, William L. 1948. *Plunkitt of Tammany Hall: A Series of Very Plain Talks on Very Practical Politics.* New York: Knopf.

Rogers-Dillon, Robin H., and John D. Skrentny. 1999. "Administering Success: The Legitimacy Imperative and the Implementation of Welfare Reform." *Social Problems* 46: 13–29.

Saegert, Susan, J. Phillip Thompson, and Mark R. Warren. 2001. *Social Capital and Poor Communities.* New York: Russell Sage Foundation.

Salamon, Lester M. 1995. *Partners in Public Service: Government-Nonprofit Relations in the Modern Welfare State.* Baltimore: Johns Hopkins University Press.

Sayre, Wallace Stanley, and Herbert Kaufman. 1960. *Governing New York City: Politics in the Metropolis.* New York: Russell Sage Foundation.

Skocpol, Theda. 1992. *Protecting Soldiers and Mothers: The Political Origins of Social Policy in the United States.* Cambridge: Belknap Press of Harvard University Press.

Smith, Greg B. 1996. "Renters, Own Up—City." *Daily News* (New York), March 24, 7.

Smith, Steven Rathgeb, and Michael Lipsky. 1993. *Nonprofits for Hire: The Welfare State in the Age of Contracting.* Cambridge: Harvard University Press.

Soss, J., S. F. Schram, T. P. Vartanian, and E. O'Brien. 2001. "Setting the Terms of Relief: Explaining State Policy Choices in the Devolution Revolution." *American Journal of Political Science* 45: 378–95.

Soule, Sarah A., and Yvonne Zylan. 1997. "Runaway Train? The Diffusion of State-Level Reform in ADC/AFDC Eligibility Requirements, 1950–1967." *American Journal of Sociology* 103: 733–62.

Stephens, John D. 1979. *The Transition from Capitalism to Socialism.* London: Macmillan.

Sundquist, James L. 1969. *On Fighting Poverty: Perspectives from Experience.* New York: Basic Books.

Vanecko, J. J. 1969. "Community Mobilization and Institutional Change: The Influence of the Community Action Program in Large Cities." *Social Science Quarterly* 50: 609–30.

Venkatesh, Sudhir Alladi. 2000. *American Project: The Rise and Fall of a Modern Ghetto.* Cambridge: Harvard University Press.

Von Hassell, Malve. 1996. *Homesteading in New York City, 1978–1993: The Divided Heart of Loisaida*. Westport, Conn.: Bergin and Garvey.

Ware, Alan. 1985. *The Breakdown of Democratic Party Organization, 1940–1980*. Oxford: Oxford University Press.

Warren, Mark R. 2001. *Dry Bones Rattling: Community Building to Revitalize American Democracy*. Princeton: Princeton University Press.

Weir, Margaret, Ann Shola Orloff, and Theda Skocpol. 1988. *The Politics of Social Policy in the United States*. Princeton: Princeton University Press.

Wilson, James Q. 1962. *The Amateur Democrat: Club Politics in Three Cities*. Chicago: University of Chicago Press.

Winston, Pamela. 2002. *Welfare Policymaking in the States: The Devil in Devolution*. Washington, D.C.: Georgetown University Press.

Zylan, Yvonne, and Sarah A. Soule. 2000. "Ending Welfare as We Know It (Again): Welfare State Retrenchment, 1989–1995." *Social Forces* 79: 623–52.

CHAPTER NINE

Nonprofits and the Reconstruction of Urban Governance: Housing Production and Community Development in Cleveland, 1975–2005

Michael McQuarrie

The relationship between nonprofits, states, and markets is changing. Our understanding of this relationship conventionally depends on the assumption of sector-specific institutional environments that, in their variety, offer an antidote to rationalization around unitary institutional logics (Friedland and Alford 1991). Many have noted that the last thirty years have witnessed the abandonment of many postwar institutional arrangements (Bluestone and Harrison 1982; Lash and Urry 1987; Harvey 1989a; Amin 1994). This shift has been based on a highly contingent process of institutional innovation and has resulted in new modes of governance that defy the traditional market-state dualism. These experiments and transformations challenge our conventional juxtaposition of states, markets, and nonprofits (Weisbrod 1977; Gronbjerg 1998). In order to understand this institutional transformation, this chapter will examine the reconstitution of urban *governance* through the analytical lens of nonprofit housing production. Although not a general argument, the case I examine does shed light on the contemporary transformation and, in particular, highlights the changing role of nonprofit organizations in institutional experimentation and new modes of governance.

The site of research is Cleveland, Ohio, where many of the initial political contests that defined institutional experimentation in housing occurred. Housing production is not simply relevant in terms of the provision of a social need. The reorganization of housing production has also served as a proving ground for new modes of governance that draw on the organizational resources, practices, and institutions of a variety of sectors and fields. These *arrangements* are increasingly necessary as economic and state restructuring, both of which are particularly evident at the urban scale, reduce the efficacy of prior political accommodations and the organizations and institutions that they produced. Indeed, some scholars of urban politics argue that there has been a wholesale shift in the "institutional logics" of governance (Clarke and Gaile 1998). The role of nonprofit organizations in the construction of these modes of governance has become increasingly significant over the last thirty years and this role should prompt us to reconsider our traditional understanding of the functional role of nonprofit organizations in constructing social solidarity or delivering mission-based services (Gronbjerg 1987; Wolch 1990; Salamon 1995; Boris 1999).

In using the term "governance" I draw on two distinctive uses: first, the use of the term in systems theory to signal arrangements that make use of the advantages of different institutional settings, such as those that prevail in different organizational fields or sectors (e.g., nonprofits, firms, and the state). Governance along these lines has been termed *heterarchic* (Jessop 1997). Second, governance can refer to self-organizing networks to achieve functional goals, such as the delivery of particular services (Powell 1991; Kooiman 1993; Rhodes 1996; Goldsmith and Eggers 2004). Often described under the rubric of "partnerships" between various actors, such networks are voluntary, not mandated. Consequently, they are dependent upon finding bases of mutual interest or, as in this case, constructing mutual interest institutionally. Both of these usages are relevant for the creation of new governance arrangements in housing. The cross-sectoral networking of these organizational actors is necessary in order to respond to social and economic uncertainty—a responsiveness that is problematic for established organizations and bureaucracies that were designed for different political and economic environments. Heterarchic governance is an advantage in this situation because it draws on the particular advantages of different institutional logics in formulating an effective programmatic response (Stark 1996; Jessop 1997; Rhodes 1997; Stoker 1998). The arrangements I describe draw on the institutional particularities of the state, markets, and the nonprofit sector and are self-organizing.

Though cooperative governance is not mandated by any authority, this is not to say that the construction of these arrangements was the product of some abnormal degree of interpersonal trust or political consensus on the need for more policy options for the production of low-income housing. The literature about public-private partnerships is often highly celebratory and seems to assume that these institutional arrangements are the product of some collective insight about a better way of doing things (Osborne and Gaebler 1993; Grogan and Proscio 2000). Nothing could be further from the truth, at least in the case of Cleveland. Institutional experimentation is politically contested, groups have different interests, and they have different capacities to realize those interests. If we focus on processes of institutional change such as diffusion, the contestation around institutional innovation will be masked— usually diffusion only occurs after the political battle has been waged (DiMaggio 1991). Lastly, the necessary experimentation often occurs in periods of crisis (Fourcade-Gourinchas and Babb 2002; Hay 2004). New governance arrangements for the community-based production of low-income housing are broadly relevant because they allow us to interrogate systems-theoretic and network examples of governance. Although never the same across policy arenas, similar arrangements have been introduced in education and employment policy as well. The coexistence of new modes of governance with older state institutions that have formal authority means that they do not constitute a wholly new set of institutional arrangements. This is true to a degree if one is considering the issue in the abstract. However, there are inflection points, events, and crises that make certain outcomes more likely.

By governance "arrangement" I mean a lash-up of organizations, practices, institutional logics, technologies, metrics, and objects that collectively produce a given outcome.[1] Such a term is necessary to move beyond idealistic conceptions of "policy paradigms" that emphasize the

---

1. *Lash-up* and *arrangement* are concepts that are derivative of related concepts in the work of Bruno Latour and Gilles Deleuze that are intentionally distinguished from related concepts such as "apparatus" or "machine," both of which imply a permanence, unity, and rigidity that I wish to distinguish from the object of analysis here (Deleuze and Guattari 1987; Deleuze 1988; Latour 1987, 2004). I also wish to distinguish what I am going to describe from a field. The governance arrangement in housing could be very loosely described as a field in Bourdieusian terms, but it is really a mechanism of "capital exchange" between fields. I have borrowed from Latour because his terminology is somewhat simpler and requires less explanation in appropriation than the Bourdieusian language of capital exchange and its role in his field theory. In short, my use of Latourian language is for heuristic purposes.

construction of new modes of intellectual and policy authority and toward seeing how institutional change actually happens in experimentation and political contestation. In my view, this is desirable on analytical grounds in general. However, it also redirects our analytical focus from bureaucrats, lobbyists, and think tanks to local organizational innovators and accidental institutional entrepreneurs (Aldrich 1999; Fligstein 2001). When we do so, nonprofits move from being contracted service providers or funders to being (1) the institutional innovators responsible for much of the content of new governance arrangements, and (2) central to the functioning of cross-sectoral cooperation. These roles challenge many of our conceptual distinctions about the differences between states, markets, and nonprofits. In heterarchic governance, nonprofits are less civil society organizations with particular ethical, moral, and other-directed values than central players in new arrangements of governance. Indeed, this is one of the central insights to be gleaned from the construction of heterarchic governance in housing: it is not just that there are exceptions to these conventional understandings, and it is not that civil society is being "colonized," it indicates that these conceptions need to be radically rethought to account for contemporary institutional developments. Heterarchic governance introduces new logics of inclusion/exclusion, new subjectivities, and new ethics. Arrangements, then, are socially productive. Indicative of this, participation in arrangements of governance is very likely to alter the practice and identity of participating nonprofits.

This chapter will outline the construction of new governance arrangements in housing during a moment of institutional crisis. Central to this story is the proactive role of nonprofit organizations. Although not uninterested, these organizations have proven to be key innovators and, more important, they have provided the key organizational gears that have enabled heterarchic governance to function. There are other important aspects to this story, such as the role of new national-level institutions and organizations, the coordination of social practices between fields, and the construction of a metrology to facilitate that, but I will mostly set these aside here in favor of establishing the relationship between political conflict, economic crisis, and the forging of new institutions and organizational ties across sectoral boundaries, or: the construction of heterarchic governance arrangements for the provision of housing (Squires 1992; Ballard 2003; Guthrie and McQuarrie 2005).

Institutional Crisis and Institutional Change

In order to understand transformations in the institutions of urban governance, we must understand the basic configurations that have prevailed in the postwar period. Harvey Molotch's characterization of the city as a "growth machine," a mechanism for population and economic growth, best sums this up (Molotch 1976; Logan and Molotch 1987). Private property in land leads to a generalized interest in real estate values. Real estate values are determined by the location of concentrated investment and, more distantly, by local demand, which, in turn, is driven by population growth. These institutional arrangements unite interests that might otherwise be divergent, such as middle-income homeowners and corporate real estate developers. Consequently, growth underpins the basic political accommodations in urban political life. It unifies a broad constituency in support of economic development and prevents a devolution into interest-based fights over resources. Other key components of this accommodation are a reliance on a Keynesian welfare state and institutionalized racism. Before 1980, a key component of welfare state policy was the use of state investment to even out the otherwise uneven geographic distribution of capital investment.[2] For example, fractured municipal government and tax policy have tended to favor suburban municipalities over central cities. However, Keynesian policy mitigated this by funneling federal resources back into central cities. Institutionalized racism also helped solve a number of potential problems with the postwar urban institutional setting. First, it provided ready-made scapegoats for those who suffered from growth, such as those who experienced increasing labor market competition. Of course, that competition was real and could put downward pressure on wages and, by extension, make the city more attractive to mobile capital. By barring African Americans from full social citizenship and isolating them geographically (on the East Side in Cleveland's case), the benefits of growth could be concen-

---

2. Growth poles are often geographically concentrated as well as being concentrated by industry. Consequently, mobile capital moves across space in search of the highest returns. Of particular relevance here was the movement, in the 1970s, of both capital investment and bank lending away from the Northeast and Midwest generally and from cities in particular. Investment flowed to the South, the West, and the suburbs. For example, banks would take deposits in inner-city Cleveland and invest the capital in mortgage loans for suburban homes in the South. The result was, inevitably, capital starvation and neighborhood decline in the Northeast and Midwest.

trated in other areas of the city. Institutional rationalization around the politics of growth proceeded apace in Cleveland in the postwar period.

The growth machine was not an institutional settlement that was without contradictions and tensions. Molotch has usually emphasized that unrestrained growth leads to a declining quality of life, which can potentially fracture growth coalitions. Although this is apparent in many places, the tension I am more interested in is what occurs when securing growth is no longer economically viable. We are very familiar with the politics of growth from the urban literature, but the politics of decline is more of a grey area. In Cleveland, the tensions in the growth machine were evident by the 1960s and became a full-blown municipal crisis in the 1970s. The emerging tensions were numerous. First, while growth has often enabled cooperation between business and labor, individual firms began fleeing unionized cities in the 1950s, leading to a constant outflow of investment that was further enabled by government-subsidized highway building (Sugrue 1996). Second, by the early 1960s African Americans were no longer willing to be denied social citizenship and initiated protest and electoral activism to secure more resources for their neighborhoods and greater representation in local politics (Moore 2002). Third, in the 1970s various macroeconomic and geopolitical factors combined to deliver a massive blow to the manufacturing economy, which was concentrated in the Northeast and Midwest, including Cleveland. By the late 1970s this was compounded by state retrenchment (Block 1977; Bluestone and Harrison 1982; Mollenkopf 1983). Fourth, in many cities, including Cleveland, declining investment radically altered the political dynamic from a concern with how to distribute the benefits of growth to how to divide up a shrinking pie (Boyte 1980; Clavel 1985; Swanstrom 1985). The result was open conflict between neighborhoods that were starved of investment and business leaders that wanted to restart growth by concentrating available dollars in the central business district. Put differently, the absence of economic growth resulted in a crisis of legitimacy for the institutional arrangements that had been organized to secure growth.

In Cleveland, as in many other cities, this opened the door to numerous mayoral and council candidates who claimed to act in the interests of the neighborhoods and in opposition to corporate and real-estate interests. Neighborhood-based protest emerged and new progressive electoral coalitions were formed. Growth-oriented elites, on the other hand, worked to revalorize downtown real estate through urban renewal and by reconcentrating state and private investment downtown. More broadly, the goal of these growth-oriented elites was to create a better business environment to attract new investment from outside the city (Harvey 1989b; Hubbard and Hall 1998).

The crisis was manifest broadly from the mid-1960s until the end of the 1970s. Among the notable moments were civil rights protest in the early 1960s, race riots in 1966 and 1968, the election of the first African American mayor of a large American city in 1967, the emergence of cross-race neighborhood organizing in 1974 (which would last until 1982), the formation of a successful neighborhood-based electoral coalition in 1977, a capital strike against the new progressive mayor in 1978, a mayoral recall campaign in 1978, municipal bankruptcy in 1979, and the election of a business-friendly mayor in 1979. In one way or another, all of these events were tied up with the distribution of resources in the city and the intensity of these conflicts indicates the collapse of the institutional settlements around the city as "growth machine" (Swanstrom 1985). The city's civic leadership faced the challenge of figuring out a mechanism for restarting growth while simultaneously securing an accommodation with the residents of Cleveland's neighborhoods.

What characterizes and distinguishes Cleveland was not so much the strategy to renew growth but the tactics and capacity to implement it. As has often been remarked, Cleveland has an extremely dense civic infrastructure (Clarke and Gaile 1998). That is, there is a broad culture of civic involvement in the corporate community and this involvement has been institutionalized in a number of local philanthropies and other organizations (Hammack 1989; Tittle 1992). Civic infrastructure is not simply characterized by a willingness to give to local causes and the construction of a dense population of organizations to further that task. Nor is it simply a mode of social leadership by economic elites (Safford 2004). More important has been the willingness of Cleveland's business and corporate elite to collectively and actively intervene in local politics to secure their own interests or, in their formulation, the interests of the city. But these strategies were intertwined with a desire to secure political order and reorganize municipal institutions—a need that was particularly pressing in the contentious climate of the 1960s and 1970s.

Out of the general dynamic of accommodation and resistance that prevailed in the 1960s and '70s there emerged kernels of new governance arrangements. Among the most notable of these was the Cleveland NOW! Campaign, a program to spend $177 million over twelve months to mit-

igate racial and economic tensions. Composed of federal, state, and local grants along with local philanthropic grants and personal donations,
the program was fully subscribed within weeks. The money was then
funneled to local nonprofit organizations and government entities that
were independent of the city council, such as the city planning commission. This was a tactic to outflank a recalcitrant, parochial, and, according to some, incompetent city council that refused to support the agenda
of Carl Stokes, the newly elected African American mayor. Effectively,
Cleveland's business leadership financed its own legislative program.
Moreover, rather than setting up an authority or other more permanent
organization, the relationship was ad hoc and had few formalized procedures for things such as governance or the distribution of funds. It was
in this context that a new organizational form, the community development corporation (CDC), was first utilized for governance when they became the vehicle for the retail distribution of Cleveland NOW! funds.
CDCs, largely an invention of their primary funder, the Ford Foundation, were organizations that adopted a bootstraps approach to revital-
izing poor communities. They were mostly locally based organizations
that combined citizen participation with some degree of fiscal and development expertise. Their primary goal was usually economic development and physical redevelopment in a given, relatively small geographic
area. Hough Area Development Corporation, an early CDC founded in
1966, became a central link between Stokes and his constituency on the
East Side. As an incorporated nonprofit organization, it also received
and distributed a significant chunk of Cleveland NOW! funds for programs such as summer employment, cooperative businesses, and the
like. This small-scale, cross-sectoral, governance arrangement quickly
came unglued when an armed black nationalist, who had been funded
by Cleveland NOW!, was cornered by police and opened fire. The event
triggered the Glenville riots in July 1968.

During the 1970s the crisis persisted and the city continued to decline
even with substantial new state investment. The result was the emergence of neighborhood-based protest in the form of "community congresses" as well as a new neighborhood-based electoral coalition under the banner of a youthful Dennis Kucinich. The combination of an
active protest movement and progressive control of the city's executive
seemed to have the potential for significant institutional innovation and
reorganization. Unfortunately, while they shared many programmatic
goals there were more than a few stylistic differences between the move-

ment and the mayor, which resulted in the mayor's isolation, near recall, and a capital strike. This outcome also meant the end of the possibility of a neighborhood-based institutional resolution to the crisis of growth. Moreover, fiscal retrenchment, which was made necessary by the city's bankruptcy, combined with the demise of federal urban policy in the 1980s, eliminated any state-centered institutional solution to the city's crisis. However, there were two outcomes in this period that would provide essential institutional building blocks in the 1980s. First, the community congresses, in alliance with similar organizations across the country, managed to secure the passage of the Home Mortgage Disclosure Act (HMDA, 1974) and the Community Reinvestment Act (CRA, 1977). Respectively, this legislation required lenders to disclose basic data about their lending practices and required lenders to initiate loans in areas where they took deposits. Effectively, it immobilized capital that would ensure some degree of private-sector investment, even in cities that would otherwise experience capital outflows. Second, the community congresses were defeated in 1982 after a long campaign to secure more proactive private investment in Cleveland's neighborhoods. Local philanthropies began to require community organizations to engage in bricks-and-mortar development to receive funding. This effectively enrolled, or "channeled," neighborhood-based nonprofits into an effort to revalorize local real estate (Jenkins 1998; Cunningham 2004).

Institutional Innovation and Crisis Resolution

The relatively static nature of institutions makes it easy to turn to theories of exogenous shock to explain institutional transformation. While Cleveland and much of urban America were subject to macroeconomic difficulties and a federal government that was abandoning its role in urban policy and investment, it is also true that the institutions of postwar urban governance were contradictory all along. Institutional arrangements are heterogeneous (Friedland and Alford 1991; Clemens and Cook 1999). Although there can be tendencies to rationalize around particular institutional logics, this does not mean all institutional arrangements do so equally or even that they do so around the same logics. All of which is to say, while there was clearly a general institutional crisis in the 1970s, one that was particularly evident in Cleveland with municipal bankruptcy and sustained neighborhood protest, that does not automatically lead to institutional innovation. Another place to turn for explaining institutional innovation is to the idealist conception of "policy paradigms" and the role of "ideas" in institutional change (Hall 1993; Campbell 2004). This is not particularly satisfying in Cleveland's case because it does not take seriously the practical experimentation that underpins institutional innovation. This experimentation was evident in early CDCs, Cleveland NOW!, and CRA, but it would only be realized with far more extensive innovations and, ultimately, a political settlement of the tensions between the neighborhoods, business leaders, and elected politicians.

When we turn to the micro-level institutional experiments that ultimately would underpin a new model of heterarchic governance, the role of nonprofit organizations is impossible to avoid. Although it is easy to attribute this to some definable institutional characteristics that are associated with nonprofits—their value rationality, other-directedness, or mission-oriented work—it becomes clear that the great advantage of Cleveland's nonprofits was their flexibility and the "social skill" of the people who ran them (Fligstein 2001; Sirianni and Freidland 2001). The need to work with organizations in a variety of institutional settings makes some nonprofit leaders particularly amenable to building institutions and organizations that operate across institutional settings. Heterarchic governance may be driven by crisis or uncertainty, but it only operates when organizations can be coordinated across institutional settings. The move to heterarchic governance is often characterized as a wholesale shift in institutional logics (Clarke and Gaile 1998; Campbell and Pedersen 2001; Brenner and Theodore 2002). However, if institutional rationalization around market mechanisms was, indeed, the whole story, then heterarchic governance would not be necessary and the role of nonprofits would not be as central as it has been. This is not to say that markets don't have a new privileged position in heterarchy—they do. It is to emphasize that the introduction of market mechanisms is not natural and depends on significant institutional reorganization and innovation. Tables 9.1 and 9.2 describe the organizational and institutional innovations that enabled the construction of heterarchic governance arrangements in housing.

Nonprofits Drive Institutional Innovation

The defeat of the community congresses ended the neighborhood challenge to the political and economic leadership of the city, but it also

TABLE 9.1. **Organizational innovations that enable heterarchic governance in low-income housing production**

Organizational Innovation	Date	Source	Significance
Community Development Corporation	1966	Neighborhoods, Ford Foundation	Organizational vehicle for neighborhood-based development
Cleveland Housing Network (local mediator)	1981	CDCs	Enables the production of housing at scale
Neighborhood Progress, Inc. (local mediator)	1989	Cleveland Tomorrow	Strategically directs CDCs toward growth agenda
Cleveland Tomorrow	1984	Corporate leadership	Strategic business organization with the capacity to work independently of electoral politics
Local Initiatives Support Corporation (national mediator)	1981	Ford Foundation	Moves community development toward physical redevelopment, connects CDCs to national corporations via syndication
Enterprise Foundation (national mediator)	1982	James Rouse (Baltimore-based real estate developer)	As above, though with some programmatic differences

TABLE 9.2. **Institutional innovations that enable heterarchic governance in low-income housing production**

Institutional Innovation	Date	Source	Significance
Program-related investments	Late 1960s	John Simon, Ford Foundation	Enabled philanthropies to make loans rather than just grants
Community Reinvestment Act (CRA)	1977	Federal legislation, neighborhood movement	Limited the mobility of bank capital; with the passage of LIHTC it would drive investment in tax credits
Lease-purchase rehabilitation	Late 1970s	Famicos Foundation	Provided a fiscal model for the provision of affordable housing that does not rely on grants
Low-Income Housing Tax Credit (LIHTC)	1986	Federal legislation, national mediators	Provided incentives for private corporate investment in low-income housing development
Tax abatements	1980–present	Voinovich administration	Subsidized new housing in Cleveland's neighborhoods
Land bank, housing trust fund, local CRA deals	1989–2001	White administration	Generally facilitated access to land and capital for neighborhood-based, nonprofit housing development

marked the beginning of community-based housing production. The key organizational form in this system is the CDC. As noted above, CDCs had been around since the 1960s. In addition to Hough Area Development Corporation, a number of new CDCs had been emerging in Cleveland. Local development corporations (LDCs) had been established as government-sponsored nonprofit economic development entities in the 1970s. While initially operating as merchants' associations, many came to have a broader community development function by the 1990s. The Famicos Foundation was established in 1967 by a Catholic nun who wished to rebuild the riot-torn Hough neighborhood. Due to a political accommodation reached in 1981 between the city council president, George Forbes, and the mayor, George Voinovich, members of the city council secured control over a large chunk of Community Development Block Grant (CDBG) funds. For council members interested in using their control over CDBG money to directly support their own electoral ambitions, the legislation required them to establish their own ward-based CDC to receive and distribute money. As a consequence, many wards now have CDCs effectively controlled by the council representative (cf. Marwell 2004). Finally, and most importantly, as the community congresses secured organizing victories on a number of issues, they began to take on a larger programmatic function. In short order, the congresses were managing city-sponsored paint and energy programs. They were beginning to rehabilitate housing and clean vacant lots. Despite taking on these new programmatic functions, the congresses wished to avoid the confusion of programmatic and organizing activities.[3] Consequently, even before their defeat, many of the congresses had established separate but affiliated CDCs.

The community congresses were designed to magnify the neighborhood voice in city politics and hold politicians and business leaders accountable for conditions in the neighborhoods. If necessary, they would protest in order to secure resources. However much it was possible to garner results from challenging business and political leaders, it was also

3. The reasoning here was clear. In an organizing capacity, the congresses were often engaged in contentious politics with the same organizations that funded development. Of course, there is the broader institutional issue: 501 (c) 3 status is necessary to receive funding for development, but it also constrains political activity. This is rarely enforced, but it is enforced. For example, an officer of the National Training and Information Center (who was one of the organizers of Cleveland's congresses in the 1970s) is currently in jail for allegedly overstepping the bounds of 501 (c) 3 status. Coincidentally, the investigation was opened shortly after an affiliated organization led a protest on Karl Rove's lawn.

clear to many of the congresses and their CDCs that there would be diminishing returns from the public sector and victories against businesses were likely to be transient. Moreover, because they devalued neighborhood property and attracted crime, the congresses were coming to view abandoned homes as "Public Enemy No. 1." As much as the congresses felt that it was not their obligation to redevelop the neighborhoods even if they had the capacity to do so, some began taking an interest in exploring what was possible and soon decided to become "developers of last resort" (Warren 1995).

It was in this context that the Famicos Foundation developed a mechanism for intervening in the physical environment of the neighborhoods. The mechanism, called "lease-purchase rehab," would facilitate the redevelopment goals of the CDCs. For financing, the system drew upon an institutional innovation in the philanthropic sector, the program-related investment. Program-related investments allow philanthropies to not only give money away (which they are obligated to do) but to invest money in program-related projects. This required a series of organizational and legal innovations that were largely carried out at the Ford Foundation in the late 1960s and early 1970s. In the lease-purchase model, the CDC would secure control over a site by purchasing it for as low a price as possible; after 1984 land was provided by the city's land bank. Rehabilitation money would come from a foundation in the form of a loan, with the rehabilitation done in part by volunteer labor. After rehabilitation, the house would be leased to a tenant for fifteen years at a rate sufficient to amortize the CDC's loan and cover costs. The occupant would then have the option of buying the home for the cost of the debt principal.

Though it was not immediately evident, lease-purchase was the kernel of an entirely new arrangement that would link for-profit business to nonprofit CDC producers via nonprofit philanthropies (with the support of incentives in the tax code). Recall that in the late 1960s low-income housing, all of it rentals, was produced by local state-run and state-financed housing authorities, while building often occurred on land cleared with urban renewal funds.[4] The financing came from the private sector via taxation and was distributed in the legislative process and through the management of the Department of Housing and Urban

---

4. Cleveland has a housing authority but never established an authority to handle urban renewal, which was supervised by the city council.

Development. In the new arrangement, nonprofit CDCs decided what to rehabilitate based on costs and the priorities arrived at in consultation with community residents. They managed the rehabilitation and managed the property while it was being leased to the occupant. Nonetheless, despite the beginnings of a working arrangement, production levels were woefully small due to a lack of funds and a lack of construction management skill (Warren 1995).

Two developments, the formation of nonprofit *mediating organizations* and the passage of the Low-Income Housing Tax Credit (LIHTC) would transform the capacity of this arrangement. The first prominent mediating organization in Cleveland was the Cleveland Housing Network (CHN), formed in 1981 out of a cooperative agreement among the CDCs that were engaged in lease-purchase housing rehabilitation. The purpose of CHN was to pool financial, construction, and management resources for the lease-purchase program (and eventually other programs as well). Its goal was to relieve the burden on individual CDCs by negotiating as a group with funders, contractors, and city government. At the same time, the CDCs retained control over property selection, design, volunteer labor, selection of occupants, and property management. CHN's activities were funded by local philanthropies and low-interest loans from the city's CDBG allocation. Eventually, as CDBG funding was cut during the Reagan administration, CHN turned to a national mediating organization, the Enterprise Foundation, for financing assistance.

The Enterprise Foundation made up for CDBG cuts and then some using the Low-Income Housing Tax Credit. LIHTC was passed as part of the Tax Reform Act of 1986 with significant lobbying pressure from Enterprise and its competitor, the Local Initiative Support Corporation (LISC) (Ballard 2003; Guthrie and McQuarrie 2005).[5] It provided what has since become the primary mechanism for the production of low-income housing. The question was: How do tax credits aid nonprofit organizations who have no tax liability? The answer, which took some time to figure out, was to distribute the credits to housing developers, including nonprofit housing developers. The developers could then sell the credits to corporations with tax liability. This system was super-

5. LISC had also been active in Cleveland since the mid-1980s and often provides financing from tax credits and loans. Like Enterprise, LISC has a syndication arm but because CHN is the largest user of LIHTC in Cleveland and CHN mostly works with Enterprise, LISC doesn't do much syndication in Cleveland. LISC closed its Cleveland office in 2004.

charged by the Community Reinvestment Act. CRA required banks to invest where they took deposits, and they were required to invest a lot, often more than they were willing to distribute in loans. LIHTC enabled banks to meet CRA requirements through the simple mechanism of buying credits. CRA ensured a market for housing tax credits. However, individual CDC and CHN projects were seen as too risky and the CDCs often did not have the connections necessary to sell the credits. This is where the national-level mediating organizations had a role to play. The Enterprise Foundation and LISC would not only sanction the expertise and reliability of the CDCs they worked with, they would also "syndicate" the credits into something like a mutual fund. Banks and other corporations would then buy into the fund and reduce their tax liability at low risk while simultaneously receiving credit for CRA compliance. This effort was further aided in Cleveland by the negotiation of even more lucrative local CRA agreements during the administration of Mayor Mike White (1990–2001).[6]

Collectively, this institutional configuration resulted in a flood of capital seeking out tax-credit-financed community development projects. The primary problem with the lease-purchase system developed by Famicos and the Cleveland Housing Network was not on the production side; it was that these innovations were starved of capital. The combination of CRA-LIHTC-mediating organization solved that problem by greatly extending the reach of the low-income housing governance arrangement. Instead of reaching from CDCs to the city government and on to the federal government, the arrangement now linked CDCs to a mediating organization (CHN) to the federal government (via tax credits), on one hand, and to another mediating organization (Enterprise), on the other.[7] Via Enterprise the arrangement was then extended to cor-

6. A number of cities made similar agreements. Nationally, these local agreements resulted in a total (paper) commitment of over $350 billion by the mid-1990s.

7. Tax credit syndication is actually handled by a for-profit affiliate of the nonprofit Enterprise Foundation, Enterprise Social Investment Corporation (ESIC). The yield of tax credits to corporate investors basically serves as a direct indicator of the competition over them and the trust that investors have developed in the system. While early funds in the late 1980s and 1990s would often yield more than 20%, at the peak of the housing bubble in 2006 credits in California yielded less than 1% more than a Treasury bill. Effectively, the market was saying that nonprofit housing development projects were only slightly more likely to fail than the U.S. federal government. Of course, it is now clear that there was a huge credit bubble and that risk was seriously mispriced—the delusion of crowds. The broader point is that nonprofits were not being stigmatized in the market; in fact, they were viewed as more trustworthy than any number of Fortune 500 companies. On a speculative note, this suggests that corporate accountants were betting that the value orientation of nonprofits was more oriented to preserving the value of their investment than the value orientation of for-profit firms. Interviews also suggest that they

porations and, when a secondary market in tax credits eventually developed in the 1990s, to capital markets. The fact that the very small-scale efforts of neighborhood-based CDCs acting as "developers of last resort" could eventually be linked in a governance arrangement to capital markets is an extraordinary social achievement that required significant institutional innovation and negotiation. Among the most important of these was the invention of organizations that could mediate between organizational actors governed by different institutional logics.

Corporate Strategy and Institutional Innovation

We must also be attentive to what Cleveland's growth-oriented elites were doing concurrently with these developments. The crisis of the 1970s made it clear that municipal government was unlikely to initiate the sort of institutional transformation that local corporate leadership felt was necessary to restart growth. The combination of neighborhood-based protest, the Kucinich administration, and the continuing economic decline of the city prompted Cleveland's business leadership to rethink how they were setting out to achieve their goals. Under the leadership of the chief executive officer of the Eaton Corporation, and in the hands of the visionary organizational innovator Richard Shatten, Cleveland Tomorrow was formed in 1982. Modeled on Pittsburgh's Allegheny Conference, Cleveland Tomorrow's membership was composed exclusively of the CEOs of the city's largest businesses. As a result, the organization was led by people who could make decisions and write checks. Moreover, Cleveland Tomorrow had immense clout with politicians and bureaucrats as a consequence of its exclusive membership. Shortly after its founding, the organization funded a strategic plan for the city and then was able to raise the funds internally to implement it. As a consequence of this concerted effort to build new institutions and organizations, Cleveland Tomorrow has become a proactive, strategic, nonprofit policymaking organization with the financial clout to implement its strategic plan (Bartimole 1995; Shatten 1995; Keating, Krumholz, and Perry 1995; Adams 1998).

In the midst of fiscal crisis and a crisis of authority in the neighborhoods, local elites shifted to a strategy that relied much less on winning

---

were betting that local governments and intermediaries would not let the projects fail and would bail them out if they got into financial trouble.

victories in the electoral arena. In contrast, even as the city made a modest recovery and a business-friendly mayor was ensconced in office, the municipal government had no significant resources for discretionary funding on policy initiatives or institutional reorganization. The fiscal crisis had made it clear that electoral victories were of declining importance for securing the goals of the city's growth-oriented elites. Instead, usually acting in concert with the Cleveland Foundation, the Gund Foundation, and other key components of Cleveland's civic infrastructure, Cleveland Tomorrow became the centerpiece of a shadow municipal government that operated outside of formal politics (Wolch 1990).

A key component of the early strategic plan was to assist in the redevelopment of Cleveland's neighborhoods, though critics would say an ulterior motive was to marginalize neighborhood-based protest (Cunningham 2004). To this end, Cleveland Tomorrow spun off and funded Neighborhood Progress, Inc. (NPI). NPI was originally intended to be the primary redevelopment engine for Cleveland's neighborhoods. However, its formation was met with significant objections and an incipient protest organization before it redesigned its model to act as a funder and technical supporter for the numerous already-existing CDCs, which were and are thought to be more accountable to neighborhood residents. Moreover, due to CHN and the lease-purchase system, the CDCs had already established themselves as able developers. Consequently, NPI backed off and filled a key niche in this arrangement: the provision of competitive and strategically targeted operating support to the CDCs via grants.

Now, NPI has four key functions. First, it retails philanthropic funds intended to support the operations of community developers. The foundations, in turn, no longer deal with CDCs directly. Money is distributed in accordance with the strategic priorities of NPI (and, by extension, Cleveland's growth-oriented elites) and the production capacity of the applicants. Second, in exchange for operating support, CDC staff are required to submit to NPI training and supervision in areas such as real estate development and construction management. Third, NPI provides capital for community development projects using funding provided by Cleveland Tomorrow and the LIHTC. In other words, NPI acts as a syndicator for the purposes of selling credits to Cleveland Tomorrow's members. Fourth, NPI engages in the design and development of autonomous projects, often over the objections of CDCs who feel they should be the developers. NPI's strategy has successfully enabled the implementation of a community development strategy that single-mindedly focuses on reviving real estate markets through physical development (Burns, Wing 2001).

The Public Sector: From Investor to Facilitator and Regulator

Finally, to get a full understanding of the emergence of new heterarchic governance arrangements we need to turn to the public sector. Obviously, the Kucinich administration did not create an environment amenable to cooperation across sectoral boundaries. Kucinich was succeeded by George Voinovich (1980–88) and Mike White (1990–2001). Voinovich was the candidate of local growth-oriented elites, but he had broad appeal and facilitated cross-sectoral cooperation and institutional innovation. He played two central roles. First, he brought Cleveland through bankruptcy. Second, he became known for his advocacy and support of "public-private partnerships," which effectively meant that he acquiesced to the leadership of real estate developers, Cleveland Tomorrow, and the Cleveland Foundation (Peterson 1981). The focus of his administration was on a downtown revival that once again began concentrating resources downtown at the expense of the neighborhoods, though he also supported the idea of partnership with nonprofit community developers. Under Voinovich, development planning was left to the private sector and economic development activity focused on subsidizing the private sector, including the extensive use of federal Urban Development Action Grant (UDAG) money for upscale retail developments. Extensive tax abatements were also provided for new stadiums, office space, and the Rock and Roll Hall of Fame, all of which was a startling policy reversal from Kucinich's platform a few short years earlier. Unlike in some other cities, there was no effort to link government investments designed to revalorize downtown real estate with investments in the neighborhoods. The key strategy appeared to be to attract suburban shoppers, workers, and entertainment dollars into downtown Cleveland. Needless to say, the neighborhoods had little role to play in this approach.

Voinovich helped move Cleveland's government in the direction of being an "entrepreneurial state," meaning that rather than using government money to run government programs, government money was increasingly used as capital for strategic investments, such as the CDBG-funded loan pool for CHN (Eisinger 1988; Keating, Krumholz, and Perry 1995). Collectively, this change amounts to a shift in the institutional logics that govern economic and community development policy in Cleveland from a "state-bureaucratic" model to a market model (Clarke and Gaile 1998). Critics have argued that these developments are characteristic of strategies that attempt to restart growth through the reconstruction of urban territories to be more amenable to capital accumulation while setting aside concern with equity or democratic deliberation; and there is plenty in the Cleveland case to support this view (Harvey 1989b; Hubbard and Hall 1998; Brenner and Theodore 2002).

It was not easy for Voinovich to get support from the city council and its powerful president for this reconcentration of resources downtown. The key component of the deal he cut was to turn over control of a large chunk of the city's CDBG funds to individual councilmembers for use in their wards. Most of the councilmembers used these dollars to fund the operating costs of ward-based CDCs. Some of these new CDCs would become part of the new development system; many others would act as patronage operations. This deal did make some CDCs less dependent on the Cleveland Foundation and, later, NPI, with the result that Cleveland CDCs are split between those aligned with the development agenda and those acting as patronage operations—a split that has governed conflicts over the direction of Cleveland's community development efforts ever since (Marwell 2004; McQuarrie 2007). What this deal also did was further extend the governance arrangement in neighborhood-based housing development to include the city council and, via the council, the Department of Housing and Urban Development.

The administration of Voinovich's successor, Mike White (1990–2001), tested and extended this shift in institutional logics and governance arrangements. While serving as a councilperson he had been instrumental in the formation of a CDC that quickly became an established presence as a community developer and part of the emerging governance arrangement in housing (with the support of White's CDBG allocation). When elected, he promptly institutionalized that arrangement in the city's executive by hiring two of the most experienced community developers to run his key development agencies. They set about reorganizing municipal government to support those activities.

The most important innovations to come from the White administration were, first, to continue and expand the use of tax abatements on new and rehabilitated housing in order to make Cleveland housing more competitive with suburban housing. Second, the city established a land bank, which greatly facilitated neighborhood development activities. The land bank accelerated establishing city control over delinquent and noncompliant properties. CDCs could then make a single application to the city for any land bank parcels they wanted control over for the purposes of development. Third, White negotiated CRA deals with Cleveland's bankers that resulted in the commitment of hundreds of millions of dollars to local community reinvestment. Fourth, the city used its CDBG allocation to establish a Housing Trust Fund, which is used to facilitate development deals by providing bridge loans and spreading risk (Yin 1998). Finally, White, who was elected with the support of the CDCs, has ensured that there would be a seat at the table for the new community developer even if he was not particularly willing to redistribute resources to Cleveland's neighborhoods. It was this central role for neighborhood-based organizations in the heterarchic governance arrangement for housing production that would represent the institutionalization of the neighborhood-based protest movements of the 1960s and 1970s.

The Heterarchic Governance Arrangement in Housing Production

This overview of the emergence of a housing-centered heterarchic governance arrangement has demonstrated how the provision of housing in Cleveland has been reconstituted to include a variety of different organizational actors from different institutional settings (figure 9.1). The outcome has been a successful engine for neighborhood redevelopment. Where the arrangement began with a few links between largely local organizations, today this arrangement links neighborhood residents and CDCs with local philanthropies, government, and businesses. Beyond the boundaries of the city, CDCs are linked with corporations, institutional investors, and capital markets. On the government side, CDCs are linked with the Ohio Department of Development at the state level (which distributes tax credits), the federal Department of the Treasury (which polices compliance with the tax credits), and the federal Department of Housing and Urban Development (which distributes CDBG money). Also at the national scale, CDCs are linked to national corporations and philanthropies via intermediary organizations such as LISC and Enterprise. Rather than our image of community-based developers as isolated organizations only able to act on a small scale, Cleveland's

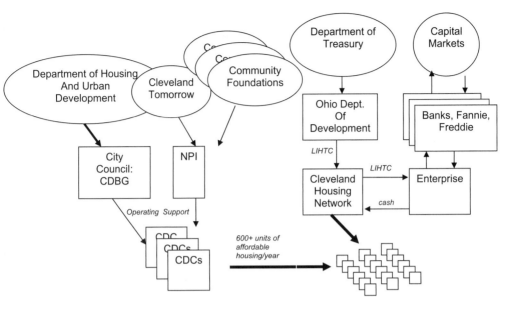

FIGURE 9.1. The low-income housing organizational lash-up.

CDCs are a central component in a governance arrangement that links neighborhoods with a number of national-level organizations and institutions. Taken together, this governance arrangement produces over six hundred homes per year—a huge expansion over the handful produced every year by CHN in its pre-LIHTC years.

After describing this arrangement and its formation, it is useful to pry it apart in order to explore the particular advantages of heterarchy. Most obviously, in Cleveland formal government plays a much more marginal role in development than it once did. The government now mostly invests its resources to facilitate and subsidize other organizations and their projects. These investments come in the form of cheap land, tax abatements, and operational funding for CDCs and mediating organizations. Finally, in a regulative move, Mike White negotiated the CRA agreements with Cleveland's banks. Despite the occasional resistance of the ward-based city council, Cleveland has become much more of an "entrepreneurial city" in which the chimera of growth is prioritized over all else. Perhaps more distinctively, Cleveland's government has reorganized a number of institutions to enable development projects, including the CRA deals, the use of CDBG money for operational support of CDCs, the speedy acquisition of land bank properties, and the overall prioritization of physical development (Eisinger 1988; Clarke and Gaile 1998; Hubbard and Hall 1998; Harvey 1989b; Keating, Krumholz, and Perry 1995). The national government has been just as instrumental, mostly by creating new institutions that made it practical and logical for organizations to cooperate across sectoral lines. Both LIHTC and CRA create powerful incentives for corporations to become partners in community development with both nonprofits and the public sector. This arrangement is not cheap. The LIHTC program, for example, is very expensive both to the taxpayer and the eventual homeowner. The advantage is that these institutions create private-sector partners in community development.

Guided by institutions such as LIHTC and CRA, and provided with specific modes of cooperation by mediating organizations, the private sector has brought capital and sector-specific modes of management and problem solving to the governance arrangement. As a result, the risks and costs of development are not exclusively borne by government and philanthropies. Moreover, a market mechanism is introduced into the process that, while only operating in isolated aspects of the arrangement such as tax credits and syndication, has created efficiencies in financing. For example, brokerage houses have largely supplanted nonprofit mediating organizations as syndicators of tax credits. As a result low-income housing must provide an annual return or the nonprofit developer will not be considered a safe manager of investment dollars. Partnership with for-profit organizations has also necessarily resulted in the introduction of fiscal controls and skills that had not been widely evident among Cleveland's neighborhood-based nonprofits. As a consequence, CDCs are no longer developers of last resort. In an environment where financing development requires the use of numerous complex financial instruments such as tax credits, layered mortgages, and risk-sharing among banks, nonprofit developers are often among the most skilled developers around. This fiscal and development skill is evident in the move of many CDCs to commercial and market-rate housing development. In short, the participation of private firms provides capital, accountability to market mechanisms, and the introduction of practices and institutions from that sector into a functional arena where it had been absent: the provision of low-income housing.

Finally, nonprofits provide a number of functions in this arrangement. Most important, they act as developers; they provide some of the funding via local foundations and they provide a forum for community participation. However, not much of this is particularly new. There are three new aspects. First, nonprofits have secured and maintained the rescaling of governance to enable a degree of community-based control and input into land use and development processes. Second, nonprofits have provided key innovations not just in service delivery and funding but in governance arrangements. It is the innovation of nonprofits that has transformed physical redevelopment practice in Cleveland as well as land use regulations and procedures generally. Third, nonprofits, in the form of mediating organizations, provide the lubricant for the many interlocking gears of heterarchic governance by finding grounds for the coordination of institutions and practices across sectoral lines.

Community control over development was a new idea in the 1960s and 1970s. For the most part, development had been a top-down affair in which residents' voices were marginalized. Indeed, the protest movements described here were, in many ways, a reaction to centralized, citywide control over development. Three things changed that. First, the community congresses established a CDC-based production system in the form of CHN and the lease-purchase system. Second, the effort to establish NPI as the primary developer with the backing of the business community failed in the face of resistance and NPI was forced to work through established CDCs. To put this into perspective, we should keep in mind a prior effort to rescale governance to the community scale, namely, the Community Action Program under the Office of Economic Opportunity during the War on Poverty. This effort to rescale decision making to urban neighborhoods and out of the hands of local growth-oriented elites was an abject failure as the program undermined local Democratic Party machines. In contrast, the governance arrangement described here did amount to an accommodation between the neighborhoods and growth-oriented elites that did rescale significant control over development. The neighborhood-based organizations gained control over resources and decision-making power in exchange for political silence on other development issues. This quid pro quo is not explicit of course. It is an outcome. As CDCs have become more focused on real estate development, they have largely abandoned their role of giving voice to residents' development priorities—a significant narrowing of the mission of nonprofit community development organizations.

NPI and CHN, like many nonprofit organizations, describe themselves as intermediary organizations. Analytically, I prefer the term *mediating organization.* Intermediary organization implies that the organization simply passes through resources and information. On the contrary, I find that NPI, for example, acts as a mediator wherein it actively repackages and reconfigures information and resources in order to further its organizational agenda—an agenda that is focused on strategic real estate development. This agenda has marginalized community development strategies that don't rely on physical development as well as the community's voice in determining the organizational priorities of CDCs, which was a key component of the day-to-day functioning of the community congresses that preceded them. In an environment where NPI retails all foundation funding, an independent course is difficult for CDCs to sustain. On a more positive note, NPI is actively involved in training the CDCs to manage complex financial deals and property development. Consequently, CDCs that are sanctioned by NPI are increasingly coming to be seen as low-risk partners even though they have no capital and do not operate as a private-sector business. CHN, on the other hand, was initially more of an intermediary that was designed to further the implementation of the lease-purchase agenda that had been collectively decided on. However, as CHN has grown it has gotten decisive control over millions in project funding. As a consequence, it has become less attentive to the specific interests of its organizational members.

By calling NPI and CHN mediating organizations, I intend to draw attention to the manner in which they proactively manage the relationship between organizational actors from different sectors and fields to ensure particular outcomes. Moreover, I believe the term flags the importance of such organizations in facilitating heterarchic governance—something which is overlooked when analysis is trumped by descriptions of a mediating organization's activities. They enable organizational actors that operate in very different fields governed by different institutional logics to effectively partner with one another to accomplish a given governance function. If the challenges of economic and state restructuring do indeed drive the move to more heterarchic forms of governance, mediating organizations act as the facilitator of cross-sectoral and cross-field cooperation (Brown 1998; Liou and Stroh 1998; Brown and Kalegaonkar 2002; Weber and Schnell 2003; McDermott 2004; McQuarrie, Guthrie, and Hess 2005; O'Mahoney 2005). Their role as facilitators and innovators, rather than producers, marks this distinctive form of cooperative governance that is organized to achieve cross-sectoral cooperation directed toward narrow functional goals. Mediating organizations are the distinctive organizational forms in heterarchic governance.

Conclusion

The emergence of Cleveland's heterarchic governance arrangement in housing was the product of a contest between different political and institutional projects that were attempting to respond to the urban crisis of the 1970s. Rapid economic decline, fiscal crisis, urban riots, and political protest were indicative of the failure of prior arrangements that were centered on growth coalitions in the electoral arena and federal funds and programs in the policy arena. The contest over institutional reorganization was most evident between Cleveland's neighborhoods and its growth-oriented elites who wanted to concentrate resources downtown, especially once it became clear that municipal government would be too fiscally constrained to engage in proactive interventions. Ultimately, a political accommodation was reached in which growth-oriented elites were able to focus neighborhood organizations on physical redevelopment rather than protesting the distribution of resources. In exchange, neighborhoods received resources and significantly expanded neighborhood control over development. More important for our purposes here, servicing this accommodation required the construction of ad hoc forms of cooperation between different sectors and institutional logics rather than the emergence of a system of governance rationalized around a single institutional setting. Of course, there are numerous advantages to such arrangements. In an environment of economic uncertainty and a crisis of institutional legitimacy, it is unclear what solutions and practices are most appropriate. In the insecure economic environment that Cleveland finds itself in, governance that is dependent on cooperation among actors in different sectors has clear advantages. This success, in turn, has depended on finding ways to organize different settings around a common strategic goal, a process that is mutually constitutive. The result is that institutional settings that were once very different can become more similar over time. Nonprofit developers, for example, start to look more and more like for-profit developers; and the investment criteria of philanthropic program-related investments start to look like the same criteria used by banks.

Whatever else one thinks of the arrangements that have emerged in Cleveland, they are interesting, innovative, and make one pause to contemplate the social achievement entailed in their construction—an achievement that was largely led by nonprofit organizations with ties to very different, indeed divergent, social interests. However, we must be cautious about joining the celebration of governance arrangements. Heterarchic governance in Cleveland has little democratic accountability and has seriously skewed the distribution of resources in the city. Houses are being built at a furious pace in a city whose school system has been deemed unconstitutional and whose economy is still bleeding jobs. Moreover, after twenty years of a system that promised to solve the city's problems through physical redevelopment, in 2005 Cleveland received the distinction of being the most impoverished big city in the country. The poverty rate has not dropped significantly from where it stood even when the city was bankrupt. Recently, the complete collapse of real estate markets in Cleveland due to the collapsing credit bubble suggests that the bet on growth via artificially funneling resources into supporting real estate markets was misdirected.

Lastly, there are significant tensions and contradictions within this arrangement that will be a challenge going forward. First, CDCs have increasingly become driven by the fee income to be garnered from market-rate housing, making it increasingly difficult to distinguish nonprofit developers from for-profit developers; this, in turn, opens the door to the elimination of the advantages of production at the neighborhood scale. In this scenario, development will increasingly move into the hands of the mediating organizations, NPI and CHN, which will, in turn, be doing a lot less mediation and a lot more production. Second, growth-oriented elites came to an accommodation that rescaled some resources and decision making to the neighborhood scale, but that doesn't mean they are particularly happy about it. Currently, they are engaged in an active campaign to rescale governance to the regional scale. Publicly, this is out of a desire to improve regional competitiveness and limit intraregional zero-sum competition. In interviews this is also characterized as a move to outflank the obstruction of the neighborhoods and their representatives on the city council who do not wish to see resources reconcentrated in regional growth poles. Third, however effective the governance arrangement in housing has been at rebuilding neighborhoods and silencing neighborhood-based protest, it has not restarted growth. Cleveland's population continues to decline and it is unclear if there are significant economic growth poles that can underpin renewed growth. There is potential in some areas and there are active interventions by strategic organizations such as Cleveland Tomorrow to facilitate this, but the road Cleveland has traveled is littered with the failure of previous efforts. Finally, as the city continues its downward slide, and as neighborhood-based organizations become increasingly accountable to funders and investors rather than community residents, it seems likely that a new round of neighborhood protest may emerge.

Regardless of the particularities and challenges that will confront low-income-housing developers in the coming years, it seems clear that this very complex form of heterarchic governance represents a serious departure from the implementation of social policy and housing policy in the past. Where once federal housing dollars were usually funneled to local housing authorities that would then build and manage housing, the role of the federal government in this system is that of an indirect financier via tax policy. In many ways, this is indicative of the "hidden welfare state," which has been so ably described by Christopher Howard (1997), and the particular political pressures and opportunities that drive such a mechanism for social provision. However, this dimension of the heterarchic governance arrangement that increasingly prevails in low-income housing is not adequately captured by that idea alone. Equally important here is the role of the particular challenges of housing development in cities with declining economies and weak economic growth. In particular, there is the problem of securing a political accommodation with neighborhoods that are starved of resources. Also central is the increasing need to draw on the resources of businesses not simply for financing (which in this case is subsidized by federal tax policy), but for introducing new mechanisms and controls for the development and management of housing.

As a whole, the arrangement was far more reliant on serendipity and the outcome of political conflict than actual planning or new "policy paradigms" arrived at in the abstract. The uncertainty of early LIHTC developments was evident to all. It has developed into a well-developed and understood tool for community developers only over time and, indeed, it is still constantly being tweaked by lobbyists and Congress. The outcome of these efforts is, however, quite clear. This arrangement has effectively drawn upon the particular advantages of a number of different institutional and normative settings to produce a policy that fulfills a public need. As such, it must be understood not simply as a policy or political achievement but as a social one as well.

References

Adams, B. 1998. "Cleveland: The Partnership City." In *Boundary Crossers: Case Studies of How Ten of America's Metropolitan Regions Work,* edited by Bruce Adams and John Parr. College Park, Md.: University of Maryland Academy of Leadership.

Aldrich, H. 1999. *Organizations Evolving.* Thousand Oaks, Calif.: SAGE.

Amin, A., ed. 1994. *Post-Fordism: A Reader.* Oxford: Blackwell.

Ballard, M. J. 2003. "Profiting from Poverty: The Competition between For-Profit and Nonprofit Developers for Low-Income Housing Tax Credits." *Hastings Law Journal* 55, no. 9: 211–43.

Bartimole, R. 1995. "Who Governs: The Corporate Hand." In *Cleveland: A Metropolitan Reader,* edited by W. D. Keating, N. Krumholz, and D. Perry. Kent, Ohio: Kent State University Press.

Block, F. 1977. *The Origins of International Economic Disorder: A Study of United States International Monetary Policy from World War II to the Present.* Berkeley: University of California Press.

Bluestone, B., and B. Harrison. 1982. *The Deindustrialization of America: Plant Closings, Community Abandonment, and the Dismantling of Basic Industry.* New York: Basic Books.

Boris, E. T. 1999. "Introduction—Nonprofit Organizations in a Democracy: Varied Roles and Responsibilities." In *Nonprofits and Government: Collaboration and Conflict,* edited by E. T. Boris and E. Steuerle, 3–30. Washington, D.C.: Urban Institute.

Boyte, H. C. 1980. *The Backyard Revolution: Understanding the New Citizen Movement.* Philadelphia: Temple University Press.

Brenner, N., and N. Theodore. 2002. *Spaces of Neoliberalism: Urban Restructuring in North America and Western Europe.* Oxford: Blackwell.

Brown, L. D. 1998. "Creating Social Capital: Nongovernmental Development Organizations and Intersectoral Problem Solving." In *Private Action and the Public Good,* edited by W. W. Powell and E. S. Clemens, 228–41. New Haven: Yale University Press.

Brown, L. D., and A. Kalegaonkar. 2002. "Support Organizations and the Evolution of the NGO Sector." *Nonprofit and Voluntary Sector Quarterly* 31, no. 2: 231–58.

Burns, T., and K. Wing. 2001. *A Decade of Development: An Assessment of Neighborhood Progress, Inc.* Philadelphia: OMG Center for Collaborative Learning.

Campbell, J. L. 2004. *Institutional Change and Globalization.* Princeton: Princeton University Press.

Campbell, J. L., and O. K. Pedersen. 2001. *The Rise of Neoliberalism and Institutional Analysis.* Princeton: Princeton University Press.

Clarke, S. E., and G. L. Gaile. 1998. *The Work of Cities.* Minneapolis: University of Minnesota Press.

Clavel, P. 1985. *The Progressive City: Planning and Participation, 1969–1984.* New Brunswick, N.J.: Rutgers University Press.

Clemens, E., and J. Cook. 1999. "Politics and Institutionalism: Explaining Durability and Change." *Annual Review of Sociology* 25: 441–466.

Cunningham, R. 2004. "What We Need to Do: The Rise and Fall of Community Organizing in Cleveland, 1975–1985." Cleveland: Neighborhood Progress Inc.

Deleuze, G. 1988. *Foucault.* Minneapolis: University of Minnesota Press.

Deleuze, G., and F. Guattari. 1987. *A Thousand Plateaus: Capitalism and Schizophrenia.* Minneapolis: University of Minnesota Press.

DiMaggio, P. 1991. "Constructing an Organizational Field as a Professional Project: U.S. Art Museums, 1920–1940." In *The New Institutionalism in Organizational Analysis,* edited by W. W. Powell and P. J. DiMaggio. Chicago: University of Chicago Press.

Eisinger, P. K. 1988. *The Rise of the Entrepreneurial State: State and Local Economic Development Policy in the United States.* Madison: University of Wisconsin Press.

Fligstein, N. 2001. "Social Skill and the Theory of Fields." *Sociological Theory* 19, no. 2: 105–25.

Fourcade-Gourinchas, M., and S. L. Babb. 2002. "The Rebirth of the Liberal Creed: Paths to Neoliberalism in Four Countries." *American Journal of Sociology* 108, no. 3: 533–79.

Friedland, R., and R. R. Alford. 1991. "Bringing Society Back In: Symbols, Practices, and Institutional Contradictions." In *The New Institutionalism in Organizational Analysis,* edited by W. W. Powell and P. J. DiMaggio, 232–63. Chicago: University of Chicago Press.

Goldsmith, S., and W. Eggers. 2004. *Governing by Network: The New Shape of the Public Sector.* Washington, D.C.: Brookings Institution.

Grogan, P., and T. Proscio. 2000. *Comeback Cities: A Blueprint for Urban Neighborhood Revival.* Boulder, Colo.: Westview Press.

Gronbjerg, K. 1987. "Patterns of Institutional Relations in the Welfare State: Public Mandates and the Nonprofit Sector." *Journal of Voluntary Action Research* 16: 64–80.

———. 1998. "Markets, Politics, and Charity: Nonprofits in the Political Economy." In *Private Action and the Public Good,* edited by W. W. Powell and E. S. Clemens. New Haven: Yale University Press.

Guthrie, D., and M. McQuarrie. 2005. "Privatization and the Social Contract: Corporate Welfare and Low-Income Housing in the United States since 1986." *Research in Political Sociology* 14: 15–50.

Hackworth, J. R. 2007. *The Neoliberal City: Governance, Ideology, and Development in American Urbanism.* Ithaca: Cornell University Press.

Hall, P. A. 1993. "Policy Paradigms, Social Learning, and the State: The Case of Economic Policymaking in Britain." *Comparative Politics* 25, no. 3: 275–96.

Hammack, D. 1989. "Community Foundations: The Delicate Question of Purpose." In *An Agile Servant,* edited by R. Magat, 23–50. New York: Foundation Center.

Harvey, D. 1989a. *The Condition of Postmodernity.* Oxford: Blackwell.

———. 1989b. "From Managerialism to Entrepreneurialism: The Transformation of Urban Governance in Late Capitalism." *Geografiska Annaler* 71B: 3–17.

Hay, C. 2004. "The Normalizing Role of Rationalist Assumption in the Institutional Embedding of Neoliberalism." *Economy and Society* 33, no. 4: 500–527.

Howard, C. 1997. *The Hidden Welfare State: Tax Expenditures and Social Policy in the United States.* Princeton: Princeton University Press.

Hubbard, P., and T. Hall. 1998. "The Entrepreneurial City and the 'New Urban Politics.'" In *The Entrepreneurial City: Geographies of Politics, Regime, and Representation,* edited by T. Hall and P. Hubbard. New York: John Wiley and Sons.

Jenkins, J. C. 1998. "Channeling Social Protest: Foundation Patronage of Contemporary Social Movements." In *Private Action and the Public Good,* edited by W. W. Powell and E. S. Clemens. New Haven: Yale University Press.

Jessop, B. 1997. "The Governance of Complexity and the Complexity of Governance: Preliminary Remarks on Some Problems and Limits of Economic Guidance." In *Beyond Market and Hierarchy: Interactive Governance and Social Complexity,* edited by A. Amin and J. Hausner. Lyme, U.K.: Edward Elgar.

Keating, W. D., N. Krumholz, and D. Perry. 1995. "Postpopulist Public-Private Partnerships." In *Cleveland: A Metropolitan Reader,* edited by W. D. Keating, N. Krumholz, and D. Perry. Kent, Ohio: Kent State University Press.

Kooiman, J. 1993. "Social-Political Governance: Introduction." In *Modern Governance,* edited by J. Kooiman. London: Sage.

Lash, S., and J. Urry. 1987. *The End of Organized Capitalism.* Madison: University of Wisconsin Press.

Latour, B. 1987. *Science in Action.* Cambridge: Harvard University Press.

———. 2004. *Reassembling the Social: An Introduction to Actor-Network Theory.* Oxford: Oxford University Press.

Liou, Y. T., and R. C. Stroh. 1998. "Community Development Intermediary Systems in the United States: Origins, Evolution, Functions." *Housing Policy Debate* 9, no. 3: 575–94.

Logan, J. R., and H. Molotch. 1987. *Urban Fortunes: The Political Economy of Place.* Berkeley: University of California Press.

Marwell, N. 2004. "Privatizing the Welfare State: Nonprofit Community-Based Organizations as Political Actors." *American Sociological Review* 69, no. 2: 265–91.

McDermott, M. 2004. "National Intermediaries and Local Community Development Corporations." *Journal of Urban Affairs* 26, no. 2: 171–76.

McQuarrie, M. 2007. "Backyard Revolution to Neoliberalism: Community Development, Civil Society, and the American Third Way." PhD diss., Department of Sociology, New York University, New York.

McQuarrie, M., D. Guthrie, and A. Hess. 2005. "Intermediary Organizations and the Coordination of Social Practices." Presentation at American Sociological Association Annual Meeting, Philadelphia, August 13.

Mollenkopf, J. H. 1983. *The Contested City.* Princeton: Princeton University Press.

Molotch, H. 1976. "The City as Growth Machine." *American Journal of Sociology* 82, no. 2: 309–322.

Moore, L. N. 2002. *Carl B. Stokes and the Rise of Black Political Power.* Urbana: University of Illinois Press.

O'Mahoney, S. 2005. "The Role of Boundary Institutions in Reconciling Convergent and Divergent Interests." Presentation at American Sociological Association Annual Meeting, Philadelphia, August 13.

Osborne, D., and T. Gaebler. 1993. *Reinventing Government: How the Entrepreneurial Spirit Is Transforming the Public Sector.* New York: Plume.

Peterson, P. E. 1981. *City Limits.* Chicago: University of Chicago Press.

Powell, W.W. 1991. "Neither Market nor Hierarchy: Network Forms of Organization." In *Markets, Hierarchies, and Networks: The Coordination of Social Life,* edited by G. Thompson, J. Frances, R. Levacic, and J. Mitchell. Newbury Park, Calif.: Sage.

Rhodes, R. A. W. 1996. "The New Governance: Governing without Government." *Political Studies* 44: 652–67.

———. 1997. *Understanding Governance: Policy Networks, Governance, Reflexivity, and Accountability.* Buckingham: Open University Press.

Safford, S. 2004. "Why the Garden Club Couldn't Save Youngstown: Civic Infrastructure and Mobilization in Economic Crises." *MIT IPC Working Paper Series* 04–002.

Salamon, L. M. 1995. *Partners in Public Service: Government-Nonprofit Relations in the Modern Welfare State.* Baltimore, Md.: Johns Hopkins University Press.

Shatten, R. 1995. "Cleveland Tomorrow: A Practicing Model of New Roles and Processes for Corporate Leadership in Cities." In *Cleveland: A Metropolitan Reader,* edited by W. D. Keating, N. Krumholz, and D. Perry. Kent, Ohio: Kent State University Press.

Sirianni, C., and L. Friedland. 2001. *Civic Innovation in America: Community Empowerment, Public Policy, and the Movement for Civic Renewal.* Berkeley: University of California Press.

Squires, G. D. 1992. *From Redlining to Reinvestment: Community Responses to Urban Disinvestment.* Philadelphia: Temple University Press.

Stark, D. 1996. "Recombinant Property in East European Capitalism." *American Journal of Sociology* 101, no. 4: 993–1027.

Stoker, G. 1998. "Governance as Theory: Five Propositions." *International Social Science Journal* 50, no. 155: 17–28.

Sugrue, T. 1996. *The Origins of the Urban Crisis: Race and Inequality in Postwar Detroit.* Princeton: Princeton University Press.

Swanstrom, T. 1985. *The Crisis of Growth Politics: Cleveland, Kucinich, and the Challenge of Urban Populism.* Philadelphia: Temple University Press.

Tittle, D. 1992. *Rebuilding Cleveland: The Cleveland Foundation and Its Evolving Urban Strategy.* Columbus: Ohio State University Press.

Warren, C. 1995. "Housing: New Lessons, New Models." In *Cleveland: A Met-*

ropolitan Reader, edited by W. D. Keating, N. Krumholz, and D. Perry. Kent, Ohio: Kent State University Press.

Weber, R., and S. Schnell. 2003. "Contracting In: How a Business Intermediary Sought to Create Supplier Networks and Jobs in the Inner City." *Economic Development Quarterly* 17, no. 2: 148–64.

Weisbrod, B. 1977. *The Voluntary Nonprofit Sector: An Economic Analysis.* Lexington, Mass.: Lexington Books.

Wolch, J. R. 1990. *The Shadow State: Government and Voluntary Sector in Transition.* New York: Foundation Center.

Yin, J. 1998. "The Community Development Industry System: A Case Study of Politics and Institutions in Cleveland, 1967–1997." *Journal of Urban Affairs* 20, no. 2: 137–57.

CHAPTER TEN

Evangelical Megachurches and the Christianization of Civil Society: An Ethnographic Case Study

Omri Elisha

Religious congregations are frequently touted among scholars and civic leaders as preeminent sites for the production of social capital in the United States, unique among voluntary associations for their longevity and the solidarity they inspire among members. An issue that has received far less attention is the cultural content of social capital in specific communities. What, for example, are the moral and ideological goals that members of distinct religious groups seek to achieve as they form new relationships and social networks? Given evangelical Protestantism's historic rise to prominence in recent years, and the steady decline of liberal mainline churches, it has become especially necessary to address such questions through interpretive and ethnographic studies of the social worlds inhabited by conservative evangelical churchgoers. The proliferation of evangelical megachurches, in particular, deserves closer scrutiny with regard to the purpose, character, and potential consequences of social capital generated therein. Rooted firmly in Christian revivalist and missionary traditions, these large and resourceful congregations are useful case studies for analyzing social cohesion in religious settings as well as the complex power dynamics that emerge as evangelical pastors and activists expand their influence in civil society through philanthropic endeavors.

That megachurches are well suited to the task of promoting community among their members is in many ways self-evident, given that one of the main features of the modern church-growth movement is its emphasis on community as a moral and religious ideal.[1] Many churchgoers are drawn to megachurches precisely because they offer the benefits of social belonging combined with the spectacle of corporate worship, as well as programs and activities catered to a variety of personal, spiritual, and professional needs. It is hardly surprising then that in a recent survey of "social capital success stories," Putnam and Feldstein (2003) include a chapter on Saddleback Church, one of the largest megachurches in America with a congregation of over twenty thousand.[2] Their analysis suggests that key elements of the congregational culture of the megachurch, including the presence of strong communitarian values and strict moral codes, are conducive to the creation of social networks defined by bonds of trust and reciprocity. The authors also note that Saddleback is a predominantly white and affluent congregation, and most relationships therefore take the form of what Putnam calls "bonding social capital," which builds on existing affinities among individuals of the same social class or group identity. Although this is an accurate assessment, missing from this analysis is a serious consideration of the extent to which the members of evangelical megachurches try—with varying degrees of success—to reach out beyond the social confines of their congregations to produce religiously inflected "bridging social capital" (staying with Putnam's terminology) with poor and minority communities.

In the following discussion, based on ethnographic research conducted in Knoxville, Tennessee, over fifteen months spanning from 1999 through 2001, I analyze just such an effort. Marble Valley Presbyterian (a pseudonym) is a conservative, suburban, and almost entirely white evangelical congregation a fraction the size of Saddleback. Beginning in the late 1990s, the deeply mission-oriented megachurch used its wealth of resources to develop an institutional partnership with a financially dependent black church in Knoxville's inner city. The partnership was meant to foster racial reconciliation as well as stimulate economic and

1. For information about American megachurches, consult Scott Thumma's comprehensive megachurch database at the website of the Hartford Institute for Religion Research (at Hartford Theological Seminary): http://hirr.hartsem.edu/.

2. Saddleback Church is located in Orange County, California, and is led by celebrity pastor Rick Warren, the author of *The Purpose-Driven Life,* which has sold over twenty-five million copies since it was published in 2002. Saddleback epitomizes the "new paradigm" of American religiosity (Miller 1997), with an emphasis on innovative ministries and worship services, doctrinal minimalism, therapeutic support groups, educational and recreational activities, and active outreach programs. Like most U.S. megachurches, Saddleback is predominantly white and middle class and theologically conservative.

community development in the inner city with the assistance of several intermediary agencies. The motives behind the philanthropic initiatives reflected a desire among leaders and congregants to see the megachurch realize its full outreach potential and enhance its public profile as a regional institution. The aim of my discussion is not to assess the merits or achievement of those efforts. Rather, I want to explore how the membership of Marble Valley Presbyterian conceived of the relationships—interpersonal and institutional—that were intended to result from intrasectoral linkages formed within networks of cooperation in which the megachurch held a position of moral authority.

I argue that when affluent conservative evangelicals engage in bridge-building activities of this kind, their efforts must be understood as qualitatively distinct from those of secular and/or progressive organizations in the nonprofit sector. This is not simply due to the commonly overstated fact that evangelicals "only help people so that they can convert them." Although the mandate to proselytize and convert is certainly foremost in churchgoers' minds, their social practices as a group—and in this case as members of a powerful local church—are rooted in an even broader and encompassing religious agenda: the Christianization of civil society. This entails more than just a desire for political or institutional dominance; it is properly understood as a kind of *cultural* Christianization, in that what evangelicals seek to do is to infuse civil society, and all relationships constituted within that realm, with religious values and moral codes stemming from the dictates of conservative evangelical Protestantism. For evangelical pastors, activists, and lay churchgoers, the production of social capital has little value in and of itself but it attains redemptive value in the context of social relationships in which the principles of "true" Christian faith are embodied and exemplified.

Of those principles, I focus on the concept of *accountability,* as it is understood by conservative evangelicals. The significance of this concept in evangelical social outreach is a useful reminder that the production of social capital means different things in different segments of society and can be mobilized for different purposes (Arneil 2006). Civic enterprises of the kind described here are, for evangelicals, animated in large part by the will to practice, reinforce, and impose what they view as biblical standards of moral, spiritual, and financial accountability: tasks that are ultimately oriented toward the loftier religious aims of evangelism and Christianization. At the same time, I argue that the formation of institutional partnerships that depend largely on the patronage of suburban megachurches leads to situations in which affluent church-goers are able to determine the conditions of benevolence and account-ability, and thereby exercise political and social power over the recipi-ent communities. In addition, they assert power in the local nonprofit sector—the power to promote conservative approaches to poverty re-lief and community development, and to effectively preclude progressive models of social and economic justice.

Studies have repeatedly shown that religious organizations make sig-nificant contributions to the health and vitality of civil society, as their members are regularly exposed to avenues of civic participation, in-cluding welfare voluntarism, community organizing, and political activ-ism (Cnaan et al. 2002; Verba, Schlozman, and Brady 1995). The ide-alization of religious organizations as "mediating structures" (Berger and Neuhaus 1977) in American society is based on the fact that they al-low people to engage in socially productive activities in the public sphere presumably unhindered by state and/or market forces. However, as the chapters in this book demonstrate, mediating structures rarely function as autonomously as an ideal model of the public sphere suggests. In the case of faith-based charity organizations, for example, it would be dif-ficult to thoroughly assess their impact on civil society without viewing such organizations within a larger systemic framework, that is, acknowl-edging that they remain embedded in elaborate and expansive networks of social, philanthropic, and political institutions (Wuthnow 2004). This applies as well to megachurches, where abundant human and material resources are concentrated and mobilized for various community-wide initiatives and social programs beyond the sanctuary walls. Adopting a systemic framework for analyzing new forms of conservative evangelical activism is particularly advantageous since those who are engaged in so-cial outreach ministries often conceive their efforts in precisely systemic terms. Although evangelicals are known as staunch individualists, at the same time their strategies of cultivating and utilizing broad-ranging social and institutional relationships are meant to advance regimes of moral governance in civil society that resonate with orthodox Christian sensibilities.

When we take the time to examine specific meanings attached to mo-tivational concepts within social groups, we can better understand how such concepts acquire the power to mobilize, justify, or impede various forms of social action. This, in turn, allows us to gain a more critical per-spective on the similarities and differences among diverse groups and institutions that interact in public life as partners, patrons, and competitors. One of the distinct values of ethnographic research, which relies on extended participant observation, is the attention to the nuances and complexities of the moral ambitions that individuals learn, enact, and revise as they engage their social world. Ethnography, in this sense, is more than just a method of describing what it is that people are doing; it is a way of bringing to light their ideals, desires, and contradictions. It is also a way of analyzing the role that cultural institutions play in shaping the social and political dynamics that define local communities, and in resolving or exacerbating tensions that arise as groups compete over the terms of civil society.

Marble Valley Presbyterian Church

Marble Valley Presbyterian Church is one of the oldest and most widely recognized churches in Knoxville.[3] The congregation began to experience dramatic growth in the 1960s, following the tide of suburbanization that overcame rural areas just beyond the city limits where the church is located. By 2002, the official membership tally was listed as 3,648, but when nonmembers and visitors are taken into account the number of weekly churchgoers is as high as 5,000. Although this is small by the standards of massive churches such as Saddleback, it is not insignificant for Knox County (pop. ~382,000), where there are many Christian congregations but only a handful of such size and prominence. Multiple worship services on Sunday, morning and evening, as well as midweek vespers, accommodate the growing number of churchgoers.

The worship style at Marble Valley Presbyterian is typically "high church," complete with cushioned wooden pews, a traditional liturgy, and classical hymns sung by a choir of singers in black robes accompanied by a pipe organ. At the same time, the megachurch regularly incorporates contemporary elements into its worship services—including "praise songs" and electronic instruments—that have made the megachurch attractive to young newcomers. In this blending of traditional and contemporary aesthetics, Marble Valley Presbyterian exemplifies many qualities that have been identified as distinctive markers of evangelical

---

3. All churches, nonprofit organizations, and individuals in Knoxville appear in this article under pseudonyms. In some cases, identifying details have been altered as well.

megachurches born of the modern church-growth movement (Thumma 1996).

Marble Valley Presbyterian occupies a large chunk of real estate near a busy commercial intersection. Over several years the megachurch purchased adjoining land and developed it into an expansive complex of church buildings, parking lots, and recreational facilities. This concentrated infrastructure allows the megachurch to provide a wide range of ministries, programs, and events that cater to the diverse interests and needs of its membership, which is composed mainly of white, suburban professionals with families. A number of the congregation's members are among the region's political, cultural, and business elite, including several prominent corporate executives, two recent city mayors, leaders of various community organizations, and a few local media celebrities. Marble Valley Presbyterian's local reputation as an affluent, even somewhat aristocratic congregation is well deserved, as many of the churchgoers I met live in upscale residential subdivisions in and around Knox County. The fact that the congregation is almost entirely white is consistent with regional patterns of racial segregation that map conspicuously along the urban-suburban divide.

Marble Valley Presbyterian belongs to a denomination called the Evangelical Presbyterian Church (EPC), which it joined after leaving the Presbyterian Church of America (PCA) because of conflicts over congregational autonomy. Both denominations reflect the megachurch's theological conservatism, but church elders believed that the more flexible denominationalism of the EPC would better accommodate their various ministry innovations and expansions. As with its worship aesthetics, Marble Valley Presbyterian blends traditional and contemporary elements in the church authority structure. Male pastors, elders, and deacons oversee church administration, but this traditional hierarchy is complemented by an elaborate network of "teams" composed of ordained pastors, paid staff, and laypeople (men and women) who carry out day-to-day functions, administrative as well as pastoral. These "accountability teams" (as they are often referred to) provide clear avenues for delegating authority and reaffirm the value of accountability as an organizing principle within the megachurch. They reflect the widespread belief that churches, no less than major corporations, function best with an integrated division of labor, ordered hierarchically, in which groups of task-oriented individuals work according to their abilities and gifts in pursuit of common goals.

Much of Marble Valley Presbyterian's success in church growth is attributed to the preaching abilities of its senior pastor, Pastor Jerry. A mild-mannered and self-possessed figure, Pastor Jerry is known throughout the region for his intellectual breadth and homiletic skills. His preaching style reflects a strategic departure from the angry Bible-thumping of Southern revivalism, and his "intentionally postmodern" approach to ministry involves an intellectual willingness to engage with diverse interpretations and opinions, within certain moral and theological parameters. Pastor Jerry explained to me that Christians should not read the Bible with blind faith in Western interpretive traditions but should learn to listen to different interpretations of scripture among Christians in other cultures (again, within certain bounds of acceptable deviance). I observed over time that this commitment to open-mindedness and cross-cultural communication—what Pastor Jerry referred to as "multiperspectivalism"—is a critical aspect of Marble Valley Presbyterian's overall ambition for itself as a congregation. Pastor Jerry and many (not all) of his congregants share the conviction that a church's ability to reach out beyond its own boundaries is essential because that is "a sign of the future kingdom."

Marble Valley Presbyterian has a strong emphasis on global missions. In 2002, 14 percent of the church's $5 million general budget and $2 million in additional donations were allocated to support missionary societies and over one hundred individual missionaries all over the world. The megachurch also supports medical missions and humanitarian relief organizations. Bolstered by its annual Global Missions Conference, a highly anticipated event among churchgoers, Marble Valley Presbyterian takes great pride in its investments in foreign missions.

A small portion of the megachurch's budget for missions is earmarked for "home missions," which includes support for missionaries and parachurch ministries in North America. Also included in this category is support for social outreach ministries, based both within the megachurch and in cooperation with local faith-based organizations that provide social services in and around Knoxville. The megachurch has supported social outreach activities for several decades, but they have never been among the congregation's top priorities. While the foreign missions budget is augmented by financial donations that churchgoers specifically designate for that purpose, the modest budget for "home missions" is assigned directly from the megachurch's general operating budget and is rarely an explicit target for congregational fund-raising campaigns. Over the last decade, however, a level of interest in social issues affecting the community at large has developed among members of the congregation, particularly with regard to problems related to urban poverty. This interest has largely been fueled by the mobilization efforts of select individuals within the congregation who have dedicated themselves, in one way or another, to the task of helping the megachurch realize its full potential as a socially engaged religious institution. These evangelical activists believe that the megachurch (and others like it) will have an extraordinary impact on the social and moral health of the region once it effectively channels its considerable resources toward sustained social outreach ministries and community initiatives. Community development in Knoxville's inner city became for Marble Valley Presbyterian one of the sites for the congregation's investment in such endeavors, and this has involved institutional partnerships that, for reasons discussed further on, have presented several practical and moral challenges for the suburban megachurch.[4]

Over the course of my fieldwork, I often heard evangelicals who attend megachurches express frustration about what they perceived as the relatively weak social impact of their congregations (that is, relative to their size) in the larger community. Unlike evangelical critics who find fault with megachurches for their explicit uses of corporate marketing strategies and popular culture (Hart 2000; Horton 2000; Pritchard 1996), churchgoers at Marble Valley Presbyterian are more concerned about the problems of social withdrawal and isolationism. Sensitive to their demographic homogeneity and relative privilege, churchgoers are self-conscious that their congregation looks to outsiders more like a country club or gated community than a church. They want neither to appear elitist nor indifferent to the world around them, and thus one can observe a certain sense of urgency as pastors and mobilizers speak of the

---

4. The whole question of whether churches should be engaged in social action of any kind is a complicated and often controversial issue among conservative evangelicals. For much of the last century, evangelicals have wrestled with the separatist ideology of Christian fundamentalism. The fundamentalist worldview is driven by antimodern, antiliberal sentiments, and influenced by premillennial dispensationalism, an end-times theology that asserts that the world is in a state of perpetual degeneration and can only be saved upon Christ's return. According to this perspective, the sole mission of the Christian church is to proclaim the gospel and indoctrinate as many new believers as possible before the Second Coming. Conservative evangelicals, many of whom are strongly influenced by fundamentalist sensibilities, proceed cautiously, if at all, with ministries that involve social interventions, especially if they appear to invoke the progressivism of the Social Gospel movement of the early twentieth century.

need to increase the megachurch's investments in social outreach and community revitalization.

The desire among white evangelicals in the suburbs of Knoxville to bridge the gaps between themselves and regional cultural strangers (i.e., minorities and the poor) is as much in response to the region's political-economic conditions as it is a theological mandate. The persistence of racial alienation and conspicuous residential segregation in Knox County offers a case in point. Most neighborhoods in the metropolitan area lean decisively toward one racial group or another. The African American population is concentrated and economically isolated within the city limits, far removed from the suburban office parks, subdivisions, and congregations where upwardly mobile whites live, work, and worship (the county population is 88% white). De facto segregation in Knoxville is the result of generations of institutional racism and social conservatism. The conditions are less severe than in other parts of the South, but the fact remains that white evangelicals typically do not acknowledge the systemic roots of racial inequality and thus seldom express any concern with instituting broad social reform.

Nonetheless, members of Marble Valley Presbyterian did express a keen interest in "racial reconciliation," an idea that gained popularity in evangelical circles nationwide during the 1990s (see Emerson and Smith 2000, 63–68). The aim of racial reconciliation, in the minds of white evangelicals, is the formation of redemptive relationships across once-impenetrable cultural boundaries. It is anticipated that such relationships will radically transform individual lives and society as a whole. Supporting and partnering with a local black church became an essential component to realizing these ideals. As we will see, the relationship that developed between Marble Valley Presbyterian and the financially dependent Harvest Glory allowed the megachurch to pursue its aims, but the relationship also reflected and reinforced regional power dynamics and social stratification. In the absence of sufficient resources from public or private sources (for example, state agencies and secular philanthropies) for struggling communities in the inner city, suburban evangelical megachurches like Marble Valley Presbyterian step in to assume patronage roles that not only allow white conservative churchgoers to feel as though they are fulfilling a religious mandate but also allow them to stake privileged claims as power brokers and moral arbiters of civil society.

Racial Partnerships and Racial Politics

In 1997, Marble Valley Presbyterian established an official partnership with Harvest Glory. The small, newly formed, black evangelical congregation was composed of churchgoers who split away from another inner-city church that members felt was weak in addressing problems in the community such as poverty, inadequate housing, and gang violence. The breakaway congregation, under the youthful and charismatic leadership of Pastor Leon, was in desperate need of financial support and some form of sponsorship that would enable the church to establish itself and develop its community ministries. Through a series of interpersonal connections, the leadership of Marble Valley Presbyterian became aware of the needs and plans of Harvest Glory. With the urging of a group of elders and churchgoers who were eager to see the megachurch develop greater racial sensitivity and social engagement, church leaders agreed to initiate a process of familiarization and encouraged members of their respective congregations to participate in a series of workshops intended to foster interracial dialogue and reconciliation.

Shortly after, a council of elders (known as the Session) at Marble Valley Presbyterian voted to approve a fund-raising campaign to underwrite a third of the costs of building a $1.5 million facility that would serve as Harvest Glory's new worship center and a base for its ministries. A number of the white churchgoers who took part in the racial reconciliation workshops were real-estate developers, bank executives, and architects, and they ended up donating valuable skills and resources to the construction of the new facility, as well as to the development of twenty-three acres of adjoining property, purchased with additional financial backing from the megachurch. The adjoining property was to become the site of a community-based housing initiative.

Eventually the two churches came to refer to one another as "sister churches." The most public expression of their newfound affinity took the form of joint worship services, staged once or twice a year, usually in the megachurch's sanctuary. At these services, Pastor Jerry and Pastor Leon shared the pulpit while choir singers from both churches stood side by side and sang a mixed repertoire of gospel music and classical hymns. (An elderly woman at Marble Valley Presbyterian commented to me that the image of a mixed-race church choir reminded her of "what heaven must look like," even though she also admitted that she never felt entirely comfortable with the exuberance of black gospel singing.) The use of the term "sister church" is revealing here for what it indexes and what it conceals. On one hand, it represents egalitarian kinship and doctrinal fellowship, with a gendered emphasis that highlights the symbolic feminization of all churches in relation to "the lordship of Jesus Christ." On the other hand, the term obscures vertical power dynamics that are intrinsic to institutional partnerships that are, in the first place, built upon social and economic inequalities. This aspect of the sister-church link, at once unspoken and glaringly apparent, caused certain tensions to emerge in the partnership of Marble Valley Presbyterian and Harvest Glory over issues having to do with the management of financial resources, and, more generally, over conflicting expectations about the precise nature of the partnership and the extent of the megachurch's authority to make practical demands.

The likelihood that tensions would develop amid all the high hopes and good intentions must have been evident from the start. For one thing, the congregations represent differing perspectives on the exact meaning and purpose of racial reconciliation. White and black evangelicals share a basic impetus toward equality and harmony, as well as an emphasis on the importance of transparency, repentance, and forgiveness. However, the social-justice inclination that typically resides in black evangelical churches like Harvest Glory conflicts with the far more conservative and individualistic attitudes found among white evangelicals (Emerson and Smith 2000). Such discrepancies became consequential as the partnership between Harvest Glory and Marble Valley Presbyterian evolved, and as members of each congregation came to understand the way that their racial counterparts interpreted racial politics and the social challenges that African Americans face. However, an even bigger source of contention—one with more immediate implications—was a problem involving notions of accountability; namely, the frustration among leaders in the megachurch over what was perceived as Harvest Glory's lack of adequate mechanisms to ensure institutional accountability.

Although the leadership of Marble Valley Presbyterian generally approached the relationship with enthusiasm, they also had doubts and deep concerns (as did churchgoers at Harvest Glory). When the Session initially approved the fund-raising campaign on behalf of Harvest Glory, they did so with the expectation that the church would eventually raise its own funds to cover the remaining balance. At the time, several prom-

inent elders expressed concern that this would not happen and warned
of the possibility that their congregation would get stuck having to alleviate the black church's financial burdens. As it happened, their fears were
somewhat justified. Harvest Glory struggled in its early years to become
financially solvent, and the relationship between the "sister churches"
was frequently strained because of the perception among members of
Marble Valley Presbyterian that Harvest Glory was willfully irresponsi-
ble with its finances. A string of crises nearly caused the partnership to
collapse, including one instance when the megachurch ended up paying
Harvest Glory's outstanding property taxes. Such problems only compounded negative perceptions already present among white evangelicals
about black culture, particularly the assumption that black communities
lack strong commitments to the virtues of accountability and fiscal sol-
vency. For white evangelicals, this is more than a practical problem; it is
viewed as a distinctly moral and spiritual one.

Given their social isolation from the black community, conservative
white evangelicals in Knoxville hold many cultural stereotypes, negative
and positive, affecting their attitudes toward African Americans. One of
their guiding preconceptions (although it is seldom made explicit, in the
interest of propriety) is the belief that the urban black community experiences persistent poverty and social dysfunction due to the absence of
a vibrant civic and entrepreneurial spirit. Echoing the logic of the well-
known (and widely criticized) "culture of poverty" thesis, white evangelicals presume that social mobility and economic sustainability is limited for African Americans primarily because urban black culture fails
to promote the values of personal responsibility, meritocratic ambition,
and moral community. Paradoxically, African Americans are perceived
by some white evangelicals as having an innate spirituality that is deeper
and more intense than that of most whites. Rooted in racial ideologies of
no less significance, such estimations contribute to the profound sense of
ambivalence experienced by white evangelicals who lament the history
of racial oppression and believe in the potential of the black church but
doubt the leadership and (implicitly) the moral competence of African
American communities.

Although many churchgoers were often uncomfortable discussing
these issues, one person who was particularly open and candid with me
was a church elder named Norman Griswall. In addition to being closely
involved in the early stages of the partnership between Marble Valley
Presbyterian and Harvest Glory, Norman aptly demonstrated the con-

flicted attitudes and expectations present among members of Marble Valley Presbyterian. Though a consistent and avid supporter of the endeavor, he confessed to a degree of ambivalence and uncertainty about the partnership. He noted, with some resignation, that among the chief problems to emerge between the two congregations was the fact that, from the perspective of the megachurch, "we wanted to hold them accountable, and they didn't want to be held accountable."

The preconceptions that guide Norman Griswall's evaluation of the situation are representative of a good portion of his fellow congregants, if not a majority. As I came to know Norman, I found him to be in many respects especially open-minded and tolerant on various intercultural issues. Like many white evangelicals, however, he struggles to reconcile his tolerance with his racial biases, a struggle he engages self-consciously and which he describes as even more challenging when his biases are reinforced in his encounters with African Americans.

On the one hand, he explained to me how he has come to realize that the urban black community displays "a spiritual depth and reliance on the providence of God" that he feels is virtually absent among middle-class whites. He has also come to believe that blacks do not obsess over money and material possessions "the way us WASPs and capitalists do," and that there are some "spiritual advantages" to having a less materialistic outlook on life. On the other hand, Norman noted that there are significant disadvantages to what he saw as a cultural predisposition among blacks to downplay the importance of financial responsibility. These disadvantages have potentially serious practical consequences for black churches, which, he observed, "live from one financial crisis to another." In seeking to explain this phenomenon, Norman attributed it to two behavioral factors that he assumes to be characteristic of urban black culture in general. First, he noted that African Americans tend to blame all of their problems on racism, which he believes causes poor blacks to develop a false sense of entitlement and prevents them from appreciating the rigors and realities of economic development. As an example, Norman pointed out that while black people complain about being turned down for bank loans, they refuse to acknowledge that banks have every right to deny loans to people who cannot provide any form of collateral. Norman's second observation is that black churches typically do not value tithing as highly as do white churches. He suggested that this tendency diminishes the possibility for black churches to build revenue, and that this is especially problematic in congregations that minister to prostitutes and drug dealers, who may decide to change their sinful ways and join the church but are not likely to become generous tithers any time soon.

Norman's first point is arguably more of an ideological assessment than an empirical observation. His perception echoes the long-held rhetoric of political conservatives who reduce economic and social ills to matters of personal responsibility and dismiss historical and systemic arguments as either misleading or deceptive. His second point, that black churches place less value on monetary giving, may reflect conditions that Norman observed at Harvest Glory or other area churches, but this is another common misconception that has been disproved by statistical evidence. Researchers have found that no significant difference exists between white and black congregations in terms of church offerings, and that variations occur along lines of income and denomination rather than race (e.g., Pressley and Collier 1999). Nonetheless, Norman's generalizations about blacks and black churches are significant, if not entirely accurate. Since his views are widely shared among churchgoers at Marble Valley Presbyterian, they no doubt have strongly affected how the megachurch approaches the partnership (and patronage) it has established with its inner-city "sister church," especially insofar as they relate directly to notions of accountability that reinforce paternalistic tendencies among white evangelicals as they reach out to cultural minorities in struggling communities.

There was, to be sure, a sincere desire to promote interracial trust and equality, to foster a "horizontal" relationship built on spiritual and cultural interdependence rather than unilateral patronage. Many members of the megachurch were emotionally invested in the partnership with Harvest Glory, and some even became personally involved, such as a retired accountant who volunteered to help Harvest Glory keep its finances in order. The issue I want to highlight here is that while the praxis of interracial Christian fellowship was conceived along ostensibly horizontal lines, the relationship between these two congregations was overdetermined by factors that reproduced vertical power dynamics stemming from existing structural inequalities. These dynamics facilitated the development of wider social and institutional networks in which white conservative evangelicals acquired the kind of political-economic leverage that they seek in order to redefine the norms of moral governance in civil society. The concept of accountability plays a key role in this regard, and so I now turn to a fuller discussion of that concept before returning to the ethnographic case study.

Constructs of Accountability

The language of "accountability" has become commonplace as an ethical paradigm in American culture, from corporate boardrooms to self-help seminars to the nonprofit sector. In the political realm, accountability has served as a conceptual linchpin for a host of recent legislative initiatives, including welfare reform, campaign finance reform, and most recently No Child Left Behind. In its various functions, the concept performs ideological work critical to both neoliberal and neoconservative agendas by stressing the ethics of personal and corporate responsibility amid increasing economic and institutional privatization. Overtones of moral authoritarianism are also present to the extent that norms of accountability require disciplines of transparency, conformity, and social control that are often regulated hierarchically. In other words, accountability is never merely a question of responsibility alone, but also a measure of a person or group's willingness to submit to a code of governance enforced by authorized peers or, more commonly, by institutionally recognized authority figures.

Among conservative evangelicals, the concept of accountability carries these connotations and takes a decidedly theological turn. It reveals the moral and religious underpinnings of much evangelical engagement in public life, demonstrating how everything from organized philanthropy to social networking assumes missionary significance. Concerned with more than ethical and financial matters, the evangelical understanding of accountability reflects on the presumed qualities of Christian faith: the disciplines of piety and submission to a transcendent (that is, divine) authority that is supposed to guide one's moral actions in this life and secure one's salvation in the afterlife. Human social and institutional relationships are crucial in this regard insofar as they are ideally understood to mediate the norms of accountability mandated by biblical orthodoxy. Although righteousness is linked to the content of one's beliefs, it is also directly related to one's placement in a network of affiliations (e.g., the church) and relationships (e.g., other believers) that reinforce conservative religious and moral standards. It is often observed that evangelical notions of eternal salvation are strongly individualistic, but it is worth noting that such notions are embedded within a relational logic of Christian fellowship and evangelism, in which other people are instrumental and indispensable.[5]

As a distinctly theological notion, the evangelical concept of accountability clearly evokes paternalistic imagery. From their readings of scripture, evangelicals believe that God the Father holds everyone accountable for their thoughts and actions. The merciful God who grants salvation to all those who embrace the Christian faith is, in evangelical theology, also a God who expects the faithful to embody the "fruits" of divine grace throughout their lives. Fulfilling God's expectations is understood to require patience, fortitude, sacrifice, and abnegation of self. The imperative to keep one's thoughts and actions constantly in line with God's will is experienced as a difficult temporal challenge, but worthwhile for the sake of one's ultimate well-being. When applied to areas of Christian ministry such as counseling and rehabilitation, child socialization, and charitable social outreach, the paternalism intrinsic to the concept of accountability is expressed through related principles such as "tough love" and "house rules," which presuppose a parental-disciplinarian role for Christian authority figures (i.e., pastors, teachers, faith-based charity workers and volunteers) who dictate the terms of moral action for others by claiming to know what is best for them (Elisha 2008).

Accountability also serves as a key organizing principle in evangelical parachurch organizations and megachurches (recall the "accountability teams" at Marble Valley Presbyterian). Its theological valences aside, accountability emerged as a major issue within American evangelicalism as the movement underwent vigorous institutionalization throughout the twentieth century, and particularly in the aftermath of the high-profile televangelism scandals of the 1980s. Still reeling from bad publicity brought about by the sexual and financial misdeeds of prominent TV preachers such as Jim Bakker and Jimmy Swaggart, today's evangelical leaders and pastors seek to enhance their public credibility by promoting corporate ethics and transparent accountability structures in churches and organizations. At the congregational level, an emphasis on accountability has the added sociological advantage of encourag-

---

5. I have elsewhere written more extensively on the evangelical concept of accountability and its paradoxical relationship to the moral imperative of compassion, as understood in the context of evangelical social outreach and welfare voluntarism. See Elisha 2008.

ing interdependence and cohesion among church members, particularly through the use of "small groups," in which members are made directly responsible for and to one another through regulated contact (usually in the form of Bible study). Whatever the context, accountability is meant to remind Christians that they are answerable to other Christians as well as to higher powers; it is meant to strengthen individual commitments to a particular system of religious belonging and authority.

Another important factor contributing to the high valuation of accountability in evangelical communities is the recent amplification of such concepts in conservative political discourse, especially with regard to issues of citizenship and welfare reform (Cruikshank 1999; Katz 1989). Along with other right-wing critics, conservative evangelicals were vocal in their opposition to the entitlement policies of the welfare state, and when congressional legislation dismantled "welfare as we know it" in 1996 the moment was hailed as a moral and political victory. Welfare reform was seen to signal the defeat of godless liberalism in the welfare arena and to pave the way for the resurgence of "traditional" community values.

A key figure in establishing this viewpoint at the grassroots of the Christian Right was Marvin Olasky, whose hugely popular book *The Tragedy of American Compassion* (1992) gave many religious conservatives a language and an ideological framework with which to challenge progressive and secular norms of governance perceived to have been politically dominant. Olasky analyzes the history of organized charity in a way that is meant to support his general argument that secular approaches to welfare fail to adequately address major social problems because they are not motivated by religious principles that promote moral discipline and accountability. His stern polemic is expressed through a narrative that romanticizes an American past when hardworking and faithful Judeo-Christians took care of the social welfare needs of their own communities, relying on "biblical" standards of charity and discernment before that authority was usurped by the morally corrupting government interventions of the New Deal. A university professor and editor of the rightwing magazine *World*, Olasky is also credited as the architect of "compassionate conservatism," the cornerstone of George W. Bush's presidential campaign in 2000. His extraordinary influence as a public evangelical is based on his role in redefining, along with others, the long-standing affinities between religious and political conservatives by articulating communitarian ideals that became popular in the 1980s and 1990s. At the same time, this development was part of a broader set of transformations in American politics and civil society toward increasingly authoritarian norms of moral governance, as well as new partnerships between religious (or "faith-based") organizations and state agencies, through which such norms are able to become fixtures of community life.

For conservative evangelicals, a nation in which people and institutions are bound together by the values of faith, compassion, and especially accountability, is a nation reanimated with biblical and thus godly virtues. They believe these to have been the defining characteristics of the first-century church of the apostles, which is the primary role model on which they base their moral vision for society. From this point of view, the efforts of contemporary evangelical Christians to establish a culture of accountability in the United States—whether through political activism, philanthropic engagement, faith-based voluntarism, or community development—are seen as having a direct spiritual affinity with the evangelizing work of Christianization to which the early apostles dedicated themselves with unqualified resolve.

My purpose in this brief digression through the ideological contours of accountability is to clarify that as an embedded cultural construct it deeply influences the manner in which conservative evangelicals engage in social enterprises and institutional partnerships, be they civil, ecumenical, economic, or political in nature. It is not the only construct mobilized in projects of cultural Christianization, but it is a critical one. Socially engaged evangelicals believe that they have a religious obligation to cultivate "redemptive relationships" in the public sphere and to create social and institutional networks that will facilitate large-scale cultural and spiritual transformations in their local communities and beyond.

With a profound sense of religious obligation, of course, also comes a sense of moral authority. This becomes all the more salient in social and institutional relationships already marked by structural inequality. The potential to exacerbate rather than ameliorate the conditions of alienation between white suburban churchgoers and cultural minorities is always present in programs of reconciliation or outreach initiated in hopes of overcoming such strains. At the same time, the active participation of white conservative evangelicals in charitable and philanthropic programs can lead to positive results for struggling communities in need of resources that are often unavailable by other means.

Christian Community Development

In 2000, Harvest Glory designated five acres of undeveloped land—part of the twenty-three acres that was purchased with the help of Marble Valley Presbyterian—to become a mixed-income residential subdivision. The project was part of Harvest Glory's vision to stimulate economic development in the inner city by creating opportunities for home ownership for middle- and working-class black families, and in turn provide a boost for social ministries spearheaded by the church. The subdivision was given the name of Harvest Homes, and the prescreened residents were all African Americans who belonged to Harvest Glory. The construction of twelve houses—a stone's throw from the new church building—was completed over the next two years. Of the twelve houses, eight were built by white contractors who subsidized most of the construction and received nominal fees to help cover their labor costs. The other four homes were built by Habitat for Humanity, with volunteer teams from several area churches, including Marble Valley Presbyterian. The Habitat homes were offered to low-income working families who met the organization's qualifications for housing assistance. As a condition of moving in to Harvest Homes, each family signed an agreement to join a neighborhood homeowner's association and actively participate in ongoing community initiatives.

A key player in the development of Harvest Homes was a local Christian nonprofit called the Koinonia Partnership of Knoxville (KPK).[6] The organization is run by Tom Frick, a leading figure in Knoxville's nonprofit sector and one of the few white members of Harvest Glory. Although Tom lives very close to the inner city, he is no stranger to white evangelical culture in the suburbs, having attended a number of suburban congregations over the years, including Marble Valley Presbyterian. Tom was an early proponent of the partnership between Marble Valley Presbyterian and Harvest Glory, and over the course of that process he has played crucial intermediary roles, describing himself in hindsight as one of several "agents of reconciliation." With direct funding from Marble Valley Presbyterian's missions budget, in addition to private dona-

---

6. *Koinonia* is a Greek word meaning "fellowship," which has come to refer specifically to Christian fellowship, or communion with God and other Christians. Contemporary evangelicals typically use the term to mean "Christian community."

tions, grants, and HUD subsidies, KPK functions as a community development corporation for small-scale development projects like Harvest Homes. Tom and his staff coordinate logistical matters among various agencies and partners, while raising funds to help qualified families earning $20,000 to $35,000 a year to obtain mortgages.

The model of community development endorsed by KPK, and implemented at Harvest Homes, is called "Christian community development," a popular faith-based approach to socioeconomic revitalization coined by a nationally renowned African American evangelical activist named John Perkins. A veteran of civil rights struggles, Perkins has founded numerous ministries addressing racism and poverty relief, most notably among them the Christian Community Development Association. His books and programs have been enormously influential among white and black ministry professionals, especially those working in urban settings with high racial tension. The essence of Perkins's ministry philosophy is summarized in what he calls "the three Rs of community development": *Relocation, Reconciliation,* and *Redistribution* (1993, 36–37). "Relocation" calls for middle-class families (including those who rose up from poverty themselves) to move into developing communities and take part in grassroots activities and organizations. "Reconciliation" refers to the process by which "the love and forgiveness of the gospel reconcile us to God and to each other across all racial, cultural, social, and economic barriers." Lastly, "Redistribution" means the sharing of "skills, technologies, and educational resources in a way that empowers people to break out of the cycle of poverty," which entails forming business cooperatives, securing corporate and government subsidies, and helping struggling families get low-interest home loans.

Of these three goals, establishing channels for resource redistribution is widely understood to present the greatest challenge, especially insofar as it requires the participation and goodwill of institutions whose members often live at a far distance, geographically and culturally, from developing communities. This is why the intermediary participation of nonprofit organizations, CDCs, and area churches is especially vital. In Knoxville, KPK is one of several Christian nonprofits that fill this role, although it is limited in its ability to advocate on behalf of the kind of long-term redistributive justice envisioned by John Perkins. Restricted somewhat by his largely conservative donor base, Tom Frick concentrates his efforts on the tasks of encouraging "indigenous" leadership at the grassroots of the inner city and ensuring that hardworking Christian families achieve homeownership and become collectively invested in the health of their community. He believes that once this is accomplished, economic growth comes naturally. "It all starts with a family or a group of families, living in a neighborhood, who value that place," he explained to me. "At some point then the market forces take over and the property values start to climb." Tom's comment is suggestive of the privileging of free-market ideology in the community development industry. At the same time, like many socially engaged evangelicals working in the nonprofit sector, Tom actively seeks ways to incorporate progressive ideas that might help bridge ideological and racial divides.

The significance of intermediary agencies in providing access to otherwise limited resources was never lost on the incoming residents of Harvest Homes. At a public ceremony marking the completion of the initial construction phase, major partners and contributors to the project were honored with plaques and words of recognition from Harvest Glory's Pastor Leon and a few of the prospective homeowners. A young father who had already moved into his new home with his family addressed the crowd of donors and news reporters, praising the tireless efforts of the various agencies that helped to make Harvest Homes a reality. He compared their combined efforts to a story in the gospel of Mark (2:1–12) in which a group of people bring a paralyzed man to Jesus to be healed. As the men arrive at the home where Jesus is staying, they find a large crowd of followers blocking the doorway. They decide to lift the paralyzed man over the house and lower him down through a hole in the roof. Jesus is moved by their actions and performs the healing miracle. By drawing an analogy to this story, the young father expressed his gratitude to organizations such as Harvest Glory and KPK that "helped us reach the people that have turned us down before." This analogy has a remarkably ambiguous subtext. On the one hand, the speaker insinuated that low- to middle-income African Americans in Knoxville who aspire to become homeowners still encounter resistance from lending institutions, resistance that is only overcome through the mediation of reputable agencies with access to economic and political resources. On the other hand, the parallel he drew to the biblical story implicitly positions those very lending institutions symbolically in the role of Christ the healer.

As we have seen, the participation of Marble Valley Presbyterian, a source of direct funding for both Harvest Glory and KPK, was a critical component in the development of Harvest Homes. Furthermore, the megachurch was a source of many informal services of consider-

able value, including the assistance of a state employee who helped
with the processing of building permits and a recent retiree who coordinated most of the Habitat for Humanity construction teams, in addition
to dozens of individual volunteers and donors. More important, a number of powerful corporate executives and skilled professionals contributed to the project, with the encouragement of committed pastors and
churchgoers. All this participation begs the question: If the black inner-
city community represented by Harvest Glory benefited from access to
resources facilitated by institutional partnerships with white-run organizations, what were the incentives for white suburban churchgoers with
the power to provide such access? Here I am less interested in the potential economic or political incentives so much as the benefits conceived by
a particular religious ideology understood to be well served by partnerships of this kind.

Aside from tax write-offs, good publicity, and other likely perks, there
was an articulated (and not insignificant) religious rationale for the participation of white churchgoers in the development of Harvest Homes.
Such philanthropic efforts are framed in part according to the language
of "Christian stewardship," which is especially meaningful for Christian
business elites who aspire to show themselves to be responsible and vir-
tuous in their use of valued resources, which ultimately belong to God.[7]
More generally, their contributions are intended not only to provide economic and moral uplift for struggling communities but also, through the
interpersonal and intrasectoral linkages that such efforts create, to advance the kingdom of God in Knoxville.

At the same time, however, I want to make it clear that the generosity
coming out of Marble Valley Presbyterian in this case was largely contingent on the fact that intermediary agencies were in place that they
believed would uphold the standards of accountability that conservative
evangelicals value so highly. In other words, contributing to the community development efforts of Harvest Glory and KPK was viewed as
meaningful and worthwhile not only because it was the "right" thing
to do but because Marble Valley Presbyterian was in a position to hold
both organizations accountable, financially as well as ideologically, ac-

---

7. The language of "stewardship" is most commonly used in reference to tithes and other financial
offerings specific to the church. Due to its connotation of "taking care of God's resources," the term
also has become central to an emergent environmental awareness movement among evangelicals.

cording to its own standards and practices. With a vertical structure of accountability in place, the members of Marble Valley Presbyterian felt free to invest themselves in charitable bridge-building activities in which their interests, both as conservative evangelicals and as members of their social class, remained at the forefront. Racial prejudices and practical concerns expressed by churchgoers in the early stages of the partnership with their "sister church" were at least partially assuaged with regard to the construction of Harvest Homes because of the perception that their resources were being administered responsibly by reputable intermediaries that could be monitored and managed. And while this structure of accountability involved a broad network of institutional partners, the pivotal status of Marble Valley Presbyterian bolstered the perception among white churchgoers that their moral preferences would continue to enjoy privileged status in the public culture of the region.

For conservative evangelicals, "faith-based" networks of cooperation and accountability, which bind together distinct institutions, transcend the divide of church and state (without *necessarily* eliminating it), and bridge boundaries of race, class, and sometimes even religion. The creation of such networks is idealized as an end unto itself, capable of aiding the circulation of orthodox Christian values in diverse milieus. To the extent that these values have become closely aligned with social and political conservatism, it is apparent that such networks can also have the effect of restraining progressive sensibilities that may otherwise be asserted on the part of community activists in the inner city. A number of black evangelical leaders and organizers in Knoxville (who are no less conservative in their theology) told me that although they generally regard the increased social engagement of white evangelicals as a positive trend, their incessant dwelling on issues of accountability makes it hard for struggling minority communities to become truly empowered. Black evangelicals embrace the tone of reconciliation but criticize the extent of its consistent depoliticization and the fact that white evangelicals tend to downplay the need to combat racial injustice and inequality through broad socioeconomic reforms. This is not merely a matter of two ideological positions coming into conflict—one oriented toward social justice, the other toward market forces, nuclear families, and personal responsibility—but rather a situation in which both positions coexist within an institutional matrix that generally precludes progressive models of development in favor of more conservative ones.

Community activists are not completely powerless, but those seeking to advocate progressive reforms in Knoxville do so cautiously, hoping to make their point without risking the indispensable support of major donors and institutions. The risks are compounded by difficulties of a practical nature. Although white conservative evangelicals view accountability as a necessary precondition for empowerment, black community organizers argue that all too often they simply lack sufficient resources to be able to prove to white benefactors that they can uphold high standards of accountability in the first place. Many black leaders are particularly frustrated by the fact that whenever resources do become available, they are funneled through intermediary agencies—not all of which are located at the grassroots—which create additional bureaucratic hurdles and new restraints on community activism and development.

Harvest Homes has come to be regarded by local observers as an example of successful community development, and as proof of a growing political climate in Knoxville favorable to developing affordable and adequate housing in urban neighborhoods. Within a few years of my fieldwork, the newly formed neighborhood association of Harvest Homes (composed of twelve households) received an award in recognition of its "civic achievements" from a municipal planning agency. Shortly thereafter, the official partnership between Marble Valley Presbyterian and Harvest Glory came to an end, although the congregations have maintained a relationship on good terms. Still, the circumstances described above reveal how existing social structures and power dynamics are reproduced as new relationships and distributive channels are formed in the postwelfare era. Although everyone, including the members of Marble Valley Presbyterian, was as committed to the community development initiative as they were to the process of racial reconciliation that preceded it, the manner in which the entire project took form reminds us that such examples of "Redistribution" are unlikely to lead to major structural reforms, any more than the language of "Reconciliation" will necessarily alleviate racial tensions beyond the lives of a dedicated few. I do not mean to suggest that under such conditions there can be no social change. My point is that in an overwhelmingly conservative regional culture, the politics of social change are tied in large part to the proclivities of elite or privileged groups who are represented by cultural institutions—such as evangelical megachurches—that actively seek to enact change on their own terms.

Conclusion

With the increasing privatization and deregulation of welfare, religious congregations with sufficient wealth to support ambitious civic and philanthropic enterprises are poised to exert considerable influence over the distribution of human and material resources in local communities.[8] Conservative evangelical megachurches, faith-based organizations, and foundations have already begun to do so in many communities, and their efforts are informed by distinctive religious and even missionary aspirations. They seek not only to generate what social capital theorists call "bridging social capital," but also in the process to redefine the very moral grounds on which social and institutional relationships are formed in the realm of civil society. Such aspirations are complex in that they are guided by an egalitarian impulse to break down social and cultural barriers, and at the same time, by ambitions of cultural Christianization, attended by evangelical concepts such as accountability that, among other effects, reinforce social stratification between those with the power to mobilize capital and those who must seek their benevolence.

Sociologist Omar McRoberts (2003) has argued that current debates over the status of social capital and civil society are useful but that much of the discussion is "misplaced." He suggests that the question with regard to civic associations should not be about "how much" but rather "what for?" In other words, "For what purposes are these associations coming into being, and to what ends are the resultant networks and skills being mobilized?" (2003, 144).[9] My discussion of the relationship between Marble Valley Presbyterian and Harvest Glory, and its consequences, has proceeded in this vein. I have focused on the attitudes, expectations, and motivational concepts of white conservative evangelicals in an effort to better understand exactly what it is they are doing, and (in the spirit of the late Clifford Geertz) what they *think* they are doing as they reach out from their congregations to make an impact in the lives of cultural strangers and, simultaneously, in the rapidly evolving nonprofit sector.

In focusing on the perspective of white middle-class churchgoers,

8. Religious institutions have, of course, always played a central role in shaping the culture of American civil society and implementing wide-ranging social reforms. In addition, church-state partnerships of the kind envisioned by Charitable Choice legislation (part of federal welfare reform) are not new to American history. See, for example, Cnaan, Wineburg, and Boddie 1999 and Skocpol 2000.

9. For a particularly astute and thorough critique of social capital theory, see Arneil 2006.

I do not mean to downplay the impact or significance of motivations and actions (including acts of resistance and reformation) among minority communities. On the contrary, my analysis is meant to encourage further investigations of the machinations of civil society, not as they may be imagined in some formulaic and universal sense, but as they are conceived within specific cultural groups and contexts. "Civil society" is neither concrete nor uniform; it is itself a concept that encompasses a diverse patchwork of communities and institutions that interact, overlap, and compete with one another, each seeking, according to their own values and ideals, to realize and even redefine the promise of a pluralistic and democratic society (see Checker and Fishman 2004).

The practical theology embraced by many evangelicals is one in which civil society is engaged as a vehicle, and perhaps even a template, for an ideal of cultural transformation that is more theocentric than theocratic. The prospect of "the Kingdom of God on Earth" is, for the average churchgoing evangelical, less of a mandate for political domination than a model for social engagement intended to unite individuals and groups under the totalizing religious authority of biblical orthodoxy— and, by extension, those who claim to uphold its moral standards. Because of right-wing shifts in American evangelicalism, this paradigm is in close alignment with social and political conservatism, which in turn has been bolstered by current political configurations and popular support for the resurgence of "faith" in public life. The politics of "faith-based initiatives" have been met with enthusiasm by conservative evangelicals because they represent legal and cultural trends that are seen as conducive to the unimpeded circulation of "the gospel" through reconstituted networks of philanthropy, charity, and civic participation. Even when linkages are formed between organizations where Christian beliefs and practices already exist (as in the case I have been describing), conservative evangelicals assume that the aims of Christianization are being advanced, especially when their own institutions and agencies hold sway over competing liberal or secular authorities.

Of course, faith-based activism as a social practice is varied and complex, and its evangelical manifestations are not necessarily always in sync with the agendas of the Christian Right. The outcomes of grassroots initiatives by religious groups cannot be predicted based entirely on the structure of formal associational networks or the theological orientations of key participants. Several of the socially engaged evangelicals I observed in the field found themselves torn between the prevailing conservatism of their home congregations and prophetic/progressive notions of social justice that they encountered when they were immersed in the realm of welfare activism. Still, it should be noted that the language of accountability, steeped as it is in an intriguing mix of neoliberal idealism, neoconservative authoritarianism, and communitarian optimism, resonates powerfully with hegemonic currents in the contemporary West. In this sense the Christianization of civil society, as evangelicals envision it, may be less of a revolutionary transformation than they expect. It may in fact represent the fulfillment of power-laden processes already in motion all around us.

References

Arneil, Barbara. 2006. *Diverse Communities: The Problem with Social Capital.* Cambridge: Cambridge University Press.

Berger, Peter L., and Richard John Neuhaus. 1977. *To Empower People: The Role of Mediating Structures in Public Policy.* Washington: American Enterprise Institute for Public Policy Research.

Checker, Melissa, and Maggie Fishman, eds. 2004. *Local Actions: Cultural Activism, Power, and Public Life in America.* New York: Columbia University Press.

Cnaan, Ram A., with Stephanie C. Boddie, Femida Handy, Gaynor Yancey, and Richard Schneider. 2002. *The Invisible Caring Hand: American Congregations and the Provision of Welfare.* New York: New York University Press.

Cnaan, Ram A., Robert J. Wineburg, and Stephanie C. Boddie. 1999. *The Newer Deal: Social Work and Religion in Partnership.* New York: Columbia University Press.

Cruikshank, Barbara. 1999. *The Will to Empower: Democratic Citizens and Other Subjects.* Ithaca: Cornell University Press.

Elisha, Omri. 2008. "The Moral Ambitions of Grace: The Paradox of Compassion and Accountability in Evangelical Faith-Based Activism." *Cultural Anthropology* 23, no. 1 (February): 154–189.

Emerson, Michael O., and Christian Smith. 2000. *Divided By Faith: Evangelical Religion and the Problem of Race in America.* New York: Oxford University Press.

Hart, D. G. 2000. "The Techniques of Church Growth." In "The Malling of Mission," a special issue of *Modern Reformation* 9: 20–25.

Horton, Michael. 2000. "The Ethnocentricity of the American Church Growth Movement." In "The Malling of Mission," a special issue of *Modern Reformation* 9: 15–19.

Katz, Michael B. 1989. *The Undeserving Poor: From the War on Poverty to the War on Welfare*. New York: Pantheon Books.

McRoberts, Omar M. 2003. *Streets of Glory: Church and Community in a Black Urban Neighborhood*. Chicago: University of Chicago Press.

Miller, Donald E. 1997. *Reinventing American Protestantism: Christianity in the New Millennium*. Berkeley: University of California Press.

Olasky, Marvin. 1992. *The Tragedy of American Compassion*. Washington, D.C.: Regnery Publishing.

Perkins, John M. 1993. *Beyond Charity: The Call to Christian Community Development*. Grand Rapids, Mich.: Baker Books.

Pressley, Calvin O., and Walter V. Collier. 1999. "Financing Historic Black Churches." In *Financing American Religion,* edited by M. Chaves and S. Miller, 21–28. Walnut Creek, Calif.: AltaMira Press.

Pritchard, G.A. 1996. *Willow Creek Seeker Services: Evaluating a New Way of Doing Church*. Grand Rapids, Mich.: Baker Books.

Putnam, Robert D., and Lewis M. Feldstein, with Dan Cohen. 2003. *Better Together: Restoring the American Community*. New York: Simon and Schuster.

Skocpol, Theda. 2000. "Religion, Civil Society, and Social Provision in the U.S." In *Who Will Provide: The Changing Role of Religion in American Social Welfare,* edited by M. J. Bane, B. Coffin, and R. Thiemann, 21–50. Boulder: Westview Press.

Thumma, Scott. 1996. "The Kingdom, the Power, and the Glory: The Megachurch in Modern American Society." PhD diss., Emory University.

Verba, Sidney, Kay L. Schlozman, and Henry E. Brady. 1995. *Voice and Equality: Civic Voluntarism in American Politics*. Cambridge: Harvard University Press.

Wuthnow, Robert. 2004. *Saving America? Faith-Based Services and the Future of Civil Society*. Princeton: Princeton University Press.

CHAPTER ELEVEN

Resolviendo: How September 11 Tested and Transformed a New York City Mexican Immigrant Organization

Alyshia Gálvez

There is a single two-lane road connecting the city of Puebla and the small town of Tulcingo del Valle in the rural area called La Poblana Mixteca, in southeastern Mexico, the region where vast numbers of Mexicans living in New York grew up. In Tulcingo, it is possible to eat New York-style pizza or use a phone in a calling center where the operators spend all day dialing numbers that begin with the three main New York City prefixes: 718, 212, and 917. It used to be that the three-hour drive was punctuated by little more than stately saguaro cacti and an occasional stray dog. But since late 2002, there is a stand at a wide spot in the road called Zaragoza where travelers can take a break for a soda, a bag of potato chips, or to eat some tamales (figure 11.1). The stand is run by a woman named Félix Martínez with help from her mother and sister, and she is often accompanied by the youngest three of her five children. Her two oldest sons are in Chicago, having migrated with help from an un-

I am grateful to the editors of this volume, Lis Clemens and Doug Guthrie, for their feedback and support throughout the process of editing this piece. I am also grateful to Ken Prewitt, David Hammack, Tracy Steffes, and Lis Clemens for their responses to an earlier version of this paper that I delivered in March 2005 at the capstone conference of the Program on Philanthropy and the Nonprofit Sector in Florence, Italy, funded by the Social Science Research Council. My dissertation research, to which this paper is related but not entirely derived from, was also funded by the Social Science Research Council's Program on Philanthropy and the Nonprofit Sector, and I received a write-up grant from the same. I am very thankful for the SSRC's repeated support of my work.

FIGURE II.I. Félix's roadside stand under construction, Zaragoza, Puebla, Mexico.

cle. This is not so remarkable in this region of "accelerated migration."[1]
But when we learn that the youngest child, who when I visited was about
ten months old, was born in Brooklyn and that this roadside stand and
Félix's house, a stone's throw up the hillside, were built with funds from
a New York City–based nonprofit organization, it is clear that there is a
story here.

Indeed, the story is a complex and tragic one. It was less than two
weeks after the tragic day of September 11, 2001, that volunteers at Asociación Tepeyac de New York, an umbrella group composed of forty
parish-based Guadalupan committees (centered on devotion to the Virgin of Guadalupe, patron saint of Mexico) that serve the Mexican immigrant community, reported meeting a woman going from hospital to
hospital, trying to find her husband, José Morales. She insisted he was

1. With respect only to migrants from the southeastern state of Puebla, who until 1995 were in the
clear majority among immigrants to New York City; from 1980 to 2000 there was a twenty-six-fold increase in the rate of international migration (which is virtually all to the United States), and between
1995 and 2000 five times as many *poblanos* came to the United States as arrived from 1980 to 1985
(Cortes 2003).

employed in the Twin Towers and missing in the aftermath of September 11. She was seven months pregnant, knew no English, could not read or write Spanish, and had flown to the border, then traveled overland, crossing the border with a *coyote,* a trafficker in human beings, to search for José.[2]

On September 11, 2001, the offices of Asociación Tepeyac on West 14th Street, about a mile from the World Trade Center, became the default refuge for many Latino immigrant workers fleeing the destruction downtown on foot. As people covered in dust and debris began streaming in over the course of the morning to use the phone, rest, and watch the news, and as Cantor Fitzgerald, AON Corporation, the Port Authority, and other agencies and businesses began to construct lists of the missing using payroll records, Tepeyac became one of the first institutions to ask, "What about the people who were working off the books?" That day, Tepeyac began to compile a second list of the missing, the invisible victims, many of whom would never appear in the "Portraits of Grief" in the *New York Times,* whose family members would never receive death certificates, and whose names will not be etched in the granite at the future WTC memorial.

José Morales had only just migrated to New York City during the summer of 2001. He was still paying off his *coyote* and had yet to send any money to his pregnant wife and their children, let alone photographs, mementos, or letters about his new life. He did call, though, and he said he was working "en las torres gemelas," the Twin Towers. Félix did not have a marriage certificate; the two children José fathered do not bear his last name; she did not even have a photograph of him.[3] Even if she had, though, these would not have been enough for her to qualify for federally funded victims' assistance without some kind of proof that he had been employed and perished in the towers.

Until the Family Assistance Center was created by the Mayor's Office of Emergency Management to offer "one stop shopping" for victims' families and the United Services Group created a single database

2. Félix's story is drawn from accounts by volunteers who worked with her, as well as media coverage of her story, including a report on CNN by Viles (2001). I did not ask her to tell me the story when I met her in the fall of 2002, because I did not wish to dredge up painful memories. All of the accounts coincide that she traveled shortly after September 11, and in Viles's account she flew to the border, then traveled overland to New York, arriving the week after the disaster.

3. In this rural region of Mexico, many couples share their lives as "common-law" spouses. Formal marriage is expensive and complicated, especially when one or both partners were previously married (as was the case with Félix), and bears relatively few benefits.

FIGURE 11.2. Félix and her daughter Wendy, October 2002.

for gathering information on all of the victims and their relatives, survivors were forced to fill out multiple forms for every possible form of assistance, and many wandered from hospital to hospital hoping a loved
one would turn up. The Federal Emergency Management Administration (FEMA) even—inexplicably—prohibited nonprofit organizations
from assisting people with completion of their forms (Coe et al. 2003,
4). If we factor in the challenges faced by Félix having only just arrived
in New York City, virtually penniless, without English or basic literacy,
and lacking documentary proof of her relationship, it is clear that her efforts to obtain information and benefits would be difficult and she was
not likely to be credible as a widow to the major victims' aid agencies.
Indeed, a volunteer at Tepeyac told me that aid workers at other organizations had at times leaned conspiratorially toward Félix and asked how
she was so sure her husband had not simply run off with another woman
and told her he was emigrating. "He could be in your neighboring town
in Mexico right now," they would say.

However, in Tepeyac, an organization composed mostly of and in service to undocumented Mexican migrants, it is known that few—if any—

people undertake a border crossing lightly, especially from a place as remote from the U.S.-Mexico border as Zaragoza, while seven months pregnant, and leaving behind four other children. That Félix had done this—and during the almost complete paralysis of mass transport in the days following September 11—was evidence in itself that she was credible and worthy of support, even while her story continued to baffle people who were accustomed to quite astonishing stories of sacrifice.

In this chapter, I analyze the role filled by Asociación Tepeyac de New York after September 11, 2001, and the ways that its success in filling a void in services for immigrant victims of the World Trade Center attacks transformed the organization. I ask whether this transformation was merely an inevitable—if hastened—stage in the organization's maturation toward greater bureaucratization and formalization of its services, or whether, in fact, the changes in the organization may have hearkened the end of its grassroots appeal and efficacy. This is a story with resonances of a long history of the growth and transformations of culture- and faith-based organizations serving immigrants reaching back to the mid-nineteenth century, even while it is also a story that could only occur in the twenty-first century in our particular globalized moment and the unique climate of expansion of "third sector" provision of services.

Over the last decade we have seen an erosion of the welfare state and a bolstering of the expectation among conservative and mainstream sectors that the philanthropic "third sector" as well as the corporate, private sector can step into the vacuum left by the state. The withdrawal of many government-based services has been accompanied by an expansion of federal funding of private sector and faith-based programs. In this chapter, I examine how a faith-based organization such as Asociación Tepeyac de New York filled an important role in this new era of service provision in the aftermath of September 11. Faith-based and community-based organizations often exhibit much greater flexibility and sensitivity than their governmental counterparts. If they are able to access federal and state funding they can sometimes direct those funds to people who are categorically ineligible for most government benefits, such as the undocumented immigrants who are the constituency of Asociación Tepeyac. However, September 11 marks both the beginning and the end of an era for Tepeyac in that it made available new sources of funding (mostly in the category of emergency, seed, and start-up grants), which fostered its growth and expansion, at the same time that they increased its dependence on outside funding and made it ineligible for some of the funding for small and underfunded organizations that had enabled it to function previously. Further, the insertion of Tepeyac into federal, state, and nonprofit funding arenas implied a necessary rationalization of its operations, programming, and message in ways we might recognize as institutional isomorphism (DiMaggio and Powell 1983).

This chapter will analyze the transformation of Asociación Tepeyac from a very local network of parish-based devotional organizations to a large, transnational organization subject to the pressures and expectations of funders and a broad swath of advisers, philanthropists, and evaluators from the foundations that both enabled and guided its transformation. To analyze this transformation, I employ Michel de Certeau's notion of strategies versus tactics, a dichotomy that enables us to contrast Tepeyac before September 11, when it was an informal grouping of community-based organizations, with the large, professionalized organization that Tepeyac has become since then, obliged by its own success to conform to the organizational structures characteristic of large, funded service agencies. Ironically, the same transformations that marked Tepeyac's success could very well spell its eventual demise, as some charge that the changes wrought took the organization away from its original purpose and that it lost legitimacy with a large part of its constituency.

In Spanish, the verb *resolver* has more complex meanings than simply "to solve" a problem, its literal translation. A musician might be admired for his ability to *resolver,* to creatively improvise when his bandmates lose the beat or forget the melody; a parent living in poverty whose children never feel deprived is said to know how to *resolver. Resolver* is comparable to the notion of *tactics* in the dichotomy de Certeau constructs between *strategies* and *tactics.* In his formulation, tactics are, by definition, subaltern, and depend "on time— . . . always on the watch for opportunities that must be seized 'on the wing.' Whatever it wins, it does not keep. It must constantly manipulate events in order to turn them into 'opportunities'" (1984, xix). He continues, "Tactics do not obey the law of place, for they are not defined or identified by it. . . . They are not any more localizable than the technocratic (and scriptural) *strategies* that seek to create places in conformity with abstract models" (1984, 29). I would argue that *strategies* correspond to the practices developed by institutions and their members to maximize resources in a climate of bureaucratization of structures, and they are implicit as an ideal form of behavior for organizations within the teleological isomorphism of institutions posited by DiMaggio and Powell (1983). In this chapter, I will examine how Asociación Tepeyac went from being a network of organizations which used tactics, in the de Certeauian sense, and in the vernacular, grassroots, activist sense, to serve the needs of its constituency to being an institutionalized nonprofit organization, pressured through both coercive and normative isomorphic processes (DiMaggio and Powell 1983) to rationalize and bureaucratize itself and thus develop strategies for long-term viability. After September 11, 2001, Asociación Tepeyac showed its ability to *resolver* around a seemingly insurmountable predicament, and as I examine here, it continues *resolviendo* on a daily basis, working to build an empowered immigrant community in a transformed political and economic landscape. Nonetheless, it has had to exchange some of its tactics for strategies, and in the process has alienated some of its grassroots base and created a distance between its constituency, leadership, staff, and volunteers, which in the early days were one and the same.

Service Provision in a Historical Context

Asociación Tepeyac's formation can be contextualized within a long history of mutual aid societies and immigrant service providers in the United States from the mid-nineteenth century forward. Its positioning as a collection of lay societies organized under the mantle of the Catholic Church help us understand how Tepeyac became an organization with a tremendous amount of legitimacy both with its members and with the larger organizational landscape of service provision, while still retaining its flexible, tactical character within the relatively inflexible, rule-bound context of the church. Historically, guilds or mutual aid societies, which were formed in the interest of mutual assistance, aid to the poor and sick, burial of members, and worship of particular patron saints, have "enlarged the great family to afford assistance to one another as one would to a brother" (Brentano 1870, 37). This is a logical consequence of industrialization for Durkheim who posits that the kinds of mechanical solidarity "natural" to preindustrial, undifferentiated societies must, in a sense, be manufactured in societies marked by a division of labor (1984, 84–85).

Confraternal organizations dedicated to saints and mutual aid were one of the key forms of popular organization and social welfare in the colonial and postcolonial periods in Latin America and continue to be an important mode for the organization of social life in urban and rural contexts. Confraternal societies provide a known model for social organization and management of collective needs that has proven useful to the church and to the nation-state in Latin America historically, as well as in periods of Catholic migration in the United States.

At the turn of the twentieth century, voluntary associations arguably had a much larger role in receiving and acclimating new immigrants in the United States than they do today (Wucker 2006). The settlement house movement, most often associated with Chicago's Hull House, sought to provide people with the tools to surmount poverty and had special programs for immigrants to celebrate their cultures at the same time they learned English. In New York City, from the mid-nineteenth century and as late as 1960, organizations such as the Sons of Herman and the Hibernian Society met their German and Irish countrymen at Ellis Island, assisting them in finding lodging, work, and housing (Wucker 2006; Abell 1952; Appel 1966; Murphy and Blumenthal 1966. For Poles, see Thomas 1918). Although some organizations like these still exist, such as the U.S. Committee for Refugees and Immigrants and Hull House, their emphasis today is on refugees and native socioeconomically disadvantaged populations respectively, and not primarily on the reception and assimilation of immigrants.

As in mutual aid societies everywhere, charity was the main business of thousands of Catholic benevolent societies organized along national lines, but this also spilled over from self-help for a community of brethren into national social movements, such as the one for temperance that resulted in national Prohibition in the 1920s (Abell 1952, 311). The Irish Catholic Benevolent Union, composed of four hundred societies, "believed that temperance and benevolence should 'go hand in hand' and endorsed the 'attractive' mutual relief features which, with scarcely an exception, Catholic societies had 'blended' into their temperance work" (Abell 1952, 315).

It is estimated that 3.5 of the five million immigrants who arrived between 1908 and 1919 were Catholic. The U.S. church placed a particularly powerful emphasis on Americanization, social welfare, and prevention of the loss of faith (McAvoy 1942, 417–18). The church was seen as a haven for the preservation of language, faith, and custom, understood to be an inseparable triad, among first-generation immigrants—at the same time that it sought to ensure the assimilation and Americanization of the second and third generations (Gleason 1987, 42). The emergence of national parishes combated the fear that loss of language preceded loss of faith, and within the same neighborhoods, different immigrant groups attended different churches. This even led to the creation of broader Catholic nationalisms, among Italians, for example, who previously had identified as Neapolitans, Sicilians, and so on (Dolan 1994, 78; Orsi 1992; Tomasi 1970, 1975).

By the time of the great Puerto Rican migration from 1946 to 1964, the Catholic Church shifted from an emphasis on national parishes to a focus on ethnicity, as a result of the largest effort ever within the Archdiocese of New York to serve a particular cultural group (Gleason 1987; see Glazer 1963 on ethnicity; McGreevy 1996). The arrival of so many immigrants, many of them from rural areas who were nominally Catholic but had little experience with the church as an institution, was called "a state of emergency" by Francis Joseph Cardinal Spellman (Dolan and Vidal 1994, 75). Rather then tend to Puerto Ricans within the old model of the national parish, in which immigrants did not necessarily attend their local parish church but attended a regional church with their countrymen in which their language was spoken, often by a priest from the "old" country, the archdiocese opted for a language-based pastoralism in which new seminarians were trained in Spanish. In addition to the regular English language mass, they gave a second, or more, masses in Spanish.[4]

In Catholic parishes in New York City, religious fraternities, prayer societies, and ethnic confraternities have found space and support for their activities. Historically, parishes have become the logical home for lay organizations comprised of immigrants, such as the *comités guadalupanos* that would only later be linked under the mantle of Asociación Tepeyac. Tepeyac could not have developed as quickly as it did without the preexisting space for organization provided both by the Catholic parish's structure for lay involvement and the diocese's assistance.

That space was not only particular to the New York City Catholic institutional landscape but also particular to the role of lay religious asso-

---

4. In parishes with multiple pastors, the church might be spatially subdivided with the main space being dedicated to the English mass, and a basement or smaller rectory chapel being home to the Spanish language mass. This separation, which seems to many to be visibly hierarchical, bothered Puerto Rican civil rights activists who complained of being relegated to basement churches (Diaz Stevens 1993). A monsignor I interviewed in a very large parish in the northern-most section of the Bronx justified this division—which persists in his parish—by saying that the Latino parishioners do not like the austere, modern design of St. Bartholomew's Church with its emphasis on the sculptural formality of the altar and architecturally maximized play of natural light, preferring the basement chapel to which the statuary of saints and the Virgin Mary were relegated after the renovation.

ciations in the United States. In his famous book on democracy in the United States, Tocqueville marvels at Americans' tendency to form associations and their necessity in a democratic state:

> They all, therefore, become powerless if they do not learn voluntarily to help one another. If men living in democratic countries had no right and no inclination to associate for political purposes, their independence would be in great jeopardy, but they might long preserve their wealth and their cultivation: whereas if they never acquired the habit of forming associations in ordinary life, civilization itself would be endangered. (Tocqueville 2004)

In the United States, religion is still considered a private matter that need not be left behind, as other cultural features and language often are, in the process of immigrant integration into U.S. society. Despite the rise in federal funding of and legal provisions favorable to faith-based initiatives, religion is still assumed in a fundamental, cultural sense, to be beyond reproach. Further, it has long been viewed to aid, not hinder, immigrant assimilation. Through participating in confraternal social organizations dedicated to the Virgin of Guadalupe, it is arguable that Mexicans in New York City are able to mobilize for immigrant rights more successfully than if they were to come forward simply as an association of undocumented immigrants. Not only does their choice of organizational modality offer powerful symbolic and discursive tools that draw from Catholic theology, it offers ready allies and, as we can see in the September 11 disaster, ways for them to access federal funds and services for which they would otherwise be ineligible. This goes beyond being a matter of "strength in numbers."

History of Asociación Tepeyac

The role Asociación Tepeyac would play following the tragic events of September 11, 2001, was unpredictable and represents a conjuncture of various elements. I focus my attention here on the organization's unique positioning and ability to respond to the crisis, and the way that response would in turn transform the organization itself. Asociación Tepeyac de New York is an umbrella organization of Catholic parish-based Guadalupan committees dedicated to "the social welfare and human rights of Latino immigrants, specifically the undocumented in New York City" (www.tepeyac.org). Although some of the member committees were formed as many as two decades earlier, the association was created in 1997 by a group of priests and Mexican community leaders who sought a concerted way to serve the needs of the very rapidly growing Mexican population in New York City, which was marked by high rates of labor exploitation, poverty, and little access to services. In the beginning, Jesuit brother Joel Magallán Reyes, the founder, and Esperanza Chacón, a community leader, sat on five-gallon paint buckets, used crates for desks, had one phone, and recruited leaders at city playgrounds and area "shape-up" sites where day laborers congregate (interview with Chacón, November 1, 2000). Eventually the archdiocese rented them a four-story dilapidated former convent on 14th Street between Eighth and Seventh Avenues. Slowly, by linking all of the existing committees, encouraging the formation of more in neighborhoods only just receiving influxes of Mexican immigrants, and appealing to otherwise disparate and disconnected recent immigrants with the familiar idioms of Guadalupan devotion, Mexican nationalism, and openness about undocumented status, Tepeyac grew into one of the largest, most known, and respected immigrants' rights groups in New York City.[5] Even before September 11, Tepeyac was so extensively discussed in the Spanish-language media in New York City, in the United States more broadly, and in Mexico that some immigrants came to its 14th Street offices seeking orientation immediately on arriving in New York City. Others carried the phone number with them when they crossed the border, calling the office from motels or rest areas on Arizona highways, seeking assistance in contacting relatives in New York City or to denounce abuses by the Border Patrol. When I began research in the organization in 2000, I would frequently hear Chacón working on cases like that of a migrant who never arrived at his brother's house in Brooklyn. She alternately spoke with the young man's mother in rural Puebla, his brother, and the Mexican consulate in Tucson, trying to retrace his movements and determine where he had last been seen.

Asociación Tepeyac's organizational strategy is premised on a universal Catholic humanism. The rights immigrants claim are seen as a function of their status as human beings, vouchsafed by the figure of the

---

5. In my book, *Guadalupe in New York: Devotion and the Struggle for Citizenship Rights among Mexicans* (New York University Press, 2009), I extensively discuss the role of these three concepts: Guadalupanismo, Mexican nationalism, and undocumented status as Tepeyac's mode of mobilization.

Virgin Mary, in her manifestation as Our Lady of Guadalupe. This articulation of rights seeks to supersede the nation-state and render moot its laws which cast undocumented immigrants as juridical *personae non grata*. In this way, immigrants disengage from the narrowly constructed and xenophobic debates about law and juridical status in which, by virtue of being undocumented, their claims for rights are always already illegitimate, and when granted, cast as a "favor" voluntarily ceded by a benevolent state and populace that owes them nothing and can at any time revoke whatever benefits might have been granted in moments of largesse or economic expansion.[6] The efforts of immigrants to imagine themselves as rights holders above and beyond the nation-state is an example of postnational or cultural citizenship, premised on "universal personhood" as theorized by Soysal (1994), Rosaldo (1997), and Flores and Benmayor (1997).

Although Tepeyac does get into the nitty-gritty of politics at the local, state, and national level, ultimately the organization's struggle for a humane reform of immigration law in the form of an amnesty that would allow undocumented immigrants already in the United States to remain, work legally, and ultimately achieve naturalization is premised on the idea that the quest for survival, for a living wage, may—and in our transnational age often does—take workers across borders. They argue that immigrant workers are fulfilling a demand for labor at the same time that they seek a living for their families, and as such, their actions should not be considered "illegal." Indeed, this assertion of rights is also corroborated by such entities as the signatories of the Universal Declaration of Human Rights, as well as the United States Conference of Catholic Bishops and the Episcopado Mexicano who wrote in a joint letter, "Strangers No Longer," of the arbitrariness of borders and their immorality if they prevent people from seeking a living wherever they may find it (United States Conference of Catholic Bishops 2003).

6. The debate over immigrant access to health care is a good illustration of this tendency to alternately grant, then withhold services to undocumented immigrants. Although it makes good public health sense for all of those living in a society to have equal access to health care, especially for treatment for infectious diseases and immunizations, immigrants' ability to obtain low-cost or state-subsidized health care is often the first thing threatened by any surge in xenophobia, such as the foiled attempt to ratify Proposition 187 in California, and similar moves in New York State, following September 11 and the subsequent "belt-tightening" of the city budget enforced by Mayor Michael Bloomberg. At the moment, New York State is one of the most generous states in terms of state-subsidized health care, offering free and low-cost health care to children and pregnant women with or without a Social Security number (generally, among noncitizens, only work visa holders and permanent residents are able to obtain Social Security numbers).

Asociación Tepeyac fulfills a significant role in serving as a collective proxy enabling engagement in civic processes by people who individually, as undocumented immigrants, are ineligible for such participation. Participating in protests and lobbying, the undocumented members of Tepeyac behave "as if they were citizens" (Bosniak 1998). These rehearsals of citizenship open up spheres of access to the civic processes of lawmaking within which immigrants hope to promote the legislation of an amnesty granting them legal status, even while they are unable to participate formally in electoral processes. In the interim, these activities prepare them for an anticipated future in which they will be fully enfranchised citizens. It is hard to imagine that the net effect of such participation would be so significant or empowering were the immigrant members of Tepeyac to take on the state and its representatives as individuals. However, channeled through Tepeyac as an intermediary and proxy, their voices are multiplied and amplified, and enable them to achieve greater legitimacy for their claims.

Asociación Tepeyac and September 11, 2001

It was logical when, on the morning of September 11, so many Latinos saw the offices of Tepeyac, literally at the border of the original catchment area cordoned off as "Ground Zero" and in sight of the smoking ruins, as a refuge. The problem was that at that point in the organization's life there were still only two computers, a handful of phones, and two paid staff members employed by the organization. Nevertheless, lacking any semblance of the kind of infrastructure necessary for such a task, Tepeyac undertook to address the needs of the disaster's invisible victims. Almost immediately, they began to develop an innovative system that has since been adopted by other nonprofit organizations to identify victims who do not leave a paper trail.[7]

As the reader will recall, initial estimates held that as many as ten thousand people perished in the disaster, and initial relief efforts, while well intentioned, sometimes missed the mark in poignant ways: only a small fraction of the thousands of body bags ordered by the city were used, funds set up for 9/11 orphans went unclaimed, and initial counts of

---

7. One organization that has adopted their methods is Safe Horizons, an organization dedicated to serving victims of violent crime and domestic violence.

the dead and missing were grossly exaggerated. In those early days, no one could know how many undocumented workers might have been at the Trade Center on the morning of September 11. Volunteers at Tepeyac began to ask people who came to them a series of questions: Where did you work? Who were your co-workers (names, countries of origin, ages, and so forth)? How many people were working that morning? Who have you been able to contact? Although undocumented workers fall under the radar of the payroll system and even their managers may not know their real names, their co-workers, it was discovered, are a rich source of information and have stores of credible information.[8] Notarized affidavits were drafted that could then be used, collectively, as alternative sources of documentation. If ten different people reported that "Chuy," a sous chef, was prepping lunch in a kitchen in the towers that morning, his widow could then rely on such testimonies as corroboration of her claims and more accurate estimates of the dead and missing could be developed. Tepeyac developed a database of employers, employees, family members, and victims with which they compiled and cross-checked cases. This system not only helped corroborate victims and survivors' claims, it also was an effective way to rule out potential fraud. Developing such a rich and detailed database of affected companies, personnel, and routines meant that the few people who came in with incongruent information were immediately detected as fraudulent. The methods Tepeyac developed for documenting survivors' claims is a perfect example of its ability to *resolver,* to flexibly respond to a changing set of conditions and improvise within and outside of existing bureaucratic structures and procedures. Perhaps precisely because of Tepeyac's formation as a grass-roots organization, not a service agency, it did not readily deploy the strategies of many of the other nonprofit agencies and foundations that responded to September 11. By skirting procedural norms, it developed responses that were creative and captured the attention of funders who wished to enable it to continue to do its work, as well as to expand it.

Tepeyac worked on 106 cases of missing persons. By conducting thorough investigations that sometimes led representatives of Tepeyac to rural homes in Puebla state in Mexico, to Guatemala, and elsewhere to

---

8. Windows on the World was one of the few employers that came forward and worked to identify all of its missing employees and through the foundation it began, Windows of Hope Family Relief Fund, worked to get their families survivors' benefits, irrespective of their immigration status (Polakow-Suransky 2001).

gather testimonies from family members, they documented sixty-seven cases, including sixteen Mexicans. They also provided services to nine hundred workers dislocated by the tragedy, 64 percent of whom were Mexican, 9 percent Ecuadoran, and most of the rest from elsewhere in Latin America and the Caribbean, virtually all of them undocumented (Coe et al. 2003; Asociación Tepeyac 2003). To date, of the sixty-seven cases documented by Tepeyac, only forty-eight families have received death certificates and only thirty-seven were eligible for federal compensation (Coe et al. 2003, 40). The discrepancy in proportions of Mexicans among those served in the two groups is because Tepeyac was one of the only organizations publicly reaching out to undocumented victims of the Trade Center attack, and thus many non-Mexican survivors also sought its services. Tepeyac was not the only organization providing services for displaced workers, on the other hand, and Mexicans were more likely than people of other nationalities to receive them because these involved a long-term commitment by recipients of aid, including mental health services, job training, computer, ESL, and GED classes if relevant, all in Spanish (except for ESL), and couched in the particularly Mexican cultural milieu of Tepeyac.[9] The likelihood of a displaced worker who was not Mexican committing to many months of interaction with an organization that asserted its collective identity in particularly Mexican idioms was less than for those who sought its assistance simply in obtaining a death certificate and emergency survivors' benefits. The organization, at the same time, also engaged in less outreach to non-Mexican displaced workers. Because funding for these ongoing services was minimal, outreach was limited and those served were likely to belong to the organization's preexisting constituent base.

Just as undocumented immigrants are ineligible for many federal- and state-funded services, including Social Security and unemployment insurance, undocumented victims of September 11 and their survivors were not eligible for unemployment insurance, workers' compensation, Social Security, or FEMA benefits. Although many of the families of those 9/11 victims who appeared on official payrolls have received pensions and death benefits, life insurance, and Social Security benefits amounting to more than a million dollars, many of the families of undocumented

9. Even the name Tepeyac is something of a code word. Mexicans are likely to understand the reference to the hill at Tepeyac outside Mexico City, site of the apparition of the Virgin of Guadalupe in 1531.

victims received nothing at all from the main sources of aid. In October 2001, the Red Cross promised to distribute aid to victims referred by Tepeyac so they could meet their immediate food and housing expenses, saying that up to $1,500 would be given to families that submitted required affidavits at the Family Assistance Center. Another $28,500 was pledged, to be divided equally among the families that could produce death certificates (Moreno González 2001). If this indeed occurred, it would have meant that each family that received a death certificate would have received a paltry $593.78. Even Luz María Mendoza (figure 11.3), who like Félix traveled from Mexico in the days after September 11 in search of her missing husband, but who came bearing check stubs and photos of her husband at his job at Windows on the World, was turned away from the Family Assistance Center and eventually required help not only from Tepeyac but also from the Mexican consulate before she received a basic survivor's benefit package. Indeed, problems in accessing aid were not experienced only by undocumented workers and their relatives; overall, seven of ten requests for housing assistance were denied by the Federal Emergency Management Administration (O'Neil 2001). Nonetheless, the problems seemed to be disproportionately experienced by those who also tend to be the most vulnerable in society: those who were already in financially precarious positions before the disaster, immigrants, non-English speakers, the disabled, and so on. For example, until criticisms resulted in protests and a congressional hearing, FEMA distributed fifteen thousand faulty aid applications in the weeks after the attack, and applications for aid were only available in English (Henriques 2002).[10]

It is typical, according to some analysts, that when donors respond to a specific incident with an outpouring of contributions, that the rules for giving are not so strictly enforced (Steurele 2003, 3). Although some lawmakers proposed various amendments to regulations, such as granting permanent residency or citizenship to the widows and children of WTC victims or suspending certain eligibility requirements, to date this has not occurred. FEMA outreach workers insisted to Tepeyac repre-

---

10. For example, aid applications for workers displaced as a result of the terror attacks did not have a space for workers to identify their place of employment or to explain the reasons why their unemployment was a "direct result" of the disaster, one of the key requirements for eligibility. One applicant, who attached a letter with his place of employment, including a phone number and supervisor's name, at a restaurant that was located *inside* the towers was denied aid when a FEMA worker was unable to get through to the place of business on the telephone (Henriques 2002).

FIGURE 11.3. Luz María Mendoza, whose husband died in the World Trade Center and who, unlike many other victims, had pay stubs and photos of her husband at work in the towers to corroborate her story.

sentatives that many of their clients did qualify for aid (U.S.-born children of victims, for example) and held workshops on how to file FEMA applications, but only one of the three hundred applications that were filed with the assistance of Tepeyac received FEMA assistance. Applicants were further dissuaded by the stern and discouraging warning on the applications that applicants who were in the country illegally would be subject to prosecution (Coe et al. 2003, 40). Indeed, in the aftermath of the disaster Spanish-language media forewarned that undocumented immigrants would be subject to greater scrutiny following the attacks, could be liable for summary deportations, and possibly forced to repay any federal aid that they might have received in the past, including emergency Medicaid for emergency room visits, workers' compensation, and so on. Unfortunately, many of these dire predictions have borne out and they certainly had the immediate effect of discouraging many victims and survivors from seeking disaster aid. For these reasons, Tepeyac was uniquely positioned to *resolver* and foresee the needs and serve the "invisible victims" of September 11.

Following September 11, analysts remarked that the diversity of charities and organizations poised to provide services proved to be the city's greatest strength in its response to the disaster: "Many of New York's charities are small and sharply focused on immigrants, for example . . . groups often overlooked by larger, more generalized agencies" (Coe et al. 2003, 13). Most of Tepeyac's WTC relief funding was from private foundations such as the American Jewish World Service, AFL-CIO, and the Robin Hood Foundation. In a blurring and overlap of sectors, as theorized by Elisabeth Clemens and Doug Guthrie in the introduction, Tepeyac's role is not simply one of funneling private funds and facilitating access to government services. In the wake of September 11, immigrants were targets of even greater xenophobia than had become normal in the era after the passage of the 1996 Illegal Immigration Reform and Immigrant Responsibility Act (IIRIRA).[11] For example, the National Association of Realtors even barred its September 11 charitable donations from benefiting non-permanent-resident immigrants (Coe et al. 2003). Even if the will had existed to do it, any major effort by FEMA or the beleaguered American Red Cross to revise their regulations and make it possible for people without Social Security numbers or legal immigration status, much less any conclusive evidence that their loved ones perished in the disaster, to apply directly for benefits would have been met roundly with criticism and might have resulted in even greater scrutiny of the evidence—or lack thereof—being provided by people like Félix.

Asociación Tepeyac played the role of intermediary between the large government and nongovernmental agencies, foundations, and im-

---

11. Among other things, the Illegal Immigration Reform and Immigrant Responsibility Act increased employer penalties for hiring undocumented workers and instituted three- and ten-year bars on reentry for immigrants who were deported.

migrants: lobbying for greater benefits; developing innovative means to corroborate the stories that victims told; referring people to services that were available to them and helping them negotiate the maze of forms, affidavits, and documentary evidence; and using monies from foundations and individual donations to provide direct benefits to victims and their families as well as to displaced workers. In this way, they represented a flexible and strategic response to a disaster that required a coordination of services like no other in history. The former chief executive officer of the September 11th Fund wrote later that "the problem was not money but coordination" (Gotbaum 2003, 2). Then–New York attorney general Eliot Spitzer likened his work to achieve coordination of relief efforts and a single survivors' database to "herding cats" (Barstow 2001). The nonprofit sector offers greater flexibility in response to a disaster than a behemoth like FEMA because of its ability to receive and distribute funds with less federal oversight. Tepeyac, as a relatively young nonprofit that nonetheless had earned a widely known and respected reputation among Latinos in the city, especially among Mexicans in the United States and Mexico, and bearing the legitimacy of archdiocesan patronage, was uniquely situated to address the needs of a sector of victims of the September 11 disaster who were not being adequately served. Precisely because of the organization's relative newness and lack of a staff schooled in negotiating the labyrinthine paths of federal funding, it was able to respond in a more flexible, tactical and, ultimately, highly effective manner than many older and larger organizations.

Asociación Tepeyac Today

Asociación Tepeyac was transformed by its involvement in the September 11 disaster and relief effort. As described previously, de Certeau contrasts tactics and strategies, associating the former with flexibility, improvisation, and subalternity and the latter with power and bureaucracy. Asociación Tepeyac shifted from a mode of operating and planning that was tactical—based on emergent human rights issues, a dedicated if constantly rotating staff and volunteer base, and an always uncertain funding environment—to being an organization with a more professionalized staff that was flooded by funders, program evaluators, philanthropists, city and federal oversight, and a high-stakes media and public relations environment. The process by which Tepeyac responded to this shift and the end result—the organization's transformation from grass-roots organization to service agency—is comprehensible within DiMaggio and Powell's theory of institutional isomorphism, by which organizations come to resemble each other in their competition for resources, customers, political power, institutional legitimacy, and social and economic fitness (1983, 150).

The responsibility that Asociación Tepeyac assumed for counting, documenting, and providing for the survivors of the "invisible" victims was much larger than its existing infrastructure could accommodate. Nonetheless, the staff and volunteers did not pause in their efforts but carried on, accomplishing with sheer will and dedication what an organization double its size would have found overwhelming. Liliana Rivera Sánchez told me that in the weeks following 9/11, she worked as a volunteer at Asociación Tepeyac for twenty hours a day, going home only to sleep for a few hours, and then returning to the task at hand. She accompanied the survivors of victims to the family assistance center and hospitals, and even more than a year later, after relocating to Puebla, Mexico, spent a great deal of time delivering funds and paperwork and checking in with Félix in Zaragoza, a three-hour drive away. In the chaotic but generous outpouring of charity following 9/11, the need for organization and channeling of assistance was even greater than the need for additional funds.

Foundations and private donors learned of Tepeyac's work, marveled at what they were accomplishing with virtually no budget, and clamored to provide them with more resources. The Robin Hood Foundation awarded Tepeyac $600,000: $420,000 for emergency cash relief to families of World Trade Center victims, and $180,000 designated to strengthen its relief services (Robin Hood Foundation 2006). The following year, the foundation awarded an additional $480,000, most of it for staffing, and it continued to fund an after-school program that Tepeyac ran in Queens for several years afterward. Nonetheless, while a half million dollars can cover several salaries for a year or two, grants like this are assumed to sustain an organization temporarily while it applies for other funding for operating expenses, salaries, and long-term growth. In addition, Tepeyac charges membership fees and a modest tuition for its ESL, computer, and GED courses, which are intended to provide it with necessary income indefinitely. However, the organization has been unable, to date, to expand its programs and constituency while at the same time securing funding sources that will enable it to operate at this expanded magnitude in the long run. September 11 ratcheted up the expectations for and the role of Tepeyac in ways that are not fully reversible, and perhaps are not reversible at all.[12] Over the past few years, most of the paid staff has been laid off or asked to revert to volunteer status. In one particularly poignant example, there is a former staff member who had been employed in a restaurant in the Twin Towers and who the morning of 9/11 ran from the smoke and debris that enveloped him when he emerged from the subway on his way to work. After seeking assistance at Tepeyac, he was hired there, first in WTC relief work, then in cultural affairs. However, after four years of full-time work at Tepeyac, he is now waiting tables again to earn a living.

In efforts to obtain grants for operating costs—often the most difficult funding category because many funders prefer funding terminal "projects," not overhead—the development director has discovered that because of two years of greater-than-a-half-million-dollar budgets following on the heels of 9/11, Tepeyac is now ineligible for the smaller $20,000 to $50,000 grants that were its bread and butter. However, it does not have the many years' long track record to qualify for or the infrastructure to manage multimillion dollar government service contracts or grants from larger foundations. This year, the director of the Queens center was told that in addition to single-handedly running a bustling community center, she needs to find money for her own salary and the center's rent while coordinating a full calendar of English, GED, and computer classes, as well as women's groups, cultural activities, and children's programming. As of this writing she was hustling to raise funds by renting the center's space to individuals and organizations for activities ranging from tax preparation to *quinceañera* rehearsals to poetry readings.

Indeed, there seems to be a structurally analogous problem occurring with Tepeyac as an organization to what occurs with its constituents as immigrants. Just as immigrants who seek services must contend with cultural and language barriers and legal bars to their eligibility because of their lack of citizenship and/or legal residency, Asociación Tepeyac, as a relative newcomer in the nonprofit world, has had to rapidly professionalize and formalize structures that emerged organically from its grassroots basis in forty parish-based community organizations; and

12. Thank you to Lis Clemens for suggesting this metaphor.

yet it still faces large obstacles in its effort to integrate into the institutional culture and elaborate governing mechanisms of "fundable" nonprofits. This can be seen in the absurdity of the development director's task of applying for funds from foundations with grant applications that she writes, and, if received, which she will administer and evaluate because the organization does not have enough personnel to spare any other staff members from their always urgent program responsibilities to fulfill these tasks. Further, with layoffs due to the organization's inability to sustain payroll for its dramatically expanded staff, the comprehensive and complex programming that the immediate post-9/11 funding enabled, including long-term mental health services, job training, and more, has had to be scaled back, and the remaining skeleton crew fulfills the work of two or three job titles apiece in order to keep the rest of its programs and services afloat.

Another consequence of the expansion and increased visibility of Tepeyac after 9/11 is that Joel Magallán has had to assume the role of "executive director" with its attendant obligations of hosting funders, public speaking engagements, lobbying, media appearances, and so on, which sometimes run contrary to how he and his constituency might have preferred to define his role as a "community leader." While he has been profiled in the *New York Times,* Spanish-language media including *El Diario* and *El Diario de México,* and on television, and awarded honors by the mayor of the city of New York, the consulate of Mexico, and the Robin Hood Foundation, he has lost the support of many of those who worked with him to create Tepeyac a decade ago. Some community leaders complain that in the past they would call or visit Tepeyac and it was Joel who picked up the phone or answered the door. Now, visitors are made to wait or are passed on to staff members, while he spends a great deal of time outside of the office on appointments, meetings, press conferences, and travel. Further, he must balance the tremendous and conflicting pressures of the expectations of funders for proper management, administration, and auditing of funds; of actors in the larger political sphere with whom he must develop and sustain relationships; and of those Mexican immigrants who have been Tepeyac's base, for sincerity and comprehension of their needs and an authentic cultural bond.

Perhaps this process was inevitable and not unique to Tepeyac. Only two months after 9/11, analysts anticipated a "day of reckoning" for newer nonprofits that had not yet developed a solid donor base. Robert F.

Sharpe Jr., a nonprofit-group consultant, predicted a significant winnowing: "A lot of the charities that were formed in recent years aren't going to make it" (O'Neil 2001). Further, Cho (2002) and Anft (2002) have signaled the difficulty of raising funds for programs and services that benefit immigrants after 9/11 because of the rise in xenophobia and increased focus on terrorism, as well as new provisions on charitable giving under the USA Patriot Act.

This process of change is predicted by DiMaggio and Powell's theorization of coercive, normative, and mimetic isomorphism (1983). Building on Hawley's description (1968), DiMaggio and Powell define isomorphism as "a constraining process that forces one unit in a population to resemble other units that face the same set of environmental conditions" (1983, 149). During the first four years of its existence, Tepeyac, apart from minimal diocesan support, was otherwise independent and, while its activities and reach were limited by an almost total lack of funding, it also did not need to answer to anyone. The (volunteer) personnel director once complained to me long before 9/11 that he was never sure if the funds for payroll would be available on payday for the few employees he needed to pay, or if they had perhaps been used to pay the electric bill or print the newsletter. Members paid dues in exchange for low-cost ESL and computer classes and other benefits, but there was little transparency about the funds' use. There has never been an accusation, to my knowledge, of misuse of the funds, and it is clear to anyone who enters the offices that funds have rarely been used to make the staff more comfortable or better equipped, and the director is known for his asceticism, but there has not been the transparency of recordkeeping required by external funders.

After September 11, 2001, however, the funding agencies that with the best intentions sought to enable Tepeyac to meet the needs of the survivors and displaced workers of the terror attacks, continue serving its existing clients, and expand its services, also imposed expectations and practices on the organization that inevitably changed it. Of the three kinds of isomorphic processes posited by DiMaggio and Powell—mimetic, normative, and coercive—the latter two seem most relevant to an analysis of Tepeyac after 9/11. Mimetic processes involve imitation on the part of organizations that model themselves after other organizations due to uncertainty. Mimesis is less relevant to Tepeyac, an organization that, until recently, had surprisingly little contact with other similar service providers and immigrant groups, and a marked lack of interest in following anyone else's example.[13] However, it is subject to coercive isomorphism: if a funding agency provides capital, it wants (and needs for accountability to its own funders and board of directors) certain assurances that the money is being used for its intended purpose. This process of coercion begins before a funder even enters into a relationship with an organization; in order to apply for a grant, an organization like Tepeyac must accommodate its mission, purpose, and its operations to the terms, concepts, and modes that are comprehensible, and ultimately, acceptable to, the external source. Although Tepeyac, as is typical of organizations only recently viewed as "fundable" and chronically short on funds, went through a phase after 2001 of applying for anything for which it could conceivably be eligible, only in the last year or two has the organization begun to weigh the potential benefit of a grant against the coercive pressures a funder might impose and chosen not to apply for some funding opportunities. Nonetheless, because of these coercive pressures, the organization has expanded its mission, "toned down" its Mexican identity,[14] and placed its greatest emphasis on programs for youth and children.

Normative pressures have also worked to further isomorphism between Tepeyac and other nonprofit organizations in the United States. Before 9/11, volunteers and a minimal staff wore many hats. The executive director rejected the notion of job descriptions and preferred to assign tasks to people based on their interests and skill sets, even if it meant their work might overlap several different project areas. After 9/11, Tepeyac organized its work into departments, composed of staff; campaigns linking staff and constituents; and "commissions" composed of board members (who are community leaders), volunteers, staff, and members of the comités. Many of the departments included highly trained professionals: lawyers (volunteer) and paralegals, psychologists, educators, and administrators. Soon, some of these new staff members turned the lack of job descriptions into a complaint about what they perceived to be disorganization and an excessive workload. Job descriptions, after all, describe one's task within an organization as much as they make a job comparable to similar positions in any like organization:

13. See Gálvez (2004) for an extended examination of Tepeyac's historic reluctance to build coalitions and alliances with other groups.

14. The development director described to me the innovation of the use of an abstract butterfly motif in its most recent annual report as a response to funders who balked at the ubiquitous images of the Mexican flag and the Virgin of Guadalupe in its previous reports as "too Mexican."

"Such mechanisms [including also professional training institutions and trade associations] create a pool of almost interchangeable individuals who occupy similar positions across a range of organizations and possess a similarity of orientation and disposition that may override variations in tradition and control that might otherwise shape organizational behavior" (DiMaggio and Powell, drawing on Perrow 1983, 152).

Instead of personal interest and the director's assessment of need in distributing responsibility, staff wished to constrain their tasks to a coherent and discrete area for which they had been trained. At the same time, because federal laws governing hiring would cast Tepeyac's efforts in the past to create and nurture a visibly and profoundly Mexican space as discrimination, the new hires, although still largely bilingual, were quite diverse in terms of national origin and ethnicity. Further, federal hiring regulations also mean that many of the people who have been core participants in the creation of Tepeyac are not eligible to be hired as staff because of their undocumented status. Of course, being able to hire a highly trained staff is important to any organization that seeks to provide high-quality services to an ever-expanding constituency, but so is the retention of continuity with the institution's original organizing principles. Nonetheless, this example of normative isomorphism is another way that the organization has been transformed.

Ultimately, the expansion of Tepeyac after 9/11, even if it ultimately cannot be sustained, has already permanently altered the organization. Should it be unable to access funding and sources of income that enable it to operate at its expanded scale, it nevertheless cannot return to being a volunteer-driven, grassroots association of parish-based voluntary organizations. Indeed, many of the core activists who had been instrumental in the organization's formation have withdrawn from it, and several of them have turned their energy to smaller, community-based organizations in the five boroughs of New York City, with different purposes, varying from cultural expression to soccer to political activism. Perhaps the most striking consequence of the untenability of the conflicting pressures and demands on the organization is that the forty parish-based Guadalupan committees that composed the Asociación now number less than a dozen, as many have seceded or disbanded. Instead, staff at Tepeyac now, and only recently, have stopped emphasizing the role of the comités and instead say that the association's base is its two community centers based in Queens and the South Bronx, which are mainly dedicated to the provision of services and are largely unaffiliated with the Catholic Church.[15] In addition to the Manhattan headquarters, these two centers offer services including financial literacy workshops, ESL, GED, and computer classes, and after-school programs to Mexican and other Latino immigrants. Even the most basic defining characteristic of Tepeyac, that it was founded to serve Mexican immigrants, has been forced to change, as funders balk at the presumed exclusionism of that mission and ask the organization to be more universal and inclusive in its outreach and constituency. Its mission statement, which previously was described as service to and mobilization of the Mexican immigrant community, now refers to "Latino immigrants."

Ultimately, it remains to be seen whether 9/11 produced, in an accelerated and dramatic fashion, a transformation of Tepeyac that was inevitable. After all, few grassroots movements can be sustained over the long term without losing members to other causes and core participants to fatigue, burnout, and better-paying jobs (cf. Edelman 1999). Perhaps the transformation has allowed Tepeyac to embark on a new path that will enable it to serve many more thousands of clients for years to come. Indeed, the creation of immigrant-serving institutions that can serve the changing needs of a population as it settles in the United States and of new arrivals who may face a different landscape than their predecessors should be considered a good thing. Nonetheless, there are many who are saddened by the transformation of Asociación Tepeyac from a movement into an institution.

Conclusion

Asociación Tepeyac illustrates a trajectory that is surely not unique in the history of institutions in the United States or around the world: it grew from being a group of loosely affiliated mutual aid societies into a movement, and from a movement into an institution. Similar trajectories can be traced with political parties, unions, and religious organizations throughout the world. The Guadalupan committees, parish-based confraternal societies, became linked into an activist movement for the rights and dignity of undocumented immigrants, especially Mexicans, in the New York area. Then, because of the events of 9/11 and its after-

---

15. Nonetheless, the South Bronx center is housed in a church building. Since this writing, the South Bronx Center was closed due to lack of funds.

math, this movement and its nascent organizational structure turned its efforts to coordinating relief, services, and long-term empowerment of the "invisible victims" of that tragic day. This abrupt expansion of its mission and its widely acknowledged and astonishing success at serving this elusive and underserved population prompted it to expand its operational capacity and led funders to shower it with the means to do so. However, that funding expanded its infrastructure very rapidly during a hectic period, and the organization's efforts to turn that infusion of capital into a solvent operating budget in the long term has yet to be successful. As such, while the organization grew beyond its founding parts—its grassroots base in the committees—it has not achieved full legitimacy in the eyes of foundations nor of its constituency in its role as an institution dedicated to service provision. Ironically, the very thing that drew funders to Tepeyac in the aftermath of September 11, its ability to creatively respond to the tragedy in ways no other agency did, to *resolver,* was precisely what would have to be changed with the infusion of foundation dollars: tactics would have to be made into strategies, and the pressures toward institutional isomorphism would become irresistible.

Nonetheless, I think this move from *associationalism,* which is such an important part of American civic life, into *activism,* and then into *institutionalization,* for people who are not actually yet "Americans" offers quite liberatory possibilities. Indeed, historically, some of the same organizations that were founded in the nineteenth and early twentieth centuries to serve the most basic needs of European immigrants in the United States have, over a century, become some of the oldest and most prestigious service providers still operating, and their missions are now typically very broad. In the meantime, too, organizations such as Tepeyac provide concrete benefits to people who otherwise would be left in the cold, unserved by the behemoth relief agencies and service providers. Indeed, as Tepeyac is made to resemble other agencies by the forces of institutional isomorphism, it could also influence other organizations to take greater consideration of undocumented immigrants and others who fall through the cracks in many existing services. Presumably isomorphism is not unidirectional. Nonetheless, it is important to contextualize this transformation within larger national and global processes of globalization, the shrinkage of the welfare state and expansion of the third sector, and a rise in the role of faith-based service providers. By examining this larger context, it becomes possible to observe how the tactics developed by Asociación Tepeyac to serve a highly exploited community of undocumented Mexican immigrants and that made it uniquely able to resourcefully address (what I call *resolver*) the sudden and overlooked needs of the "invisible" victims of 9/11 were consequently redirected. When the tactics were transformed into strategies, Asociación Tepeyac became a larger, more efficient, and more fundable institution at the same time that it was alienated from its base. It remains to be seen whether this transformation was ultimately for the best.

References

Abell, Aaron. 1952. "The Catholic Factor in Urban Welfare: The Early Period, 1850–1880." *Review of Politics* 14, no. 3 (July): 289–324.

Anft, Michael. 2002. "Immigrant-Rights Organizations Face Fallout from September 11." *Chronicle of Philanthropy* 14 (January 10): 18–19.

Appel, John. 1966. "American Negro and Immigrant Experience: Similarities and Differences." *American Quarterly* 18, no. 1 (Spring): 95–103.

Asociación Tepeyac. 2003. "WTC Relief Program: Providing Help for Invisible Victims." New York: Asociación Tepeyac.

Barstow, David. 2001. "A Nation Challenged: Compensation; Victims' Families Lack Voice in Effort to Coordinate Relief." *New York Times,* December 15, A1.

Bosniak, Linda. 1998. "Citizenship of Aliens." *Social Text* 56: 15–30.

Brentano, Lujo. 1870. *On the History and Development of Guilds, and the Origin of Trade-unions.* London: Trübner & Co.

Casimir, Leslie. 2000. "Market Workers Win 100g Award." *Daily News* (New York), August 31, 36.

Celestino, Olinda, and Albert Myers. 1981. *Las cofradías en el Perú, región central.* Frankfurt am Main: Verlag Klaus Dieter Vervuert.

Certeau, Michel de. 1984. *The Practice of Everyday Life.* Berkeley: University of California Press.

Cho, Eunice. 2002. "Building Communities, Defeating Fear: Organizing for Immigrant Rights after September 11." *Nonprofit Quarterly* 9 (Spring): 32–35.

Coe, Natalie, Jennifer Furl, Kevin Kinsella, Mitch Nauffts, and Rick Schoff. 2003. *September 11: Perspectives from the Field of Philanthropy.* New York: Foundation Center.

Cortes, Sergio. 2003. "Migrants from Puebla in the 1990s." In *Immigrants and Schooling: Mexicans in New York,* edited by Regina Cortina and Mónica Gendreau. Staten Island, N.Y.: Center for Migration Studies.

DiMaggio, Paul, and Walter W. Powell. 1983. "The Iron Cage Revisited: Institutional Isomorphism and Collective Rationality in Organizational Fields." *American Sociological Review* 48, no. 2: 147–60.

Dolan, Jay P., and Jaime Vidal. 1994. *Puerto Rican and Cuban Catholics in the United States, 1900–1965.* Notre Dame, Ind.: University of Notre Dame Press.

Durkheim, Emile. 1984. *The Division of Labor in Society.* New York: Free Press.

Edelman, Marc. 1999. *Peasants against Globalization.* Palo Alto: Stanford University Press.

Flores, William, and Rina Benmayor. 1997. *Latino Cultural Citizenship.* Boston: Beacon Press.

Gálvez, Alyshia. 2009. *Guadalupe in New York: Devotion and the Struggle for Citizenship Rights among Mexicans.* New York: New York University Press.

Glazer, Nathan, and Daniel Patrick Moynihan. 1963. *Beyond the Melting Pot: The Negroes, Puerto Ricans, Jews, Italians, and Irish of New York City.* Cambridge: Harvard University Press.

Gleason, Philip. 1987. *Keeping the Faith: American Catholicism, Past and Present.* Notre Dame, Ind.: University of Notre Dame Press.

Gotbaum, Joshua. 2003. "Compassion and Competence: A Nonphilanthropist Reflects on the Contributions of Philanthropy." In *September 11: Perspectives from the Field of Philanthropy,* edited by Natalie Coe et al., 1–11. New York: Foundation Center.

Greenhouse, Steve. 2002. "Korean Grocers Agree to Double Pay and Improve Workplace Conditions." *New York Times,* September 18, 1.

Hawley, Amos. 1968. "Human Ecology." In *International Encyclopedia of the Social Sciences,* edited by David Sills. New York: Macmillan.

Henriques, Diana. 2002. "Change in Rules Barred Many from Sept. 11 Disaster Relief." *New York Times,* April 16, 1.

Herberg, Will. 1960. *Protestant, Catholic, Jew: An Essay in American Religious Sociology.* Garden City, N.Y.: Anchor Books.

Kintz, Linda. 2007. "Performing Imperialist Fundamentalism(s)." In *Performing Religion in the Americas: Devotion, Media, and Politics in the 21st Century,* ed. Alyshia Gálvez. London: Berg.

Lenkowsky, Leslie, and Sheila Kennedy. 2004. *Social Equity Issues in President Bush's Faith-Based Office Initiatives and Charitable Choice Provisions of Recent Welfare Reform Legislation.* http://www.napawash.org/aa_social_equity/SocialEquityIssuesinFaith-BasedWelfareReform.pdf.

McAvoy, Thomas T. 1942. "The Catholic Church in the United States between Two Wars." *Review of Politics* 4, no. 4 (October): 409–31.

McGreevy, John T. 1996. *Parish Boundaries: The Catholic Encounter with Race in the Twentieth-Century Urban North.* Chicago: University of Chicago Press.

Moreno Gonzalez, John. 2001. "Red Cross Begins Outreach Program." *Newsday,* October 2.

Murphy, Ruth, and Sonia Grodka Blumenthal. 1966. "The American Community and the Immigrant." *Annals of the American Academy of Political and Social Science* 367 (September): 115–26.

Office of the Press Secretary. "2005 Fact Sheet: Compassion in Action: Producing Real Results for Americans Most in Need." http://www.whitehouse.gov/news/releases/2005/03/20050301–1.html.

O'Neil, John. 2001. "Tough Times, Tough Choices: Charities Get a Big Helping of Uncertainty." *New York Times,* November 21, G11.

Orsi, Robert Anthony. 1992. "The Religious Boundaries of an In-between People: Street Feste and the Problem of the Dark-Skinned Other in Italian Harlem, 1920–1990." *American Quarterly* 44: 313–41.

Polakow-Suransky, Sasha. 2001. "The Invisible Victims: The Undocumented Workers at the World Trade Center." http://www.racingmix.com/word/victims.htm.

Robin Hood Foundation. 2006. "Asociación Tepeyac." http://www.robinhood.org/programs/relief_profile.cfm?recipientId=8.

Rosaldo, Renato. 1997. "Cultural Citizenship and Educational Democracy." *Cultural Anthropology* 9: 402–11.

Soysal, Yasemin. 1994. *Limits to Citizenship: Migrants and Postnational Membership in Europe.* Chicago: University of Chicago Press.

Steurele, C. Eugene. 2003. "Managing Charitable Giving in the Wake of Disaster." In *September 11: Perspectives from the Field of Philanthropy,* ed. Natalie Coe et al., 1. New York: Foundation Center.

Thomas, William. 1918. *The Polish Peasant in Europe and America.* Chicago: University of Chicago.

Tocqueville, Alexis de. 2004. "Of The Use Which The Americans Make Of Public Associations In Civil Life" (from *Democracy in America,* vol. 1). http://xroads.virginia.edu/~HYPER/DETOC/ch2_05.htm.

Tomasi, Silvano. 1970. "The Ethnic Church and the Integration of Italian Immigrants in the United States." In *The Italian Experience in the United States,* ed. Silvano Tomasi and Madeline Enge. Staten Island, N.Y.: Center for Migration Studies.

———. 1975. *Piety and Power: The Role of the Italian Parishes in the New York Metropolitan Area, 1880–1930.* Staten Island, N.Y.: Center for Migration Studies.

United States Conference of Catholic Bishops and Conferencia Del Episcopado Mexicano. 2003. *Strangers No Longer: Together on a Journey of Hope.* http://www.ucsb.org/mrs/stranger.shtml.

Viles, Peter. 2001. "Families of Undocumented Victims Find Help Scarce." CNN, November 3, http://www.cnn.com/2001/US/11/03/rec.who.knew.jose/index.html.

Wucker, Michelle. 2006. "Becoming American." In her *Lockout: Why America Keeps Getting Immigration Wrong When Our Prosperity Depends on Getting It Right.* New York: Public Affairs Press.

Contributors

ELISABETH S. CLEMENS is Professor of Sociology and Master of the Social Sciences Collegiate Division at the University of Chicago. Building on organizational theory and political sociology, her research has addressed the role of social movements and voluntary organizations in institutional change. Her first book, *The People's Lobby: Organizational Innovation and the Rise of Interest Group Politics in the United States, 1890–1925* (Chicago, 1997) received awards in both organizational and political sociology. She is also coeditor of *Private Action and the Public Good* (Yale, 1998), *Remaking Modernity: Politics, History, and Sociology* (Duke 2005), and the journal *Studies in American Political Development.* She is currently completing *Civic Nation,* an account of the role of voluntarism in American governance.

OMRI ELISHA is Assistant Professor of Anthropology at Queens College/ City University of New York. He received his PhD in Anthropology from New York University in 2005, and was Resident Scholar at the School for Advanced Research in Santa Fe, New Mexico, in 2007–08. His publications include research articles on American conservative evangelicalism in the journals *Cultural Anthropology and Social Analysis,* and editorials for media/academic blogs such as the Revealer and the Immanent Frame (SSRC). His book on the moral ambitions of evangelical social engagement is forthcoming from University of California Press.

JAMES A. EVANS is Assistant Professor of Sociology at the University of Chicago and member of the Committee on the Conceptual and Historical Studies of Science. His work explores how social and technical institutions shape knowledge—science, scholarship, law, news, religion—and how these understandings reshape the social and technical world. Evans is particularly interested in the relation of markets to science and knowledge more broadly. He has studied how industry collaboration shapes academic science; the web of individuals and institutions that produce innovation; and markets for ideas and their creators. Evans has also examined the impact of the Internet on knowledge in society. His work uses natural language processing, the analysis of social and semantic networks, statistical modeling, and field-based observation and interviews. Evans's research has appeared in *Science, Administrative Science Quarterly,* and other publications.

ALYSHIA GÁLVEZ is Assistant Professor of Latin American Studies at Lehman College/City University of New York. She is a cultural anthropologist (PhD, New York University, 2004) whose work focuses on the efforts by Mexican immigrants in New York City to achieve the rights of citizenship. Her book on this topic is *Guadalupe in New York: Devotion and the Struggle for Citizenship Rights among Mexican Immigrants* (NYU Press 2009). Other publications include *Performing Religion in the Americas: Media, Politics, and Devotion in the 21st Century* (Berg/Seagull 2007) and articles in *Social Text, International Migration, e-misférica,* and *Revista Enfoques* (Chile). She is conducting a research project, an intervention into the so-called Hispanic birth weight paradox, examining the experiences of Mexican women with New York's public health system.

DOUG GUTHRIE is Professor of Management and Daniel P. Paduano Faculty Fellow at the NYU-Stern School of Business and Faculty Director for Global Executive Education. In addition to his duties at Stern, Guthrie also holds an appointment as Professor of Sociology on NYU's Faculty of Arts and Sciences. He also is Academic Director of the Berlin School of Creative Leadership. Professor Guthrie's areas of expertise lie in the fields of management, leadership, corporate governance, and economic reform in China. His research has been funded by the Ford Foundation, the Alfred P. Sloan Foundation, and the Social Science Research Council. He has also served as the Director of the Business Institutions Initiative and the Program on the Corporation as a Social Institution at the Social Science Research Council. He received his BA degree in Chinese Literature from the University of Chicago and his PhD in Organizational Sociology from the University of California, Berkeley.

MARK HENDRICKSON received his PhD in History from the University of California at Santa Barbara and is Assistant Professor of History at the University of California at San Diego.

NICOLE P. MARWELL is Associate Professor of Public Affairs and Sociology at Baruch College and the Graduate Center of the City University of New York, as well as a faculty affiliate of the Baruch College Center for Nonprofit Strategy and Management. Her research, exemplified by her 2007 book *Bargaining for Brooklyn: Community Organizations in the Entrepreneurial City* (University of Chicago Press) sits at the intersection of urban, organizational, and political sociology, with a substantive focus on nonprofit organizations, local and state politics, and Latina/o communities. Professor Marwell's ongoing research includes a study of the Latino middle class and an analysis of government contracting to nonprofit organizations in New York City; the latter is supported by the National Science Foundation.

MICHAEL MCQUARRIE received his PhD from New York University and is currently Assistant Professor of Sociology at the University of California at Davis. He has published numerous articles on low-income housing, community organizing, and the role of corporate investment and philanthropy in an era of welfare state retrenchment.

JOHANN N. NEEM is Associate Professor of History at Western Washington University and author of *Creating a Nation of Joiners: Democracy and Civil Society in Early National Massachusetts* (Harvard, 2008).

ALICE O'CONNOR is Professor of History at the University of California at Santa Barbara. Her many publications include *Social Science for What? Philanthropy and the Social Question in a World Turned Rightside Up* (Russell Sage Foundation, 2007), *Poverty Knowledge: Social Science, Social Policy, and the Poor in 20th Century U.S. History* (Princeton University Press, 2001), and *Urban Inequality: Evidence from Four Cities,* coedited with Chris Tilly and Lawrence Bobo (Russell Sage Foundation, 2001).